Turning Points in Modern History

Vejas Gabriel Liulevicius, Ph.D.

THE
GREAT
COURSES

PUBLISHED BY:

THE GREAT COURSES
Corporate Headquarters
4840 Westfields Boulevard, Suite 500
Chantilly, Virginia 20151-2299
Phone: 1-800-832-2412
Fax: 703-378-3819
www.thegreatcourses.com

Vejas Gabriel Liulevicius, Ph.D.

Lindsay Young Professor of History
University of Tennessee, Knoxville

Professor Vejas Gabriel Liulevicius was born in Chicago, Illinois. He grew up on Chicago's South Side in a Lithuanian American neighborhood and spent some years attending school in Aarhus, Denmark, and Bonn, Germany. He received his B.A. from the University of Chicago. In 1989, he spent the summer in Moscow and Leningrad (today St. Petersburg) in an intensive Russian-language study program. His dissertation research was funded by a German Academic Exchange Service fellowship and took him to Freiburg in Germany's Black Forest region and to Vilnius, Lithuania. He earned his Ph.D. in European History, specializing in modern German history, from the University of Pennsylvania in 1994.

After receiving his doctorate, Professor Liulevicius spent a year as a postdoctoral research fellow at the Hoover Institution on War, Revolution, and Peace at Stanford University. Since 1995, he has been a history professor at the University of Tennessee, Knoxville. He teaches courses on modern German history, Nazi Germany, World War I, 20th-century Europe, diplomatic history, and the history of espionage. He has won both of the University of Tennessee's top teaching awards: the Provost's Excellence in Teaching Award in 2003 and the Chancellor's Award for Excellence in Teaching in 2012. In 2005, he was awarded a prestigious National Endowment for the Humanities Research Fellowship. He currently serves as Director of the Center for the Study of War and Society at the University of Tennessee.

Professor Liulevicius's research focuses on German relations with Eastern Europe in the modern period. His other interests include international history and the history of the Baltic region. He has published numerous articles (which have also appeared in French, Italian, and German translations), and his first book, *War Land on the Eastern Front: Culture, National Identity and German Occupation in World War I* also appeared in German

i

translation in 2002. His second book is a study of German stereotypes of Eastern Europeans and ideas of a special German cultural mission in the East over the past two centuries, entitled *The German Myth of the East, 1800 to the Present.*

Professor Liulevicius has recorded four other Great Courses: *Espionage and Covert Operations: A Global History; War, Peace, and Power: Diplomatic History of Europe, 1500-2000; World War I: The "Great War"*; and *Utopia and Terror in the 20th Century.*

Professor Liulevicius lives in Knoxville, Tennessee, with his wife, Kathleen, and their children, Paul and Helen. ■

Table of Contents

Table of Contents

Table of Contents

SUPPLEMENTAL MATERIAL

Turning Points in Modern History

Scope:

Since 1400, crucial turning points have jolted the world's modern history. These critical moments, and the waves of change they unleash, have defined what makes modern history different from all that preceded it. Our course tracks these crucial turning points in the areas of politics, scientific development, social transformation, technological innovation, startling intellectual challenges, economic advance, and military triumph and disaster.

All these transformative moments have one basic thing in common: They sparked profound changes in how humans viewed their world, what humans might be capable of, and even the essence of human nature. In this course, we examine the deepest human impact and change in worldview precipitated by these key historical turning points. Whether covering a turning point in technological change (such as the invention of the printing press or the atomic bomb), political history (the establishment of nation-states as a default mode of world politics), social transformation (the abolition of slavery or the recognition of women's right to vote), and many, many more—in each case, we focus on the impact of the turning point on the worldview and general outlook of contemporaries, what they hoped or feared would be the effects.

This course begins by confronting a striking, inescapable contrast. In premodern societies, tradition and the time-hallowed ways of the ancestors held great authority, while innovations were seen as suspect, as deviations from how things had always been done. Traditional societies did not welcome that which was new and revolutionary but, instead, longed for the restoration of a mythic golden age. By contrast, in modern societies, newness is celebrated and hope is placed in progress. Modern people often look for the "new and improved" and eagerly anticipate the "next big thing." The difference could not be more stark. How did this fundamental shift in outlook take place, historically?

This course shows how the decisive turning points of the last 500 years have, in fact, combined to create the world as it is today, shaping the condition of modernity as we know it and live it now. The elusive concept of modernity is often described as a new way of life marked by the growth of technology, the autonomy of the individual, recourse to experimentation and science over the dictates of tradition, new concepts of popular sovereignty and equality, and new interconnectedness on an increasingly global scale. To get at the evolution of this modernity, in each of our lectures, we investigate changing concepts of authority, what is seen as legitimate and true.

As we zero in on the 24 most important turning points of modern history, our course presents an astonishing and memorable cast of characters: from a Chinese eunuch admiral of the Ming dynasty sailing the Indian Ocean to an Italian physicist seeking to create the first sustained manmade atomic reaction, from a New Zealand crusader for women's votes to a Dutch scientist laboring in obscurity whose findings amazed learned scholars, and many others. The story of this course is global in reach, traversing the Galapagos Islands, Jamaica, China, the Spice Islands of Indonesia, and Africa and even reaching into the cold vastness of outer space.

Surprisingly, we will see how many of the turning points of modern history are linked in startling ways, often building on one another or woven into a common web overlaid on the modern age. This interconnectedness, increasingly on a global scale, also is an emerging hallmark of modernity.

Most exciting of all is when our course considers turning points that are still turning! These are developments that are still in the process of unfolding in our lives today, with their consequences discernible (to the trained eye) in the events and dynamics of the present world. Ultimately, by tracking these evolutions, transformations, and connections, this course offers a better understanding of what it means to be modern. As a result, we can better understand ourselves and where we stand in the grand sweep of world history and the human project.

The final message of this course is an optimistic one: We reveal the astonishing capacity of human beings for creative responses to meet change and the shock of the new. Ordinary individuals, as well as great inventors and thinkers, have encountered changes and not only turned them to positive uses but also pushed these transformations onward.

This course, in sum, is an astonishing voyage into the meaning of modernity in our world—its origins, challenges, perils, and rewards. Together, we will make a quest of discovery! ∎

1433—The Great Voyages of Admiral Zheng He
Lecture 1

Under the Ming dynasty, Zheng He, a eunuch admiral, sailed a great Chinese fleet to India, the Middle East, and Africa. Almost 30 years after they had begun, these voyages were mysteriously curtailed, but if they had continued, world history might have been very different. As we'll see, Zheng He's voyages were not about discovery or exploration but most likely meant to assert the symbolic authority of the Chinese emperor; they were called off when a sign from heaven appeared—a giraffe!—to affirm the good government of the dynasty.

A Turning Point That Didn't Happen

- Imagine how world history would have changed if a huge fleet of ships from China had landed in the Americas 50 years before the voyages of Christopher Columbus. This could have been the moment when the hemispheres of the globe, previously largely isolated from each other, were united in one great historical encounter.

- On the deck of the flagship, directing this moment of global history, would have been standing a huge man, the Chinese admiral Zheng He, commanding a vast naval expedition to lay claim to this new world and bring it into the cultural orbit of the Ming dynasty.

- In the centuries to come, the ancient civilization of China would overspread North and South America in a dynamic process that would shape all of world history to come. The smaller European kingdoms, such as Portugal, Spain, or England, would be overshadowed and wouldn't even set forth to explore the oceans. But this was a turning point that didn't happen.

Defining Our Terms

- We should begin by asking: What is a turning point? A turning point marks a decisive moment that shapes later developments. If it had not happened, or had happened differently, matters would have taken an entirely different course in history. In this course, we'll look at crucial moments that have transformed the worldview of vast parts of humanity.

- What about the word "modern"? Modernity is a notoriously slippery concept because what is modern now soon becomes the past. The concept of "modern" is often applied to a historical period, starting in about the 15th century.

- Most often, attributes of modernity are thought to include the growth of technology, the autonomy of the individual, recourse to experimentation and science over the dictates of tradition, new concepts of popular sovereignty and equality, and new interconnectedness on an increasingly global scale.

- In a fascinating history entitled *The Birth of the Modern World*, historian C. A. Bayly adds another quality, arguing that "an essential part of being modern is thinking you are modern." Thus, modernity involves a mindset that stresses novelty and breaks with the past.

- Paradoxically, the very concept of a contingent turning point—the organizing theme of our course—is itself quite modern. The term "turning point" was apparently first used in English in 1836. An awareness of change marks modernity.

- In this course, we will seek to trace how the attributes of modern life have developed by looking closely at shifts over time in what are seen as the true sources of authority.
  - What makes authority legitimate and trustworthy? Here is a key attribute of modern life: the concept of change as progress. In a modern society, change and progress have authority: They are looked to, invoked, hoped for.

  - By contrast, in traditional societies, time-hallowed ways were authoritative. Newness was not a recommendation or a merit but immediately suspect. In reality, traditional societies were not unchanging and frozen, but even when something new was introduced, it would be presented as a revival of an earlier practice.

- By contrast, in modern societies, progress is sought in the new and the cutting edge. How did this shift take place, from novelty as suspicious to desirable? We will seek to follow how this inversion came to pass through each of our turning points.

Background to the Voyages of Zheng He

- By the start of the 15th century, China had thrown off its earlier Mongol ruling regime and a new dynasty had commenced, the Ming dynasty, which would rule until 1644.

- A key concept that undergirded authority in China was the idea of the "mandate of heaven," a concept that went back to the 4th century B.C. and was introduced by Confucian scholars.

From their capital in Beijing and the new Forbidden City, Ming emperors ruled over what they considered the central kingdom, backed by the authority of 4,000 years of continuous Chinese culture.

- o The heavenly mandate meant that when a ruler or a dynasty ruled in accordance with the laws of harmony in nature, its virtue would produce prosperity, well-being, and a government that was good for the people at large.

- o By contrast, rulers whose misrule violated the mandate of heaven would bring down social disorder and natural disasters: floods, famines, plagues.

- • After the disruptions that had passed under previous Mongol rule, the Ming dynasty prized stability and order—deeply Confucian values. The name of the emperor, Yongle, meant "perpetual happiness."
  - o At this time, Ming China had the most wealth and population of any economy in the world.

  - o Chinese leaders thought of their realm as self-sufficient. And indeed, at the time, China presented a dramatic contrast with Europe—an advanced civilization compared to a society that remained relatively primitive.

- • This conviction of the centrality of China was expressed in many ways. Among them was the view of commerce with neighboring countries. Trade was seen not as a mutually beneficial exchange but as a form of tribute sent to China, which the Chinese answered with magnanimous gifts.

- • The Ming dynasty was not isolated or intellectually incurious, and its earliest rulers were adventurous. Emperor Yongle fought against the Mongols, invaded Vietnam, and ordered his great admiral, Zheng He, to launch a series of voyages across the Indian Ocean.

The Life of Zheng He

- • What we know about Zheng He is disappointingly fragmentary. He was born in 1371 amid troubled times. At that point, his name was Ma, and he was from the Muslim minority in Yunnan, in southwestern China. His father and grandfather had both borne the title *hājjī*, signifying that they had made the pilgrimage to Mecca.

- As a 10-year-old boy, Zheng He was captured by the armies of the first Ming emperor, who was fighting against the Mongols. He was taken into the imperial court and castrated to serve as a eunuch official, part of the ruling elite of the imperial household.

- At the court, Zheng He became a close adviser to the son of the first Ming emperor, who went on to become Emperor Yongle. Unlike other eunuchs, Zheng He grew into an imposing figure, supposedly seven feet tall and powerfully built.

Zheng He's Voyages

- At the orders of his emperor, Zheng He sailed on seven voyages throughout Asia. The first of these took place in 1405 and the last in 1433. The fleets sailed to Malacca, Java, Sumatra in Indonesia, Thailand, Sri Lanka, Siam, India, the Persian Gulf, the Red Sea, Somalia, Zanzibar, and perhaps, Kenya.

- These fleets must have been imposing to see! Along with many smaller boats were the great treasure ships, 400 feet long with up to nine masts, watertight bulkheads, multiple cabins and decks, and huge crews. Europeans at this point had nothing that could compare.

- The voyages had many different purposes, but common to all was the projection of an image of power throughout the region to impress the claims to China's centrality and the emperor's authority.

The End of the Voyages

- In 1433, these diplomatic voyages were stopped. This seems a tantalizing moment: What if the fleets had continued and had ranged even further? What if they had rounded the southern tip of Africa and continued westward to discover the American continents? Or what if they had headed beyond Java to come at new worlds from the east?
    - The author Gavin Menzies has claimed in his book *1421: The Year China Discovered America* that they did just that, landing in present-day Oregon. Menzies further argued that Chinese fleets visited Australia and Italy, touching off the Renaissance.

- o Almost no historians agree with this argument, but it sums up the tantalizing sense of global possibility.

- Why were the voyages discontinued? First, Zheng He himself died in 1433. A tomb exists today in his hometown of Nanjing, but it is empty and, for many years, was all but forgotten.

- But even more than a matter of the fate of the eunuch admiral, the project of the voyages fell victim to the bureaucratic intrigues of the imperial court.
  - o There, a professional civil service class of Confucian scholars wrestled with the eunuch class for control of the agenda of government. The scholars claimed that the travels were a waste of funds and lives, and they won. The voyages were called off, and the great fleet was left to rot at the docks.

  - o Economic pressures may also have played a role as internal improvements made domestic trade more profitable than speculative overseas trade.

- This leaves us with a deeper question: Why did the voyages not go further afield, as part of a larger campaign of discovery?
  - o The reasons for this have everything to do with the theme of authority that we will pursue in this course. From the start, these voyages were not about exploration or discovery of new lands, nor the scientific collection of specimens or mapping. In fact, the fleets traveled routes that were already familiar to private Chinese merchants and traders.

  - o The real point of the voyages was to awe with what we today would call "soft power": the glory, impressiveness, and riches of Chinese culture, which the imperial elite saw as central to the world as a whole. The expeditions were about confirming something that was already known: the universal authority of the Chinese emperor and China's civilization.

- One particular passenger of the treasure fleets makes vividly clear that the voyages were about the assertion of authority. This was an African giraffe, brought back to China as tribute.

  o The giraffe seemed marvelous and exotic, but it was not considered fundamentally new or unprecedented; learned scholars said that it was, in fact, an animal already known from Chinese myth.

  o This rare beast was said to appear only at times of good government, when the emperor ruled in such a way as to bring order and prosperity. It was a sign of the mandate of heaven.

  o With the imperial Chinese authority so dramatically vindicated by the favor of heaven, the mission of the voyages was accomplished.

Suggested Reading

Bayly, *The Birth of the Modern World, 1780–1914.*

Dryer, *Zheng He.*

Levathes, *When China Ruled the Seas.*

Questions to Consider

1. Given that we know little about Admiral Zheng He, what do you see as his most important character traits?

2. If you were a member of the Ming court, how might you have argued for continuing these voyages?

1433—The Great Voyages of Admiral Zheng He
Lecture 1—Transcript

Hello. My name is Vejas Liulevicius. Welcome to this course on the great turning points of modern history: those particular discoveries, inventions, political upheavals, or great ideas which have transformed the history of the world since 1400. As we begin our examination of these top 24 transformative moments, let's begin with a turning point that was a turning point precisely because it did *not* happen. But perhaps could have. Imagine how much of world history, right down to our own times, would have been entirely different if this imaginary scenario had actually taken place.

It's the 1440s, a half century before the voyages of Christopher Columbus to the Americas. A huge fleet of enormous ships, far larger than any ever launched by the European kingdoms, approaches the forested American coast! This could be the moment when the hemispheres of the globe, east and west, previously largely isolated from one another, are united, in this one great historical encounter.

On the deck of the largest ship, the flagship of this huge navy, directing this moment of global history, stands a huge man, who entirely towers over others on the ship. But what sets him apart even more than his stature is his unflinching, focused, stern gaze. He is the Chinese admiral Zheng He, and he commands this vast Chinese naval expedition, which will lay claim to what seems to them a new world, bringing the Americas into the cultural orbit of the magnificent Ming dynasty, ruled over by an emperor who enjoys the favor of heaven itself.

Then, in the centuries to come, the ancient civilization which China represents will overspread the North American and South American continents, in a dynamic process which will shape all of following world history. Eventually there may be no need for the smaller European kingdoms like Portugal, Spain, or England to set forth and explore the oceans, now that they've been so completely overshadowed! No need for a Christopher Columbus.

In the centuries that follow, all of the global international system, as it evolves, will depend on the fortunes of the Ming dynasty in China. An emerging global civilization will be founded on the basis of Chinese Confucian values. Centuries later, this very lecture you are listening to right now might instead be delivered in elegant, learned Mandarin. But this did not happen. We will examine shortly the background and reasons for this turning point that did not turn.

We should really begin by asking, what is a turning point? How can a turning point be defined? A turning point marks a decisive moment which shapes later developments. If it had not happened, or it happened differently, matters would have taken an entirely different course in history. For the purposes of our course, to make that very tough call concerning what are the top 24 turning points of modern history, I want to add further this emphasis: We will choose those crucial moments which have jolted how vast parts of humanity have viewed their world. We'll zero in on those moments when how humans perceive their world has been radically changed, when their entire worldview has been upset and transformed, when their mental map of the world is reconfigured.

Whether covering a turning point in technological change (like the invention of the printing press or the atomic bomb), or of political history (like the establishment of nation-states as essentially the default mode of world politics), or of social transformation (like the abolition of slavery or the recognition—finally—of women's right to vote), and many, many other turning points—in each case, we'll focus on the impact that this had on the worldview and general outlook of contemporaries. What they hoped or feared would be the effects of this turning point.

This of course does not mean that in every case, the thinking of each and every living person at the time was changed in the same way, or that everyone saw a newly transformed world in the exactly the same terms. Human beings are far too complicated for that. Often indeed, older worldviews still persisted and lingered. Our focus here will be on how turning points were lived and experienced by large aggregations of people, on the ground so to speak.

On this score, there's a very hopeful and positive note that comes out of our course. We'll see how, in spite of the repeated shock of the new, human creativity in adapting to new worlds is astonishing and ultimately very hopeful. Thus, the turning points this course covers are not the same as merely the greatest events of history. Rather, most profoundly, these are the moments of true change in worldview!

Another useful point to note is that this course specifically looks at how these turning points have shaped the *modern* world, since 1400. This raises a key question: What is modern? What does that mean, as opposed to the ancient or premodern? What is "modernity"? Modernity is a notoriously slippery concept, because, obviously, what is modern now will soon become the past, as time marches relentlessly forward.

The very word "modern" in fact simply derives from the Latin word *modo* for "just now," in distinction to the past. Yet the concept of "modern" is often applied to an entire historical period, starting about when our course begins, the 15th century. Most often, attributes of modernity are thought to include the growth of technology, the autonomy of the individual, a recourse to experimentation, and science instead of trusting the dictates of tradition. It includes new concepts of popular sovereignty and equality, and also a new interconnectedness on an increasingly global scale.

In a fascinating history entitled *The Birth of the Modern World*, historian C.A. Bayly adds another quality, arguing that, "an essential part of being modern is thinking you are modern. Modernity is an aspiration to be 'up with the times.' It was a process of emulation and borrowing." So modernity as a process involves a mindset that stresses novelty and breaks with the past.

Indeed, consider this beautiful paradox: The very concept of a contingent turning point that could have gone different ways, the organizing theme of our course, is itself very modern. The term "turning point" was apparently first used in English in 1836. An awareness of change is ultimately what marks modernity. In our course, we will seek to trace how the attributes of modern life (as we know it) have grown up and developed by looking closely at shifts over time in what are seen as the true sources of authority. What makes an authority legitimate and trustworthy? Here, we'll argue, is a key defining attribute of modern life: the concept of change as progress, and thus a source of authority. In a modern society, change and progress possess authority. They are looked to, they are invoked, and they're hoped for.

What a contrast with traditional societies, where time-hallowed ways were authoritative. These societies would say, "We do this in this way because that is how it has always been done." In a traditional society, newness was not a recommendation, or considered a merit. Something that was new was, on the contrary, immediately suspect just for that reason. Now in fact, traditional societies in the past, in reality, were never unchanging or frozen, but they were marked by this reverence for tradition. Even when something new was introduced, it would be presented as a revival of an earlier practice, a positive return to the original "good old days."

By contrast, in modern societies like our own, progress is sought in the new, that which is cutting edge, the latest thing, or the next big thing. Think of the constant refrain of advertisements: "new and improved." We want to ask in this course, how and why did this shift take place, from novelty as something that's suspicious and dubious, to the new as desirable and good? We'll investigate this. We will seek to follow how this huge total inversion came to pass, through each of our turning points with growing intensity.

Coming back to our turning point that did not happen, what's the background to this fascinating story? By the start of the 15th century, China had thrown off its earlier Mongol ruling regime and a new dynasty had begun, the Ming dynasty, which would rule all the way until 1644. The name of the dynasty, Ming, meant "brightness," to contrast its rule with the dark, unhappy recent times. From their capital in Beijing, and their splendid new Forbidden City there, the Ming emperors ruled over what they considered the "central kingdom," of the world, backed by the authority of four thousand years of continuous Chinese culture.

A key concept that undergirded the authority that was exercised in China was a particular idea, the idea of the "mandate of heaven." This was a concept that went back to the 4th century B.C. and was introduced by Confucian scholars. The mandate of heaven meant that when a ruler, or a dynasty, ruled in accord with the laws of harmony that were all throughout nature, the virtue of the ruler would produce prosperity, well-being, order and a government that was good for the people at large. Naturally by contrast, rulers whose misrule violated the mandate of heaven would bring down social disorder and natural disasters: floods, famines, and plagues. They wouldn't rule for long.

After the disruptions that had just passed under the previous Mongol rule, the Ming dynasty prized, above all, stability and order, deeply Confucian values.

The name of the emperor, Yongle, meant "perpetual happiness." That's what they hoped for. At this time, Ming China had the most wealth and population of any economy in the world, and the prospects looked good. China in a word was the superpower of its times, and knew it.

Think for a moment of the worldview, the image of the surrounding world that all of this implied. Chinese leaders thought of their realm as complete, self-sufficient, not needing anything from outside. The rest of the world was the periphery, as they saw it. Indeed, at the time, China presented a dramatic contrast with Europe. China was an advanced Asian civilization, while European civilization remained in many ways relatively rough-hewn and primitive by comparison. This had already been true in the days of Marco Polo when he made his journeys a hundred years previous.

This conviction of the centrality of China was expressed in many ways. Among them was the way in which commerce with other neighboring countries was presented in China not as trade with foreigners, a mutually beneficial exchange, but instead as a form of tribute that was being sent to China, which then would be answered by magnanimous, generous gifts in turn (but not in exchange). Merchants were not highly valued in Confucian tradition, nor was commerce.

The Ming dynasty, it needs to be said, was not isolated and intellectually incurious—on the contrary, the printing of books and especially of a famous huge encyclopedia, the *Yongle Encyclopedia*, attest to this face. The emperor Yongle had commissioned this encyclopedic work as a summation of all knowledge as known in his realm.

The earliest rulers of the Ming dynasty also were venturesome. Emperor Yongle fought against the Mongols and invaded Vietnam to bring it back into the Chinese orbit. Most dramatically, the emperor did this: He ordered his great admiral, Zheng He, to launch a series of great voyages across and around the Indian Ocean. From 1405 to 1433, this man, who would later be called by some the "Chinese Columbus," travelled far and wide.

Who was he? In fact, what we know about him is disappointingly fragmentary, but here it is. Zheng He was born in 1371, in troubled times. At that point, his name was Ma, and he was from the Muslim minority in Yunnan, in southwestern China. His father and his grandfather had both carried the title *hājjī*, which in Muslim civilization honors someone who has made the Haj, the pilgrimage to the holy site of Mecca, which is a religious duty for the faithful. So perhaps from the very beginning this boy had travel and the crossing of vast distances right in his bones.

But the man who would become that great Chinese admiral grew up far from any sea. As a ten-year-old boy, Zheng He was captured by the armies of the first Ming emperor, who at that time were fighting against the Mongols, whose rule they had overthrown. The young boy was taken into the imperial court—his talents were recognized. There, he was castrated. He was to serve as a eunuch official, part of the ruling elite of the imperial household. These eunuchs were the advisors to the emperor, trusted because it was assumed that after their castration, their loyalties would lie only with the emperor. Not having the ability to establish families of their own, the eunuchs would (at least in theory) have no other rival loyalties or attachments that would distract them from the service of the emperor.

At the court, Zheng He became a close adviser to the son of the first Ming emperor, and that son would go on to become Emperor Yongle. Unlike other eunuchs who remained small in size, Zheng He grew into an imposing figure. He is supposed to have been seven feet tall and powerfully built. Some records say that his voice was "as loud as a huge bell."

Now, at the orders of his emperor, Zheng He sailed on seven great voyages throughout Asia. The first of these voyages took place in 1405, the last in 1433. The fleets sailed to Malacca, Java, Sumatra in Indonesia, Thailand, Sri Lanka, Siam, India, the Persian Gulf, the Red Sea, and East Africa, down to Somalia and Zanzibar, and perhaps even to Kenya. They covered and retraced a distance of 9,000 miles and visited more than 30 countries. These fleets must have been imposing to see! They had many smaller boats, but the great features of these fleets were the great treasure ships, some 400 feet long (making them longer than an American football field), with up to nine masts, watertight bulkheads, many cabins and multiple decks, and huge crews.

By contrast, Europeans at this point had nothing that could compare. These treasure ships were the largest ships on the seas until the days of Industrial

Revolution, indeed the largest wooden ships ever put to sea. The largest of these Chinese treasure ships is estimated to have weighed 7,800 tons, making it three times bigger than contemporary European ships, and indeed remained so for the next three centuries. All of those famous ships of Columbus could have easily fit inside the storage areas of just one of the great treasure ships.

Each trip involved some 300 ships sailing in a fleet, with about 30,000 participants involved. By contrast, when the Portuguese explorer Vasco da Gama sailed in this same area later, it was with four ships and about 170 men. The Chinese crews of the treasure fleets included doctors, translators (especially for Arabic, a language of commerce in the area), astrologers, astronomers, and even pharmacists. The ships employed the compass to navigate. The great ships were accompanied by many others that were in a supply function: junks with water and rice, combat ships, and troop transports. The ships are said to have even had floating gardens that were maintained to provision the vast force as it sailed.

The voyages had many different purposes, but common to all was the projection of an image of power through the region, to vindicate and impress on everyone the claim to China's centrality and the Yongle emperor's authority. The early voyages may also have been charged with another mission, hunting down a rival claimant to China's throne who had fled abroad. Zheng He also took time to suppress piracy in the strategic Malacca Strait area, that seaway between Malaysia and Sumatra in Indonesia, between the Indian Ocean and the Pacific, which then, as now, is one of the key geopolitical points and shipping routes in the world.

Most of all, the voyages visited country after country on a diplomatic mission, receiving tribute and bestowing gifts in exchange. The aim of these missions was not to impose one faith, in contrast to the European explorers that we'll discuss later. In fact, Zheng He placed stone monuments to commemorate the visits that he made, like one in Sri Lanka, which invoked each of the major religions of the area: Buddhist, Hindu, and Muslim. Local rulers from foreign countries would sometimes be brought to China aboard these ships to honor the emperor on official visits.

Just imagine for a moment what the impact of one of these visits might have been for a local ruler—in fact, suppose for a moment that you are that ruler.

You've been minding your own business, concerned with the many details of administering your kingdom. You're certainly aware of Chinese civilization, far away though it might be, because after all, individual Chinese merchants have been making regular trips to bring desirable goods to your kingdom.

Then one day, without any advance word or warning, on the ocean horizon appears a fleet of Chinese ships so vast and numerous that it looks more like an approaching monsoon. It's sailing directly towards you. The eunuch admiral commanding this fleet will arrive at your court with greetings and gifts of silk and other precious things, but the message of China's power and prestige that was communicated by your just seeing that fleet for the first time will always be unforgettable.

Then, in 1433, these great voyages stopped. This seems a tantalizing moment: What if the fleets had continued and had ranged even further? What if they had rounded the southern tip of Africa and had continued westwards, to discover the American continents? Or what if they had headed beyond Java eastwards, to come at new worlds in that way? The author Gavin Menzies has claimed precisely this in his book, entitled *1421: The Year China Discovered America*. He claims that the Chinese landed in present-day Oregon, and also has argued that Chinese fleets visited Australia, and also Italy where they touched off the Renaissance. Almost no historians agree with this argument, but it sums up the tantalizing sense of global possibility—what might have been. How do we explain this mystery?

Why were the voyages discontinued? First, the imposing figure of Zheng He himself passed from the scene, dying of illness on the seventh voyage, on his way back home in 1433. A tomb exists today in his hometown of Nanjing, the old capital, but it's empty and for a long time was all but forgotten. Oddly enough, the memory of Zheng He endured in some overseas Chinese communities, where he came to be revered as a god. In that way at least, he achieved a kind of immortality after all. But even more than the matter of the fate of this one eunuch admiral, the project of the voyages fell victim to what we might call office politics, the bureaucratic infighting of the imperial court. There, a professional civil service class of Confucian scholars (who studied classics that were already 2,000 years old) was engaged in a conflict with the class of eunuchs (who handled Chinese commercial relations). At stake was control of the agenda of government. The Confucian scholars claimed that the travels were a waste of funds and lives, and in this dispute the scholars won. The voyages were called off. The great fleet was left to rot in place at the docks. One story suggests that these bureaucrats, to prevent anyone in the future reviving the idea of the voyages, even went so far as to destroy the records of Zheng He's travels in 1477.

They went further. By 1500, the imperial government declared that anyone who built a ship with more than two masts, able to travel far, would be condemned to death. In 1525, the government went further and just made it illegal to build any ship to sail the high seas. Admittedly economic pressures may have played a role in some of these decisions as well, as internal improvements within China made domestic trade more profitable than speculative overseas commerce. But this leaves us with a deeper haunting question: Why did the voyages not go further afield, as part of a larger campaign of discovery? The reasons for this have everything to do with the theme of authority which we'll pursue throughout this course. From the start, these voyages were not about exploration or the discovery of new lands. Not about the scientific collection of specimens or mapping of territories. In fact, they covered routes that already were familiar to many private Chinese merchants and traders.

The real point of the voyages was to spread awe, to communicate what we today would call China's "soft power": the glory, the impressiveness, and the riches of Chinese culture, which the imperial Chinese elite saw as central to the world as a whole. The expeditions were not about finding something new but about confirming something that was already known: the universal authority of the Chinese emperor and China's civilization. As a later official history put it, the voyages had happened because the emperor "wanted to display his soldiers in strange lands to make manifest the wealth and power of China." To make manifest, to announce to the world with authority, to make clear to one and all!

As Zheng He prepared for the seventh voyage in 1431, he actually set up a stone monument which explained his travels from his perspective. Let's listen to his words. The voyages, he said, had been about spreading the influence of the Ming dynasty, which he said, "has unified the lands within the four seas and under the canopy of Heaven. From the edge of the sky to the ends of the earth, there are none who have not become subjects and slaves."

The voyages of the fleet went so far afield into remote regions that they met foreigners whose languages needed what Zheng He called double translation— their language needed to be translated into another language that was known to Chinese translators, and only then into Chinese. These were people far afield. Such barbarians that did not recognize the superiority of the Ming and their civilization had to be captured and persuaded otherwise.

One particular passenger of the treasure fleets makes vividly clear that the voyages were about the assertion of authority. That was an African giraffe that was brought back to China as tribute. Actually, there were several of them. When they were displayed in China, they seemed marvelous and exotic, but not fundamentally new or unprecedented: Learned scholars in China said that these were in fact an animal already known from Chinese myth, the miraculous Qilin. It was said to be a kind of Chinese unicorn, with a horn, the hoofs of a horse, the tail of an ox, and the body of a deer, and skin that was dappled with spots. This rare beast, the Qilin, would appear only at times of good government, when the emperor ruled so as to bring order and prosperity, so the Qilin was a sign of the mandate of heaven.

An official of the Imperial Academy addressed the emperor on this topic: "The ministers and the people all gathered to gaze at it and their joy knows no end. … This," meaning the Qilin, "shows that Your Majesty's virtue equals that of Heaven; its merciful blessings have spread far and wide so that its harmonious vapors have emanated a Qilin, as an endless bliss to the state for a myriad myriad years. … Oh how glorious is the Sacred Emperor who excels both in literary and military virtues. Who has succeeded to the Precious Throne and has accomplished perfect order and imitated the Ancients!" Who wouldn't enjoy praise like that?

The voyages had been thus about authority, and now that the imperial Chinese authority was so dramatically proved by the favor of Heaven, the mission was accomplished. Yet, turning back those treasure fleets left a power vacuum in the Indian Ocean, which would in short order be filled by the Portuguese, then the Dutch, then the British. This was a turning point that could have happened, but did not, with decisive consequences down to our own times. After examining this turning point that did not turn, we direct our attention to one that did, the fall of a great and seemingly permanent empire, in our next lecture.

1453—The Fall of Constantinople
Lecture 2

Many educated people think they know about the fall of the Roman Empire. They believe that Rome collapsed when it was sacked in 410 and again in 455 or when Germanic tribes slouched into the imperial capital and deposed the last Roman emperor in the west in 476. Those bare facts are true, but the real end of the Roman Empire as a whole took place 1,000 years later, at the dawn of our modern age, with the fall of the imperial city of Constantinople to the Ottoman Turks. Today, this is the city of Istanbul in Turkey; in 1453, it was the focus of a dramatic turning point.

Byzantium
- Part of our difficulty in recognizing that the fall of Constantinople was the true fall of the Roman Empire is that later historians imposed a name on the surviving empire in the east that was not used by the people who inhabited it themselves: Byzantium.

- In fact, long after the Roman Empire in the west had fallen, the survivors in the east thought of themselves as the true Romans and saw their state as, self-evidently, the real Roman Empire.
  - Constantinople had been established in 330 by Emperor Constantine, not far from where legendary Troy had once stood. It was to be the Roman capital of the east and so it remained.

  - It was set on a pivotal geopolitical spot, the meeting place of two oceans and two continents. Whoever ruled in this city seemed to bestride much of the known world.

- But all this came crashing down in 1453, as the last remnants of the Roman Empire in the east crumbled and fell. Why did the fall of Constantinople matter? In what sense is this a turning point of modern history? The answer is threefold.

○ First, the end of the Roman Empire haunted modern consciousness and echoes into our own times. Our very word "empire," from *imperium* in Latin, means "authority." The seemingly universal empire of Rome had been a key source of political and symbolic authority, and what would now replace it?

○ Second, the fall of Constantinople would prompt desperate bids to inherit the mantle of universal empire—even into modern times! It would be an abiding dream of men of destiny to revive the glory that had been Rome.

○ Third, the collapse of this Christian empire in the east redrew the world's political map in fundamental ways and touched off the European voyages of discovery that would lead Columbus to what for Europeans was a new world.

Constantinople before 1453

- By 1453, Constantinople was in bad shape, but centuries before, it had flourished. Traders from across Europe and Asia mingled in its streets. Throughout the city were splendid churches, glowing with gold icons and crosses. The imperial palaces were dreams of marble, radiating power. But by 1453, this picture was much reduced.

- In 1204, in a terrible irony, a Crusader army had sacked Constantinople, and fellow Christians devastated the city.

Many tourists admire the bronze horses atop the Basilica of Saint Mark in Venice, but few know that those horses were stolen from Constantinople.

- Next, Constantinople faced the onslaught of the Ottoman Turks, who swiftly conquered the Eastern Roman Empire's lands in the Near East, until Constantinople was reduced to its city limits.

- In these crises, Constantinople could not hope for help from the West, because doctrinal questions had separated the Western Latin Christians from the Eastern Orthodox Christians in the Great Schism of 1054.

The Fall of the City

- Determined to capture Constantinople, a young Ottoman sultan, Mehmet II, and his armies began a siege on Easter Monday, April 2, 1453. Inside the walls, Emperor Constantine XI was determined to hold out, even if the situation was hopeless.

- The siege lasted eight weeks. The city's defenders strung a huge chain, floated on barrels, across the entrance to the inlet and harbor—the Golden Horn. They hunkered down behind the 1,000-year-old walls of their capital. Seven thousand defenders were matched against some 80,000 invaders.

- Outside the city was mustered the huge Ottoman army, which included Christian forces and the Janissaries, elite shock troops. A Hungarian artillery expert named Orban gave the Ottomans a dreaded new weapon, a 27-foot cannon that used gunpowder. It must have been deafening when fired; this was the sound of a military revolution, making stone walls, towers, and battlements obsolete.

- The defenders were delighted when some reinforcements arrived from the commercial city-state of Genoa, including an expert in fortifications. The Genoese expert helped the Byzantines rebuild or reinforce crumbling parts of the city wall by night after they had been pounded by cannon during the day. Further, Genoese ships managed to break through the Ottoman blockade and reach the harbor.

- But then, in an amazing military feat, the Ottomans lifted some of their own ships out of the water and rolled them two or three miles over land. Eventually, they set the ships down in the water on the far side of the chain across the harbor, circumventing that defense.

- Through it all, Emperor Constantine XI refused to surrender and rallied both locals and Latin Christians fighting in defense of the beleaguered city, gathering them for shared worship at the Hagia Sophia. In a way, it was a truly remarkable moment—after centuries of doctrinal division within Christianity, in the last days of this besieged city, ecumenical unity appeared. But it could not stop the inevitable.

- After long weeks of siege and the relentless pounding of the cannon, the walls of Constantinople fell. The Janissaries raced in to exploit the breach, and the defenders fell back. The city fell on May 29, 1453, and was sacked by the forces of Mehmet.

- The news of the fall of Constantinople took some time to spread, but when it finally reached the West, it was met with shock, disbelief, and horror. Some refused to believe it or were certain that it must be reversed.

The Ottoman Victory as a Turning Point

- As we said, Constantinople was already well past its glory days before the arrival of the Turks. Its fall was inevitable, only a question of time. How, then, is this a turning point? Apart from the historical event itself, its effects, especially how it was viewed by contemporaries, were shattering. They had become used to the notion that Constantinople was always under threat, perpetually in crisis, and yet it had always somehow survived.

- There were three main results of this turning point related to how the world was seen, with consequences to the present. The first of these is that after this final fall of the Roman Empire, much of the world would be haunted by the ghost of the memory of what Rome had been, what it had once achieved and represented.
  - In this earlier age, thinking about the implications of the fall of Constantinople was based on the medieval concept

of *translatio imperii*, the "transfer of rule," as an organizing principle of history. European scholars looking out at the world concluded that history was based on a succession of empires, one following the other, based on divine favor.

- When one empire had played out its role, a new empire would arise to take its place. Babylon had given way to Persia, Persia to Greece, and Greece to Rome. Now that Rome was gone, what new power would follow? The vacuum left by the fall of Rome at Constantinople in 1453 was the turning point.

- The second result of this moment would be the recurring bids to inherit universal empire. Most strikingly, the Ottoman Turkish sultans saw themselves as the legitimate successors of the Romans. Indeed, after Mehmet had seized Constantinople, he next laid plans to capture Rome in Italy.

  - In a way, for the city of Constantinople, this eagerness of the new rulers to assert continuity with what went before was lucky. Instead of just fading into oblivion, the city dramatically revived under Ottoman rule, again becoming a center of authority, trade, and commerce.

  - The dream of inheriting the empire also was deeply influential in Russian history because Russia had received its Orthodox faith from Constantinople. This spiritual and historic link was expressed in the potent idea of Moscow as the "Third Rome." The desire to ascend to this position led to a durable impulse in Russian foreign policy—an expansionist impulse that impelled Russia to grow in the following centuries.

  - In the German lands, the Holy Roman Empire, as it came to be called, claimed to be the successor to Rome. In the 19th century, the French leader Napoleon, as he swept across Europe, set about creating a Grand Empire, also outfitted with Roman symbols. Even as late as the 20th century, the dream of Rome endured. The German dictator Adolf Hitler's attempt at a world empire also looked back to Roman models.

- Finally, the third result of the fall of Constantinople was the redrawing of the world map in the minds of men.
  - The decline and fall of that great imperial city contributed to a movement already taking place in Europe: the Renaissance. The texts brought out of Constantinople in the years leading up to 1453 fed a second wave of Renaissance activity that was based on the rediscovery of Greek texts. Most important of all was the teaching of the Greek language to the Italian humanists.

  - Further, the fall of Constantinople presented a geographic problem for Europeans. Trade routes with the Orient were now largely in the hands of the Ottoman Turks. The desire to outflank the Turks and find alternate routes for trade spurred European voyages of discovery, including the voyage that led Columbus to what was for him a new world.

  - This drive to outflank the Turks also had a strategic and religious dimension that recalled the Crusades: The key geopolitical location of earlier authority, Constantinople, had been lost, and the religious and political imperative was to find a way around that fact. In a real way, the loss of Rome opened a gap in the mental map of the world, and that gap was what became this turning point.

Suggested Reading

Brownworth, *Lost to the West*.

Crowley, *1453*.

Questions to Consider

1. What do you consider the greatest legacy of the Roman Empire that affects our times?

2. Do empires tend to die with a whimper or a bang?

1453—The Fall of Constantinople
Lecture 2—Transcript

Let me ask you a fascinating and rather strange question: What is the sound of a civilization as it collapses? What sound does an empire make when it comes crashing down? Imagine that we are standing on the ramparts of an ancient imperial city. It's a spring day in the year of 1453, and below us are uncountable, shouting, surging crowds of enemy soldiers who are massing for an attack on our city. High above those frenzied masses, we are standing on great thick walls that are already a thousand years old. Until now, the walls have always held, repelling siege after siege, attack after attack.

But shortly, we will hear a new sound, louder and more frightening than any we have heard before—the booming thunder of siege cannon, beginning to pound, shatter, and then breach these great walls. That rumble of great cannon we hear in the distance announces the true end of the Roman Empire.

Many educated people think they know about the fall of the Roman Empire, long ago at the start of the medieval period. They believe that the glory that was Rome collapsed when in 410, the Visigoths sacked Rome, or in 455 when the Vandals sacked Rome again, or when finally in 476 Germanic tribes slouched into the imperial capital in Italy and simply deposed the last Roman emperor in the west.

Those bare facts are true, but the real story is much more complicated, and actually comes much later. The real end of the Roman Empire as a whole actually happened a thousand years later, at the dawn of our modern age, with the fall of the great imperial city of Constantinople to the Ottoman Turks. Today this is the city of Istanbul in Turkey. In 1453, it was the focus of a dramatic turning point.

Part of our difficulty in recognizing that this was the true fall of the Roman Empire is that later historians imposed a name on the surviving Roman Empire in the East that was not used by those people themselves. Historians called it Byzantium and referred to the Byzantine Empire. The name comes from the older Greek name for the settlement that had stood on that spot before. But in fact, the so-called Byzantines, at their time called themselves Romans. Long after the Roman Empire in the west had fallen, the survivors in the great Roman Empire in the east thought of themselves as the true remaining Romans (even as they mostly spoke Greek). They saw their state as, self-evidently, the real Roman Empire.

Constantinople had been established in the year 330 by Emperor Constantine, not far from where legendary Troy had once stood. Constantinople was to be the Roman capital of the East, and so it remained. It was set on a crucial, pivotal geopolitical spot, the meeting place of two oceans and two continents. This one spot straddles Europe and Asia, and the Turkish Straits (also called the Dardanelles and Bosporus) link the Black Sea and the Mediterranean Sea. These were key places in the horizons of the ancient, classical world. Whoever ruled in this city seemed to bestride much of the known world. But all this came crashing down in 1453, as the last remnants of the Roman Empire in the east crumbled and fell. Why did the fall of Constantinople matter? In what sense is this a turning point of modern history? The reasons are threefold.

First, the end of the Roman Empire, the glory that had been Rome, would continue to haunt modern consciousness, and echoes into our own times. Our very word "empire," from the Latin word *imperium*, means authority, the ability to command. As we already suggested in our previous lecture, this theme of authority and how it changes will be a recurring theme in our course. The seemingly universal empire of Rome had been in its day a key source of political and symbolic authority. When it was gone, what would now replace it? Second, the fall of Constantinople would prompt repeated, desperate bids to inherit the mantle of universal empire, reaching into modern times. It would be an abiding dream of men of destiny to revive the glory that had been Rome. Third and finally, the collapse of this Christian empire in the east redrew the world's political map in really fundamental ways, and touched off as a result the European voyages of discovery that would lead Columbus to what for Europeans was a new world.

So what did this glorious capital look like as the turning point of 1453 approached? An essential fact to keep in mind is that by 1453, once-great Constantinople was in very bad shape. Centuries before it had flourished. Imagine for a moment what its streets and market squares had been like when it was at its height. Here, where trade routes crossed, you could hear a multitude of languages of Europe and Asia. Walking in the alleyways, you could smell exotic spices imported from far away, wine of the very choicest vintages. Throughout the city were splendid churches, with dark interiors glowing with gold and rich icons and crosses. You could hear the chanting of monks, and smell the wafting of incense. The imperial palaces radiated power: They were, in a way, dreams of marble and gold and silk in the imperial purple color.

But all that was before—by 1453, this picture was much reduced, and much poorer. The last two centuries had not been kind to Constantinople. In a terrible irony, in 1204 a Christian Crusader army had actually sacked Constantinople, fellow Christians devastating a Christian city. The Venetians, whose navy had brought the Crusaders on this mission, engaged in a massive pillaging of relics and art from Constantinople. (Today, many tourists in Venice admire the bronze horses atop the Basilica of St. Mark, but few know that those horses were robbed from Constantinople.)

Next, Constantinople faced the onslaught of the Ottoman Turks, a new force who swiftly conquered the Eastern Roman Empire's lands in the Near East, until eventually Constantinople was reduced essentially just to its city limits, a capital without its empire! In these crises, Constantinople could not really hope for help from the West, because doctrinal questions and theological disputes had separated the Western Latin Christians from the Eastern Orthodox Christians in the so-called Great Schism of 1054.

The Ottoman Turks for their part were determined to capture the splendid city. Their nickname for it was the "Golden Apple," the ultimate prize. Like New York, the "Big Apple" of our times, Constantinople, the Golden Apple, was seen at the time as the ultimate metropolis, the ultimate object of desire. Given all this, it was clear that eventually the city must fall, and the real wonder is how long it had held out, given its deeply weakened state. The young Ottoman sultan, Mehmet II, and his armies began their siege on Easter Monday, April 2, 1453. Inside the city walls, Emperor Constantine XI was determined to hold out, even if the situation was hopeless.

Afterwards, this would seem like an eerie symmetry, that the last emperor, like the first emperor who had established the city, were both named Constantine. It was like a destiny coming full circle. But there were other events that were feared at the time as bad omens for the city. There was a lunar eclipse, there were mysterious dense fogs, and people were horrified to see strange lights dancing above the church dome of Hagia Sophia during the night. The siege, once it began, lasted for eight weeks. The city's defenders strung a huge metal chain, floated on barrels, across the entrance of the harbor, the Golden Horn. The defenders hunkered down behind the huge thousand-year-old walls of their capital, and waited. Seven thousand defenders were matched against some 80,000 invaders.

Outside the city was mustered the huge Ottoman army, which in fact even included some Christian forces who were fighting with the Ottomans as allies. The elite of the Ottomans were the Janissaries. The Janissaries were what we today would call shock troops, who as boys had been taken from their Christian parents in the Balkans, under Ottoman rule, had been converted to Islam and then conscripted into the Ottoman army, where they were a kind of supersoldier. One other figure would be decisive as well, and that was a Hungarian artillery expert, by the name of Orban, who gave the Ottomans a dreaded new weapon, a monster cannon using gunpowder. Gunpowder, with its explosive potential, was actually a Chinese invention, from around the 9th century. Knowledge of gunpowder had reached Europe around the 12th century. Once this technology was perfected by people like Orban, it would devastate the certainties and the traditions and the way of life of the medieval age. Think of the Middle Ages, and one of the first things that probably would leap to mind for us are castles, those immense, strongly fortified structures that were the power bases of their day. Artillery would change all of that, as the shattering of the walls of Constantinople was about to demonstrate.

The young artillery expert Orban at first offered his services to Constantinople. His native Hungary was a Christian country after all, so there was this religious affinity, and for awhile Orban worked for Constantinople. But then the money to pay him ran out, so Orban went over to the Turks because they offered him a better salary. Nothing personal—better financial incentives. Now, Orban the professional artillery master constructed a monster cannon, the largest yet seen, that would be used to pound the ancient walls of Constantinople. The cannon was 27 feet long, and it was able to shoot a 1,500-pound stone ball at the defenses of the beleaguered city. When this huge artillery piece was actually cast and constructed in faraway Adrianople, it had to be hauled, physically moved, more than a hundred miles to be moved up to the besieged city. Hundreds of Turkish soldiers and teams of oxen dragged it there, moving two and a half miles every day.

When it finally had been dragged and put into position, the sight must have been awe-inspiring, and clearly very bad news for the defenders of Constantinople. With deafening thunder, the cannon fired. In fact, the cannon could only be fired seven times each day, because it needed to be cooled off in between; otherwise, it might explode. But in addition to this monster gun were many other smaller cannon that continued the bombardment that had begun. This was the sound of a military revolution, making stone walls and towers and battlements largely obsolete.

The defenders were delighted when some reinforcements from the West actually did arrive in spite of the theological differences. These reinforcements came from the Italian commercial city-state of Genoa, and among their number was an expert in fortifications. That Genoese fortifications expert in fact, remarkably, helped the Byzantines to rebuild or reinforce crumbling parts of the city wall by night, after they had been pounded by cannon during the day. During the night, the damage of the day would be made good. Further Genoese ships actually managed to break through the Ottoman blockade and reach the harbor, bringing reinforcements and supplies.

But then, in an amazing military feat, the Ottomans actually lifted some of their own ships out of the water, and rolled them, over land and surrounding mountains for some two or three miles, using logs as rollers, by brute force transporting them over the terrain. Then, they set the ships down on the water on the far side of the chain that had been drawn across the harbor. The Ottomans had circumvented that famous defense. To demoralize the defenders and to stir fear inside the city, the Turks also impaled prisoners within sight of the walls. The Byzantines responded by throwing Turkish prisoners to their deaths from the ramparts.

Through it all, Emperor Constantine refused to surrender, and rallied both local inhabitants of the city and Latin Christians from Venice and Genoa, who were merchants who had worked in the city, all fighting together in defense of the beleaguered metropolis. In fact, the defenders gathered for shared worship at the beautiful church of Hagia Sophia. In a way, this was a truly remarkable moment within a crisis. After centuries of doctrinal division within Christianity, in this besieged city, in its very last days, ecumenical unity had appeared at the last moment. But even this could not stop the inevitable. After long weeks of siege, after the relentless pounding of the cannon that had been set up and directed by the Hungarian professional Orban, the walls at last broke. The Ottomans' elite forces, the Janissaries, raced in to exploit the breach, and the defenders started to fall back from the walls. The city was about to be taken. Emperor Constantine did something dramatic. He shouted out to all who could hear, "The City is lost, but I live." With that, he tore off the emblems of his imperial rank, what marked him as the emperor, and like an ordinary soldier rushed into the thickest part of the fighting, and he was never seen alive again.

The city of Constantinople fell on May 29, 1453. Mehmet's forces sacked the city, and sold the surviving inhabitants into slavery. The sultan Mehmet entered Hagia Sophia, what had been a church, and now turned it into a mosque. Geometric designs were painted over the famous mosaics of Hagia Sophia, and verses of the Koran were placed where earlier holy icons had been hung. Henceforth, the victor of this siege would acquire a new nickname. He would be known as "Mehmet the Conqueror." He would also be called the "Sultan of Rum," that is to say, the Sultan of Rome, of the lands of the expired Roman Empire. In the rest of Europe, the news of the fall of the city took some time to spread given what communications were like, how slow they were in those days. In fact, given the confused situation of war, news of the capture of Constantinople only reached Rome and Italy more than a month after it had happened! But when the news did spread in the West, it was met with shock, disbelief, and a growing sense of horror. Some contemporaries simply refused to believe it, as if the news must be wrong. Others accepted it but were certain that this must be reversed; it must be changed. In fact, fascinating rumors circulated that sort of reinforced the strength of this conviction.

Such rumors are worth considering because they tell us deep truths about what people at the time were feeling, fearing, or wishing. Let me offer two examples. Because as I've mentioned, the emperor Constantine had rushed into battle without insignia, his body was never identified after the fighting. As a result, legends circulated that the emperor Constantine did not die, but had miraculously been saved, and had fallen into a mystical sleep. The rumors continued; even now, the emperor Constantine is sleeping in a secret underground chamber under the city gates of Constantinople, waiting for the chance to reclaim his empire. Another legend referred to the church of Hagia Sophia. This story concerned priests who were in the middle of holding Christian services as the siege reached its climax. These priests, according to the legend, were not done with their service as the Turkish warriors broke into the church, and the priests didn't flee. Instead, they were somehow absorbed into the walls of the church. Someday, the story ends, those priests will step out of the walls, to complete their rituals after a hiatus of hundreds of years.

Here we confront a big paradox. A skeptic might say, in what sense was this really a turning point? Constantinople was already far gone even before the arrival of the Turks, weakened beyond recognition compared to its earlier glory days as the Eastern Roman Empire. Its fall was inevitable, really only a question of time. But this is the crux of the matter: Apart from the historical event itself, its effects, especially on how it was viewed by contemporaries, were shattering. Contemporaries had become used to the notion that Constantinople was always under threat, perpetually in crisis, and yet it had always somehow survived.

Until now. There were three main results of this turning point in how the world was seen, with consequences that do endure to the present. The first result is that after this final fall of the Roman Empire, much of the world would be haunted by the ghost of the memory of what Rome had been, what it had once achieved and represented. Rome had been a universal authority, the archetype of what an empire was and should be. Indeed, it still is the archetype: Think of the Roman neoclassical architecture of government buildings in Washington DC.

In this earlier age, thinking about the implications of the fall of Constantinople was based on a medieval concept, that of *translatio imperii*, the transfer of rule or authority, as an organizing principle of history. This transfer of empire resembled the Confucian idea of the mandate of heaven, which we saw with the Ming dynasty in our previous lecture. European scholars looking out at the world at the time concluded that all of history was based on a succession of empires, one following on the other based on divine favor and divine will.

When an empire had played out its role, or had lost what in Chinese tradition would have been called the mandate of heaven, by misrule, a new empire would arise to take its place. In this scheme of history, the empire of Babylon had given way to Persia, Persia had given way to Greece, and Greece gave way to Rome. Now that Rome was gone, what new power would follow? Here is the essence of this lecture: The gap, the vacuum left by the fall of Rome as Constantinople in 1453 fell, was the turning point.

So the second result of this moment was to be a further effect of recurring bids to inherit the universal empire. Most strikingly, as we saw, the Ottoman Turkish sultans saw themselves as new Roman emperors, the legitimate inheritors of Rum. Indeed, they called themselves the "Sultans of Rum" to announce this claim. In fact, Mehmet the Conqueror, after he had captured Constantinople, next made plans to capture Rome in Italy, to complete his victories. As it turns out, he did not capture Rome in the West and finish this continuity; it was just too big an ambition. But what if he had? How different European history and the history of the world would be today.

In a way, for the city of Constantinople, the eagerness of the new Ottoman rulers to assert the fundamental continuity with what went before was lucky, because instead of just fading into oblivion as a heap of ruins, the city actually and dramatically revived under Ottoman rule, again becoming a center of authority, trade and commerce, and assuming once again a pivotal position. Eventually, the city came to be popularly known as "Istanbul," which may be a Turkish rendering of a Greek phrase meaning "to the city" (*eis tin polin*), but officially it still retained its name of "Konstantiniyye" until the fall of the Ottoman empire after World War I. It only officially became Istanbul in 1930.

The longstanding dream of inheriting the empire also was deeply influential in Russian history, for Russia had received its Orthodox faith from Constantinople. This spiritual and historic link was expressed in the potent idea of Russia as the "Third Rome." As Constantinople fell, Russian monks announced to the Tsar— or Emperor—of Moscow, that the first Rome had fallen (the actually city of Rome in Italy), and now Constantinople the second Rome had fallen as well. This meant that now the power of Muscovy would be the third, eternal Rome. The marriage of Tsar Ivan III to a niece of the last Byzantine emperor was also intended to strengthen this claim. The idea of the Third Rome soon took on a messianic fervor, and endured for centuries. The Russian coat of arms, of the Russian empire or of the Russian federation today, shows a double-headed eagle, which had earlier been the emblem of the Byzantine Empire.

That desire to be the Third Rome led to a durable impulse in Russian foreign policy, the striving to capture Constantinople, or as it was called in Russian, *Tsargrad*, or "Caesar City." Over the centuries, Tsars and Tsaritsas (especially Catherine the Great) would make this goal one that they would pursue, a spur to the expansionist impulse that has impelled Russian foreign policy to grow in the following centuries.

Not only the Tsars of Russia were moved by the dream of standing at the end of the line of succession of the Roman Empire. Many others would find this to be an ambition that deeply stirred them as well. In the German lands, the Holy Roman Empire as it was called in the Middle Ages, claimed to be the successor to Rome. Later, in the 19th century, the French leader Napoleon, as he swept across Europe, set about creating a Grand Empire, also outfitted with Roman symbols. In a way, it was perfectly apt that Napoleon thought about how he could capture Constantinople as well. When Russia suggested to Napoleon that they could trade some territories, and Russia could take over Constantinople from the Turkish Empire, Napoleon refused. He announced that whoever holds that city of Constantinople has the key to global power: "It is the empire of the world," he said, adding, "Ultimately, the question is always this—who shall have Constantinople?" He wanted it for himself. It was a geopolitical pivot point of great strategic power. As late as the 20th century the dream of Rome endured. The German dictator Adolf Hitler, in his attempt at a world empire, also looked back at Roman models. His Nazi storm troopers stretched out their arms to give the Roman salute. His Nazi empire, which was expected to last a thousand years, also was outfitted with neoclassical architecture that evoked those days of Roman power. Ultimately, memory of Roman glories has been a spur to many different ambitious leaders and groups throughout modern times.

Finally, the third result of the fall of Constantinople was the redrawing of the world maps in the minds of men. The decline and fall of that great imperial city contributed to a movement that was already taking place in Europe, the Renaissance. Older history textbooks used to claim a simple formula, that Greek-speaking scholars, writers, and intellectuals had fled Constantinople as it fell, taking with them their most treasured possessions, ancient classical texts, and that these texts fired the Renaissance, that passionate movement to revive classical models and humanistic learning.

Actually, historians point out now, the picture is far more complicated. Canny and realistic intellectuals had actually been leaving Constantinople long before 1453 and the disaster of that year. They'd been transferring texts and their personal knowledge a long time. It's estimated that of the 55,000 texts of ancient Greek writings that we possess now, about 40,000 of them come to us by way of Constantinople. The texts that Byzantine scholars brought with them to the West didn't so much cause the Renaissance, which had already been going on and earlier had emphasized Roman literature. What their Greek texts did was to feed a second wave of Renaissance activity, which was based on the rediscovery of Greek texts. Most important of all was that the Greek scholars who arrived in the West taught the Greek language to the Italian humanists and enriched their understanding.

Further, the fall of Constantinople presented a geographic problem for Europeans. Trade routes with the Orient, which had run through the Byzantine Empire, were now in the hands of the Ottoman Turks. These routes were not entirely closed because trade continued, in part helped by the merchants of Venice and Genoa trading with the Turks. But the desire of Europeans to outflank the Turks and to find alternate routes for trade would spur European voyages of discovery, including the voyage which led Columbus to what was for him a new world (and will be the subject of a coming lecture).

This drive to outflank the Turks also had a strategic and religious dimension, which recalled the Crusades—the key geopolitical location of earlier authority, Constantinople, had been lost, and the religious and political imperative was to find a way around that fact, the end of the Roman Empire. The loss of Rome had created a gap in the mental map of the world, and that gap was the turning point.

In this lecture, we have seen the trauma that the loss of Constantinople produced at the start of the modern period. It produced a ferment of ideas, anxieties, fears, and hopes that marked the age. These would also be reflected and amplified by a new technology, the printing press, and we will explore that in our next lecture.

1455—Gutenberg's Print Revolution
Lecture 3

Some have called Johann Gutenberg's innovation of printing with movable type the single most important transformation of the modern world. From this beginning, the printed word launched the modern media and modern mass audiences for new information and ideas. In this lecture, we'll examine how the print revolution supercharged movements that we are well familiar with and that have shaped our modern world: the Renaissance, the Reformation, and the Scientific Revolution. Even more basically, we'll trace how the printed word changed concepts of authority—what was trusted and true.

The World before Print

- What was the world like without print? In the beginning was the word—spoken and remembered. In both classical and medieval times, much effort was devoted to training the memory to allow people to categorize and recall stores of information and texts.

- The philosopher Socrates had misgivings about the effect of being able to rely on the written word; he predicted that writing would create "forgetfulness in the learner's souls because they will not use their memories," leaving them with "the show of wisdom without the reality."

- Written texts were preserved on scrolls of papyrus or vellum (animal skins). In the monasteries, cathedrals, and universities of the medieval Christian world, these texts were not recorded in the vernacular language but in the holy language of Latin, narrowing access to the learned.

- The libraries of monasteries were repositories of rare, unique texts. If a copy needed to be made, this was done in the scriptorium, where a monk would reproduce, as closely as possible, the original text but inevitably yielding a product with its own differences and errors.

- Even in this timeless work of copying books by hand, there were transformations. One crucial one, largely complete by the start of the Middle Ages, involved the shift from a scroll to a codex, which is the form of our hardcopy books today: pages not rolled up but folded or stacked between covers.

- Bookselling became more of a business in the later Middle Ages. Stationers opened up shops around the young universities that arose in medieval Europe from around 1350, and there, scribes would produce copies of needed texts. What was a constant was the laborious process of copying by hand.

The Life of Johann Gutenberg

- Gutenberg was perhaps born in 1394. He came from a notable family in Mainz, part of the elite, and became a skilled goldsmith, learning technical skills he later used for his invention.

- Gutenberg's innovation was in bringing together separate elements into one process. These elements included the printing press itself, individually cast type (as opposed to woodblocks), and a hand mold to produce individual type in a method resembling the minting of coins. Finally, he perfected an oil-based ink that would work best with these methods to print on paper or vellum.

- There had been precursors to these methods, notably in China and Korea, but Gutenberg seems not to have known about these advances. He called his project "the work of the books," a deliberately vague phrase, to hide his innovation, although he initiated some others into his secret as a way of getting them to invest. One such person was Johann Fust, a prosperous merchant in Mainz, who bought into Gutenberg's proposal.

- Gutenberg's business model probably involved religious authority. The Catholic Church had been in a state of turmoil for centuries, rocked by the Western Schism of 1378 to 1417, when rival popes asserted their claims to spiritual authority over Christendom. Even after a council had settled the matter, the unity of Christendom seemed uncertain. What better way to achieve unity of religious practice and belief than issuing a uniform and approved Bible?

- Gutenberg set about printing the Bible and other texts with an eye to the religious market. Included in his output were pamphlets that spoke to the great issues of the day and indulgences, forms issued by Catholic authorities that could be purchased to release the buyer from sins.

- In 1455, just as Gutenberg hoped that he was about to make a commercial success of his printing of the Bible, his partner Fust lost patience with not getting repaid on his investment and took Gutenberg to court, where Gutenberg lost all his equipment; Fust took over the business.

- Gutenberg seems to have reconstructed his process and kept printing. His work included the ambitious encyclopedia the *Catholicon*, a "book of universal knowledge." He died in 1468 in Mainz, unheralded but remembered—in spite of being a shadowy figure—for the change he introduced.

The Print Revolution

- Printing revolutionized the speed and range of distribution of texts. A text that might have earlier taken several months to produce could now be delivered in 500 copies in one week. Costs came down with this proliferation, so that a printed book probably cost one-eighth of its former price.

- Earlier, texts had been the province of religious institutions, but now, access was democratized. The result would eventually be a large reading public, a mass audience for the printed word in the form of books, newspapers, journals, and pamphlets. Gutenberg's invention also contributed to preserving and fixing texts. Hand-copied texts had all been different, even in the work of the most careful transcriber. But printed texts were increasingly standardized. Printers promised that their texts were purged of scribal errors, carefully proofread and examined, and thus, closer to the originals.

- The social changes provoked by printing, in addition to democratizing access, involved the creation of new forms of community around the common reading of printed texts and discussion of new ideas. A new kind of person, the intellectual, no longer necessarily a cleric or religious, emerged and communicated with others who had shared interests.

- From its German origins, printing spread at a fantastic rate in Europe and then worldwide. By 1465, German printers introduced printing to Italy and began a great wave of printing of classical authors. Paris had its first press in 1470; Cracow, in 1474; and Moscow, in 1555.

- The level of production also increased exponentially. It is estimated that by 1500, in all of Europe, some 40,000 individual titles had been published, and there were already some 20 million copies of printed books.

- At the same time as this turning point was vividly visible, it was not total. In fact, innovators of the printed word worked to reassure contemporaries that in some ways this was not so new or radical. Some printers specifically chose to call their craft "artificial writing" or tried to make their books look like traditional manuscripts.

Contemporary Views of Printing

- The contemporary reactions to printing were mixed. Some called it a "divine art" because it promised to spread religious doctrine more consistently, uniformly, and authentically.

- Others, however, probably including many scribes, saw it as something from the devil. In at least one legend, Gutenberg's partner Fust seems to have been confused with Faust, a legendary scholar who sold his soul to the devil to win total knowledge.

- The fact that print was not flawless—despite the claims of the printers—may have fueled contemporary anxiety. A famous case in England was the so-called Wicked Bible of 1631, in which the printers accidentally rendered the Seventh Commandment as "Thou shalt commit adultery," having left out "not."

Outcomes of the Print Revolution

- Among the biggest outcomes of this turning point were the later Renaissance, the Reformation, the Scientific Revolution, and the growth of national communities. The Renaissance and the intellectual movement of humanism predated the printing press but were supercharged by its potential. The humanist concern with regaining and reviving classical knowledge and wisdom was assisted by the new availability of classic texts.

At the time of the Reformation, German printers were producing about a million books a year, and a third of them were by Luther—the first modern best-selling author.

- A half century after its invention, printing also supercharged the Protestant Reformation. In 1517, the Catholic priest Martin Luther announced his famed Ninety-five Theses, calling for changes in the church. What made this call different than earlier ones was that Luther's writings were disseminated with great speed, thanks to the printing press.

  o In a sense, the fit between medium and message here was perfect. Luther's message of *sola Scriptura* ("scripture alone") as the true source of legitimate authority worked well with the new power to print Scripture. The spiritual significance of print was deep for Protestants, who stressed how vitally important it was for all believers to read the Bible themselves, as God's word.

  o Reading that word in an unmediated way, as a source of direct authority, meant being individually responsible for one's own salvation and relationship to God. The printing revolution was key for the Protestant movement, because it meant that access to the Bible, now mass-produced and readily available, was possible.

- The Scientific Revolution, which introduced new knowledge about the observed world, was also sped along by print. One of the launching texts of this movement was a work published by Nicolaus Copernicus in 1543, in which he argued that the earth revolved around the sun, not the other way around.

- Printing also shaped the linguistic communities that we know and belong to today. To cater to mass popular audiences, printers moved beyond the Latin of learned texts to print in vernacular languages, the everyday speech of the people. In the process, they standardized these languages, giving them a form and fixity they had not possessed earlier.

- Historians also argue that the medium of print created a new sense of national community. Reading together, whether newspapers or novels, gave people a sense of belonging to what the historian Benedict Anderson has called an "imagined community" of the nation, united linguistically and by print.

- Of all the changes this turning point unleashed, let's conclude by underlining the rich paradox at the heart of early printing: Printers announced that they offered ancient authoritative texts, accurately transmitted, cleansed of scribal errors—both old and "new and improved" at the same time. Paradoxically, in the pursuit of ancient wisdom, newness could be desirable. And it might, in the process, unexpectedly open up new worlds, as would be the case in the journeys of Christopher Columbus, which we consider in our next lecture.

Suggested Reading

Eisenstein, *The Printing Revolution in Early Modern Europe.*

Man, *Gutenberg.*

Questions to Consider

1. Do you agree with those who call Gutenberg the most important man of the millennium?

2. Was Marshall McLuhan right in arguing that "the medium is the message"?

1455—Gutenberg's Print Revolution
Lecture 3—Transcript

In our previous lecture, on the fall of Constantinople to the Turks in 1453, we started by asking what the sound of a civilization falling was like. In this lecture, let's move forward by just two years, to 1455, and ask: What sound does a communications revolution make?

For the answer to that question, let's stroll through the city of Mainz, Germany, in the beautiful Rhineland, in the Holy Roman Empire. Mainz is not a huge city, but a rich and important one with some 6,000 inhabitants. At the center of the city is a great, imposing cathedral in the Romanesque style, and next to it the lively and bustling marketplace. Around the cathedral are many streets and narrow alleyways, monasteries and convents, and a welter of businesses and private homes.

Inside one of these medieval buildings is a former goldsmith, with the amazing name Johann Gensfleisch zur Laden zum Gutenberg. We'll just call him Johann Gutenberg. He is deploying his secret invention, one that he has been working on for years while keeping it jealously hidden. That invention is the printing press, equipped with moveable type, and he and his skilled employees are printing sacred texts. The sound of a media revolution, then, is like this: It's a ratcheting sound, followed by a click, click, click, as the press moves up and down, as paper is put in and removed, in a cascade of words such as the world had never seen before, and which will grow and grow into a flood of publication that has never stopped since.

What we are hearing is a turning point which some have called the single most important transformation in the modern world. From this beginning, the printed word launched the modern media—even today, in the days of blogs and online publications, we still talk about the work of journalists as "the press," and treasure what we call the "freedom of the press." Also growing up at the same time, enabled by this new technology, were modern mass audiences for ideas, literature, art, for information of all sorts, from the practical to the fanciful.

Moreover, we'll examine in this lecture how the print revolution supercharged and added more force to movements that we're already well familiar with, that have shaped our modern world: the Renaissance, the Reformation, and the Scientific Revolution. Even more basically, we'll trace how the printed word changed concepts of authority, what was seen as true and trusted.

Some have even argued that print changed fundamentally how we perceive the world. Back in 1962 Marshall McLuhan published his book *The Gutenberg Galaxy*. He followed his oft-quoted coinage that "the medium is the message," and following that phrase of his, McLuhan saw print as having defined the modern world, until the present day. He saw this as a transition point when electronic media were ushering in what he called a new "global village." These are really vast claims made for print.

But to really appreciate and sense the depth of the print revolution, we need to survey and understand what came before, what the change replaced in other words. What was the world like without print? In the beginning, was the word—the word spoken, and remembered. For the ancient Greeks, their goddess of memory, Mnemosyne, was the mother of all the other muses. In classical as well as in medieval times, much effort was devoted to training one's memory. These were the so-called arts of memory, like mentally conjuring up a memory palace in your head, which would allow people to categorize and recall small bits of information that they had stored in different places of this imagined structure.

This is a world very foreign to us, that of memory, because we're used to looking things up and not having to rely on memory. The philosopher Socrates had already had misgivings in his day about the effect of our being able to rely on the written word. He predicted that writing would create "forgetfulness in the learners' souls because they will not use their memories." They will be left, he worried, with "the show of wisdom without the reality." But for all these misgivings, the written word remained the preserve of elites in society, those who had the special knowledge of writing, especially clerics and monks. These written texts were preserved on scrolls of papyrus or of vellum, animal skins. In the monasteries, cathedrals, and universities of the medieval Christian world moreover, these texts were not recorded in the ordinary everyday language—the vernacular—but in a holy, special language, Latin, which further narrowed access to the learned possessed of Latin skills.

The libraries of the monasteries were repositories of rare, sometimes unique texts. If a copy needed to be made, this was done in a special place, the scriptorium, the room of the scribes, where a monk would reproduce, as closely as possible, the original text he was copying, but inevitably this yielded a product with its own slight differences and very often errors. Yet such copying was seen as a holy labor, and many men devoted all of their lives, and their eyesight, to this task. Some of these copies could be beautiful products: Think of the famous Book of Kells, from around the year 800, and its ornate, twisting Celtic decorations.

But even in this timeless work of copying books by hand, there were changes; it wasn't unvarying. A crucial transformation, largely complete by the start of the Middle Ages, involved the shift from the ancient use of scrolls, to the use of a codex. A codex is the form that our hardcopy books use today: pages not rolled up as in a scroll, but folded or stacked between covers. Some historians of the book even argue provocatively that this shift to the codex was more significant as a change in book usage even than printing. They argue that the shift to the codex reduced the wear and tear that was inevitable in unrolling and rolling scrolls, gave easier access, and was all-around more efficient as a way of reading.

Bookselling also was becoming much more of a full business in the later Middle Ages. Stationary shops opened up around the young universities that were arising in medieval Europe from around 1350, and there, scribes would produce copies of needed texts on an individual basis, what we today would call print-on-demand. What was a constant in all of this, however, was the laborious and long process of the actual copying. A scribe would on average only be able to produce at most several pages a day. This was the world of the "manuscript"—literally, that which is written by hand.

Who then was Gutenberg, and how did he change all of this? Remarkably, we actually know very very little about a man who has been frequently called by historians the most important man of the second millennium. What we do know about him actually comes from records of his legal disputes in the Rhineland. This in and of itself is suggestive—he was a man of business, a practical man who was at law, an entrepreneur who was trying to perfect a new mode of production. Gutenberg was born (probably) in 1394. He came from a notable family in Mainz; he was part of the elite, and became a skilled goldsmith, in the process learning technical skills that he would later use for his special invention. He worked on the printing press for many years, in Mainz as well as in nearby Strasbourg. It took him a long time to perfect the new method and get it just right.

For his invention, he brought together separate elements into one process. These included the printing press itself—presses had been around for centuries to press olives, or to press grapes, or to make paper, or to bind books, or to imprint designs on cloth. Another crucial element was moveable type. Prints made by woodblocks also had a longer history, but individually cast type that broke down the component parts of text into the elements of the alphabet was newer. To produce these in huge quantities, and to make them interchangeable so they could be reused, Gutenberg created a special hand mold to produce individual type in a method that resembled the minting of coins. Finally, Gutenberg also perfected a special oil-based ink that would work best with these methods, to print on paper or vellum.

There had been precursors to these methods. In China for instance, block printing had been common since the 8th century. It included the paper money that Marco Polo had observed in his travels, and yet, the complexity of rendering Chinese characters (or "ideograms" as they're called) in moveable type was a serious obstacle. There also had been printing in Korea for instance. But Gutenberg seems not to have known about these Asian advances as he set about his own project. He called it by a euphemism: *das werck der bucher*—"the work of the books," a deliberately vague and veiled phrase that he used to hide the innovation that he was working on. Gutenberg did initiate some others into the secret as a way of getting them to invest into his project, as financial partners. One such person was Johann Fust, a prosperous merchant in Mainz who bought in to Gutenberg's proposal. They went into business together.

It seems likely that Gutenberg's business model involved religious authority. The Catholic Church had been in a state of turmoil for centuries already, rocked by the Western Schism of 1378 to 1417, a period of turmoil within Christendom when rival popes—at one point in fact, three rival popes—asserted their claims to be the spiritual authority over Christendom. Even after a council had settled the matter, the unity of Christendom seemed to many at the time an uncertain thing, and reformers called out for more internal unity and cohesion. What better way to achieve unity of religious practice and belief than being quite sure about the texts that were being used, especially the Bible, so that all of them would be uniform, proper and approved? Authoritative. The cathedrals and monasteries of Europe would be the perfect market for an invention like the printing press, demanding improved and recognized printed texts.

Now, Gutenberg set about printing the Bible and other texts besides, always with a practical view to the market. These productions included pamphlets that spoke to great issues of the day. They included, for instance, a papal proclamation calling for a Crusade against the Turks, who had just taken Constantinople in 1453, as we discussed in our last lecture. Other printed products of Gutenberg's included indulgences. These indulgences were special official forms issued by Catholic authorities, in exchange for acts of penance and a monetary payment. These indulgences were believed to release the buyer from sins.

Funds from these indulgences were to be put for a special purpose: the Crusade against the Turks. Gutenberg also produced a special "Turk calendar" as it was called, with monthly calls for Crusade against the Turks. I'm sure that you start to see the pattern that's forming here: The first productions of print responded to the trauma of the advancing Turkish power, which had just toppled Constantinople! Other early printed products included playing cards as well as images of saints. Then, in 1455, just as Gutenberg hoped that he was about to make a commercial success of his printing of the Bible, which was then underway, his partner Johann Fust lost patience with Gutenberg not repaying him his investment and took Gutenberg to court, where, as a result of the trial Gutenberg lost all of his equipment, and Fust took over his business.

This was shattering, and yet Gutenberg seems to have reconstructed his process and resumed printing. His work included the ambitious encyclopedia called the *Catholicon*, the "book of universal knowledge." Gutenberg died in 1468 in Mainz, unheralded, largely unknown by contemporaries, but eventually remembered—in spite of being such a shadowy figure—for the change that he had introduced. But if Gutenberg the man was not appreciated or recognized at the time, the results of his invention were enormous. In our own times the historian Elizabeth Eisenstein has called this phenomenon a "print revolution," and that term seems very apt. Let's examine the ways in which this was a turning point.

Printing revolutionized the speed and range of distribution of texts. Now, a text that might have taken several months to produce by hand copying could be delivered in 500 fresh copies, in one week. Potentially, the age of the bestseller had arrived! Historians also estimate that costs came down as print proliferated, so a printed book could cost one-eighth of the former price in the handwritten version. In a real sense, this implied a certain democratizing of access to texts, which earlier as we'd pointed out, had been the province of religious institutions and limited access. Eventually, public libraries would become available (the first one in Florence, in 1571). Bookselling now grew and grew as a business, most brilliantly on display at the famous annual Frankfurt book fair, which in fact still operates today after having been started over 500 years ago as Gutenberg was developing print! The result would eventually be the creation of a large reading public, a mass audience for the printed word in the form of books, newspapers, journals, and pamphlets.

Gutenberg's invention in fact went further: It also contributed to the preservation of texts and their "fixing," one might say, in a new way. Hand-copied texts, as we pointed out, had all been different, even in the work of the most careful transcriber, all different. Printed texts instead were increasingly, if not perfectly, standardized. It became possible, for instance, to offer an index which made printed texts "searchable" we would say today, in a way that manuscripts had not been. Printers also promised that their texts were purged of scribal errors, that they were carefully proofread and examined, and thus, they suggested, closer to the originals.

So the possibility of a more faithful transmission of ancient authoritative texts was real. Thus for instance, we see the introduction of something that hadn't been around before: quotation marks, which were a sign of the new care that was being given to textual detail, to getting it exactly right. These first stages of printing have actually impressed themselves on our language up to the present, even to the days of e-mail and URL addresses. One example of an early convention that developed then that we still follow today is when we speak of "lowercase" letters, or "uppercase" letters, even for e-mail addresses. In fact, these terms refer to the actual cases or boxes from which typesetters took the type they needed: uppercase from an upper box, lowercase from a lower box.

The social changes that were provoked by printing, in addition to democratizing access, involved the creation of new forms of community around the common reading of printed texts and the discussion of their new ideas. So it was that a new kind of person, the intellectual, arose, no longer necessarily a cleric or someone in religious orders, but someone who communicated with others on the basis of shared interests, ideas, reading, and writing. This very-often-international network of intellectuals went by many different names in the centuries that followed; it was a kind of virtual community. It was sometimes called the Learned Commonwealth, at other times the Republic of Letters, and was in a sense a kind of homeland for readers, a homeland of the mind. Printing shops and bookshops were key gathering places for such people, and printers took on the role of being public intellectuals. A splendid example would be, in the American case, Benjamin Franklin as a printer and public intellectual.

From its German origins, printing spread at a fantastic rate in Europe, and then quickly worldwide. By 1465, German printers had introduced printing to Italy, and began a great wave of printing of classical older authors: Cicero, Caesar, Livy, and Pliny. In Venice, it was the work of ancient Greek authors specifically, brought by intellectuals before the fall of Constantinople, that became sort of a famous specialty product of Venetian publishers. Paris had its first press in 1470, Cracow in Poland in 1474,

Moscow in Russia in 1555. So it was also that the level of production also increased exponentially, in a veritable print explosion. It's estimated that by 1500, in all of Europe, some 40,000 individual titles had already been published. Also by that year, 1500, it's estimated that there were already some 20 million copies of printed books in Europe.

At the same time as this turning point was so vividly visible, it was not a total turning point. In fact, innovators of the printed word—those who were publishing these new texts—worked to reassure their contemporaries that in some ways what they were doing was not so new, not so radical. Some printers specifically chose to call what they were doing "artificial writing," instead of using some new technical term, because artificial writing sounded more familiar, more in continuity with earlier familiar practice. Similarly, printers tried to make their new books look like traditional manuscripts. They followed scribal design, for instance having two columns on a page for ease of reading. The work of scribes did not vanish overnight, either; this is a fascinating thing to observe. A suggestive statistic is that today we have, in archives and libraries, still nearly as many manuscript texts from the half century after the invention of the printing press as from the half century before. The printing press didn't wipe out handwritten texts. The prestige of beautiful handwritten texts still endured, especially at the high end of the market, because more status attached to the hand-copied text, as more exclusive, more rare, and thus more valuable to the discerning customer. So the change didn't come all at once, and there were unsuspected continuities: Some scribes actually worked at copying printed books in order to meet demand, strange as it is to think about that.

How did contemporaries view printing? Their reactions were actually quite mixed. Some were enthusiastic and called it a "divine art," because printing promised to spread religious doctrine more consistently, uniformly, and authentically. Others, probably including many scribes whose livelihoods were being undermined, saw print as something from the devil. There's one legend from this period that really is suggestive of this, and it concerns Gutenberg's business partner—the guy who sued him—Johann Fust. It is said that some people suspected that Fust had supernatural powers, because he was able to suddenly appear with texts produced with magical speed. This particular legend seems to confuse Fust with another legendary German figure, Doctor Faust, a scholar who, in his legend (fired by boundless ambition) sells his soul to the devil to win total knowledge. This confused linking of Fust and Faust, whose names obviously are very close, suggests that some people at the time were made nervous by the new potential of the mass-produced and printed word.

There seemed to be plenty of things to be anxious about in this area. Print was not flawless, even if printers did make claims for the accuracy of their works. One very famous case in England of an accident in printing was the 1631 book, the so-called Wicked Bible, in which the printers accidentally rendered the seventh commandment as, "Thou shalt commit adultery." They accidentally left out the "not." They were fined severely by the King, who was very scandalized, and unsold bibles were confiscated, but the remaining ones have turned into treasures for bibliophiles and book collectors; they fetch huge prices. Not only holy texts and first-class literature were printed—a lot of trash also poured forth to meet popular demand, along with many pirated and plagiarized texts, because centuries would still have to pass before laws of copyright were introduced.

Among the biggest outcomes of this turning point were the later Renaissance, the Reformation, the Scientific Revolution, and the growth of national communities. The effects of these well-known movements are with us still. The Renaissance and the intellectual movement of humanism predated the printing press, but were supercharged by its potential. The concern of humanists with regaining and reviving classical knowledge was helped by the sudden new availability of classic texts. So here's a really nice paradox: A new technology helped revive antiquity, older learning, and its authoritative writings.

A half century after the invention of printing, it also supercharged the Protestant Reformation. In 1517, the Catholic priest Martin Luther announced his famed Ninety-five Theses, calling for changes in the Church, not least the abolition of the indulgences like those Gutenberg had been printing.

Now here's the key point: For centuries past, there had been repeated calls for reform and change within the Church, and slowly such calls had either been accepted, or ignored. What made this movement different and soon tremendously successful? In this case, instead of the reform message just evaporating, the new invention of the printing press actually worked to disseminate Luther's impassioned writings with fantastic speed and directness and force. Luther's arguments had an electric effect and found an eager response throughout Europe.

The eagerness with which Luther's message was greeted was astonishing. At this time, German printers were printing a million books a year, and one-third of those were written by Luther, so Luther was really the first modern bestselling author! Little surprise: By 1600, about half of Europe was Protestant. In a sense, the fit between medium and message was perfect. Luther's message of *sola Scriptura*, or "scripture alone," as the true source of legitimate authority worked very well with the new power to print scripture, for the masses. The spiritual significance of print was thus understandably very deep for Protestants, who stressed always how vitally important it was for all believers to read the Bible themselves, as God's direct word.

Reading that word in an unmediated way, as a source of direct authority, meant being individually responsible for one's own salvation and one's own relationship to God. The printing revolution thus was key for the Protestant movement, as it meant that access to the Bible, now mass-produced and readily available, was possible. What began as reform within the Church led to a break within the Christian community itself, pitting Protestants against Catholics. Each side used the printing press to argue for its beliefs in a propaganda war of leaflets, and there was also much burning and banning of books that were judged heretical. The ensuing divisions within the Christian community were at first marked by stunning violence, in religious wars and slaughters, and the confessional divide endures to this day. Without print, the Reformation would perhaps not have lasted.

More pacifically, the Scientific Revolution, which introduced new knowledge about the observed natural world, was also sped along by print. Conventionally, one of the launching texts of this movement is seen as the astronomer Nicolaus Copernicus's work in 1543, published just as he was dying. In that work, the astronomer argued that the earth revolved around the sun, not the other way around. Traditional cosmology would need to be rethought, and once this was done, many other traditional conventions were being thrown into doubt as well.

Finally, printing also shaped the linguistic communities that we know and belong to today. To cater to mass popular audiences, printers moved beyond the Latin of learned texts to print in vernacular languages, the everyday speech of people. In the process they standardized these languages, giving them a form and fixity that they had not had before.

Luther's German bible, for instance, did this for the German language. In England, William Caxton published the first book in English in 1475—it was a collection of stories about ancient Troy, near the spot of recently fallen Constantinople. For that book, he chose to use the dialect of London, a choice that echoes into our present-day usage of English.

Historians also argue that the new medium of print created a new sense of national community. Reading together, whether newspapers or novels, allowed people a new sense of belonging to what historian Benedict Anderson has called an "imagined community" of a nation, united linguistically and by print—people who one might never meet in person, but to whom one felt one was bound to and linked.

So considerable were these changes that after centuries of disregard and rival claimants, Gutenberg was again recognized as a key historic figure. Statues were erected to him in his native Germany. Today, in Mainz, you can visit a great museum bearing his name in his hometown. A vast digital library of public domain books is called the Project Gutenberg, honoring this man about whom we unfortunately know so little.

Of all the changes this turning point unleashed, let's conclude for the purposes of our course by underlining that rich paradox at the heart of early printing. Printers announced that they were offering ancient authoritative texts, accurately transmitted, cleansed of the errors of scribes, at the same time old *and* new and improved. Paradoxically, in the pursuit of ancient wisdom, newness could be desirable. It might in the process unexpectedly open up new worlds, as would be the case in the journeys of Christopher Columbus, which we'll consider in our next lecture.

1492—The Columbian Exchange
Lecture 4

Without meaning to, Christopher Columbus initiated an event that has been called the most important historical turning point of modern times: the beginning of the binding together of the globe. This development took place not just politically and culturally but also environmentally, in ways that were both deeply productive and deeply destructive and that continue to work themselves out in our own day. Indeed, we are not even always sure what to call the achievement of Columbus. It was a discovery for him but not for the peoples of the Americas. Historians now often use the more neutral term "encounter," and as we will see, it was a world-changing one.

The Cosmology of Medieval Europe

- Almost no educated European thought that the world was flat at the time of Columbus. This story was propagated by Washington Irving and others who sought to establish Columbus as a man of science, resolutely modern, and struggling against what they condemned as the outmoded religious orthodoxies of the Catholic Church. In the process, however, these partisans of Columbus actually distorted both Columbus and his contemporaries.

  o Ancient authorities, back to the days of the great classical Greek philosophers, had understood the world as a sphere. Eratosthenes, for instance, in the 2nd century B.C., not only understood that the world was round but even constructed an ingenious experiment that yielded a remarkably reliable estimate of the circumference of the world!

  o The work of the man often considered the father of geography, Ptolemy, in 2nd-century Egypt, also used this model and sought to find ways of representing the earth's curvature on maps.

- o This understanding had endured. Among their badges of office, medieval kings and queens were shown holding a scepter and an orb, a representation of world rule.

- Another key representation of the medieval worldview was a particular kind of chart or map called a *mappa mundi*, "map of the world," of which more than 600 survive. These were not accurate, scientifically determined outlines of geography but renderings of the world in spiritual terms, drawn on information from ancient authorities, especially Scripture.
  - o Most often, the maps took the form of "T-O maps," so called because their appearance is just that—a letter O with a capital letter T inside, dividing the world into three sections.

  - o Of the directions, east was seen as most important and was placed at the top. That meant that above the top of the T was Asia, with Europe below to the left and Africa below to the right.

  - o The spiritual center of the Christian faith was Jerusalem, so it was most often placed at the center of the map. The Garden of Eden, lying somewhere unknown to the east, surmounted the map as a whole.

  - o In the cosmology of medieval Europe, this world was, in turn, surrounded by seven spheres of the heavens.

The Life of Columbus
- Columbus was born in Genoa, a seafaring republic of northern Italy, in around 1451 and lived to 1506. In his youth, he gained experience as a sailor to Africa, England, and Iceland and was on a ship that was sunk by the French off Portugal.

- At the time, Portugal was the center of expansive voyaging. The Portuguese had begun sailing down the coast of western Africa, probing to find some access to the spice trade that the fall of Constantinople had placed in Muslim hands. Their aim was to head eastward.

Columbus calculated the distance to Asia by a series of hopeful leaps and bounds, as well as citations from ancient geographic writers, which he cherry-picked when they agreed with his theory.

- Inspired, Columbus set about educating himself, focusing his energies on gathering information for a different project: sailing westward to reach Asia and its alluring treasures in Japan, China, and India. The stories of Marco Polo were his constant companion, along with other compendia of fantastic travels.

- Fired by his religious self-understanding, Columbus developed a sense of himself as having a divine mission, as a bearer of Christianity. After the reverses of the failed Crusades and the fall of Constantinople in 1453, he felt a calling to somehow turn the tables geopolitically, to find new riches and convert populations that would allow Christians to regain the lost Jerusalem.

- The last element that enabled Columbus's venture was a fateful and decisive geographical mistake. Many contemporaries agreed that in theory it should be possible to reach Asia across the Atlantic, but they also argued that the distance of empty sea was so great that such a voyage was impractical or impossible. Columbus, by contrast, calculated that the distance was much shorter.

- From 1484, Columbus tried repeatedly to find a patron for his voyage. Finally, after eight years of pleading, Queen Isabella of Spain agreed to fund Columbus, and his project was launched.

The Voyage to the "Indies"

- At the age of 41, Columbus set sail with three ships from Spain on August 3, 1492. The winds driving the ships westward were so brisk that the crew feared not that they would fall off the edge of the world but, more simply, that they would never reach home again, forced out into the vast waters.

- Columbus was driven to a deception, keeping two ship logs in order to calm his crew and underestimating what he told them of their distance traveled. After 33 days of tense sailing, the ships sighted land on October 12.

- Columbus was convinced, and remained convinced, that he had reached Asia. In fact, he had landed on an island of the Bahamas; he then visited Cuba and what is today Haiti and the Dominican Republic but was sure that he had found his goal.

- After three months, the expedition headed home, and Columbus wrote a letter to his royal patrons, announcing his success and promising more soon. Over the next 12 years, Columbus made three more trips across the Atlantic, always convinced that he was in Asia. He died in 1506 in Spain, sure to the last that his dream had been fulfilled.

Amerigo Vespucci and the Naming of America

- It would take some time for contemporaries to realize what it was that Columbus had, in fact, found. And it is for that reason that we do not call these continents North and South Columbia today but the Americas.

- The name came from Amerigo Vespucci (c. 1454–1512), an Italian sailor who was, at different times, in the employ of Spain and Portugal. Little is known about him, but he seems to have made several trips across the Atlantic about a decade after Columbus. Like his precursor, Vespucci was concerned above all with access to Asia.

- On his return to Europe after one of his voyages, Vespucci wrote some letters to friends about his travels. An unknown person then used text from these letters to fabricate a sensational account of what he had found. This text was entitled "Mundus Novus" ("New World") and appeared in print around 1502. What the title conveyed was that the continent across the Atlantic was not Asia but a previously unknown landmass.

- A German geographer, Martin Waldseemüller, was impressed by this new geographic account. He and his colleagues in a small printing establishment in France incorporated these insights into a new map of the world, and Waldseemüller named the new lands after the Latinized name of Vespucci, "Americus"—in a feminized form, America.

The Columbian Exchange

- The physical fact of the meeting and travel between what came to be called the Old World and the New World was a significant environmental turning point. The term "Columbian exchange" has been used to describe the resulting mixing of people, introduction of deadly diseases, exchanges of crops and animals, and flow of goods and trade.

- One of the first consequences of the Columbian exchange was the devastation of native American populations by diseases, including typhus, diphtheria, malaria, influenza, cholera, and smallpox. By 1650, it is estimated that 90 percent of the native American populations had died. This depopulation destroyed traditional societies, sapped their powers of resistance, and mightily aided the European conquest and eventual immigration.

- Another consequence of the Columbian exchange involved the exchange of crops and animals. European crops and domesticated animals (pigs, sheep, and cattle) were introduced to America, along with weeds and pests, while American species, including potatoes, tomatoes, and corn, entered the European diet. In fact, these improvements in diet enabled a huge growth of the European population in the centuries to follow.

- Columbus's American discoveries prompted further exploration in an accelerating process of competition. The lure of expansion and treasure was great and grew stronger. In 1519, Ferdinand Magellan, a Portuguese mariner in the employ of Spain, set out on an expedition that circumnavigated the globe by 1522, revealing the Pacific and the full extent of the globe. Spanish conquistadors toppled the Aztec and Inca empires with astonishing speed.

- The conquest and carving up of new lands also resulted in transatlantic slavery. The African slave trade, originally run by Africans and Arabs, was built up by the Portuguese, Dutch, and English as they carried Africans in bondage across the Atlantic for plantation agriculture. Up until the mid-19th century, this cruel trade would involve the forced movement of an estimated 15 million Africans.

Lasting Impact of the Encounter
- As the contours of the new discoveries came into sharper focus, the kingdoms of Portugal and Spain turned to the pope to help divide the world among them. With papal mediation, a line was drawn in the Atlantic, with Spain assigned all the possessions to the west and Portugal, the newly claimed lands to the east.

- It's remarkable to think that this appeal went to the pope. But we should also note that other European kingdoms did not passively accept this division of the globe. Instead, a fierce competition would ensue over the question of who was in control.

- Harder to pin down but still important was the intellectual impact of the New World. European ideas of the New World paradoxically presented it as either better than the old or debased and inferior. For some observers, it was a new Eden, populated by "noble savages." For others, the Americas and Americans would never quite measure up to the Old World.

- This discovery of Columbus became a lasting archetype of a stunning encounter—yet we have seen that it was not what Columbus had set out for. This is an example of what is called "serendipity." The origin of this poetic term actually lies in the mysterious East that Columbus was seeking. A Persian fairy tale told of the "three princes of Serendip," who were always making unexpected discoveries.

Suggested Reading

Bernstein, *A Splendid Exchange.*

Brook, *Vermeer's Hat.*

Crosby, *The Columbian Exchange.*

Lester, *The Fourth Part of the World.*

Questions to Consider

1. If you had to choose one particular aspect of the Columbian exchange as the most important, which would it be?

2. In what ways has your everyday life been affected by the Columbian exchange?

1492—The Columbian Exchange
Lecture 4—Transcript

Christopher Columbus was a man with a dream, and on October 12, 1492, at 2 am in the morning, that dream seemed to have come true. After weeks of sailing across the Atlantic, one of his tiny fleet of ships spotted something ahead in the darkness, and then, the dim outlines of land appeared before them. At this point, Columbus had to call a halt to the sailing, until dawn would break and they could really see what it is they had encountered.

Can we imagine a more frustrating or difficult wait that lay ahead? When finally dawn arrived, this proved to be the first durable contact with the American world, but that's not what Columbus thought was about to happen. That was not his dream. On the contrary, Columbus was convinced that he had arrived in Asia, off the coast of Japan, or of China. Columbus's venture was founded on a series of misunderstandings. There's a deeply significant insight here: Some discoveries are made while searching for something else entirely!

Without meaning to, Columbus initiated an event that has been called the most important historical turning point of modern times: the beginning of the binding together of the globe, not just politically and culturally, but also environmentally, in ways that were deeply productive and deeply shattering and destructive at the same time, a process indeed which continues to work itself out into our own day. We're not even always sure about what to call this event. It was a discovery for Columbus, but not a discovery for the peoples of the Americas, who obviously knew where they were. Historians for that reason now often call this by the more neutral term, "encounter," and it was a world-changing encounter.

But we need to ask, what was Columbus thinking? What was going on in the minds of Columbus and his contemporaries at this world historical moment? This is another way of asking what the cosmology, or mental map, of the European explorers, merchants, and scholars was at this time. The very first thing one has to do is to refute the later myth that was spread by the American writer Washington Irving that claimed that the knighted contemporaries thought that the world was flat, and that among those many

many people, only the brave and visionary Columbus, who ventured forth, revealed that the world was round.

The reality is that almost no educated European thought that the world was flat at the time. Washington Irving and others propagated this story because they wanted to build up a heroic image, a rendering of Columbus as hero, and as rebel that would establish him as a man of science, resolutely modern, and always struggling against what Irving and others condemned as the outmoded religious orthodoxies of the Catholic Church. In the process of building up this image, however, these partisans of Columbus actually severely distorted both Columbus and his contemporaries and what they were thinking.

Instead, in fact, ancient authorities back to the days of the great classical Greek philosophers had understood the world as a sphere. The Greek philosopher Eratosthenes, for instance, in the 2nd century B.C., not only understood that the world was round, but even went on to construct an ingenious experiment that involved measuring the Sun's rays that yielded a remarkably reliable estimate of the true circumference of the world! Likewise, the work of the man often considered the father of geography, Ptolemy, in 2nd-century Egypt, also used the spherical model and sought to find ways of representing the Earth's curvature on maps.

This understanding of the world as a sphere had endured. Among their badges of office for instance, medieval kings and queens were shown holding a scepter and an orb, a round representation of world rule, held in the palm of their hand. Another key representation of the medieval worldview was a particular kind of chart, or a map. These maps were called called *mappa mundi*, or "maps of the world," of which more than 600 survive. They offer us a view in on the psychology of the worldview of contemporaries. These were not accurate, scientifically determined outlines of geography that were rendered in map form, but rather renderings of the world in spiritual terms, drawing on information from ancient authorities, especially holy scripture.

Most often, such maps took the form that cartographers called T-O maps. They're called this because their appearance is just that—the letter O with a capital T inside, dividing the world into three sections. Of these directions, traditionally east was seen as most important and was placed at the top, unlike our present convention of placing north at the top of maps. This makes the reading of these older maps a little bit confusing to modern eyes. What this meant was that above the top of the letter T was Asia, with Europe below to the left, and Africa below to the right.

In these maps, the spiritual center of the Christian faith was Jerusalem, the focus of the drama of salvation for all mankind, and so it was most often placed at the center of the map. The Garden of Eden, lying somewhere unknown to the east, surmounted these map as a whole. Then, once these features had been put in, other features could be filled in as well, from the news of travelers, or from tradition, or even from imagination. For example, details from the fabled voyages of Marco Polo could be worked in to some of these medieval maps.

Often included as well were the haunting rumors that persisted for centuries that somewhere, either in Asia or in Africa, there lived a mysterious Christian king, known as Prester John. ("Prester" in this case simply meant "priest.") Priest John, a king who could aid embattled Christendom in its standoff with Islam. In the cosmology of medieval Europe, this world, from its central location, was in turn surrounded by the universe, which was made up of seven spheres of the outer heavens. This notion of there being seven spheres of the heavens in which celestial bodies move is the origin of a phrase that we sometimes still use today, about being so happy that one is literally "in seventh heaven." That meant being in the highest transports of delight in the most perfect outer spheres of creation. If this was Columbus's mindset, worldview, and expectations, how did they lead to a voyage that encountered the Americas?

Columbus himself lived from around 1451 to 1506. He was Italian, born in Genoa, a great seafaring republic of northern Italy. From youth, Columbus gained considerable experience in travel. He worked as a sailor on voyages to Africa, to England, and even to Iceland. He almost didn't make it in some of these voyages; at one point he was on a ship that sank off of Portugal, having been attacked by the French. But this very wreckage that he survived was fortuitous, because he landed in Portugal, and that tiny kingdom of Portugal was actually the center of expansive voyaging at just this time. The Portuguese had begun their own tremendous explorations of sailing down the coast of western Africa. They were probing southwards, ever southwards, to find some access to the spice trade. Remember that the fall of Constantinople had placed older trade routes in Muslim hands. The aim of the Portuguese was to find a way to the East and its riches and its spices.

Inspired, Columbus set about educating himself, to learn in order to become part of this venture. He had not had much formal schooling before, so he focused his own individual energies on gathering all the information he could about a great project, but one that differed from the one that Portuguese were imagining at the time. His project was to sail in the opposite direction, westwards, to reach Asia, and to encounter and meet its alluring treasures, the riches of Japan, China, and India. Predictably enough, the stories of Marco Polo were Columbus's constant companion, and he read many other compendia about fantastic travels. They inspired him in his mission.

Columbus was also fired by a religious self-understanding; he developed, in the process of thinking about this mission, a sense of himself as having a divine calling. He felt that he would be a bearer of Christianity to other lands (in fact, the literal meaning of his first name, Christopher, was "the bearer of Christ"). After the reverses of the failed Crusades, and after the fall of what had remained of the Eastern Roman Empire with Constantinople in 1453, Columbus felt a calling to somehow turn the tables geopolitically—to find new riches and new convert populations in other lands which would allow the Christians to regain what had been lost, to regain the lost Jerusalem, and this motivation would stay with Columbus to his very death.

Finally, the last element that enabled Columbus to envision his venture was, paradoxically, a fateful and as it turns out decisive geographical mistake. Many contemporaries argued that in theory, it should be possible to reach Asia across the Atlantic Ocean, but they also argued that the vast distances of that empty sea were so great that such a voyage would be impractical, or perhaps even impossible. Keep in mind, no one in the West at this point knew of the intervening American continents. (I should add that the Scandinavian Vikings had already earlier reached the northern part of North America, but at this point their voyages had been almost entirely forgotten.) The result was that they envisioned a vast empty space between Europe and Asia across the Atlantic, far too great for a human voyager.

Columbus, by contrast, disagreed. He calculated that the distance between Europe and Asia across the Atlantic was actually much, much shorter. He did this calculation of his by a series of really very optimistic and hopeful leaps and bounds of logic, as well as using any citation he could from ancient geographic writers. What he did was to cherry-pick those facts that agreed with his theory and work them into his sense of mission. All of these elements gave to Columbus the inner conviction that he needed to be a salesman for this journey to the "Indies," that is to say to the East, Asia, by sailing west.

From 1484, Columbus tried and tried and tried repeatedly to convince someone to be his patron. He tried the monarchs of Portugal, then the monarchs of Spain (three times), France, and England, but in all cases was rebuffed, in spite of there being at first some initial interest. Columbus's timing it turns out was terrible: Soon after Columbus started this agitation campaign for a patron, the Portuguese sailor Bartolomeu Dias had arrived with exciting news that he had rounded the Cape of Good Hope in southern Africa, showing a clear eastward path to India. This news made the whole project that Columbus was suggesting less urgent. Except for one thing: the Portuguese discovery did something to stir the rival impulses of Spain, which now thought that it might be worthwhile to find out whether Columbus's plan was practical, and sort of emboldened them to risk the resources that were necessary to find this alternate route.

Thus, after eight years of pleading, finally Queen Isabella of Spain agreed to fund Columbus and his project was launched. As Columbus sailed from Spain, a crusading spirit was raging in that kingdom. With the fall of the last Muslim kingdom in Spain, Grenada, in early 1492, also this brought the completion of the *Reconquista*, the re-conquest of Spanish lands from Muslim rule. The "most Catholic Monarchs" as they were called, of Aragon and Castile, Ferdinand and Isabella, celebrated. On the very day

67

when Columbus sailed, the monarchs expelled the Jews of Spain as a non-Christian religious minority as well.

At the age of 41, Columbus now set sail with three ships from Spain on August 3, 1492. His fleet was tiny—three small ships, nothing like the great treasure fleets of Zheng He some 50 years earlier. The voyage was an uncertain one. The winds driving the crew westwards were so brisk and energetic that the crew feared, not as many people think in popular accounts, that they would fall off the edge of the world. Instead they were more simply afraid that they would be driven out into the vast open space of the Atlantic, and never able to reach home again.

Columbus was actually driven to a deception. He actually kept two different ship's logs. He did this in order to calm his crew by underestimating in the official log the actual distance that they had travelled, lest they become too anxious. Finally, after 33 days of tense sailing, the ships, on October 12, sighted land.

Columbus was now convinced that he had finally reached Asia, and he *stayed* convinced. Even though Columbus had landed in an island of the Bahamas, and then afterwards visited Cuba, and what is today Haiti and the Dominican Republic, he remained sure that he had found his goal of reaching Asia. When he surveyed the plant life of these islands, for instance, he concluded that clearly these were Asian plants and Asian spices. Even though the Arabic-speaking interpreter that Columbus had brought along could not communicate with the local people they encountered (which probably would've happened if he'd reached Asia), Columbus nonetheless, in spite of the evidence, called them Indians, denizens of India, a name which has stuck to the present day.

After three months, the expedition headed home, and Columbus wrote a letter to his royal patrons announcing his success, and promising many more successes soon. This letter soon became public and was printed. It became an early bestseller, with its announcement of a new path to the Indies.

Over the next twelve years, Columbus made three more trips across the Atlantic, always convinced that he was in Asia, even when on his fourth voyage he landed on the mainland of the continent, in what is today Honduras. Columbus died in 1506 in Spain, sure that he had fulfilled his dream to the very last.

It would take some time longer for contemporaries to actually realize and figure out what it really was that Columbus had in fact found. It is for that reason that we do not call these continents Northern and Southern Columbia today, but rather call them the Americas. That name came from the sailor Amerigo Vespucci. Vespucci was Italian, born in Florence, and at different times in the employ of Spain or Portugal. We don't really know much about him, but he seems to have made several trips across the Atlantic about a decade after Columbus. Like his precursor, Vespucci was concerned above all with that key question: access to Asia. Vespucci died in 1512, and today America bears his name—not just one continent, but two continents. This naming of the Americas was not his own doing; he did not deliberately steal the glory and name the place after himself.

In reality, the naming was something of an accident, and it shows the growing authority of print, which we discussed in our previous lecture. On Vespucci's return to Europe, he wrote some letters to friends about his travels and what he'd seen. Then, someone (we don't know who, but it apparently was not Vespucci himself) used text from these letters to fabricate a new document, a sensational account of what Vespucci had found. This text was entitled *Mundus Novus*, the "New World," and it appeared in print around 1502. What the title itself already conveyed was that the continent across the Atlantic was not Asia, but a previously unknown landmass.

At this point, a German geographer who had been trained at the University of Freiburg in the Black Forest in Germany, a geographer by the name of Martin Waldseemüller, was impressed by his reading of this new geographic account. Waldseemüller and his colleagues in a small printing establishment in the Vosges mountains in northeastern France incorporated the insights that had been written about in this text and used them to create a new map of the world as it was then known. Waldseemüller in this new map named the new lands after the Latinized name of Vespucci, his first name, Amerigo, "Americus," but rendered them in a feminized form, as America.

The Waldseemüller map that resulted is really quite mysterious. It also shows the outline of South America on the Pacific side, which had not yet been charted. Historians still don't really know how this is possible—perhaps it was just a conjecture, or an educated guess. The new map, published in 1507, was a blockbuster, and as a result, the name given to the continent, America, came into popular usage. There's kind of a footnote here: After publishing that map, Waldseemüller had second thoughts; he had regrets about whether the choice of name for America was really appropriate and he tried to rescind it, but it was too late. Once in print, the idea and the name of America had taken hold. We see here that the process of print was really showing its vast power.

The physical fact of the meeting and travel between what came to be called the Old World and the New World was in fact a huge environmental turning point, which has been given the name of the "Columbian exchange," the mixing of people, deadly diseases (that devastated Native American populations), crops and animals, goods, and trade flows. The term "Columbian exchange" was coined by the historian Alfred Crosby in a book by that name in 1972, subtitled *Biological and Cultural Consequences of 1492*.

The result of this exchange amounted to an environmental revolution, the most important of human history it's been claimed. One of the first consequences was the sweeping through Native American populations of epidemics—diseases that Europeans had acquired immunities to, which devastated the populations of the Americas: typhus, diptheria, malaria, influenza, cholera, and especially smallpox. As Europeans travelled in lands new to them, epidemics preceded them, often wiping out more than half the people.

By 1650, it is estimated that 90 percent of the Native American populations had died. This produced a depopulation of millions that destroyed traditional societies, sapped their powers of resistance, and really helped the European conquest and eventual European immigration. Syphilis, by contrast, may have been a disease that headed in the opposite direction, but there is still some debate on this question.

It's probably also necessary to note at that this time the importation of illnesses was not somehow intended by Columbus and other explorers, or necessarily unique to him. Recalling the very start of our course, when we spoke of the voyages of Zheng He and mentioned speculations about where further voyages might have taken him, perhaps to the Americas, the same would have applied. If Zheng He's fleets had made landfall on the Pacific coast, a similar wave of epidemics from Asia would have been seen, and we might instead be speaking of the Zheng He-ian Exchange, rather than the Columbian exchange.

Another vast dimension of this phenomenon involved crops and animals, and went both ways. European crops and domesticated animals (like horses, pigs, sheep, and cattle) were introduced to America (in the case of horses, actually reintroduced), along with weeds and pests (like the everyday dandelion), while American species like potatoes, tomatoes, and corn (or maize) entered the European diet, enriching it to the point of enabling a huge growth of population in the centuries to follow because of these improvements. Not just European diets were affected—the sweet potato for instance, contributed, it's been argued to the doubling of China's population in the next three centuries.

Of the elements of this exchange, an especially telling one to focus on just for a moment is the potato. It was new and a very productive crop from the Andes. Because potatoes were able to grow in soils that traditional European wheat could not thrive in, the potato became a staple of European agriculture, essentially doubling the European food supply. This was especially so in places like Ireland, until disaster struck from 1845, when the potato blight hit, creating a famine. What most people do not know is that the Irish potato blight was in turn also a product of the Columbian exchange, transported to Europe by ships that brought guano (bird droppings essentially) as fertilizer for European fields. As a result of the famine, two million Irish fled in desperation, many of them to the United States.

Columbus's American discoveries prompted further exploration, in an accelerating process of competition. The lure of expansion and treasure was great and grew stronger. In 1519, Ferdinand Magellan, a Portuguese mariner in the employ of Spain, set out on an expedition that traveled around the globe by 1522, revealing the Pacific and the full extent of the territories between. Spanish conquistadors toppled the Aztec and Inca empires with astonishing speed.

This conquest and carving up of new lands also from the first had a tragic dimension: transatlantic slavery. As an ancient institution, slavery had a long, long history worldwide. Columbus on encountering the Indians already had surmises about enslaving them, and took captives himself. Later, when the use of Native American slaves did not suffice, Africa was drawn in. The African slave trade, originally run by Africans and Arabs, now successfully was built up by the Portuguese, Dutch, and English, as they carried Africans in bondage across the Atlantic for plantation agriculture. This cruel trade, over the centuries until the mid-19th century, would involve the forced movement of between 12 and 15 million Africans it's estimated.

In terms of how this new expanded world was viewed, and how authority over it was understood, we need to note a remarkable fact. As the contours of these new discoveries came into sharper focus, the kingdoms of Portugal and Spain turned to the Pope to help divide the world among them. With papal mediation, a line was drawn across the Atlantic and then extending on the other side, the Pacific, with Spain assigned all the possessions to the west of the line and Portugal assigned newly claimed lands to the east. The Treaty of Tordesillas of 1494 drew the line west of the Azores islands. Later discoveries showed that part of South America bulges out beyond that line, which meant that the vast lands of Brazil fell to Portuguese rule, essentially by coincidence.

Stop for a moment to let this all sink in: what a vivid testimony to religious authority in the Christian West, that this is how the appeal went, to a religious authority, to the pope! But we also need to note that times were already changing, and that other European kingdoms did not passively accept this division of the globe—instead, a fierce competition would break out over this question of who was to control newly discovered territories.

Harder to pin down, but still important, was the intellectual impact of what was considered the New World. European ideas of the new world paradoxically presented it as either better than the old, or inevitably debased and inferior! For some observers, this was essentially a new Eden, populated by so-called noble savages, people who were living in harmony with nature. For others by contrast, the Americas and Americans would never quite measure up, would always be second class, would instead always be seen as uncultivated, barbarous, and at best sort of cheap imitations of the Old World.

In general, the very existence of the new world in some ways undermined the traditional authority of the ancients and of classical thought—the ancient authorities, who were supposed to be authoritative, had not even known about the Americas; they had been incomplete in their knowledge, it was revealed Clearly, their explanations of the world were not comprehensive, and had to make room for new facts, like the sudden appearance of entirely new continents. Nor for that matter, had the Bible revealed this New World, a fact that could be very disturbing to readers accustomed to its authority in describing all of creation.

So this discovery of Columbus became the lasting archetype of a stunning encounter—and yet we've seen it was not what Columbus had set out for. This was an example of what's called serendipity, meaning finding something other than what you're looking for. The origin of this beautiful and poetic term "serendipity" actually did lie in the mysterious East Columbus was seeking. A Persian fairytale told of three princes of Serendip. "Serendip" was the Persian name for today's Sri Lanka, at that point called Ceylon.

Incidentally, Serendip or Ceylon lay in the Portuguese part of the world as carved up by the Treaty of Tordesillas with Spain, so this was in fact part of the very prize which the Iberian kingdoms were dividing up among themselves. In this Persian fairytale, the three princes of Serendip were always making unexpected discoveries, so this phenomenon has come to be called serendipity. The next time you find yourself or someone else using the term, take a moment to remember the remarkable lineage of that word! Ultimately, Columbus may not have reached the Asia of his dreams, but he did find serendipity.

Obviously, Columbus was not the only one to be enchanted by dreams of the East. Continuing his yearning for the riches of Asia, a whole new group of merchant adventurers (organized into the English East India Company) would likewise seek the East, and in the process—also serendipitously—invented the modern corporation, as we will see in our next lecture.

1600—The British East India Company
Lecture 5

This lecture examines the founding and growth of the English East India Company (later the British East India Company). We will see how it beat out its main rivals, the Dutch East India Company and the French East India Company. This turning point put Britain on the road to establish an empire on which the sun never set. It also saw the birth of the modern corporation, stock shares, and the commercial binding together of the globe. Globalization, much discussed today, is in fact quite old, and the year 1600 was a key moment in that ongoing process. Profit, trade, and capital would assume crucial authority in new flows of goods, people, and wealth.

The Search for Spices

- Around the time of Columbus, Portuguese mariners had set off east—the opposite direction from Columbus—sailing down the

Spices made the preserved meat of Europeans palatable and were a great prize; pepper, cinnamon, ginger, cloves, nutmeg, mace—all could bring great wealth.

west coast of Africa in search of a way to the Indies. These mariners sought riches in the form of spices.

- In 1488, the Portuguese rounded the Cape of Good Hope, opening the path to the Indies. They established the Goa trading colony on the west coast of India in 1510.
  o They then headed further east to the "Spiceries," the Indonesian archipelago of 13,000 islands.

  o The Portuguese built forts and trading posts in the Moluccas, establishing a vast trading empire across Asia and Africa.

- Portugal's traders had successfully outflanked the Islamic states, which had controlled the trade in luxury goods from the east. But now other maritime powers from Europe, the English and Dutch, would seek to outflank the outflankers!

- A global trade war ensued in the years around 1600. The English and Dutch advanced on the east, following the principle that even though there might be peace in Europe, there was "no peace beyond the line," east of the Azores or south of the Tropic of Cancer.

- The English also attempted to discover another passage to Asia, either across the northernmost reaches of Russia or across the top of North America. The Dutch headed straight for the Spice Islands, and one of their mariners discovered the wind patterns across the Indian Ocean, allowing for accelerated travel to Indonesia.

- There, the Dutch found local populations who welcomed them, eager for competition in the trade with Portugal. Among the early Dutch ships that returned from the Indies, one made a 400 percent return on investment! Predictably, with profits like this, swarms of ships were soon heading off to the Indies, both Dutch and English. Their competition touched off a hot commercial war that would last for two centuries.

Chartered Monopolies

- The vehicles for this competition and trade were chartered monopoly companies—the first multinational corporations. Because a trading venture was too large for one investor to take on alone, resources would be pooled in companies. To make the risk worth taking for commensurately high reward, European monarchs gave monopolies to these ventures. Many such companies came into existence in England, the Netherlands, France, Denmark, Sweden, Austria, Spain, and even Scotland.

- What made these companies a real advance in commerce was the notion of limited liability.
  - Earlier, merchants who cooperated on some speculative venture formed a partnership. If the venture was successful, the profits would be divided. But in case of failure, such as a shipwreck, the partners would be held liable for the losses, which could lead to bankruptcy.

  - But when investments were pooled in joint stock, investors could lose only what they had invested. As this practice developed over time, the stock would be devoted not just to individual voyages but to the business of the corporation on a much longer-term basis.

- On New Year's Eve in the year 1600, a group of 218 London merchants was granted a royal charter, giving them a monopoly on trade east of the Cape of Good Hope for 15 years. The English East India Company (EIC) was launched.

- The first voyages undertaken by the EIC were called "separate voyages" because each was individually financed; the investments plus profits were returned to investors. After 1612, these separate voyages were replaced by joint stock voyages. After 1610, the English established trading stations on the Indian coast.

Rivals of the EIC

- Initially, a far bigger and richer rival of the EIC was the Dutch East India Company (known by the acronym VOC). It had capital resources 10 times larger than the EIC. Its power reflected the tremendous wealth and achievements of the Netherlands.

- The Dutch had the most commercially oriented society in the world. They had grown rich on trade, even as they fought for their independence from Spain, and enjoyed a Golden Age from around 1600 to 1720.

- The VOC was ahead of its rivals in its organization and financing. It was the first to establish permanent share capital and the first to issue stocks. It drew in a great number of investors from many parts of society. The Dutch government gave the company the right to make war or peace and sign treaties on behalf of the Dutch state.

- The VOC eventually built up a fleet of some 150 merchant ships and 40 warships. It had about 50,000 employees, including a private army worldwide. The company's headquarters in the east was the city of Jakarta in Java, which the Dutch had fortified and renamed Batavia in 1619. By about 1650, it is estimated that the VOC controlled half of Europe's foreign trade.

- At first, the English and the Dutch were able to coexist in the Indies, but the rivalry soon tipped over into open war. As the Dutch established their own spice monopoly in the Banda Islands, they increasingly saw the English as rivals to be excluded by force.

- These tensions finally boiled over in an infamous violent act: the 1623 Amboyna Massacre.
    o On the island of Amboyna (today Maluku, Indonesia), English and Dutch company outposts lay close to one another; the island itself was prized for its clove plantations.

    o Dutch traders arrested a Japanese mercenary working for the English and tortured him until he declared that the English were preparing a surprise attack. The Dutch surprised the English and took them captive, subjecting some to water torture and executing 10 Englishmen.

o   When news of the incident reached Europe, the English erupted. Mutual hatred led to a series of Anglo-Dutch wars in the period 1652 to 1784.

Redirection of the EIC

- As a result of the violence in the Spice Islands, the EIC redirected its focus to trade in India, which previously had been more of a way station on the route to the east.

- At this point, the main power in India was the Mughal Empire, ruled by descendants of the Mongols, who had swept into India from the north in the 16th century. By the 1700s, the Mughal Empire seemed in decline, and the EIC found itself in a competition to pick up the pieces with a new rival, the French East India Company.

- Throughout the preceding century, the EIC had continued to evolve. This was a period that saw tremendous change in English politics: A civil war raged between the king and Parliament in the 1640s, ending with the beheading of King Charles I and the establishment of a Commonwealth under Oliver Cromwell; this was followed by the restoration of the monarchy in 1660, the overthrow of another king in the Glorious Revolution of 1688, and the union of Scotland and England in 1707 to form Great Britain.

- Throughout these changes, the EIC survived, sometimes barely. Jealous merchants from towns other than London argued against its monopoly, and the renewal of its charter was often in doubt, but the company persevered.

- From its new base in India, the EIC built up an effective and efficient administrative apparatus. The company was led by 24 directors and an overall chairman, who was elected by the stockholders. Armed East Indiaman ships were formidable presences on the seas, carrying tremendous cargoes of porcelain, cotton and silk cloth, tea and coffee.

Political Rule of India

- The growth of the EIC took a quantum leap with its assumption of political rule in India. In this, it contended against the French East India Company, chartered in 1664, which had established its own bases in Chandernagore in Bengal and Pondicherry (now Puducherry) near Madras.

- The rival companies trained and deployed armies recruited from locals, called "sepoys." They increasingly involved themselves in Indian politics, favoring one or another prince.

- In these local wars, a figure named Sir Robert Clive took on a new military role and rose through the ranks of the EIC. In 1757, he defeated the far larger army of an Indian prince aligned with the French at the Battle of Plassey. The British installed their own loyal prince to rule Bengal.
  - The richest province in India now came under the control of the EIC, which ran its taxation and civil administration.

  - In the coming decades, the Indian holdings of the company expanded, forming the basis for the British Empire.

- The company had severe critics in its home country, including Adam Smith, who argued against monopolies as an impediment to free trade, and Edmund Burke, who condemned the damage to Indian traditions and the corrosive effects that the new wealth flowing back to Britain would have on British society.

The Birth of Global Connections

- In the final analysis, the turning point represented by the founding of the EIC in 1600 went on to produce new global connections based on the authority of trade and profit. By the end of the 18th century, the EIC had outpaced its Dutch rival by diversifying its trade beyond spices to include textiles and tea.

- The lives of some of the officers of the EIC were also global in a sense. One man who prospered in service to the EIC was Elihu Yale, an American-born merchant who became the governor of the Madras settlement. In 1718, Yale College was named in his honor. According to his tomb, Yale was born in America, bred in Europe, traveled in Africa, and married in Asia. This sort of life was a new testimony to early globalization.

- An eccentric figure known as Walking Stewart, a former employee of the EIC, later argued that humans had no fixed identity but lived like a river, with everything constantly forming and dissolving. His personal philosophy underlined connections in a world of motion and his criticism of the EIC's oppression of the Indians represented a very modern awareness of this new globalization.

Suggested Reading

Bernstein, *A Splendid Exchange*.

Bown, *Merchant Kings*.

Brook, *Vermeer's Hat*.

Lawson, *The East India Company*.

Robins, *The Corporation That Changed the World*.

Questions to Consider

1. Do you consider the East India Company heroic, exploitative, or both? Why?

2. What aspects of early capitalism seem most unfamiliar today?

1600—The British East India Company

In our times, military metaphors abound in the business world, as we say that companies battle for market share, advance into new markets, or retreat. But what if these were not just metaphors? What if companies actually went to war? Imagine for instance the troops of McDonald's fighting against the armies of Burger King, or the Coca-Cola navy sailing forth to attack the Pepsi fleet!

Yet that was the reality when the first multinational corporations were founded, around 1600. We speak today of "corporate raiders," but that's actually what the reality was at the start. We speak of "trade wars," but indeed world commerce was shaped by the clash of companies.

In this lecture, we examine the founding and astonishing growth of the English East India Company. I should note that after 1707 (when England and Scotland were united to become the United Kingdom of Great Britain), it became the British East India Company. Here I will refer to it as the East India Company or by its acronym, EIC. We will see how it beat out its main rivals, first the Dutch East India Company, and then the French East India Company.

This turning point, the founding of the East India Company in 1600, put Britain on the road to establish an empire on which the sun never set. It also saw the birth of the modern corporation, stock shares, and the commercial binding together of the globe. Globalization, a phenomenon much discussed today, is in fact not new but quite old, and this was a key moment in that ongoing process. Profit and trade and capital would assume crucial authority in new flows of goods, people, and wealth.

Just as with the voyage of Columbus, it all began with dreams of Asian riches. Around the time of Columbus, you will recall, Portuguese mariners had set off to the east, in the opposite direction from Columbus—they had felt their way down the west coast of Africa, trying to find a way around the continent to head towards what were called the Indies. There, they sought riches in the form of spices. Spices made the preserved meat of Europeans palatable, made the food interesting, and were a great exotic prize. Pepper, cinnamon, ginger, cloves, nutmeg, and mace, all could bring great wealth and in some cases were literally worth their weight in gold. But Europeans knew little of where these exotic wares came from: They came from the mythical "Spiceries" or "Spice Islands" of the Indies.

The Portuguese headed off to search for these locations, eventually reaching the routes followed by Zheng He 50 years before. In 1488, they rounded the Cape of Good Hope at the southern extremity of Africa. The path to the Indies was open. Recall that the Treaty of Tordesillas in 1494 had assigned these mysterious regions to Portugal. In India, Portugal established the Goa trading colony on the west coast in 1510 (and the Portuguese held this for some 450 years, until independent India annexed it in 1961).

The Portuguese then headed further east to the Spiceries, the Indonesian archipelago, a collection of 13,000 islands, chief among them the Moluccas in what today is Indonesia. They were known as the Spice Islands (among them for instance, the Bandas were the world's sole source for cloves and nutmeg and mace, only to be found there—nowhere else). The Portuguese established forts and trading posts in these islands, asserting their monopoly, total control. The Portuguese traded with China and with Japan, so that ultimately the small country of Portugal was building a vast trading empire, across Asia and Africa.

In a historic turn, Portugal's traders had successfully outflanked the Islamic states which had controlled the trade in luxury goods from the East. But now soon, other powers from Europe would seek in turn to outflank the outflankers! These new powers were the growing maritime countries of northern Europe, especially the English and the Dutch.

A global trade war ensued, in the years around 1600. The English and the Dutch advanced on the East following the principle that even though there might be peace in the current time in Europe, there was "no peace beyond the line," as the phrase went, in these more exotic locations east of the Azores or south of the Tropic of Cancer. Moreover, as Protestant countries, England and the Netherlands totally rejected the papal decision that was embodied in the Treaty of Tordesillas, and also brought their religious motives to the struggle against Catholic Portugal and Catholic Spain.

There was certainly plenty of hatred to go around. In 1588, the English under Queen Elizabeth had just defeated the Spanish Armada that was sent against them, and they took the initiative at sea. The Netherlands meanwhile had revolted against Spanish rule in 1566 and continued a long, long war of independence that lasted until 1648.

Now, the English and the Dutch combined piracy with trade ventures. Indeed, this was the great age of piracy. The English also attempted to discover another passage to Asia, either across the northernmost reaches of Russia, or across the top of North America, with not-marked success. The Dutch headed straight for the Spice Islands on their own, and one of their mariners made a fascinating discovery: the wind patterns across the Indian Ocean known as the Roaring Forties. If you could catch those winds, you could achieve accelerated travel to Indonesia.

Following these winds, the Dutch found local populations who welcomed them, eager for competition in the trade with Portugal. Among those early Dutch ships that returned from the perilous voyage to the Indies, they made great profits. One indeed, one ship made a 400 percent return on investment! Predictably, with profits like this, soon swarms of ships were heading off to the Indies, both Dutch and English, to get a share of that wealth. Their competition touched off a hot commercial war that would last two centuries.

The vehicles for this competition and trade were chartered monopoly companies, in essence the first multinational corporations. Because a trading venture was too large for one investor to finance on his own, resources would be pooled in companies. Indeed, the word that we use today "company," originally simply meant a group of people who shared bread, who ate the same bread, *companio*. To make the risk worth taking for these tremendous rewards, European monarchs encouraged these companies by giving monopolies to these ventures so they alone would be able to fulfill this role.

There would be many such companies. In England alone, there was the Muscovy Company trading to Russia, the Virginia Company trading to North America, and the Royal African Company. The Dutch had not only the Dutch East India Company, but also the Dutch West India Company which worked in the Americas, and founded New Amsterdam (today's New York), and carved out a huge share of the Atlantic slave trade. To exploit the East Indies, there were also other companies: the French, Danish, Swedish, Austrian, Spanish, and even Scottish East India companies.

What made these companies a real advance in commerce was a financial tool: the notion of limited liability. Earlier, a handful of merchants who cooperated on some speculative venture formed a partnership. If it was a success, they would divide the profits. But in case of failure (let's say a shipwreck), the partnership, and thus the partners individually, would be held liable for the losses, which could lead to a businessman being entirely bankrupted, losing everything as a result of this speculation.

By contrast, with limited liability, when investments were pooled in joint stock, an investor might lose, but only the sum that had been invested, not all of his personal fortune. As this practice developed over time, the stock that grew up would be devoted not just to one voyage, but to the larger business of the corporation on a much longer-term basis.

So our turning point, which got this whole process rolling, involves the founding of the East India Company, in England, on New Year's Eve, 1600. A group of London merchants met and planned how to break in on this profitable Indies trade, and then with their plan in hand hurried to the royal court. On December 31, 1600, Queen Elizabeth formally granted these 218 merchants a royal charter, for 15 years, in their capacity as the company, "The Governor and Company of Merchants Trading into the East Indies." They were allowed a monopoly on trade east of the Cape of Good Hope, and then essentially left to their own devices: The company would have to defend itself; it was given the right to punish so-called interlopers, those who were trying to sneak in and violate their monopoly; and the company in general would have to seek its fortunes as best it could.

The business model of the corporation, which we sketched earlier, took time to develop in the EIC. The first voyages after 1600 were called separate voyages, because each was individually financed, made great gains, and then the investments plus profits were returned to the investors. Then after 1612, joint-stock voyages took their place, so the whole process became more regular and more efficient. English ships successfully made their journeys and established a special trading station, known as a "factory" (that's where our current name for a manufacturing center comes from) in Java, at Bantam, in 1602. From 1610, the English established more stations on the Indian coast for trade, as a way station on the way to the real prize, the Spiceries.

It's at this point that we need to consider the initially far bigger and richer rival of the EIC, the Dutch East India Company. In Dutch, this was called the *Vereenigde Oost-Indische Compagnie*, and it went by its acronym, the VOC, which has been called in fact the first global business brand, because those initials, VOC, appeared on their buildings, ships, and their coinage. The Dutch company was founded just two years after the EIC, but soon built up a huge lead. The Dutch company had capital resources 10 times bigger than the EIC. Its power reflected the tremendous wealth and success of the Netherlands, or as they were known at the time, the United Provinces, or the Dutch Republic.

At this point, the Dutch had done something amazing: They had created the most commercially oriented society in the world. The Dutch had grown rich on trade even as they'd fought for their independence in rebellion against Spain. In a later lecture, we're going to discuss these achievements more fully, so here let me just note that this was the Dutch Golden Age, from around 1570 to around 1720.

The VOC was ahead of its rivals in its organization and its financing—this was a key to its success. It was the first to establish permanent share capital. It was the first to issue stocks, and drew in a great number of investors from many different parts of society, the high as well as the lowly. The Dutch government gave the company the right to make war or peace, and even to sign treaties on behalf of the Dutch state. The company itself was directed by the Seventeen Lords, with representatives chosen from the different cities of the united provinces.

The VOC eventually built up a huge fleet of some 150 merchant ships and 40 warships. It had about 50,000 employees, including a private army that was stationed worldwide. In all, the VOC would send about a million Europeans to the East, in order to help with their trading activities. Only about half of them survived—it was a dangerous occupation. The great headquarters of the VOC in the East was the city of Jakarta in Java, which the Dutch had fortified and renamed "Batavia" in 1619. (Batavia is the classical Latin name for the Netherlands.) By about 1650, it's estimated—an astonishing figure—that the VOC controlled half of all of Europe's foreign trade.

At first, the English and the Dutch, as they worked to outflank the Portuguese, were able to coexist in the Indies, but this rivalry soon tipped over into open war. As the Dutch established their own spice monopoly in the Banda Islands, they increasingly and naturally saw the English as rivals, and decided that they needed to be excluded, by force.

As one of the governor generals of the Dutch East Indies put it in a report that he wrote back home to the Seventeen Lords of the VOC, he said: "Your Honours should know by experience that trade in Asia must be driven and maintained under the protection and favour of Your Honours' own weapons, and that the weapons must be paid for from the profits from the trade; so that we cannot carry on trade without war, nor war without trade."

These tensions finally boiled over in an infamous international incident, the 1623 Amboyna Massacre. On the island of Amboyna, today Maluku, Indonesia, English and Dutch company outposts lay very close to one another, and in fact they looked out suspiciously at each other. The island was a prize for its precious clove plantations.

At one point, Dutch traders from their trading post spotted a Japanese mercenary who was working for the English, who they thought was skulking about suspiciously. They arrested him, and tortured him, until he declared that the English were preparing a surprise attack on the Dutch. The Dutch surprised their English neighbors and took them captive, subjecting some of them to water torture, and extracted many other improbable confessions, and then executed 10 Englishmen.

When news of this got back to Europe, the English erupted, and the story was told and retold, emphasizing Dutch cruelty and rapacity. A battle of pamphlets ensued in the press, with titles like *A True Relation of the Unjust, Cruel, and Barbarous Proceedings against the English at Amboyna*, which included woodcuts of the torture scenes to inflame passions even further. The Dutch responded with pamphlets of their own, defending their actions. This incident had two important results: It fueled English-Dutch tensions which tipped into wars, and it also led the EIC to reorient its business.

Mutual hatreds led to a whole series of Anglo-Dutch Wars. This included Anglo-Dutch wars of 1652–54; 1665–67; 1672–74; 1780–84. You get the idea. There was a whole series of this, a constant animosity. Curiously, this English antipathy towards the Dutch is still imprinted in the English language, in fact in some expressions whose origins are obscure to most people even if they use them. Thus for instance, to speak of a "Dutch treat" means splitting the cost of something, which allegedly was characteristic of the cheap and miserly Dutch enemy, while the phrase "Dutch courage" means kind of an artificial resolution or courage that's been fired by alcohol, masking underlying cowardice. To call somebody a "Dutch uncle" used to mean someone who is unhelpful, super critical, completely ungenerous, the very opposite of what a true loving uncle should be.

Another outcome of this series of wars was the English capture of New Amsterdam in 1664; they renamed it New York. The other outcome of this violent reverse in the Spice Islands—the Amboyna Massacre—was that the EIC turned away from the Spice Islands to concentrate on trade in India, which until this point had been more of a way station on the route to the east. In India, the EIC expanded its trade in goods like pepper, indigo, raw silk and raw cotton, as well as textiles like silk cloth and calicoes, and saltpeter, a chemical (potassium nitrate) that's needed for the production of gunpowder.

At this point, the main power in India was the Mughal Empire, ruled by the descendants of the Mongols (hence the name Mughal), who had swept into India from the north in the 16th century. One of the Mughal emperors built the Taj Mahal in Agra from the 1630s, one of the greatest architectural monuments of the world. But by the 1700s, the Mughal Empire in India seemed in decline, and the EIC found itself in a competition to pick up the pieces—competition with a new rival, the French East India Company.

Throughout the preceding century, the EIC had continued to evolve. This was a period that saw tremendous and even shocking change in English politics: A civil war had raged between the king and Parliament in the 1640s, ending with the beheading of King Charles I; a commonwealth had been established under Oliver Cromwell; and then the monarchy had been restored in 1660. Then in 1688 the Glorious Revolution had seen the overthrow of another king. In 1707, Scotland and England had been united to form Great Britain.

Through all these changes, the EIC survived, sometimes barely. Jealous merchants from towns other than London argued against its monopoly, and the renewal of its charter at regular intervals and its monopoly were often in doubt. But across these changes of regime, the company did get its charter renewed. It was experiencing success. The directors used considerable cunning: When a rival company was permitted in 1691 that would cut in on their trade, the EIC bought a share of its stock and infiltrated it from within, then absorbed it. A constant tool in gaining rechartering was the use of gifts, or bribes, to gain support from the monarchy and the Parliament, and all this came on top of the customs revenues which the company's trade was bringing in and that were most welcome to the state.

Indeed, just surviving led the EIC to grow, especially from the new base in India. The EIC built up an effective and efficient administrative apparatus. The company itself was led by 24 directors, who conducted administration by committees, and the overall chairman was elected by the stockholders of the company. Below these top officials were different ranks of officers of the company, called servants of the company. Their ranks went all the way from the most junior, called writers, up to the post of senior merchant. The servants were not paid large salaries, but instead when they were posted abroad, they were allowed to engage in trade on their own. This could produce new fortunes but also complicated incentives and loyalties given this dual role of servants in foreign lands.

Armed East Indiamen ships were formidable presences on the seas, carrying the goods of the EIC: tremendous cargoes of porcelain, cotton and silk cloth, tea and coffee. The company's famous flag was a large red and white horizontal-striped flag with the British flag in an upper corner. Does that sound familiar? What other flag do we know that has horizontal red and white stripes? Obviously, the United States flag, which in early versions was almost identical to that of the company.

So formidable was the EIC as a corporate personality that it was even jokingly spoken of as if it were a person, and called, John Company. The formal title was The Honourable Company.

Then, unexpectedly, it grew even larger, taking a quantum leap with its assumption of political rule in India. The EIC in India contended against the French East India Company, which had been chartered in 1664, and which had established its own bases in India, in Chandernagore in Bengal and Pondicherry near Madras. The rival companies trained and deployed private armies recruited from the local populations, called sepoys. They increasingly involved themselves in Indian politics, favoring one or another prince.

The key role here was ultimately played by a larger-than-life-size figure, Sir Robert Clive. An unruly and unpromising youth from Shropshire nobility, Clive was sent by his family to India to make something of himself, as a lowly writer at the age of 18. Some historians believe that he suffered from bipolar disorder, which was evidenced in exalted highs and corresponding lows of depression. In these local wars, Clive took on a new military role and achieved fame and rose with meteoric speed through the company's ranks, gaining the honorifics "Heaven-born General" and "Clive of India."

Most famously in 1757, he defeated a far larger army of an Indian prince, the Nawab, who was aligned with the French at the famous Battle of Plassey. Clive's thousand English troops, along with 2,200 sepoys, faced an opposing army of 50,000, with war elephants and cannon, at the battle site north of Calcutta. Clive, however, had used his negotiating skills to get the military commander of the Nawab, his enemy, Mir Jafar, to actually agree to change sides during the battle, and this tipped the outcome. After this famous victory, Mir Jafar was named the new Nawab of Bengal, and he ruled with British patronage.

Bengal, the richest province in India, now was under the control of the EIC, which ran its taxation and civil administrative systems. What a spectacle: a private company taking over a country! In coming decades, the Indian holdings of the Company would expand even further, and this would form the basis for the British Empire.

Men like Clive, who made new fortunes as adventurers in the employ of the EIC, were nicknamed "nabobs" (after the Mughal name for a governor). Nabobs were sort of cartoonish figures, examples of nouveau riche and social climbing and ambition. Some may recall in American politics how Nixon's vice president Spiro Agnew once referred to intellectuals as "nattering nabobs of negativism."

The company had severe critics in its home country, scathing about its corruption and abuses, including Adam Smith. This economist argued against monopolies as an impediment to the kind of free trade he saw as most productive. Edmund Burke, the parliamentarian and father of conservative thought, condemned the damage that was being done to Indian traditions and the corrosive effects that the new wealth of the nabobs who returned to Britain was having on British society

In the final analysis, the turning point represented by the founding of the EIC back in 1600 went on to produce new global connections, based on the authority of trade and profit. By the end of the 18th century, the EIC outpaced its Dutch rival by diversifying its trade beyond just spices, to include commodities like textiles and especially tea, which became a central feature of British life.

The daily ritual of teatime was a global one, yet had tragic dimensions. That tea from China would be sweetened with sugar from the West Indies cultivated by slave labor. Fine china, like that produced by the Wedgwood company, was part of a ritual that testified to these global connections. Similarly, as another example of connections, today curry is considered the national dish of Britain, part of this dynamic interaction.

The lives of some of the servants of the EIC were also global in dramatically new ways. One man who prospered in company service was Elihu Yale, an American-born merchant (born in Boston), who became the governor of the Madras settlement in India. In 1718 Yale College was named in his honor because of the gifts he had made to that institution, and even today Yalies are also known as "Elis." When Yale was buried in Wales, his tomb marker stated that he was born in America, bred in Europe, travelled in Africa, and married in Asia, and it was now hoped was in heaven. This sort of global life spanning continents was a new testimony to early globalization.

So too, but in a different way, was the life of a man nicknamed "Walking Stewart," who was once a great celebrity, but now is forgotten. John Stewart was a London-born youth, who was sent out as a humble writer to Madras in India in 1763. He fell out with his employers in 1765 and had had enough. He decided he wanted to go home, so he set out to walk back home. He walked through Persia, through Turkey, Ethiopia, North Africa, Russia, and Europe until he finally reached London. He is supposed to have been the human being at that time who had walked the greatest distance, and later it's said that he even went on an additional walking tour of the United States and Canada.

In London, he was a famed eccentric, dressing exotically. He was tall and lean (a vegetarian who ate only one meal a day), and always scribbling mystic poetry. An urban legend from London claimed that he was able to be in several places at once because you'd meet him on your way there, and then meet him again headed in another direction. In 1822 when he died his obituary said there must have been three of him, because he was everywhere. He even appears in the poetry of Wordsworth as a mysterious traveler.

As he walked, Stewart meditated and created a distinctive personal philosophy. Stewart argued that we all have no one fixed identity, but rather our lives are like a river, with everything constantly being formed and dissolved, with everything always existing in relation to something else. His personal philosophy underlined connections, in a world in motion. Also, he had apparently fallen out with the EIC over what he saw as pretty important human issue: the cynical oppression of the Indians, exploited without the foreigners, the English being interested in their languages or cultures, Stewart felt. Here was a very modern awareness of a new globalization as well as a critical perspective on the phenomenon of globalization.

This lecture examined a turning point in building economic structures, the multinational company. Next we'll move to examine the building of political structures, for international peace, in the 1648 Treaty of Westphalia, in our next lecture.

1648—The Treaty of Westphalia
Lecture 6

The world we know seems almost to have a default mode of international organization: the sovereign state as a political powerhouse. But how did this international order come into being? In this lecture, we will examine a key turning point in international politics that had a global impact. This turning point came at the end of the Thirty Years' War in Europe in 1648, a war that itself came at the end of about a century of religious slaughter and warfare in the Western Christian world. The peace settlement that ended the Thirty Years' War—the Peace of Westphalia—pointed international politics in a new direction.

Authority in the Middle Ages

- Much of earlier history is a contrast to our current model of divided sovereignties and authority. The earlier ideal was that of universal authority, often expressed in empire. For much of human history, empire was a more common form of political organization than the nation-state or republic.

- In the Middle Ages in Europe, authority was seen as divinely sanctioned and universal in its claims and reach. Of course, the fact that both church and state appealed to divine authority could lead to conflicts. Two institutions of the Middle Ages in particular exemplify this conflict: the pope and the Holy Roman Empire.

- The church and the imperial state were intertwined in a vivid way: The emperor often controlled who became pope in Rome, while only a pope could crown a Holy Roman Emperor. Who would dominate in this relationship? Both sought to inherit the authority of the Roman Empire.
  - During the 11th and 12th centuries, as part of a movement for reform, a series of popes made claims to temporal authority, creating what has been called a "papal monarchy." In 1075, Pope Gregory VII claimed that the pope had the right

to depose the emperor. These claims led to the so-called Investiture Controversy.

o In the 12th century, the Roman Catholic Church was at the height of its political and secular power. When new monarchies arose to challenge that power, especially the king of France, Pope Boniface VIII announced a ringing assertion of papal primacy in the bull *Unam Sanctam* (1302). Shortly thereafter, French soldiers arrested the pope!

o Later popes were pressured to rule under French supervision in Avignon. Rival popes claimed authority, at one point three at one time. Such scenes damaged the political credibility of the papacy.

• The Holy Roman Empire had its own claims and problems, as well. This institution had been founded when Charlemagne was crowned by a pope in Rome in the year 800.

The crowning of Charlemagne as Holy Roman Emperor was an act meant to revive the glories of the Roman Empire in the west.

o The name "Holy" conveyed the spiritual power ascribed to the Christian empire. Theoretically, the Holy Roman Emperor was to have primacy over all other kings and princes in Christendom.

o Symbolically, that might be true, but in practice, the empire had weakened and its borders had shrunk to mostly German lands. The throne was not hereditary but an elected office, which gave power to the nobles who elected the emperor.

o At a time when such kingdoms as England, France, and Spain were starting to centralize, the Holy Roman Empire remained a feudal jumble of overlapping and multiple principalities, kingdoms, free cities, territories, and noble estates.

• In contrast to the papacy and the Holy Roman Empire, monarchs of centralizing kingdoms were on the rise in the early modern period and were not shy about reaching for religious legitimation themselves.

Religious Warfare
• The theological debate that was launched by Martin Luther in 1517 was carried out initially from pulpits and in print but later erupted in warfare, offering the scandalous spectacle of Christians killing Christians over points of doctrine.

• Germany was hit first, a country divided between Catholics and Protestants.
o Protestant princes banded together to oppose the Catholic emperor. The war ended inconclusively, but the emperor was forced to acknowledge the Lutheran princes.

o The Peace of Augsburg (1555) established the formula of *cuius regio, eius religio* ("whose rule, that person's religion"). By this, a prince could choose which faith to establish officially in his lands, and those of a different faith could either convert or emigrate.

- France was next, where the Wars of Religion lasted from 1562 to 1598 and included such atrocities as the Saint Bartholemew's Day Massacre of thousands of French Calvinists in Paris.

- Religiously inflected war also erupted in the Netherlands, which had been under Spanish rule. The Calvinist Dutch revolted against their Catholic rulers in 1568, the start of the Eighty Years' War for independence for the Dutch, only achieved in 1648 at the Peace of Westphalia.

- Then, the Thirty Years' War broke out in the Holy Roman Empire and the German lands in 1618. This war has been called the "outstanding example in European history of meaningless conflict."

The Thirty Years' War
- The war started absurdly, with imperial messengers being thrown out of a window in Prague by Protestant leaders in Bohemia defying the Catholic emperor—the famous Defenestration of Prague. The war spread into the German lands proper as Protestants and Catholics rallied to their princes.

- In the first years, things went so well for the Holy Roman Emperor that he must have been exultant, thinking that perhaps his universal claims might not be so impractical after all. But precisely for this reason, outside powers were dragged in. The kingdoms of Denmark and Sweden entered the war as Protestant champions against the emperor.

- What had started as a religiously colored conflict mutated and became something less coherent. Catholic France also entered the war against the emperor and against Spain, his ally. Eventually, more than 200 states were drawn in.

- The war grew ever more muddled, with the Dutch-Spanish war folded in. Conflict even extended beyond Europe: There fighting between the Dutch and the Spanish in Brazil, and a Dutch admiral captured the Spanish treasure fleet in Cuba in 1628.

- To many ordinary people caught up in this war, the claims and counterclaims, political and religious, seemed increasingly pointless when set against their own suffering.
  - The German lands were destroyed in this manmade disaster. Germany became the playground for huge mercenary armies, fighting for whoever would pay best and living off the land, plundering, pillaging, raping, and killing.

  - Some million soldiers took part, and it is estimated that about a third of them died. But the civilian losses were far greater. Current low estimates put the deaths at about 15 to 20 percent of the German population, more than three million.

Negotiating a Peace

- Understandably, a great and general longing for peace grew. Because the war was not decided by one final and conclusive victory, it would need to be a peace of compromise and be based on principles other than the religious orthodoxies that had sparked so much conflict.

- Negotiations opened in the western German land of Westphalia in 1643, a mixed Catholic and Protestant area. But the fighting continued even as negotiations went on, which complicated the discussions immensely.

- The negotiations took place in two separate towns, Münster and Osnabrück, which were diplomatically exempted from warfare. Some 200 rulers and thousands of diplomatic officials participated.

- The negotiations dragged on for five years, in part because nothing quite like this had ever happened before: a peace congress for all of Europe. Diplomatic ceremony and etiquette were symbolic matters that this age took very seriously.

- Crucially, this conference was not presided over by a universally recognized authority—neither the Holy Roman Emperor nor the pope.

Emergence of a New Order

- The resulting treaties confirmed that rulers of territories would have superiority in all matters ecclesiastical and political in their own lands.

- The religious compromise essentially repeated the formula of the Peace of Augsburg from almost a century before, although the new formula recognized the Calvinists and guaranteed the ability of religious minorities to practice their religion.

- In general, the treaties moved toward sovereign independence for territorial rulers as a practical solution, not as a theoretical model. The United Provinces and Switzerland were recognized as independent, and within the Holy Roman Empire, its princes also gained the power to make peace and war at will (but not war against the emperor).

- All this weakened the remaining structures of the Holy Roman Empire, as did the loss of German territories to France and Sweden. In many ways, Germany would remain a power vacuum until national unification in the later 19th century.

- The treaties were ceremonially signed on October 24, 1648. When news of the peace spread, church bells were rung in Prague, and celebration feasts were organized in countless villages and towns in Germany.

The Significance of Westphalia

- The Westphalian international system involved the recognition that world politics would not be under the rule of one universal authority but, instead, would be a constant, dynamic interplay of states, seeking to preserve their sovereignty and their own advantage.
  - The worldview of contemporaries increasingly saw international politics not in terms of a divinely ordained hierarchy but in terms of balance. Indeed, the concept of the "balance of power" would be a key model for how the world works, politically, up to our times.

o Some scholars today ask whether we are now moving past the Westphalian settlement. The European Union, for instance, involves ceding or pooling individual countries' sovereignty to achieve a more perfect union. The Internet and the forms of community that can be built in cyberspace are no longer territorial. Where does that leave the territorial sovereign state?

o Others pose questions about sovereignty itself, which excludes the outside interference of other powers in domestic issues. What happens when a sovereign state uses its powers to abuse those under its control? May outside powers justifiably intervene? Such questions are urgent in our own times.

• This turning point was not carefully and consciously planned. The most immediate priority for the negotiators was simply ending the torment of their continent.

o The changes introduced by the peace happened not for theoretical reasons but out of pragmatism, which means that the Peace of Westphalia was not a singular moment where everything happened at once. Rather, the movement toward sovereignty as a model predated 1648 and continued after.

o This was not an absolute and clean break but nonetheless a turning point. At the ground level, for ordinary people, this new model eventually brought authority closer to their lives.

• The Peace of Westphalia also had lasting effects as a precedent for later peacemaking. It did not end future wars, but it provided a template for how to negotiate. The very institution of an international peace congress could now be duplicated, and was, at the negotiations for the Treaty of Versailles after World War I or in countless summit meetings in our own times.

Suggested Reading

Wedgwood, *The Thirty Years War*.

Wilson, *The Thirty Years War: Europe's Tragedy*.

Questions to Consider

1. What are the greatest inherent strengths and weaknesses of the Westphalian international system of territorial sovereignty?

2. Do you think that the Westphalian international system is being transformed now and, if so, into what new system?

1648—The Treaty of Westphalia
Lecture 6—Transcript

Many people have a passport. We dutifully show it when we cross borders, but do we take a moment to stop and think about what it really means? In fact, that passport is visible proof of how our world is organized now: divided up into different territorial units. In this modern state system, at least theoretically, these units are sovereign, meaning that they possess their own authority: They have supreme and independent rights (like the right to control their territory and make you show your passport in order to enter their territory). In this respect, states are equals on the international plane.

This is the world we know, and it almost sometimes seems like the natural or default mode of international organization: the sovereign state as a political powerhouse, *the* actor on the international stage. Indeed, this concept is written into the United Nations charter of 1945, which declares, "The Organization is based on the principle of the sovereign equality of all of its Members." Or think of watching the Olympic Games, where we see teams of athletes representing their individual countries march in following their individual national flags.

But how did this international order come into being? It was not always so. In this lecture, we will examine a key turning point in international politics with a global impact. This turning point came at the end of the long and traumatic Thirty Years' War in Europe in the year 1648, a war that itself came at the tail end of about a century of religious slaughter and warfare in the western Christian world.

The peace settlement that ended the Thirty Years' War (called the Peace of Westphalia) pointed international politics in a new direction. This international order has been called the Westphalian system, denoting a system of sovereign states interacting with one another.

Now probably very few people very think to themselves in their daily lives, "Well, here I am, living in a Westphalian international system," but it is worth thinking about what this means, as in fact it's one of those hidden assumptions that actually structures our world up to the present, whether we're aware of it or not!

In our course on turning points then, this is a different kind of turning point than many others we have seen. It is one caused not by willed or creative invention, or discovery; rather, it's a turning point that came out of sheer exhaustion, the exhaustion of religious warfare. As a result, earlier appeals to religious authority in politics were downgraded. Increasingly, the initiative would pass to new monarchies and some republics as the source of authority. In terms of how contemporaries viewed the world after this turning point, what their mental maps looked like, increasingly the world appeared to be one of states in a shifting balance of power, instead of being subjected to one, overarching, universal authority.

Let's consider in turn how authority had been understood before this point in Europe, then view the horrific impact of an age of religious warfare, and then assess the peace of exhaustion itself, and its unexpected results. Much of earlier history is a contrast to our current model today of divided sovereignties and divided authority. Instead, the ideal that had great appeal at the start of the modern age was that of universal authority, often expressed in empire. For much of human history, empire has been a more common form of political organization that people have lived under, more common than a nation-state or a republic.

Just look back at the lectures from the start of our course. We recall China's Ming empire, the "central kingdom" which was supposed to embody order and the mandate of heaven, and thus was seen as globally central and authoritative. Or the Roman Empire, surviving in the East, in Constantinople until 1453, continuing the glory that was Rome. So too in the European Middle Ages, authority was seen as divinely sanctioned and universal in its claims and reach. This link to the divine gave tremendous legitimacy.

Now that was theory, the general mindset. Practice would be much more complicated and messy, inevitably. In this period, church and state were intertwined in Europe, because both appealed to this source of divine authority, and this would lead to conflicts. Two institutions in the Middle

Ages in particular had shown this earlier: the Pope of the Roman Catholic Church, and the Holy Roman Empire.

The Church and the imperial state were intertwined in a vivid way that would be unfamiliar to us in the present: The emperor often controlled who became pope in Rome, while only a pope could crown a Holy Roman Emperor, making his rule official. Who would dominate in this relationship? Both sides sought to inherit the authority of the Roman Empire, which had expired in the West by 476.

During the 11th and 12th centuries, as part of one of those frequent movements for reform, a series of popes made large claims to temporal authority, creating what has been called essentially a papal monarchy. For instance, in 1075, Pope Gregory VII had announced that "The Roman church was founded by God alone," and that only the pope "can with right be called universal," and went on to claim that the pope had the right to depose the emperor. These claims led to the so-called Investiture Controversy with the Holy Roman Emperor, in which ultimately the emperor backed down, but not very sincerely.

In the 12th century, the Roman Catholic Church was at the very height of its political and secular power. When new monarchies arose to challenge that power, especially the king of France, Pope Boniface VIII in 1302 announced a ringing assertion of papal power in the papal bull labeled *Unam Sanctam*. He declared, "The temporal authority ought to be subject to the spiritual power," and, "If the earthly power errs, it shall be judged by the spiritual power." Ironically, this expansive statement came just at the point when the pope's position had become untenable, because French soldiers arrested the pope! Later popes were pressured to rule under French supervision in Avignon. Rival popes claimed authority as well; at one point there were three rival popes at once. Such scenes did much to damage the political credibility of the Papacy.

The Holy Roman Empire had its own claims and its own problems as well. This institution had been founded when Charlemagne was crowned by a pope in Rome in the year 800, to revive the glories of the Roman Empire in the west. The name "Holy" in Holy Roman Empire conveyed the spiritual power that was ascribed to this Christian empire. Theoretically, thus, the emperor of the Holy Roman Empire was to have primacy over all other kings and princes in the rest of Christendom. Symbolically he might have, but in practice the Holy Roman Empire had weakened and weakened, shrinking in its borders mostly just to the German lands. The throne of the empire was not hereditary but rather an elected office, which gave power to the nobles who periodically elected the emperor.

At a time when kingdoms like England, France, and Spain were trying to centralize, this state, the Holy Roman Empire, remained a feudal jumble of overlapping and multiple principalities, kingdoms, free cities, territories of bishops and of monasteries, and noble estates, many of them tiny in size. There were more than 300 of these units, an incredible diversity and decentralization. The Holy Roman Emperor could make vast symbolic claims to authority in Europe, but those claims would be hard to enforce with this kind of power base (no wonder that later comedians would announce that the Holy Roman Empire in fact had been neither holy, nor Roman, nor really an empire).

In contrast to the papacy and the empire, in the early modern period, monarchs of new centralizing kingdoms were on the rise, and they not shy about reaching for religious legitimation themselves. The monarchs of Spain called themselves like the "Most Catholic" monarchs. The kings of France called themselves the "Most Christian" monarchs, and the English kings were known as the "Defenders of the Faith."

Add to this mix the explosive impact of the religious division of Christians in Europe with the Reformation. Since the onset of the Reformation, the breakdown in the theoretical unity of Christianity, religious wars were wracking Europe, and even extended to other parts of the globe where European explorers or traders ventured and ran into one another. This sort of religious warfare was not what Luther had expected at first when he had launched his message of religious reform within the Catholic Church in 1517. At first, the struggle was a rhetorical one, carried out from pulpits expressing different points of view, and especially in print, using the new power of Gutenberg's printing press. Within weeks of Luther announcing his Ninety-five Theses, printed copies were flying all around Germany. Luther's writings were mass-produced. Then, the opponents of Luther in the Catholic Church produced their literature in turn, and one saw a war of fliers.

In German, the word for a flier is *flugblatt*, literally a "flying sheet of paper," and these fliers, circulating throughout Germany, often decorated with vivid illustrations and easy to post on walls as handbills, really accelerated and increased the temperature of the debate. The debate then became even more complex when divisions appeared in the camp of the reformers, as Calvinists urged a doctrine of predestination, disagreeing with the interpretations of the Lutherans.

Then fatefully, this theological debate in print erupted into warfare, and one saw the scandalous spectacle of Christians killing Christians over points of doctrine. Germany was among the places hit first, as sort of the ground zero of this ferment, a country divided between Catholics and Protestants. Protestant princes banded together to fight against the Catholic emperor. The war ended inconclusively, but the emperor was forced in sort of a ceasefire to acknowledge the Lutheran princes' right to exist in Germany.

This happened with the so-called Peace of Augsburg in 1555, which established as official the formula of, in Latin, *cuius regio, eius religio*: "whose rule, that person's religion." (The prince gets to determine the religion of his territory.) A prince could choose which faith, Catholic or Lutheran, to establish officially in his lands (Calvinists, by contrast, were not recognized), and those who were of a different faith could convert, or could emigrate. This severe formula at least gave a temporary respite for some decades before conflict flared anew.

France was next in line. There, the French Wars of Religion lasted from 1562 to 1598, and included horrific atrocities, like the famous St. Bartholemew's Day Massacre, when thousands of French Calvinists were murdered in Paris. Religiously inflected war also erupted in the Netherlands, which had been under Spanish rule. The Calvinist Dutch population rose up in revolt against their Catholic Spanish rulers in 1568, and this was the start of the so-called Eighty Years' War for independence for the Dutch, which they finally only achieved in 1648 at the Peace of Westphalia.

Religious war and crusade were in the air; even the disastrous launching of the Spanish Armada against England in 1588, which failed, was seen by the Spanish as a kind of holy fight or crusade against English heretics. Then, the Thirty Years' War broke out in earnest in the Holy Roman Empire in the German lands in 1618. You will be relieved to hear that I will spare you a blow-by-blow account of this grinding, unending, and ultimately indecisive war. In her classic history of this war, British historian Dame Veronica Wedgwood called it the "outstanding example in European history of meaningless conflict." If you know something about European history, you know that that's really saying something!

Let me just offer a brief overview. The war started absurdly, with imperial messengers being thrown out of a window in Prague by Protestant leaders in Bohemia who were defying their Catholic Emperor (this is the famous Defenestration of Prague, the throwing out of a window. The messengers, by the way, miraculously survived this ordeal). Then the war was on, spreading from Bohemia into the German lands proper, as Protestants and Catholics rallied to their princes and war was engaged.

In the first years, things went so well for the Catholic emperor that he must have been exultant, thinking that perhaps his universal claims to authority might not be so impractical after all, if things continued to go this way. But ironically, precisely because the emperor was doing well, other outside powers got dragged in to balance him. The kingdoms of Denmark and Sweden entered the war as Protestant champions, to save their co-religionists fighting against the emperor.

But increasingly, something strange was happening: What had started as a religiously motivated conflict mutated, and over time became something less coherent—rather than a religious conflict with clear lines, more of a multisided battle royale. Exhibit A for this is that Catholic France also entered the war, but not on the Catholic side. It entered the war against the emperor and against Spain on the side of Protestant allies. Eventually, more than 200 states great and small were participating in the Thirty Years' War.

The war grew ever more muddled, with the Dutch-Spanish war folded in as well. The conflict even extended beyond Europe, worldwide. For instance, there was fighting between the Dutch and the Spanish in Brazil, and a Dutch admiral actually captured the famous Spanish treasure fleet in harbor in Cuba in 1628 in a great victory. The war went on and on and on.

So let me state the obvious: To many ordinary people caught up in this war, the claims and counterclaims, political as well as religious, seemed increasingly meaningless, when set against their own experience of suffering. The German lands were destroyed thoroughly in this manmade disaster. Germany became the playground for huge mercenary armies, fighting no longer out of conviction but rather for whoever would pay best, and living off the land, plundering, pillaging, raping, and killing.

These mercenaries, by the way, did leave one tiny cultural contribution which endures into our own times. In fact, men's neckties originated with Croatian mercenaries who wore colorful cloths knotted around their necks (in parts of Europe to this very day, neckties are sometimes still called *cravats*, which simply means a Croatian or something in the Croatian style).

In this war, some million soldiers took part, and it's estimated that about a third of them died. But keep this in mind: The civilian losses were far greater. Historians are still having a vigorous debate today about just how hard Germany at the center of all this was ravaged by the war. But even if you take current, lower estimates, that still puts the deaths at about 15 to 20 percent of the entire German population at the time, over three million people. Some areas were hit harder than others: When Swedish armies captured the hometown of Gutenberg, Mainz, that city lost 40 percent of its people. The city of Augsburg lost half its population. Many cities were occupied repeatedly, over and over again; most notoriously, when the besieged city of Magdeburg, held by the Protestants, was captured by the Catholic imperial forces, the population was put to the sword.

There's no wonder that one anonymous German poet sighed with a deep, deep anguish that we can still hear in his verses today: "The houses are burned out / The churches are destroyed / The villages are looted / The food has been eaten / One sees the cities, the hopes of the land, in flames / No one can recognize any more the splendor of the land."

Understandably, a great and general longing for peace grew. Because the war was not decided by one final and conclusive victory that gave decisive victory to one side or another, this would need to be ended by a peace of compromise, and obviously it would need to be based on principles other than the religious orthodoxies that had sparked the conflict to begin with.

So negotiations opened in the West German land of Westphalia in 1643. It was an area of mixed Catholic and Protestant population. But oddly enough, the negotiations coincided with fighting—the fighting continued even as talks were going on, which complicated the discussions immensely. You can imagine this: If one side was winning, it was a lot less likely to make concessions, and vice versa. Strangely enough, war-making and peacemaking were going on at the same time!

The negotiations took place in two separate towns, Münster and Osnabrück. These towns were diplomatically exempted from any further warfare. The empire's negotiations with Sweden took place in Osnabrück and the negotiations with France and Spain in Münster, running in parallel. Some 200 rulers and thousands of diplomatic officials participated (these delegations could be huge, and in fact the Swedes brought their own personal shopper, just to have him along).

The negotiations dragged on for five years as well. In part, this was because it was unprecedented. Nothing quite like these negotiations had ever happened before. This was a peace congress for all of Europe, to establish a *pax generalis*, a general peace. Diplomatic ceremony and etiquette, questions of who had precedence over whom in entering a hall for instance, were symbolic matters reflecting authority that this age took very seriously. So, the first six months were taken up with these precedence questions. For instance, the representatives of the Dutch Republic scandalized some old-fashioned diplomats by insisting on being called Excellency, just like the representatives of kings. This seemed outrageous to conservatives. Such disputes inevitably prolonged the negotiations.

Crucial, however, it to notice that this conference was not presided over by a universally recognized authority. It was not presided over by the Holy Roman Emperor. After all he was one of the parties to the war. Nor were these negotiations presided over by the pope, because the pope refused to recognize agreements with the Protestants, who in turn rejected his claims to authority.

What a contrast to the way in which Spain and Portugal had called on the pope to settle a political question, to mediate their Treaty of Tordesillas in 1494 after Columbus's voyages, essentially to divide up the world. The claims to authority of the emperor and Pope clearly were not central to these proceedings, so what new order did emerge?

The treaties that were arrived at confirmed that rulers of territories would have superiority in all matters, religious as well as political, in their own lands. The religious compromise of this treaty essentially repeated the formula of the Peace of Augsburg of 1555, almost a century ago. This must have been a sad thing for keen observers to recognize: There had been all this war and suffering, and the result was essentially something that had been arrived at about a century ago?

In fact, the new formula did recognize some changes; the Calvinists, for instance, were included in the settlement. The settlement also guaranteed the ability of religious minorities to the practice of their religion in territories, so it already represented a gesture towards recognizing the rights of minorities.

In general, these treaties moved towards sovereign independence for territorial rulers, as a practical solution, not as a theoretical model. The United Provinces and Switzerland were recognized as independent, and within the Holy Roman Empire, the princes of the empire were given the right to make peace or war at will (just not to make war against the emperor).

All this further weakened the remaining structures of the Holy Roman Empire, as did the loss of German territories to France and Sweden. In many ways, Germany would remain a power vacuum until it was nationally unified later in the 19th century. It is not a coincidence that Adolf Hitler and the Nazis would later often rant about the Thirty Years' War and the unjust Peace of

Westphalia as Germany's humiliation that must never be repeated (and then of course the Nazis went on to bring about just such a disaster themselves!).

The negotiations were followed anxiously by a general public, and this further showed the impact of the print revolution. The first newspapers were started in Germany in this time, and they reported to a wider public how the peacemaking was going.

The treaties were finally ceremonially signed on October 24, 1648. What actually happened when news spread of the peace? How do you end a thirty-year span of war? In Prague, in Bohemia (today the Czech Republic), where the war began, the church bells rang and rang in long, deafening peals of joy.

In Germany, in countless villages and towns (assuming of course they were still standing), special celebration feasts were organized. Commemorative coins and prints featured one symbol in particular: the dove with an olive branch, a symbol for peace that's still current today.

But the good news travelled very slowly to places that were further away. In the Moluccas, the Spice Islands, the Dutch actually beat the Spanish in a great battle in 1649, a year after the treaty had been signed establishing peace, because none of them had yet heard the news from Europe!

When Pope Innocent learned of this treaty, he condemned it. In the papal bull entitled *Zelo domus Dei*, he declared it "null, void, invalid, iniquitous, unjust, damnable, reprobate, inane, and devoid of meaning for all time." That's a pretty harsh review. He didn't like it. But this protest does not mean that the treaty produced a new secular politics, some sort of total break with the past. In fact, the opening text of the treaties started with the pious and shared hope, "That there shall be a Christian and universal peace, and a perpetual, true, and sincere amity." Religion remained important.

So, what was the ultimate significance of this turning point? First, the Westphalian international system, as it has been called, involved the recognition that world politics would not be under the rule of one universal authority, whether the Pope or the Holy Roman Empire. Instead, there would be a constant, shifting dynamic interplay of states, seeking to preserve their sovereignty and their own advantage. The negotiators had not aimed to create a new world around a new model—if you spoke to them about the Westphalian model they were creating, they would not have understood what you were talking about. Rather, they were seeking a pragmatic solution, and yet their pragmatic solution pointed towards a new conception of international order and authority.

Now, the worldview of contemporaries increasingly saw international politics not in terms of a divinely ordained hierarchy, but rather in terms of balance, the interaction of these sovereign states. The concept of the "balance of power" would be a key model for how the world works, politically, up to our own times. Just check the front pages of newspapers.

Some scholars today ask whether we are now moving past the Westphalian settlement. Some examples: The European Union involves ceding or pooling individual countries' sovereignty, to achieve a more perfect union. Another example: The Internet, and the forms of community that can be built in cyberspace, they're no longer territorial. So where does that leave the sovereignty of the territorial state?

Other scholars pose questions about sovereignty itself. Sovereignty excludes outside interference of other powers in domestic issues. What happens when a sovereign state uses its powers to abuse people under its control, or to commit genocide? May outside powers justifiably intervene? Or is there in fact, as some have suggested, a duty to intervene and to protect? These kinds of questions are urgent in our own times, and are still being worked out.

Second, this turning point was not one that was carefully and consciously planned. The most immediate priority for the negotiators was just ending the torment of their continent, to craft a peace of exhaustion, and end the scandal of doctrinal slaughter. The changes that they introduced happened not for abstract theoretical reasons, but out of pragmatism. So the Peace of Westphalia was not the singular moment where all of this happened at once; rather, it started a movement towards sovereignty.

The movement towards sovereignty as a model predated 1648 and continued afterwards. This was not the case of an absolute and clean break, but it was nonetheless a turning point. At the ground level, for ordinary people, this new model of territorial sovereignty brought authority closer to their own lives, but only slowly and over time. To begin with, the main emotion of everyday people was simply relief that war was over at last.

Third and finally, the Peace of Westphalia had lasting effects as a precedent for later peacemaking. Obviously, the Peace of Westphalia did not end future wars, but it did give a template for how to negotiate. The very institution of an international peace congress could now be duplicated, and was, at the negotiations for the Treaty of Versailles after World War I, or in countless summit meetings in our own times.

The desire for peace and the will for peace that had been powerfully demonstrated in 1648 remained relevant. Also very relevant for peacemaking was the intellectual shift that the horrors of war produced: The very notion of using violence to impose and enforce religious truth had become increasingly delegitimized. Yes, wars continued, and religion remained important, but this shift was an important and necessary one to begin.

In this lecture, we surveyed a vital turning point that, unbeknownst to most people today, still shapes how we live, how international politics are done today. That's big! By contrast, we'll consider the discovery of small worlds, especially as seen through the revolutionary power of the microscope during the Dutch Golden Age, in our next lecture.

1676—Van Leeuwenhoek's Microscope
Lecture 7

W hat does it look like when an entire new dimension of existence is discovered—not just a continent, as in Columbus's encounter with the Americas, but an entire world never seen before by humans? In 1676, Antonie van Leeuwenhoek was the first to see bacteria under a microscope, and he later catalogued a wide range of microorganisms. This lecture will demonstrate that discoveries such as Leeuwenhoek's take place in a double context: They come out of both the individual inquiry and work of particular people, but they also fit into a wider social or cultural context that determines whether they are recognized and used or denounced, forgotten, and discarded.

The Golden Age of the Dutch

- Leeuwenhoek first made the discovery of bacteria on April 24, 1676, in Delft, the third largest city in the Netherlands (the United Provinces). Dutch society was in the midst of a Golden Age, often defined as the period from 1570 to 1700. It was a new kind of commercial society, marked by a degree of religious toleration and tolerance for new ideas that were remarkable at the time.

In the Golden Age of the Dutch, the graceful blue-and-white pottery known as Delftware was produced as a homegrown version of exotic Chinese porcelain.

- Dutch society was also plugged in to an emerging world economy through global trade networks, especially those of the VOC. Vast cargoes of pepper, cinnamon, cloves, coffee, sugar, and tobacco flowed in to the Netherlands, to be transshipped or consumed there.

- This society produced financial masterpieces in its new economy: its stock market and the Amsterdam bank. With a population of only some two million, the Dutch enjoyed a standard of living that was the envy of most of the world.

- The Dutch were also a military power, having won their independence from the Spanish Empire after a war lasting 80 years. Further, they were most distinctive politically; the United Provinces was a republic, not a kingdom—a federation of lands with a merchant elite.

- The Dutch produced both masterpieces of visual art and technical equipment of the highest standards, especially for sea voyages. Both the telescope and the microscope were developed in Middleburg.

The Scientific Revolution

- Leeuwenhoek's discovery demonstrates a broader shift that was taking place at the time in intellectual authority concerning material things. Earlier, classic texts by such authors as Aristotle, Ptolemy, and Galen or Scripture were seen as the final word on the natural world. But now, authority was shifting (slowly) from ancient texts to experiment—to what could be demonstrated by the scientific method.

- Scientific explanation pushed aside theological or literal scriptural explanations of the natural world. In this sense, it precipitated a significant transformation in human thinking, which some have argued was even more profound than the Reformation. One could argue that we are still in this period now, seeking to assimilate the latest developments in many different fields of science.

- This intellectual earthquake began more than a century before Leeuwenhoek's experiments. A key area was astronomy. The astronomer Nicolaus Copernicus, born in Poland, overturned the small and tidy medieval universe described in our lecture on Columbus, those celestial spheres harmoniously turning around the earth.

o   In place of this earlier scheme, Copernicus offered a model of the solar system, published in 1543. Protestant and Catholic religious authorities criticized his model, which seemed to upset the traditional place of humans and the divine.

o   The Italian astronomer Galileo Galilei entered the debate when he learned of the Dutch work on telescopes, built one himself, and turned it on the nighttime skies to make direct observations. He saw mountains and craters on the moon, the moons of Jupiter, and sun spots.

o   Galileo's work suggested that the universe was a material thing and far larger than had been understood before. For his championing of Copernicus's model of the solar system, Galileo was brought before the tribunal of the Roman Inquisition of the Catholic Church in 1633 and placed him under house arrest for the rest of his days.

o   The work of the English scientist Sir Isaac Newton was a synthesis of, and advance on, these earlier revolutionary ideas. In his masterwork, the *Principia* of 1687, he outlined the principles of classical mechanics and his three laws of motion, as well as the universal law of gravitation.

o   With Newton's work, the world itself came to appear ever more regular, more mechanically efficient, and orderly, explained mathematically on the basis of universal laws. This worldview has been called "Newton's world machine" and typified how the world was seen until the impact of quantum physics at the start of the 20th century.

The Life of Antonie van Leeuwenhoek

•   Leeuwenhoek was born in 1632 in Delft, Holland. His parents were middle-class artisans. In 1648, just as the Peace of Westphalia was signed, Leeuwenhoek left his hometown for an apprenticeship with a cloth merchant in Amsterdam. He then returned to Delft, where he ran his own store.

- He did not have extensive formal education and spoke only Dutch at a time when Latin was the language of truly learned discourse. In 1660, he was appointed manager of the city hall and made an inspector of weights and measures and a surveyor, all testimony to the trust placed in his skills for exact observation.

- Over the next 20 years, Leeuwenhoek took up lens grinding and became a master. He produced tiny lenses, less than an eighth of an inch across, of tremendous power and made hundreds of microscopes.

- More important than the equipment he made was Leeuwenhoek's methodical use of it. He set about making fine observations of almost everything he could get his hands on: the head of a fly, the eye of a whale, the compound eyes of beetles, his own skin. People in his neighborhood apparently saw him as either a magician or a fantastical storyteller, spinning crazy tales about mythical invisible creatures he had seen.

- At this point, the collective character of science entered the picture. The Royal Society of London had been formally chartered by the king in 1662, and Isaac Newton was among its members. One of its international corresponding members was Regnier de Graaf, a doctor in Delft.
  - Graaf was astonished with what he saw in Leeuwenhoek's study, and in 1673, he urgently pressed the Royal Society to request that this man write to them about what he had found.

  - At first, Leeuwenhoek was not believed, but when others in England duplicated the experiments he described in his letters, he was made a full Fellow of the Royal Society in 1680.

- Over the course of 50 years, Leeuwenhoek wrote hundreds of long, rambling, astonishing letters to the Royal Society. His experiments never ceased. He examined lake water, the plaque of his own teeth, human sperm, and blood. He discovered red blood cells and was the first to see the nuclei of those cells.

- In his observations, he engaged in painstaking measurements, using units the size of a grain of sand or the eye of a louse! Through it all, he seems not to have suspected that microbes can be a source of disease; certainly, as we now know, he saw bacteria that were both helpful and harmful to human life.

- Leeuwenhoek remained profoundly critical in his outlook, always willing to change his own ideas when proof was found to the contrary. He argued against those who believed in so-called "spontaneous generation," the notion that rotting cheese automatically produces maggots or that piles of dirty clothes spontaneously generate mice.
  - In part out of his religious conviction that God had once and for all created a universe whole and entire—without such ongoing creation—he was convinced that all creatures had parents like themselves and life cycles all their own.

  - To observe those life cycles, Leeuwenhoek walked around with worms in his pocket and asked his wife to keep insect eggs warm under her dress in the chilly Dutch climate. He even kept a colony of lice inside his stockings to observe them, but the itching became unbearable and that experiment was called off.

- When Leeuwenhoek died at the age of almost 91, his will ordered that 26 of his microscopes be sent to the Royal Society. This bequest was generous, because he had never shared them before. But while alive, he had avowed that his work was not for financial gain or fame but for "discovering the things that are buried from our eyes" and to satisfy a "craving after knowledge."

The Context of Leeuwenhoek's Work

- The specific social context into which Leeuwenhoek's work fit was the Dutch Golden Age. The Dutch were proud of having formed their land out of constant struggle—both the struggle for independence from Spain and the battle against nature itself.
  - The Netherlands struggled to reclaim low-lying lands from the tides, to hold them back by dikes, and to pump them dry using

the windmills that soon became a national symbol. Because these territories were newly won, they were national property, not the holdings of a feudal aristocracy.

- o In the revolt against Spain, many fiery leaders had been Dutch Calvinists, but not all the Dutch were of that confession. There still remained a sizable and patriotic Catholic minority, as well as other branches of Protestants.

- o The result was that the Dutch showed a measure of religious toleration and intellectual openness that set them apart from the rest of Europe. This famous toleration became a magnet for religious refugees, especially Jews fleeing persecution.

- Dutch society was also something new in economic terms, a society oriented toward commerce instead of agriculture. The Dutch first dominated the Baltic grain trade, then the shipping trade between northern Europe and the Mediterranean, and then they went global. How astonishing that so small a country would become the dominant trading power of Europe!

- In general, wealth flowed into the Netherlands, which created moral problems for a society often dedicated to the austere religious doctrines associated with Calvinism. At least one historian has noted that Dutch society in the Golden Age was marked by a troubled conscience about the enjoyment of wealth versus the religious call to repent and deny oneself.

- Leeuwenhoek's turning point had striking long-term effects. His recognition of the microscopic world was crucial to the development of microbiology, especially the later development of germ theory. Perhaps his greater accomplishment was in giving intellectual authority to that which is seen, measured, observed, and assessed over the earlier authority of classic texts.

Suggested Reading

Brook, *Vermeer's Hat.*

Schama, *The Embarrassment of Riches.*

Waller, *The Discovery of the Germ.*

Questions to Consider

1. Which was more important in leading to the discovery of the microscopic world: Leeuwenhoek's character or the cultural context of the Dutch Golden Age?

2. Do eccentrics make the best researchers and inventors?

1676—Van Leeuwenhoek's Microscope
Lecture 7—Transcript

What does it look like when an entire new dimension of existence and life is discovered? Not just a continent, as in Columbus's encounter with the Americas in 1492, but an entire world never seen before by humans? This is how the scene appears.

It is April 24, 1676, in Delft, the third-biggest city in the Netherlands, the United Provinces as they are called. Delft is a clean city with canals (indeed the name of the town itself means "canal"). These canals carry high-quality beer and an immense variety of trade goods, especially Delftware, that graceful blue and white pottery made here in Delft as a homegrown version of the exotic and infinitely expensive Chinese porcelain which Dutch traders are bringing back to the Netherlands.

Together, we stroll through Delft and look in on the study of the cloth merchant Antonie van Leeuwenhoek, as he examines an experiment he had launched, using a microscope. The microscope has already been around for decades, but Leeuwenhoek has improved the design through years and years of personal effort.

The aim of his original experiment was to find out why pepper tastes spicy. His hypothesis was that pepper had tiny, almost invisible, but sharp hooks, and that this is what gives the distinctive bite to a spicy dish. This is an awesome theory, but unfortunately it turned out to be wrong.

Leeuwenhoek, however, discovers something else while testing his theory. He had soaked pepper in water for three weeks in order to soften it up, and then looked at it using his very basic microscope. In the water, he's astonished to see many living things in motion! In fact, there are four different kinds, all amazingly small. He estimates that if he took a hundred of them and laid them all end to end, they still would not be as big as one grain of sand. Leeuwenhoek was the first to see bacteria, and in his lifelong occupation of exploring the microscopic universe, the smallest world, he cataloged varieties, their habits, motions, lifecycles, and previously inconceivably small sizes. Leeuwenhoek was the first to see microbes or microorganisms, red blood cells, bacteria, sperm cells, and mold spores.

There's a nearly perfect symmetry to this discovery taking place here, in the Netherlands. Dutch society is in its Golden Age, often defined as 1570–1720. This is a new kind of commercial society, marked by a degree of religious toleration and tolerance for new ideas which are remarkable for their times. This society is also plugged in to an emerging world economy through global trade networks, especially those of the VOC, the Dutch East India Company, that deadly rival of the English East India Company, which we discussed in an earlier lecture. Vast cargoes of pepper, cinnamon, cloves, coffee, sugar, and tobacco are flowing in, to be transshipped or consumed here. This society is producing financial masterpieces in its new economy— its stock market, and the Amsterdam bank. With a population of only some two million, the Dutch enjoy a standard of living that is the envy of most of the world.

The Dutch are also remarkably a military power, having won their independence from the Spanish Empire after an eighty-year-long war, only ended in 1648 at the Peace of Westphalia. They are also most distinctive politically—the United Provinces are a republic, not a kingdom with a dynasty, but rather a federation of lands with a merchant elite.

This is a society also producing masterpieces of visual art, the paintings of Rembrandt and—here in Delft—those of Johannes Fermeer. The Dutch also produce technical equipment of the highest standard, especially when it's useful for their sea voyages, equipment like telescopes. Around 1600, the first telescope was developed in Middelburg, when a craftsman discovered that two glass lenses, like those used for spectacles or for eyeglasses, put together could magnify far-off objects. These new telescopes were at first actually called Dutch trunks, because of the box-like shape of the first telescope. (Actually, "telescope" does sound much more scientific, doesn't it?) The same technology was also used in Middleburg to produce the microscope.

It was this Dutch innovation that Leeuwenhoek used to discern things that no one else had ever seen before, because of their tininess. In ways, this presented a bigger discovery even than that of Columbus. That, obviously, was a discovery to Columbus and Europeans, but those who inhabited the Americas knew very well where they were. Leeuwenhoek's smallest world, by contrast, was a discovery for all mankind. As a founder of microbiology, his discoveries resonate to our own times and our own bodies.

This lecture will demonstrate that discoveries take place often in a double context. On the one hand, they come out of the individual inquiry and the hard work, genius, and application of particular people. On the other hand, these discoveries also fit into a wider social or cultural context, and it's that context which determines whether the discoveries are recognized, used, and exploited, or perhaps denounced, forgotten and discarded.

This turning point was about new ways of looking at the world and the universe at large, with vast implications for the status of the human being. One further thing which this turning point did was to assert the dignity of the small. In contrast to the saying "bigger is better," in our own times we hear the counterpoint argument that "small is beautiful." The modern environmentalist idea of sustainability expresses this thought as well.

It was not always so. Earlier, in traditional art, especially before the use of visual perspective, if an artist wanted to suggest to his viewers that symbolically that something is important, or more important than other elements in the picture, often the way to do this was to depict that person or thing as really big, dwarfing other features of the picture. This conveyed its spiritual or moral importance in terms of physical size.

The appreciation of the small, however, was already anticipated during the Renaissance in Leonardo da Vinci's attention to anatomy and the astonishing details to be found in nature. Leeuwenhoek's inquiries would also be followed by microbiologists and especially by atomic scientists alike, centuries later.

What this turning point demonstrates is a broader shift in intellectual authority concerning material things. Earlier, classic texts by great scholars like Aristotle and Ptolemy (or Galen for medicine), or holy scripture, were seen as the final word on the universe, on the natural world. But now, by degrees rather than all at once, authority increasingly passed from those ancient texts to experiment, to that which can be demonstrated by the scientific method, in a shift called the Scientific Revolution.

The Scientific Revolution was ultimately really about new ways of looking at natural phenomena. Some historians argue we should really avoid the term "revolution," which sounds fast, for what was really a long, drawn-out process, and that instead we should speak of a broad "scientific movement." Whatever term we use, it was a crucial shift.

Scientific explanation pushed aside theological or literal scriptural explanations of the natural world. In this sense, it precipitated a huge transformation in human thinking. Some have argued in fact that this transformation was even more profound than the Reformation itself. One could argue that we are still very much in this period now, seeking constantly to assimilate the latest developments in many different fields of science at once.

This intellectual earthquake began more than a century before Leeuwenhoek's experiments. A key area was astronomy. The astronomer Nicolaus Copernicus, born in Poland, overturned the small and tidy medieval universe we described in our lecture on Columbus, those celestial spheres harmoniously turning around the Earth in perfect order. In place of this earlier comfortable scheme, Copernicus offered a model of the solar system, published in 1543, when he was on his deathbed. Protestant and Catholic religious authorities criticized his model, which seemed to many to upset the traditional place of humans as well as the divine.

The Italian astronomer Galileo Galilei entered this debate when he learned of the Dutch work on telescopes (remember the Dutch trunks). Finding the specifications, Galileo built one himself, and turned it on the nighttime skies, to make ever keener observations of what was actually out there, not just theorizing from texts but working from observations. Galileo saw mountains and craters on the moon; he saw moons around Jupiter, and saw sun spots.

These observations suggested that the universe was a material thing, and also that it was far larger than had been understood before, with countless stars—infinitely bigger than those cozy harmonic spheres. For his championing of Copernicus's model of the solar system, Galileo was brought before the Roman Inquisition of the Catholic Church before their tribunal in 1633, and they placed him under house arrest for the rest of his days. (Much later—much later—in 1992, Pope John Paul II expressed regret for the errors in the proceedings against this great scholar.)

As a crowning achievement, the work of the English scientist Sir Isaac Newton was a synthesis of, and advance on, these earlier revolutionary ideas. In his masterwork, the *Principia* of 1687, Newton outlined the principles of classical mechanics and his three laws of motion, as well as the universal law of gravitation. Now, the world itself came to appear ever more regular, more mechanically efficient, and orderly, explained mathematically on the basis of universal laws. This world view, replacing the earlier medieval one, has been called Newton's world machine, and typified how the world was increasingly being seen until the impact, at the start of the 20th century, of discoveries of quantum physics that would upset this earlier scheme as well.

Now clearly, these are familiar cases (Copernicus, Galileo, and Newton), and very often they're chosen as turning points in courses on turning points, but I choose in this lecture to focus on Leeuwenhoek because of how he shows, with such unexpected eloquence, these new ways of seeing, observing, and measuring—the basis of what would come to be called the scientific method. The first systematic champion of the scientific method was an English scientist, Sir Francis Bacon, who argued for rebuilding human knowledge by the inductive method—proceeding from small and detailed observation of particular things, and then making generalizations outward, rather than deducing from grand, great abstract principles. He was sure that this would yield new human powers, useful to humanity. How did Leeuwenhoek exemplify and embody this new science?

We don't know as much as we would like about some key actors in these turning points, like Zheng He and Gutenberg, and so it is with Leeuwenhoek.

His life and work remain surrounded by several mysteries, but what testimonies we do have are very expressive.

Antonie van Leeuwenhoek was born in 1632 in Delft, Holland. His parents were middle-class artisans—he was not a noble. His father was a weaver of baskets, perhaps baskets used to transport that famous Delftware. The Leeuwenhoek family lived on a street called Leeuwenport, or "Lion's Gate" in English. Like the case of Gutenberg in Mainz, the family name probably came from where they lived: "Hoek" means a corner, so Leeuwenhoek is a corner on Lion's street.

In 1648, at just that time when the Peace of Westphalia which we discussed in a previous lecture was signed, Leeuwenhoek left his hometown for an apprenticeship with a cloth merchant in Amsterdam. He did well, and then he returned to Delft to run his own store. Leeuwenhoek, given his humbler origins, did not have extensive formal education. He only spoke Dutch at a time when Latin was still seen as needed for truly learned scholarly discourse. In 1660, Leeuwenhoek was appointed manager of the city hall of Delft, which meant that in some sense he had become a janitor. But he was also made an inspector of weights and measures and a surveyor for the city, and all of this seems to have been testimony to the trust that others placed in his skills for exact observation.

Over the next 20 years, Leeuwenhoek took up, perhaps at first as a hobby, the business of grinding lenses, and he became a master without equal. He produced tiny little lenses, less than an eighth of an inch across, that were of tremendous power. They were nearly spherical in shape, which gave them added potency. Leeuwenhoek, using these lenses, produced hundreds of microscopes. As with Gutenberg, who had been so secretive about his project, the "work of the books" as he called it, we really don't know in detail how Leeuwenhoek even did his craft, because he kept it absolutely secret.

The instruments that he was producing were not complicated and sophisticated mechanisms like the compound microscopes of multiple lenses used in more recent times; rather, this was what was called a simple microscope, with one lens about the size of a pinhead, set in a metal casing only a few inches in size, that were to be held up to the light. The sample to be viewed was set on a pin that was attached to the microscope. The best of Leeuwenhoek's handmade microscopes magnified 266 times over, or even better.

But even more important than the equipment was the methodical use which Leeuwenhoek made of it. He set about years and years of fine and repeated observation of almost anything he could get his hands on: the head of a fly, the eye of a whale that had washed up in the Netherlands, the compound eyes of beetles, even his own skin. Just to prove that no prophet is honored in his own country, we need to mention that people in his neighborhood thought he was crazy. They apparently saw him as a magician, or believed him to be a fantastical storyteller who was always spinning crazy fairytales about all sorts of mythical invisible creatures.

It's at this point that the collective character of science enters the picture, and it involves English scientists. This very fact is all the more remarkable considering the Anglo-Dutch wars and the tensions between the English and Dutch trading companies that we talked about in an earlier lecture were raging at precisely this time, and yet scientific interest could bridge these tensions.

The Royal Society of London had been formally chartered by the king (just like the English East India Company had been). It had been chartered in the year 1662, and Sir Isaac Newton was among its members. One of the international corresponding members of the society was Regnier de Graaf, a doctor in Delft in the Netherlands. Dr. de Graaf was astonished with what he saw in Leeuwenhoek's study. In 1673, he urgently pressed the Royal Society by letter to request that this man write to them about what he had found. At first, when Leeuwenhoek did write letters about what he had discovered, he was not believed by the English scientists, but then, when others in England were able to duplicate his experiments and match his results he had described in his letters, he was honored, and made a full Fellow of the Royal Society in 1680.

Over the course of 50 years, Leeuwenhoek wrote hundreds of long, rambling, astonishing letters to the Royal Society. He wrote in Dutch, because he couldn't write in Latin, and the letters would be translated into English and then would be published in the journal of the society. The printing press, in this case as in so many others, helped to spread word of the new discoveries with great speed.

Leeuwenhoek, however, did not give the society his microscopes, though they implored him to do so. He always remained very secretive about them, and when demonstrating them to visitors, he always proudly said that these were OK, but there were even better ones that he used only himself! You really get the sense that he tremendously enjoyed tantalizing and even teasing his fellow scientists.

His experiments never ceased. He examined lake water and found it teeming with animalcules, as he called them. Today we would say one-celled protists. It was becoming increasingly clear that the heretofore invisible world outnumbered the visible world of plants, animals, and people.

In 1683, Leeuwenhoek experimented by flossing his teeth. At the age of 50, his teeth were untypically sound and healthy, because he did something really unusual in those days: He cleaned them daily. What he discovered, on examining scraped plaque from his teeth, was that there were (as he put it) more teeming microorganisms in his mouth than there were people in the Netherlands.

When Leeuwenhoek suffered an episode of diarrhea—you guessed it—he examined the results with his microscope and predictably found life there as well. Leeuwenhoek examined human sperm and discovered red blood cells and saw the nucleus of those cells, the first to do so.

In his observations, which he repeated again and again just to verify his results, he constantly engaged in painstaking measurements. This raised a problem: What standard do you use to measure such tiny things? He used units the size of a grain of sand, or the eye of a louse! Through it all, Leeuwenhoek seems not to have suspected that microbes might actually be a source of disease—certainly, as we now know, he was seeing bacteria that were helpful to human life as well as ones that were harmful.

Leeuwenhoek remained always profoundly critical in his outlook, always willing to change his own ideas if proof was could be shown to the contrary. Leeuwenhoek argued against those who believed at the time in so-called spontaneous generation. This was the notion that, for instance, rotting cheese automatically produces maggots, or that piles of dirty clothes that have been left around spontaneously generate mice.

In part out of a deep religious conviction that God had created once and for all a universe that was whole and entire, without such ongoing, sort of spontaneous creation, Leeuwenhoek was convinced on the contrary that all creatures had parents like themselves, and lifecycles all their own as well (if you could only observe them). To observe those lifecycles, Leeuwenhoek walked around with worms in his pocket, and examined them now and again. He asked his wife to keep insect eggs warm under her dress in the chilly Dutch climate. (It's very clear that his wife was a long-suffering, maybe even saintly spouse.) Leeuwenhoek even kept a colony of lice inside his own stockings to observe them, until finally the itching became unbearable and that experiment got called off.

As his fame grew, many notables came to visit the man who was called the great man of the century. These visitors even included Peter the Great of Russia and the Queen of England. When Leeuwenhoek died at the age of almost 91, his will ordered that 26 of his microscopes be sent to the Royal Society. This was a tremendously generous gesture, as you'll remember he had never shared his microscopes before. While alive, Leeuwenhoek had vowed that his work was not for financial gain or to win fame, but rather as he put it, "discovering the things that are buried from our eyes" and to satisfy a "craving after knowledge."

Let me point out how Leeuwenhoek's work fit into a specific social context. That context was the Dutch Golden Age. The Dutch were proud of having formed their land out of constant struggle, a struggle with two dimensions. First was the 80-year revolt against Spain, with many bloody clashes and atrocities. They finally won independence in 1648. Second was the battle against nature itself, against the sea. The Netherlands struggled to reclaim low-lying lands from the tides, to hold them back by building dikes and to pump them dry using those windmills that soon became a national symbol. This had an important implication. Because these new territories were newly won, they were national property, shared, not the holdings of a feudal aristocracy alone.

In the revolt against Spain, many fiery leaders had been committed Dutch Calvinists, but not all the Dutch were of that confession. There still remained a sizeable and patriotic Catholic minority, as well as other branches of Protestants as well. The result of this was that the Dutch showed a measure of religious toleration and intellectual openness which set them apart from the rest of Europe. This famous toleration became a magnet, especially for religious refugees, in particular Jews fleeing persecution. Amsterdam came to be a famous melting pot of diverse influences.

The United Provinces also were something new in economic terms, a society oriented towards commerce most of all, not towards agriculture as had traditionally been the case. The Dutch first came to dominate the Baltic grain trade in northern Europe, then the shipping trade between northern Europe and the Mediterranean, and then they went global! How astonishing it is, to observe that so small a country could become *the* dominant trading power. The Dutch East India Company, the VOC, was but one prominent example of that Dutch worldwide economic power as they quested for prosperity. In fact, Leeuwenhoek was involved. The day before he died, Leeuwenhoek was writing to the VOC about some geological samples they had sent him in their quest for gold overseas.

The Dutch thinker Hugo Grotius, called the founder of international law, actually crafted the doctrine of free trade on the seas at the express request of the VOC. They felt they had most to gain from this philosophical statement. This famous Dutch commercialism could also have its lapses, as during the famous tulip craze of 1637, when a kind of mass hysteria set in in the Netherlands as ordinary people, as well as the very rich, speculated wildly on the wealth represented by exotic tulip flowers, a market that eventually crashed.

But generally, the wealth just flowed and flowed, and oddly enough this created moral problems for a society often dedicated to austere religious doctrines that were associated with stricter Calvinism. The character of this society and its complexities is analyzed in a brilliant book by the British historian Simon Schama, entitled *The Embarrassment of Riches*. Schama sees Dutch society in the Golden Age as being marked by a kind of troubled conscience about, on the one hand, the enjoyment of wealth; on the other hand versus the religious call to repent and to deny oneself. One symptom of this complex was the famed Dutch cleanliness, which struck contemporaries as extreme and even bizarre—the omnipresent sweeping and scrubbing of the streets was an example. Clean and ordered home life, according to Schama, was a coping mechanism, a way of dealing with with the worldliness, the global riches that were swirling about the society.

In the rich Dutch visual art, the paintings of Johannes Fermeer in Delft stand out, and indeed speak to us today across the centuries, with their sparkling use of light and their symbolic use of detail. Many of Fermeer's evocative artworks fit into the tradition called genre painting, the depiction in art not of haughty aristocrats and court life, but the lives of ordinary people living in Dutch interior scenes. Actually, Fermeer and Leeuwenhoek were apparently close friends. When Fermeer died in poverty at a young age, he appointed none other than Leeuwenhoek as his executor. Many art historians also believe that the figure of the geographer in a famous painting of Fermeer's is actually Leeuwenhoek posing for the picture. Some, but not all, experts also argue that while Leeuwenhoek was experimenting with the microscope, his friend Fermeer was trying out other innovative ways of seeing on his own for his art, using the camera obscura, an early optical projection device, as part of his painting technique, to use it to compose those powerful scenes that he rendered in his paintings.

Leeuwenhoek's turning point had striking long-term effects. His recognition of this microscopic world was key to the development of microbiology, especially the later development of germ theory. Writing later in 1890, the German scientist Robert Koch would develop his famous postulates of germ theory, and the recognition of the power of microbes for health or for death would spread. Ironically, in terms of public health, the wider spread of the practices of that famed Dutch cleanliness were even more important, in particular the simple increased use of soap: so elementary, but producing a radical improvement in public health! Other scientists would launch into further investigations into that smallest world, in terms of atomic theory. Their work would of course be quite distinct from the work of Leeuwenhoek, but was another aspect of the appreciation of the small.

What Leeuwenhoek's discoveries, which fit into that far larger trend of the Scientific Revolution or scientific movement, had accomplished was to give intellectual authority to what could be seen, measured, observed, and assessed, over the earlier authority of classic texts. This in turn would encourage our next turning point, the democratization of such findings and discoveries through the quintessential project of the Enlightenment, the encyclopedia, giving authority to that which is useful, as we will see in our next lecture.

1751—Diderot's Enlightenment Encyclopedia
Lecture 8

Unlike the Dutch society discussed in our previous lecture, France in the early 18th century was not marked by toleration and openness; it was a place where so-called heretics could be executed for their words and ideas. Nevertheless, Denis Diderot and his fellow writers in France produced a daring work, an encyclopedia, that proved to be a turning point for modern history. It was not the first encyclopedia, but it led to profound changes in the worldview of contemporaries that we associate with the Enlightenment, a general movement to replace tradition and faith with reason and science.

The Birth of the *Encyclopédie*

- In 1745, a rich publisher named André Le Breton had hired a young Englishman in Paris to translate a two-volume English dictionary so that it could be published in French. Le Breton was so enthusiastic about the project that he invested his own money in it, but he later learned that the Englishman wasn't equal to the task and had made no progress.

- The publisher then approached a young writer in Paris, Denis Diderot, to undertake the work, along with the young mathematician Jean le Rond d'Alembert. In short order, the project changed into something quite different and incomparably more ambitious.

- The book was to be sold by subscription, with subscribers receiving the volumes as they were produced. At a time when print runs were small, the *Encyclopédie* garnered many subscriptions, some 4,500 in France and across Europe. As the work progressed, additional volumes became necessary, beyond what had originally been promised. Eventually, there would be 17 volumes of text and another 11 of illustrations.

- The *Encyclopédie* was the largest reference work and publishing project of its time. It was read by individuals, families, and reading clubs and societies, and all of them took in its message of enlightenment.

The Enlightenment
- The Enlightenment was an intellectual, social, and political movement that aimed to take the scientific method out of the laboratory or scholar's study and apply it to all spheres of life.

- The imperative was to break with the past to create progress. Reason, science, and utility were the watchwords of Enlightenment thinkers, or *philosophes*, lovers of knowledge. These values were opposed to traditional revealed religion, which these thinkers considered to be organized superstition and fanaticism.

- Inspired by Newton's discoveries and the image of a "world machine" that obeyed natural laws, many *philosophes* were Deists, believing that a supreme being had ordered the universe and then stepped back to let it run, like an absent watchmaker. The business of rational beings was to understand the scientific truths encoded in the world and, on the basis of these laws, to improve and perfect human existence!

- The Enlightenment, then, offered a comprehensive explanation of how the world worked and what it meant. It was the first of the modern secular ideologies, to be followed by liberalism, nationalism, socialism, fascism, and so on. The movement was international but was strongest in France.

Coded and Explicit Messages
- Beyond an assertion of comprehensive knowledge, the Enlightenment message was encoded in the *Encyclopédie*. Diderot and his friends wrote under censorship and needed to be careful in expressing themselves.

- It has often been pointed out that anyone who now reads the original *Encyclopédie* expecting wild, revolutionary statements will be disappointed. Instead, these thoughts were smuggled in or slyly hinted at.

    o Consider the explanation that the editors gave for how all human knowledge was structured. They offered a diagram of all branches of knowledge as a tree—astronomy, geology, zoology, and so on. They called this their world map, or *mappemonde*.

    o Recall from our lecture on Columbus that a *mappa mundi* was a cosmological depiction of the medieval worldview. The map in the *Encyclopédie*, in contrast, was a cosmology or worldview of the Enlightenment.

    o If one looked closely, this diagram revealed a subversive message. Religion is somewhere in the tree's outer branches, along with "superstitions," "fortune-telling," and "black magic." What in earlier centuries had been a supreme authority was set aside by the *philosophes*.

- Especially subtle and telling was the editors' use of cross-referencing as deliberately subversive and ironic commentary. In the most famous example, the entry on "cannibalism" directed readers to other entries for the Christian sacrament of the Eucharist.

- Beyond such veiled meanings, the explicit message of the text was that practical trades and crafts were noble and useful and that usefulness was a source of authority.

- Throughout the text, especially in ironic comments, contributors added criticisms of the status quo and established power, whether religious or political. They carefully scorned despotism or the divine right of kings in favor of a reformed political system in which the monarchy would be sensitive to its subjects. Raising up the dignity of craftsmen and workers also meant lowering the exalted social positions of aristocracy and clergy.

- To dignify usefulness as a virtue, the writers of the *Encyclopédie* sought to capture the techniques and secrets of the trades of artisans. The many detailed and careful engravings showing artisans at work celebrated their productive work.

- Another shocking aspect of the *Encyclopédie* was its unapologetic novelty. In earlier times, even innovative thinkers harkened back to the classics for authority. But the editors of the *Encyclopédie* insisted on the modernity of their project. In the introduction, Diderot stated that only this age could have produced the *Encyclopédie*, that it "could only have been the endeavor of a philosophical century."

Diderot and the *Philosophes*

- Denis Diderot was born in 1713 in Langres into a lower-middle-class family. These origins did much to shape his outlook and agenda. His father was a master cutler but had hopes for his intelligent son to advance by entering the Catholic Church as a cleric. He sent his son to Paris to be educated by Jesuits and to make a career in the church.

- Instead, Diderot set out to become an independent writer. His first works were translations of English philosophical and scientific works. His own early writings were not well received by the authorities, especially for his criticism of religion. This man who had been on the path to the priesthood turned decisively against Christianity.

- As the years went by, Diderot's atheism became stronger, and he avowed a materialistic view of the world. One of his essays provoked the authorities and, in 1749, led to his being imprisoned for three months. Later, he would write philosophical novels, plays, treatises on drama, and art criticism. He grew fierce in his condemnation of European imperialism and slavery as great crimes.

- Diderot's coeditor to begin with was d'Alembert, the illegitimate son of a minor noble, who went on to become a talented scientist. The editors recruited more than 160 other contributors, including

Voltaire and Rousseau. Less well known but deserving of mention was Louis de Jaucourt, who increasingly carried the work of the *Encyclopédie*. Some estimate that he wrote about 27 percent of all the entries.

Controversy Surrounding the *Encyclopédie*

- The *Encyclopédie* had many enemies. In part, the controversies it unleashed were deliberate—the *philosophes* enjoyed antagonizing those they saw as opponents of progress, and such scandal actually stimulated general interest in the *Encyclopédie*.

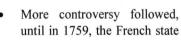

- But this could be a dangerous game. Royal orders threatened death for those writing, publishing, or selling works that were seen as treasonous. The Jesuits (who also had their own rival encyclopedia) charged Diderot's work with plagiarism and sedition. The *Encyclopédie* was allowed to continue under the supervision of three theologians.

Another fan of the *Encyclopédie* and patron of Diderot was Catherine the Great of Russia, although she believed that the work was too subversive to be shared with her subjects.

- More controversy followed, until in 1759, the French state revoked authorization for the work. But the chief censor, friendly to the project, worked out a way for it to continue being produced.

- Pope Clement XIII condemned the work, and the Catholic Church placed it on the Index of Forbidden Books. The pope ordered all copies owned by Catholics to be turned in to be burned.

The Impact of the *Encyclopédie*

- The *Encyclopédie* was reprinted in multiple editions, reaching an estimated 25,000 sets. Scores of pirated and plagiarized editions followed, spreading the message even further. The success of the *Encyclopédie* inspired an English language project, the *Encyclopedia Britannica*.

- In the long term, the *Encyclopédie* pointed toward the Industrial Revolution. Practical craft, utility, improvement of quality, and technical progress would be key values of that transformation of economics and production.

- More broadly still, it announced and encouraged changed views of authority. Diderot himself had written, "No man has received from nature the right to command others." Any political authority needed to be agreed upon, as in a contract, and rational. The "laws of reason" were paramount.
  - Not everyone agreed with this understanding of the Enlightenment or this reconfiguration of authority. The statesman and philosopher Edmund Burke, often considered the founder of conservatism, worried that the abstract theorizing and universal principles of the *philosophes* threatened to dissolve those attributes of society that were not founded on reason but still valuable: ties of tradition, conviction, and faith.

  - The German Enlightenment thinker Johann Gottfried von Herder feared that the universalizing tendencies of the Enlightenment would devastate cultural diversity, the mosaic of a thousand different ways of being human: different languages, literatures, and ways of life. This debate would continue, and does, down to our own day.

- For his part, Diderot, toward the end of his life, actually believed that he had failed, that the *Encyclopédie* had not succeeded in becoming what it might have been. He had been devastated to discover that his publisher, Le Breton, had secretly toned down some of his controversial entries. This colored his perception of the whole.

- Yet the impact of the *Encyclopédie* was enormous. When Diderot died in 1784, his last words were: "The first step toward philosophy is incredulity," not to believe. This was a radical message, prompting the testing of everything. In the decades to come, when empires and kingdoms were tested, in part by the ideas of the *Encyclopédie*, the result would be revolutions.

Suggested Reading

Blom, *Enlightening the World.*

Fowler, ed., *New Essays on Diderot.*

Himmelfarb, *The Roads to Modernity.*

Questions to Consider

1. What gave Diderot's encyclopedia so much more resonance than other encyclopedias?

2. Did censorship in France hamper the *philosophes* or spur them on?

1751—Diderot's Enlightenment Encyclopedia
Lecture 8—Transcript

We usually think of Paris in such positive terms: a capital of style, the glamorous and sophisticated "City of Light," alive with sparkling new ideas, dynamism, elegance! All that is true, but long ago it was also something else: a capital of censorship and the shutting down of ideas.

Consider this scene from 1746 in bustling downtown Paris. We stand at the *Place des Grèves*, in front of the city hall. This is where public executions take place, in front of a vast crowd of jeering, cheering, and enthusiastic onlookers. We stand in just such a crowd today. We smell a fire that has been lit, and hear crackling flames. Then a hush falls on the crowd, as the city's hangman steps forward. He raises up a pamphlet high in the air, and then, with a grunt, he tears it in half, then tears those pieces, and then the pieces of those pieces, and finally throws all of the tattered shreds of paper into the fire.

This was the fate which the authorities of the city of Paris had ordered for a pamphlet, mildly entitled *Philosophical Thoughts*, that was critical of traditional religion. Its young author, Denis Diderot, was not burned that day, but he would spend time in prison and lived in fear of official persecution. Unlike the Dutch society we discussed in our previous lecture, France in the early 18th century was not marked by toleration and openness.

The tone had been set decades earlier by the Sun King, Louis XIV, the very model of an absolutist ruler, who proclaimed, "I am the state." He revoked toleration for Protestants and punished critics of his rule. France was a place where so-called heretics could be executed for their words and ideas.

Nevertheless, over two decades, Diderot and fellow writers went on to produce a daring major printed work, the Enlightenment encyclopedia, that proved to be a turning point for modern history. From 1751 to 1772, Diderot and his fellows worked to produce the *Encyclopédie*, subtitled *a Systematic Dictionary of the Sciences, Arts, and Crafts, by a Company of Men of Letters*, with Denis Diderot and Jean le Rond d'Alembert as editors.

It was not the first encyclopedia, or comprehensive reference guide, but nonetheless it was decisive and led to profound changes in the worldview of contemporaries, which we associate with the movement of the Enlightenment, a general movement to replace tradition and faith with reason, science, and the ideal of useful knowledge. The avowed aim of the *Encyclopédie* was nothing less than "to change the way people think," the most ambitious change of all.

This was not a new technology. Rather, it was a use of an earlier revolutionary technology, Gutenberg's printing press, for an ambitious project of making accessible and useful all of human knowledge: The world might be comprehensively knowable and accessible. This project of making human knowledge useful helped speed the Industrial Revolution.

Accessibility was key. The *Encyclopédie* aimed to reach all of humanity as a potential audience. This was in stark contrast with premodern ages when a class of clerics or scribes held secret knowledge, or when a guild of artisans held the secrets of their craft or trade. Looking forward, there are parallels also in our own times, as the Internet and the instant availability of information is held up as an ideal. The great promise held by both the Enlightenment and the project of the *Encyclopédie* was, in a word, progress. In our examination in these lectures of shifting sources of authority, and the advent of that problematic thing we call modernity, this was a decisive moment. Where earlier ages had looked to the authority of the past, now progress in the future was invoked to shift authority to the future itself!

To put this project into context, we should note that there had been many earlier encyclopedias. Obviously, the idea of collecting all known things in a comprehensive way is very attractive. An astonishing Chinese version actually appeared in the time of the voyages of Zheng He, during the Ming dynasty. This was called the *Yongle Encyclopedia*, and when completed in 1408 it was the largest encyclopedia of the age. Thousands of scholars had worked to produce more than 22,000 manuscript rolls in what was to be a complete collection of all of Chinese literature and texts. Among many other such ventures in the Christian world was a notable encyclopedic work in Latin that Gutenberg had published with his early printing press, the *Catholicon*, or "universal dictionary."

The Enlightenment reinforced what we might call the encyclopedic urge to catalog, to classify, and order by means of reason. In the 18th century, there were more than 50 such encyclopedia projects. But the *Encyclopédie* stands out apart from all these, for reasons we will discuss.

For starters, none of the other encyclopedias started with a fistfight. In 1745, a rich Parisian publisher named André le Breton had hired a young Englishman who was in Paris to translate a two-volume English dictionary for him, so that it could be published in French. Le Breton was so enthusiastic about the project that he invested money in it.

Then, later, he learned with horror that after a long time almost nothing had been done. The young Englishman turned out to be both very lazy and also endowed with very bad French skills, and these were both very negative traits in a translator. In fact, the young man didn't even own a copy of the book he was supposed to translate, so it's not really surprising that he'd made so little progress. Furious out of his mind at learning of this, Le Breton went after the Englishman, and worked him over with his hands and with a cane. Afterwards. the young Englishman tried to sue Le Breton for this assault, but the court sided with the publisher, feeling he'd been provoked.

Now, Le Breton had to worry about saving his project. With three other partners, he approached a young writer of talent in Paris, Denis Diderot, to undertake the work, in cooperation with the young mathematician d'Alembert. In short order however, the project morphed, changing into something quite different and incomparably more ambitious. Instead of just a translation of an English text, why not produce something original and strikingly new? The investors were intrigued, they agreed, and so plans went ahead.

As was customary at the time, the book was to be sold not at bookshops, but by subscription, with subscribers receiving the promised multiple volumes as they were produced until they had the full set. At a time when print runs were small, this project by contrast garnered many subscriptions, some 4,500 in France and across Europe more generally. As you can see, this was an international audience; in fact, more than half of the subscriptions for the project came from outside France.

As the work progressed, additional volumes became necessary, more than had been promised in the original prospectus for subscribers (in fact, later, one set of subscribers tried to sue for breach of contract, given that the final product cost much more than they'd been told to begin with, but they also were not successful in their lawsuit). Eventually, there would be 17 volumes of text and another 11 volumes of illustrations.

The scope was vast. The *Encyclopédie* had 72,000 entries and more than 2,500 plates of illustrations. This was the largest reference work and publishing project of its time. It was read by individuals, families, by reading clubs and societies, and all of them took in its message of Enlightenment.

What was this exciting and new set of ideas called the Enlightenment? The first thing to note is that the very name, "Enlightenment," proclaimed that a new age was dawning, setting it off by implication from the alleged darkness of the past! Beyond this, one slogan of the Enlightenment as a movement was, "Dare to know!" What might humans not achieve if only they dared to use their reason and use their rational faculties? The Enlightenment was an intellectual, social, and political movement that aimed to take the scientific method, as exemplified by Leeuwenhoek in a previous lecture, out of the laboratory or out of the scholar's study, and to apply it to all spheres of life.

The imperative was to break with the past in order to create possibilities for progress. To reject old ways, those habits and traditions of the past, to make anew, on the basis of reason. Reason, science, and utility or usefulness were the watchwords of Enlightenment thinkers, or *philosophes*, lovers of knowledge as they liked to be called. These values were opposed to traditional revealed religion, which the *philosophes* considered to be organized superstition and fanaticism.

Inspired by Newton's discoveries and the image of a "world machine" that obeyed natural laws, many *philosophes* were Deists; that's to say, they believed not in Christian dogma but that a supreme being existed, who ordered the universe, and then stepped out of it, like an absent watchmaker. His work would continue to work on the principles he'd laid down. Then, the implication was that the business of rational beings was to understand the scientific truths that were encoded in the world, and on the basis of these laws, to improve and perfect human existence!

This would be the enchanting promise of human progress. The Enlightenment, then, was offering a comprehensive explanation of how the world worked, and what it all meant. It was in a sense the first of the modern secular ideologies, later to be followed by liberalism, nationalism, socialism, fascism, the whole series of "isms" that have shaped the modern world. The movement was international, but was strongest in France.

Enlightenment ideas permeated the *Encyclopédie* through and through. The very word "encyclopedia" conveyed a particular vision of the world: It meant that the world was knowable. The several parts of the word *Encyclopédie* were from Greek, from *kyklos*, or "circle" on the one hand, and *paideia*, or "knowledge," so that an encyclopedia—this is what the word meant—was a chaining together of what is known, an establishing of connections and interrelations. The editors of the encyclopedia were convinced all knowledge is interconnected. By a splendid coincidence, this very assertion is also one of the aims of our course, to show connections in history!

Beyond this assertion of comprehensive knowledge, the Enlightenment message also was encoded, rather than out in the open. Diderot and his friends needed to be quite careful. They were writing under censorship. Books that were printed in the Netherlands, famous for their freedom of ideas, could afford to be open, but this project was set in Paris of all places, under the eye of the authorities. In fact it's often been pointed out that anybody who now goes to the library reads the original *Encyclopédie* expecting to discover wild revolutionary statements in the text is going to be very disappointed. Instead, these radical thoughts were smuggled in or only slyly hinted at.

Consider for example, the explanation that the editors gave for how all human knowledge was structured. They offered in the *Encyclopédie* a diagram of all of the branches of knowledge—knowledge as a tree, essentially. Different branches were astronomy, geology, zoology, applied sciences, the humanities, and so on. Remarkable, they called this their world map, or *mappemonde*. Recall from our lecture on Columbus that the *mappa mundi* had been cosmological depictions of the medieval worldview. This was the Enlightenment's version. This was a cosmology or worldview of the Enlightenment, and to look closely at the diagram reveals a subversive message. In the tree, religion, earlier a source of authority, is set somewhere way out on the outer branches of the tree, next to the branches for superstitions, fortune-telling, and black magic. What in earlier centuries had been a supreme authority was being set aside by the *philosophes*.

The alphabetical order of entries, rather than grouping them by topic or by some other principle, was in fact both democratizing and systematic, and the editors were really pleased by it. But it had some challenges. It meant that the editors would have to have a comprehensive plan for all of the volumes from the outset so that they wouldn't miss particular topics.

Especially subtle and telling was how the editors used cross-referencing as a tactic. That had not been common in earlier reference works. They used their cross-referencing in a way that was deliberately subversive and ironic. It was really a form of sardonic commentary on what their true, hidden opinions were. To give the most famous example, consider the entry in the *Encyclopédie* on "cannibalism." The cross-reference to cannibalism directed readers to other entries in the *Encyclopédie* for the Christian sacrament of the Eucharist, which for many Christians was the partaking of their savior's body and blood for salvation.

Beyond such veiled, subversive meanings, the explicit message of the text did have huge implications. That message was that practical trades and crafts were noble and useful, and that usefulness was a source of authority. The fact that Diderot himself was the son of a master craftsman clearly shaped his strong conviction. As Diderot wrote, "Too much has been written on the sciences; not enough has been written well on most of the liberal arts; almost nothing has been written on the mechanical arts." That meant for Diderot that useful people were being demeaned and slighted. As he exclaimed at a later point, "What bizarre judgments we make! We require that people are usefully occupied, and we despise useful men."

The implications of this conviction were vast. The *Encyclopédie* would feature in its pages craftsmen and artisans and technical experts, and would have very little to say about kings and warlords and saints. In fact, the *Encyclopédie* had no biographical entries. Throughout the text, especially in ironic comments, contributors added criticisms of the status quo and of established power, whether that power was religious or political. They carefully scorned despotism or a divine right of kings, arguing in favor of a reformed political system, where a monarchy would be sensitive to its subjects in society—but they never called for revolutionary overthrow. Raising up the dignity of craftsmen and workers would mean lowering the exalted social positions of aristocracy and clergy, and careful readers saw this.

To dignify usefulness as a virtue, the writers of the *Encyclopédie* sought to capture in their pages the techniques and secrets of the trades of artisans. To do this, they visited workshops and consulted with the tradesmen to get the details just right. Many detailed and careful engravings in the *Encyclopédie* also showed artisans at work and celebrated their productivity and their usefulness. Ironically, some of these very guild craftsmen who were being observed by encyclopedia writers resisted giving away their secrets of the trade. They feared the spreading of this knowledge.

Another first-rate demonstration of how utility was celebrated connects up with an earlier lecture of ours, on 1492 and the Columbian exchange, and that key example of the transplantation, involving the Columbian exchange, the potato. Let's look at what the entry for "Potato" had to say about what was still at this point a rather new and unpopular root vegetable for Europeans.

The *Encyclopédie* did not praise the potato's taste. It said that a potato really was not very enjoyable, kind of tasteless and starchy, and not much improved no matter how you cooked or prepared it. Also, it was said to cause flatulence. So this was clearly not a very ringing endorsement. But, the *Encyclopédie* still concluded that the potato was useful for those who wanted nutritious and healthy food to fuel work, and thus was a very suitable dish for peasants and laborers!

Another shocking aspect of the *Encyclopédie* was its unapologetic novelty. In earlier times, even innovative thinkers would harken back to the past, to the classics, to make a claim for authority. Recall the Renaissance, a rebirth or recovery of classical knowledge. Or remember how the earliest printers following Gutenberg had sought to present even this innovation as something in continuity with handwriting, artificial writing. By contrast, the editors of the *Encyclopédie* insisted on the modernity of their project, its fundamental discontinuity with the past. In his introduction, Diderot stated that only this age, his time, could have produced such a thing, that it "could only have been the endeavor of a philosophical century; this age has dawned." It takes "more intellectual daring" than earlier ages had had to produce such a product.

Diderot also declared: "All things must be examined, debated, investigated without exception and without regard for anyone's feelings. ... We have for quite some time needed a reasoning age when men would no longer seek the rules in classical authors but in nature." Shocking sentiments.

Who was this man who announced such new claims so boldly? Denis Diderot was born in 1713 in Langres, out in the French provinces, into a lower–middle class family. These origins actually did much to shape his outlook and agenda. His father was a master cutler, but had hopes for his intelligent son to advance in life by entering the Catholic Church as a cleric. The father sent his son to Paris to be educated by Jesuits, and to make a successful career, he hoped, in the Church.

Instead, once in Paris, Diderot set out to become an independent writer, a man of letters. He married, against his father's wishes, but this relationship soured as he pursued mistresses. Diderot's first works were translations of English philosophical and scientific works. His own early independent writings, as we saw at the opening of the lecture, were not well received by the authorities, especially for his criticism of Christian religion. This man, who had been on the path to the priesthood, instead turned decisively against Christianity.

As the years went by, his atheism became stronger, and he avowed a materialistic view of the world. One of his essays provoked the authorities, and in 1749, led to his being imprisoned in the fortress of Vincennes for three months. Later, Diderot would write philosophical novels, plays, treatises on drama, and art criticism. He grew increasingly fierce in his condemnation of European imperialism and slavery, as great crimes being imposed on the rest of the world.

But we must not forget that the *Encyclopédie* was emphatically not a project of one man, not just Diderot. Diderot's coeditor to begin with was d'Alembert, the illegitimate son of a minor noble, who went on to become a talented and famous scientist. These editors recruited more than 160 other contributors, fellow encyclopedists. They were a diverse group of men (and there were perhaps a few women there, hiding under pseudonyms). They included priests, aristocrats, middle-class and lower-middle-class writers, all participants in that "Republic of Letters" that had grown up with the world of the new printing press. They were proud of the title *philosophe*. Let's hear what the entry on *Philosophe* in the *Encyclopédie* had to say: "Reason is to the philosopher what grace is to the Christian. Grace causes the Christian to act, reason the philosopher." Further, the text announced, while others walk in darkness, steered by their passions, the *philosophe* has reason to light his way.

Contributors to the *Encyclopédie* also included celebrities, like Voltaire and Rousseau. Less well-known but still deserving of mention was Louis de Jaucourt, who increasingly and selflessly carried the real work of the *Encyclopédie*. He was eventually writing eight entries a day! Some historians estimate that he may have written about 27 percent of all of the entries of the encyclopedia.

The *Encyclopédie* had many enemies. In part, the controversies which it unleashed were deliberate—the *philosophes* enjoyed antagonizing those whom they saw as opponents of progress, and scandal like that actually stimulated even more general interest in the *Encyclopédie*. But this could be a dangerous game. Royal orders threatened death for those whose writing, or publishing, or selling of works were seen as treasonous. The Jesuits (who also had their own rival encyclopedia project going at the same time), charged the Enlightenment *Encyclopédie* with plagiarism and sedition. The *Encyclopédie* was allowed to continue under the supervision of three theologians, who were ready to censor it at a moment's notice. Then, more controversy followed, until finally in 1759 the French state simply revoked totally the authorization for this work. But, and this is astonishing, one key person friendly to the project worked out a way for it to continue being produced. That person was none other than the French chief censor himself. He and other authorities looked the other way as work continued.

Why? In part, some of them sympathized with the *philosophes*, but another motivation was actually economic. A thousand printers, bookbinders, and booksellers in Paris were employed by this big undertaking, and to shut it down would have represented a great economic blow to the city. Here we see the economic motive at work, as in our lecture about the rival international trading companies of this age. When the last 10 volumes of text appeared, they bore false publication information, alleging that they had been produced in Switzerland.

Pope Clement XIII condemned the work, and the Catholic Church placed it on the Index of Forbidden Books. The Pope ordered all copies of the *Encyclopédie* owned by Catholics to be turned in to be burned, but few were.

Another exalted fan of the *Encyclopédie* combined support with censorship. This was Catherine the Great of Russia, the Empress, the greatest of the enlightened despots of the age. On hearing that Diderot had fallen on hard times and lacked money, she bought his personal library, and then turned around to employ him as her librarian—the books were to stay with him in Paris as long as he was alive. This was a generous gesture. It was an example of elegant patronage, yet Catherine did not spread the ideas of the *Encyclopédie* among her subjects. These ideas were too subversive to be shared in Russia.

So what was the greatest impact of the *Encyclopédie*? The *Encyclopédie* was reprinted in multiple editions, reaching an estimated 25,000 sets. In addition, scores of pirated and plagiarized editions also followed (remember this is the age before copyright), all of which spread the message even further. The success of the *Encyclopédie* inspired an English language project, the *Encyclopedia Britannica*.

In our own times, in 2010, the *Encyclopedia Britannica* published its last print edition, going online. The *Encyclopédie*, interestingly enough, is also available online for you to consult. Diderot would have been very pleased, as the thought of the *Encyclopédie*, as he conceived of it, was a knowledge machine; today we might say, a kind of search engine. It is probable that Diderot also would have been delighted with Wikipedia, as a vast open, accessible, encyclopedic project!

In the longest term, the *Encyclopédie* pointed towards the Industrial Revolution. Its emphasis on practical craft, on utility, the improvement of quality, the encouragement of technological progress, all of these would be key values of that later transformation of economics and production, the Industrial Revolution. More broadly still, the *Encyclopédie* announced and encouraged changed views of authority. Diderot himself had written, "No man has received from nature the right to command others." Any political authority needed to be agreed upon, as in a contract, and it needed to be rational. The laws of reason were paramount.

Obviously, not everyone agreed with this understanding of the Enlightenment, or this reconfiguration of authority. The Irish-born British statesman and philosopher Edmund Burke, often considered the founder of conservatism, had his doubts. Recall from our lecture on the East India Company that Burke had castigated British colonial rule in India for destroying ancient customs and ways of life. He worried also that in Europe, the abstract theorizing and universal principles of the *philosophes* threatened to dissolve, in irony and the cold light of reason, those attributes of society that are not founded on reason, but are still valuable: ties of tradition, feeling, conviction, and faith.

Similarly, the German Enlightenment thinker Johann Gottfried von Herder feared that the universalizing tendencies of the Enlightenment that he was participating in could devastate cultural diversity, that mosaic of a thousand different ways of being human—different languages, literatures, and ways of life. It could all be melted down into one universal culture and that, he thought, would be a loss. The debate would continue, and the debate still continues, down to our own day.

For his part, Diderot towards the end of his life actually believed that he had been a failure, that the *Encyclopédie* had not succeeded in becoming what it might have been. Why? When the *Encyclopédie* was nearly completed, he was devastated to discover that his publisher had actually secretly toned down some of his controversial entries. This colored how he viewed this entire project.

Yet, the impact of the *Encyclopédie* was enormous. When Diderot died in 1784, his last words were: "The first step toward philosophy is incredulity," not to believe. This was a radical message—testing everything was necessary. In the decades to come, when empires and kingdoms were tested, in part by the ideas in the *Encyclopédie*, the result would be revolutions. We will consider one of those, the American Revolution and the Constitution it produced, in our next lecture.

1787—The American Experiment
Lecture 9

In the worldview of the 18th century, republics were not generally seen as desirable or natural. A republic to most thinkers meant a form of government that was small, weak, and temporary. But the American revolutionaries challenged and overthrew such assumptions. After winning independence, they set about building a republic that would stand the test of time. To do so, they constructed a Constitution that separated powers, balanced contending interests, and was flexible enough for the future of a growing nation. The American Revolution and the building of its durable constitutional order launched a modern political project: the republic based on popular sovereignty—government of the people, by the people, and for the people.

The American Identity

- Paradoxically, the revolt of the English colonies in North America was sparked precisely because the colonists thought of themselves as Englishmen with full rights. Only slowly, over time, would a self-understanding of being distinctively American arise. And the bases for that American colonial identity had already been laid decades before by three factors.

- First, from their founding, the colonies had largely been left in a state of benign neglect by British administration rather than centralized oversight. Practices of colonial self-administration grew vigorous.

- The second factor involved religion. The immigration of many settlers had been motivated by the desire to escape the authorized and established official churches of Britain and elsewhere in Europe.
  - In the period from 1700 to 1750, many colonists were swept by a spirit of religious revival that later was called the Great Awakening, emphasizing individual conversion and piety as a way of life above fine points of doctrine and church authorities.

- This also had a political dimension: It was a call to self-administration in spiritual life. John Adams, one of the crafters of the American project, later made a bold claim: "The Revolution was in the minds and hearts of the people; a change in their religious sentiments of their duties and obligations."

- The Great Awakening led to the third key factor, the growth of education and general literacy in the colonies: To read the Bible and to receive its authority demanded schooling, even on the frontier. It was this learning that would make colonists receptive to political debate in a new—and modern—way.

The Seven Years' War
- The immediate cause of the colonial revolt lay to a great extent in the Seven Years' War of 1756–1763. This was a world war that pitted Great Britain against France, each nation with its respective allies.
  - The war started near the spot that would become Pittsburgh, Pennsylvania. British forces and the Virginia Regiment, led by a young officer named George Washington, clashed with French forces, contending for the key strategic location on the Ohio River.

  - The war then spread globally to the colonial possessions of France and Britain, from West Africa to Newfoundland. It concluded in 1763 with a great British victory. France was humiliated, losing most of its overseas empire. Britain at a stroke gained territories in India, Canada, and Florida.

- Britain's world empire now loomed internationally, with a power not seen since the days of the Roman Empire. Yet the expenses of this war would lead to crisis; victorious Britain would have to pay for its success.

- On a personal level, the victory dashed the hopes of George Washington to become a British officer. He was an imposing young man, dignified and controlled yet with a driving ambition. He was from the gentry of Virginia, but this mattered little to the nobles in

London, to whom Washington and other Americans were merely rustic bumpkins from the provinces.

"Taxation without Representation"

- The results of the Seven Years' War were felt keenly in the British North American colonies. The colonists felt more secure with the removal of the French threat, but the expense of the war prompted the British government to launch attempts at fiscal reorganization that provoked the colonists.

  o Britain's debt had doubled from 1756 to 1764, not least because of the expense of maintaining security in the colonies. From the perspective of British imperial administrators, why could the American colonies not be more like India, where the British East India Company was turning a profit?

  o In 1765, a new tax called the Stamp Act was imposed by Parliament on the American colonies. All printed materials would need to bear a stamp showing that the fee had been paid. This measure obviously antagonized the printers and writers of the colonies—dangerous enemies to make—but also galvanized many colonials who objected to "taxation without representation."

  o Colonial merchants organized boycotts of British goods to protest the Stamp Act and additional taxes on sugar and other imports. Protestors organized themselves into secret groups called Sons of Liberty to coordinate opposition and demonstrations.

- The stamp tax was never effectively collected and was repealed, but Parliament insisted that it had the right to legislate for the colonies. British troops were sent to the colonies in increasing numbers, resulting in such clashes as the 1770 Boston Massacre.

- A key moment in the unfolding process involved tea and the British East India Company.

  o The British East India Company was experiencing a downturn. To help it, Parliament passed the Tea Act in 1773, which granted the company a monopoly on the sale of tea in the American colonies. A small tax would be imposed on the tea, but it would still be cheaper than the smuggled tea that many Americans drank at the time.

○ Ironically, the colonists focused more on the imposition of a new direct tax on which they had not been consulted and on the institution of a trade monopoly than on the price of tea.

○ Colonial threats meant that the great East Indiaman ships that arrived in American ports were not allowed to unload their tea chests, except in Boston, where the governor insisted that they do so.

○ On the night of December 16, 1773, some 130 Sons of Liberty, dressed as Mohawk warriors, boarded three ships and threw the tea into the harbor. No one was killed or injured, but this was clearly a call to wider revolt.

• Even at this point, few colonists were driving for independence. Most wanted restoration of their rights as Englishmen, and a number of leading British political figures, including Edmund Burke, sympathized with them.

• But at this juncture, British authorities took a hard line. When British troops were sent to disarm colonial volunteer militias, fighting broke out. The ensuing American Revolutionary War lasted eight years, from 1775 to 1783.

The Irish-born parliamentarian Edmund Burke spoke out against imperial policies that antagonized loyal subjects in America.

The Power of Print

- Still, it took 15 months before the Americans issued a Declaration of Independence, spurred on by the power of print. In January 1776, the British political agitator Thomas Paine published a pamphlet, *Common Sense*, that changed history. In it, Paine argued for American nationhood and for independence from the British Empire.

- In July 1776, a Declaration of Independence, authored by Thomas Jefferson, was presented to, and accepted by, the Continental Congress in Philadelphia. It was an address to the world, from "a decent respect to the opinions of mankind," to explain the reasons for the break.

- The text cited self-evident truths of equality and inalienable rights to life, liberty, and the pursuit of happiness. Governments, it continued, are established by the consent of the governed to secure these rights, and when they are violated, the right of the people is to institute new government.

- This reasoning derived from a key figure of the English Enlightenment, John Locke. In his 1690 *Two Treatises of Government*, Locke wrote of a political contract between a people and the state, but a conditional one. This relation had to respect the innate and natural rights of individuals; otherwise, there was a right to rebel. And that time had come.

The Course of the War

- The war dragged on as General Washington's forces contended against the British. Washington kept the army together by the tremendous force of his personality.

- Europeans who were enthusiastic for the American cause joined the effort. Among their number was the marquis de Lafayette, who arrived in America in June 1777. After the American victory at the Battle of Saratoga in 1777, Lafayette assisted in arranging more aid from France, which now saw an opportunity to be avenged for the Seven Years' War.

- This aid was decisive. French and American forces trapped the British at Yorktown in 1781. The war was finally concluded with the Treaty of Paris in 1783.

A Perilous Moment in History

- Even though the war was won, 1783 was a perilous moment in American history. American officers were embittered at not receiving their back pay from Congress, and some began to plot to seize control. Washington traveled to the camp of the officers in Newburgh, New York, and passionately counseled them not to revolt.

- An even more forceful proof of Washington's character followed. Faced with the daunting task of building a new nation, some in America hoped that the general would become king. Instead, in December 1783, Washington went before Congress and resigned his military duties, declining to take power. His self-denial in the name of his country was a great gift to the young nation.

- The United States that emerged from the conflict was, however, a weakly structured union of sovereign states. It was bound together only by the weak Articles of Confederation, without a federal executive or judiciary, without the power to tax, and unable to keep order, as was made clear by the revolt known as Shays's Rebellion. As these flaws became more evident, many felt the need for a new model.

- A new Constitution was crafted in 1787 in Philadelphia. The Constitutional Convention was supposed to discuss reforms to the Articles of Confederation but rose to the greater task of building a new framework.

- The Constitution was ratified by 1789. It established a federal system, with power separated among three branches of government.

It featured checks and balances and separation of powers, not centralization of authority.

- A Bill of Rights added to the Constitution further enumerated protections due to the individual. This was the product of vigorous debate between the Federalists and Anti-Federalists. The possibility of amendments to the text gave crucial flexibility for the future.

- The American revolutionary settlement was beset with contradictions, including the continuation of slavery and refusal to grant the franchise to women. Yet the Constitution was remarkable for its time and endures today as the first such document adopted by a large state and the oldest written constitution still in operation in the world.

Suggested Reading

Himmelfarb, *The Roads to Modernity.*

Winik, *The Great Upheaval.*

Questions to Consider

1. Why do you think the American Republic has endured?

2. Given that republics were seen as weak and temporary, why do you think the Founders wished for a republic?

1787—The American Experiment
Lecture 9—Transcript

History, like lightning, *can* strike twice in the same place. It's 1787, and it's a beautiful fall day in the city of Philadelphia. On this very spot, where earlier the American Declaration of Independence had been signed back in 1776, now another crucial event has just taken place, of even greater importance. Delegates from the states have gathered, and throughout this summer they've worked to put the young nation on a sounder footing, by writing a new Constitution which will replace the weak and ineffectual Articles of Confederation. By September 17, 1787, they were done, and prepared to present their plan to the public.

One of my very favorite historical stories starts right here: That day, the elderly and world-famous scientist and Enlightenment philosopher Benjamin Franklin is leaving Independence Hall along with his fellows after months of hard work. Franklin's health has been poor, but he has suffered through all of those long debates and discussions about the future of his country because he feels it's worth it. As Franklin steps into the street, a lady shouts out to him, "Well, Doctor, what have we got—a Republic or a Monarchy?" Benjamin Franklin turns to her slowly, and with that characteristic sly smile of his, he replies, "A republic, if you can keep it."

To me this story is perfect. It shows awareness of the new, a sense of the noble and modern achievement of creating self-rule. Indeed, self-rule is what a republic means, from the Latin *res publica*, "the public or common matter." And yet Franklin's quip also has a keen sense of historical precariousness. The outcome is not certain. So we can ask, how did the Americans keep their republic?

Actually the best place to start is to ask why anyone would *want* to keep a republic. In the worldview of the 18th century, around the world, republics were mostly seen as not desirable or even natural. A republic to most sophisticated thinkers meant a form of government that was small, weak, and in the end temporary. Republics contrasted sharply with the apparent power and superior organization and authority and the sheer glory of absolutist kings and queens. In ancient times, the Greek city-state republics had fallen.

The Roman republic had become an empire. Italian city-state republics of the Renaissance had also collapsed.

The commonwealth of Poland and Lithuania, a veritable republic for aristocrats, was infamous at this time for being too democratic to survive. Even the Dutch Republic, whose Golden Age we discussed in a previous lecture, had been a dynamic and strong mercantile state, but now was in terminal decline politically and economically. The Swiss Confederation was too small and remote to really be held up as a model generally for everyone. In a word, republics seemed fated to failure.

That makes the story of this lecture all the more compelling. The American revolutionaries challenged these assumptions and overthrew them. After winning independence, they set about building for themselves a republic that would stand the test of time. To do so, they constructed, through debate and compromise, a new Constitution that separated powers, balanced contending interests, and proved flexible enough for the future of a growing nation.

What was envisioned by the revolutionaries was authority based on popular sovereignty, not on the will of one arbitrary ruler. This was to be a government of laws, not of men. But—and to me this is a beautiful paradox—in order for this new Constitution to survive and become established and cemented in a sense, this government (of laws and not men) actually needed the right man to serve it. That indispensable man was George Washington, who really had to invent the role of being father of his country, and president.

The American Revolution, and the building of that durable constitutional order, launched a very new modern political project, the republic based on popular sovereignty—government of the people, by the people, and for the people, we might call it. At the deepest level, the project of popular sovereignty was a new turning point that was built on top of an earlier turning point which we examined in a previous lecture, that is, the movement towards sovereign states from the Peace of Westphalia of 1648. As the American Experiment evolved, many thinkers and political leaders worldwide were transfixed, observing this daring undertaking. In our next lecture, we will consider another event that also pointed in this direction, but turned out very differently: the French Revolution.

American and French events went in radically different directions, establishing two different models of popular sovereignty for the future, with global effects into our own day. These crucial events, just a few years apart, had factors in common. They shared a common origin in a world war, the impact of the printing press electrified both, and they were inspired by Enlightenment ideas, though not always the same ideas from that movement. Also, some people were actors in both sets of events; in our lectures, we'll observe some of those lives that bridged the revolutionary processes.

So how did it come to pass that English colonies in North America found themselves in revolt? Paradoxically, the revolt was sparked precisely because the colonists thought of themselves as Englishmen, with full rights of Englishmen. Only very slowly, over time, would a self-understanding of being something new and different—Americans—finally arise.

The bases for that distinctively American colonial identity actually had been laid decades before, even if slowly, and gradually, and unconsciously, by three particular factors. First, from the time of their foundings, the American colonies had largely been left in a state of what we might call benign neglect by the British administration, rather than being subjected to really centralized oversight. As a result, practices of colonial self-government grew vigorous.

The second base involved religion. Many settlers in the colonies had immigrated, motivated by the desire to escape the authorized and officially established churches of Britain and elsewhere in Europe. In the time from 1700–1750, many colonists in the Americas also were swept by a spirit of dramatic religious revival that later was called the Great Awakening. The Great Awakening emphasized the individual experience of conversion and piety as a way of life, much more than fine points of doctrine and the rules of church authorities. This also had a political dimension: It was a call, as the Great Awakening would have suggested, a call to self-administration in spiritual life as well. John Adams, who was one of the crafters of the American project, later in retrospect argued that this had been key. He made a bold claim about his experiences: "The Revolution was effected before the war commenced. The Revolution was in the minds and hearts of the people; a change in their religious sentiments of their duties and obligations."

The Great Awakening led to the third key factor, the growth in the American colonies of education and general literacy. After all, to read the Bible and to directly receive its authority demanded schooling, even on the frontier. It was this learning which would make the American colonists receptive to political debate, in a new (and we would say very modern) way.

The immediate cause for the colonial revolt lay to a great extent in the Seven Years' War of 1756–1763. In the United States we refer to this as the French and Indian War. This war pitted Great Britain against France, with their respective allies, in what was really a world conflict. It in fact has been called the first truly global war, since clashes took place in the Americas, in Europe, in India, and in Africa. For that reason it is also sometimes known also as the Great War for Empire.

Yet this world war actually started in Pittsburgh, Pennsylvania, or rather around the spot that became what is Pittsburgh today. There, British forces and the Virginia Regiment, led by a young colonial officer named George Washington, clashed with French forces. They were contending for the key strategic location at the Ohio River.

The war now spread globally to the colonial possessions of France and Britain, from West Africa to Newfoundland. In an earlier lecture, we actually had already discussed a key battle of this war. That was Sir Robert Clive's victory in 1757 at the Battle of Plassey against the allies of the French. This was when we were following the British East India Company and its capture of Indian lands.

The war concluded finally in 1763, with a great British victory. France was humiliated, losing most of its overseas empire. Britain, at a stroke, had gained territories in India, Canada, and Florida. Britain's world empire now loomed internationally with a power not seen since the days of the Roman Empire, or China of the Ming dynasty. It was the leading colonial and naval power worldwide. Yet the expenses of this war would lead to crisis. Ironically, victorious Britain would now have to pay a dear price for its success.

On a personal level there was another irony. This victory dashed the fondest hopes of young George Washington, and that was his dream of becoming a British officer. The British army simply ignored him. He was an imposing young man, who towered over contemporaries standing at six foot two; he was marked also by a special kind of dignity of bearing and immense self-control. He also had, inside, deep driving ambition, which he kept gracefully concealed. Washington's family were from the gentry of Virginia, but that kind of background mattered very little to the great nobles in London, for whom he and other Americans were really rustic bumpkins from out in the provinces, without the needed connections at court. So, a man who might have become a servant of the British global empire instead grew alienated, and eventually Washington became its nemesis.

The results of the Seven Years' War were felt keenly in the British North American colonies. The colonists now after victory felt far more secure because the French threat had been removed. Just now, however, the mother country, Great Britain, called upon the colonists to share the costs of victory and of empire. The expense of the war prompted the British central government to launch attempts at overall fiscal reorganization. These reforms provoked the colonists. Britain's debt had actually doubled from 1756 to 1764, not least because of the expense of maintaining security in the colonies—those costs had grown five times over. So, from the perspective of British imperial administrators in London, why couldn't the American colonies be more like India? In India, the British East India Company was turning a wonderful profit, rather than draining the British treasury.

In 1765 thus, a new tax called the Stamp Act was imposed by Parliament on the American colonies. All printed materials would now need to bear a special stamp showing that the fee for this tax had been paid. This measure obviously antagonized one group in particular: the printers and writers of the colonies. They turned out to be very dangerous enemies to make. Also galvanized were many colonials who objected to principle of what they called taxation without representation.

Colonial merchants organized what we today would call boycotts of British goods to protest this and other taxes on sugar and other imports. The protestors organized themselves into secret groups that were called Sons of Liberty to coordinate opposition and demonstrations against these imperial policies.

In fact, the stamp tax was never effectively collected and ended up being repealed, but Parliament still insisted that it had the right to legislate for the colonies. British troops were sent out to the colonies in increasing numbers, and this produced clashes with the colonists like the 1770 Boston Massacre.

A key moment in the unfolding process actually involved tea, and the British East India Company, whose growth we followed in a previous lecture. The British East India Company was experiencing at this point an economic downturn, so to help the company, Parliament in London passed the Tea Act in 1773, which granted to the East India Company a monopoly on the sale of tea in the American colonies. This tea would sell at very low prices, as the Company had a large backlog to sell off, and a small tax would be imposed on that cheaper tea. The result was that tea, now sold by the East India Company, would be even cheaper than the smuggled tea which many Americans drank at the time.

Ironically, the colonists focused much more on the imposition of a new tax that they had not been consulted on on tea, and the institution of a trade monopoly, which they felt outrageous. Colonial threats meant that the great ships, the East Indiaman vessels of the company, that arrived in American ports were not even allowed by colonists to unload their famous tea chests, except in Boston, where the colonial governor insisted that the shipments would be unloaded.

So, on the night of December 16, 1773, some 130 Sons of Liberty, dressed up as Mohawk warriors, boarded three ships and threw all of the tea into the harbor, tea worth some one million dollars in today's money. Yet no one was killed, no one was injured—this was symbolic violence, and a challenge. This "Boston Tea Party," as it was christened later, was a call to wider revolt.

But even at this point, few colonists were actually driving for full independence. Most of them on the contrary actually wanted what they saw as restoration of their rights as Englishmen. Indeed, there were numbers of leading British political figures in London who sympathized with the American colonists. A key example was the Irish-born parliamentarian Edmund Burke, whom we've mentioned in earlier lectures. He had spoken out against the way in which imperial policies in America were, he felt, antagonizing naturally loyal subjects. Earlier, he had criticized the East India Company's rule in India, and these themes of not trying to impose direct intense management from outside were really the same. Burke argued against what he called a "rage for regulation and restriction."

But instead, at this juncture, British authorities decided to take a hard line with the colonists. When British troops were sent to disarm colonial volunteer militias, real fighting broke out. There ensued an American revolutionary war lasting for eight years, from 1775–1783.

But even then it took 15 months before the Americans actually issued their declaration of independence. Many colonists still wanted recognition of their rights, not total separation. This may be the symbolic meaning of the early American revolutionary flag, from which the current stars and stripes flag has evolved. The red and white stripes appeared on earlier banners of the Sons of Liberty to symbolize the individual colonies. To them was added, in the upper left corner, the Union Jack emblem of Britain's flag. This so-called Continental Union flag, as we recall, was nearly identical to that of the British East India Company, but the real meaning seems to have been a hope for reconciliation, somehow. However, this led to confusion: When the new American military commander George Washington hoisted the flag, his British opponents apparently believed he was in the process of surrendering. Soon, the British emblem in the corner was replaced by the more-familiar stars on a blue field.

It was especially the power of the printing press that moved the colonial cause towards the goal of independence. In January 1776, the British political agitator Thomas Paine, who had come to the American colonies, published a pamphlet that changed history. Paine was recently arrived, but took up the American cause, and with typical radicalism, he pushed it further than many

Americans were at the time. His booklet, entitled *Common Sense*, argued for American nationhood and national identity, and also urged independence from the British Empire.

According to Paine, this American venture of independence would be proof that the world can be made anew, because, as he put it, the cause of the Americans was the cause of human liberty worldwide. Significantly, recalling the effect of the Great Awakening, the irreligious Paine actually used religious appeals to his audience in his pamphlet, arguing that royalty was really a form of idolatry, an abomination before the Lord. Using simple and very direct language, this booklet had a huge readership and a galvanizing effect on opinion in the American colonies.

In July 1776, a Declaration of Independence, authored by Thomas Jefferson, was presented to and accepted by the Continental Congress in Philadelphia. It was an address to the world at large, from "a decent respect to the opinions of mankind" to explain the reasons for this break. This revolutionary text cited what it called self-evident truths of equality and inalienable rights to life, liberty, and the pursuit of happiness. Governments, it continued, are established among humankind by the consent of the governed to secure those rights, and when those rights are violated, the right of the people is to institute a new government.

This reasoning actually derived from a key figure of the English Enlightenment, John Locke. In his 1690 text, *Two Treatises of Government*, Locke wrote of there being a political contract between a people and the state or government, but it was a conditional one. This relation between people and government had to respect the innate and natural rights of individuals. Otherwise, they had a right to rebel, and that time had come.

It needs to be noted that not all colonists agreed with this statement. In fact, a real civil war raged within the colonies, as some one-third of the colonists favored independence, a third remained loyal to the Crown, and the third in the middle simply sought to keep out of the way of this conflict. The war dragged on, as General Washington's forces contended against the British. Washington kept the army together by the tremendous force of his own personality. He displayed at all times Olympian calm and confidence. At other times when it was necessary, he was capable of staging carefully timed explosions of his famous temper.

Europeans who were enthusiastic for the American cause came to join their effort. Among their number was the marquis de Lafayette, who arrived in America in June of 1777, and soon was almost an adopted son to General Washington. After the American victory at the battle of Saratoga in 1777, Lafayette was able to help arrange for more aid from France, which now saw a tremendous opportunity to finally gain vengeance for its defeat in the Seven Years' War against Britain. France signed an alliance with the Americans, and it was joined by other rivals of Britain from Europe, such as Spain and the Dutch Republic. Their motivation was not some love of democratic ideas, but rather the dictates of power politics. Dutch loans also provided funding to the Americans. It's fascinating to think that some of that wealth that the Dutch East India Company had amassed since we first encountered them in previous lectures now went to this project! This aid was decisive. French and American forces finally trapped the British at Yorktown in 1781. The war was finally concluded with the Treaty of Paris in 1783.

Even though the war was over, 1783 was still a perilous moment in American history. American officers were embittered at not having received their back pay from Congress and some of them actually began to plot to seize control. This threatened to become the one and only military coup in American history. Hearing this news, Washington travelled to the camp of those officers in Newburgh, New York, and passionately counseled them not to revolt, to remain loyal.

When his arguments did not convince, Washington prepared to read a letter from a Congressman promising help to the officers—to make sure that their back pay was paid. In order to read this letter, Washington pulled his spectacles from his pocket (he almost never wore them in public). As he did so, he added, "Gentlemen, you will permit me to put on my spectacles, for I have not only grown gray but almost blind in the service of my country." When he said this, the officers were thunderstruck by his simple words and simple gestures. Some of them were actually moved to tears. Immediately, all talk of military revolt stopped. The force of Washington's example and character had won out.

Then there followed an even more forceful proof of Washington's character. The victorious colonies now faced the daunting task of building a new nation. At this point, there were some who hoped that Washington would become the American king, or would rule as a dictator. Instead, in December of 1783, Washington went before Congress and officially resigned his military duties, returning to private life. This was a crucial act of abstaining from power. In this Washington was imitating a classical Roman example, that of Cincinnatus, an aristocratic Roman general who had saved Rome in war, and then immediately gave up his dictatorial powers to return to his farm.

When the British king George III was told of Washington's act, he said some words that were very powerful. He announced, "If he does that, he will be the greatest man in the world." One needs to pause here and think about this deeply. Washington showed restraint when he might have seized power. A childhood illness had apparently left Washington unable to have children; if that had not been the case, would the thought of establishing a dynasty perhaps have tempted him? This is a counterfactual that we cannot answer, but what did happen—Washington's self-denial in the name of his country— was a great gift to the young nation.

The United States that emerged from the conflict was, however, a very weakly structured union of 13 sovereign states. It really should have been called the Disunited States of America, because they were bound together only by the very weak Articles of Confederation, without a federal executive or judiciary, without the power to tax, dependent on voluntary contributions from the states, and really unable to keep order, as was made clear abundantly by a farmer's revolt in New York known as Shays's Rebellion (after one of its leaders). As all of these flaws became ever more evident, many felt the need for some new model.

A new Constitution was drafted in 1787 in Philadelphia. Washington presided over the convention, after being unanimously chosen for that role. The convention was supposed to discuss reforms to the Articles of Confederation, but rose to the greater task of building an entirely new framework. It did so in really remarkable secrecy, so that leaks would not imperil a really wide-ranging and productive internal debate, all of this under the intellectual leadership of James Madison of Virginia.

Most of the delegates to the convention were lawyers, and this gave the Constitution its very strong emphasis on procedure, its insistence on being a government of laws, not of men. Its compromise character was also patent in how the interests of small and large states were balanced by the creation of a House of Representatives on the principle of representation by population, and a Senate where each state had equal votes.

The Constitution was ratified in 1789. It established a federal system, with power that was separated between three branches of government. It also featured crucial checks and balances, and the separation of powers, not centralization of authority. A Bill of Rights added to the Constitution further enumerated protections that were due the individual. This was the product of the vigorous debate between the Federalists and Anti-Federalists. The very possibility of amendments to the text of the Constitution also gave crucial flexibility for the future.

The American revolutionary settlement was beset with contradictions, as in the case of continued slavery—this was a most compromising compromise. Nor were women, half the population, allowed to vote. Yet, the Constitution was remarkable for its time, and endures today as the first constitution adopted by a large state, and the oldest written constitution still in operation in the world.

In 1789, Washington was chosen as the first executive, again unanimously. As he served two terms, Washington really needed to invent, on the spot, the role of president. He was literally our unprecedented president. Take something as simple as how the president should be addressed by others. John Adams suggested this version: "His Highness, the President of the United States of America and Protector of their Liberties." Instead, ultimately, the simple and more austere title of "President of the United States" was used. In Washington's tenure in office, by his example, and in his farewell address in

1796, Washington always stressed that faithfulness to the Constitution would ensure that Americans would keep their republic.

Increasingly and by a long process, citizens would identify themselves not by their state, but as Americans. American national identity, based on the ideas and ideals and ideas of the Declaration of Independence and the Constitution, not on kinship lines or ties or ancestry, is really a unique and continuing experiment.

At this time, another experiment in politics, the French Revolution, was also unfolding across the Atlantic, and we turn to that in our next lecture.

1789—The French Revolution
Lecture 10

The French Revolution began in 1789 with high hopes for restructuring the state but descended into a Reign of Terror. When the violence finally burned itself out, a dictator such as the world had never seen before took power: Napoleon Bonaparte, who turned what had been the French Republic into the French Empire and then set out to conquer Europe. How had a movement for liberation from the *ancien régime* gone so wrong, producing a trajectory that led to a despotism bloodier than the one that had come before? In this lecture, we will see how the French Revolution diverged radically from the one in America, setting up a different trajectory for political modernity that still resonates today.

Background to the Revolution

- In the years leading up to the Revolution, France was increasingly caught in a systemic crisis of the state. It was ruled by a monarch, Louis XVI, whose power was, in theory, absolute, but whose state was seizing up and whose society was seething.

- France had been almost constantly at war for more than a century, and military expenses consumed three-quarters of the budget. The royal debt had doubled in the reign of Louis XVI, yet the aristocracy paid no taxes; that burden fell on the lower classes.

- At the same time, society was in ferment, with authority subject to ever more corrosive criticism. A popular underground press produced a torrent of pamphlets denouncing the king and the profligacy of his court at a time of economic crisis. Anger especially focused on the queen, Marie-Antoinette, denounced as a foreigner and a hypocrite.

- In desperation, King Louis gathered an Estates-General in 1789 to approve new taxation. This representative body had not met since 1614 but now developed a momentum of its own, with representatives of the common orders gaining confidence and making new demands. When nonaristocratic representatives resolved to write a constitution, Louis ordered that their meeting hall should be locked.

- When the delegates discovered the lockout, they went to a nearby indoor tennis court, and there—angry at the clumsy royal gesture—they took what came to be called the Tennis Court Oath. They vowed that they would remain together until they had written a new constitution, whether the king approved or not. This was a pivotal moment in the larger turning point of the French Revolution.

- The king's weakness was provocative. The National Assembly challenged traditional royal authority outright, and the king gave in. All was in flux, and all seemed possible. Yet these days of revolutionary change were also haunted by fear. When rumors spread that the king was massing troops, a mob in Paris stormed the Bastille fortress on July 14, 1789, bringing royal authority down with it.

Declaration of the Rights of Man and of the Citizen
- On August 4, 1789, the National Assembly, in one memorable night, abolished feudalism and the privileges of the *ancien régime*. On August 26, it issued the Declaration of the Rights of Man and of the Citizen, modeled on the American Declaration of Independence and Bill of Rights.

- But there were contrasts in the documents about which ideals were emphasized, which would take pride of place in the new authority under construction.
  o The Enlightenment inspiration that informed the French Revolution came most from a contributor to Diderot's *Encyclopédie*, the *philosophe* Jean-Jacques Rousseau.

  o In his 1762 book, *The Social Contract*, Rousseau argued for popular sovereignty, embodied in the "general will," in which individuals find their highest fulfillment and are subsumed.

Thus, the French Declaration of Rights announced, "Law is the expression of the general will."

- The new state was being established, and the marquis de Lafayette, as a prominent figure, was put in charge of the National Guard. But shortly, he was to experience worrying doubts.

Progress of the Revolution

- In October, the Paris mob was on the move again, marching to nearby Versailles and surrounding the royal family. Lafayette arrived with troops, hoping to shield the king and his family, but the mob took the family hostage and brought them to Paris.

- The revolutionaries also turned on the church. This policy was another significant contrast to what had taken place in America, where free exercise of religion was enshrined in the Constitution.
  - In France, at a stroke, all church property in land was taken away and priests were subordinated to the state as civil servants.

  - The effects of this nationalization were explosive. Because most clerics refused the measure, a civil war threatened. The state was centralizing its authority, perhaps unconsciously imitating the royal absolutism it had replaced.

- Internationally, opinion on the French Revolution was mixed. Some praised it as a new age of mankind, and some American revolutionaries were proud that the movement seemed to be following their example. But Edmund Burke had darker premonitions; he predicted that the revolution would end in cataclysmic disorder and that the ensuing anarchy would be followed by a dictatorship.

- On the night of June 20, 1791, the French royal family made a break, but the king was recognized the next day, and the family arrested and returned to Paris. A new constitution was enacted, creating a constitutional monarchy, but unrest was accelerating fast.

- Revolutionary France went to war with the monarchies of Europe in 1792, and when fear grew that foreign armies might win and restore the *ancien régime*, the Paris mob stormed the Tuileries Palace, on August 10, 1792.

- In September, France was declared a republic, and the monarchy was abolished. This was also the month of the September Massacres, when prisoners held in overcrowded jails, especially priests, were killed, forced to run a gauntlet of men wielding swords, bayonets, knives, and axes.

The Reign of Terror

- After September, the violence increased even more and became systematic in what came to be called the Reign of Terror, lasting 10 months, from 1793 to 1794.

- The revolutionaries executed the king and queen and established a Committee of Public Safety to rule France, dominated by Maximilien Robespierre. Under his stern guidance, the committee advocated "revolutionary terror," defined as prompt, total justice to produce a "republic of virtue." Thousands were sent to their deaths on the guillotine.

The guillotine was praised as humane, the embodiment of Enlightenment utility; the condemned supposedly felt only a rush of air on the neck and then nothing.

  - In areas that revolted against the revolutionaries, such as the city of Lyon or the Vendée region, the mass murder was ruthless and energetic, on a scale far greater than the individual guillotine.

  - Even revolutionaries were suspected. Lafayette, increasingly aware that he was distrusted by the Committee of Public Safety, escaped the country. Thomas Paine was arrested by the state, perhaps because he had pleaded that the king should be exiled, not executed.

- o   All this was in the service of obliterating the old regime and creating a new, purified society.

- At long last, the terror burned itself out. Robespierre was betrayed by associates and executed in 1794. The revolution itself was ended in 1799, when a young general who posed as the defender of the new regime declared his own military dictatorship.

The Rise of Bonaparte

- Napoleon Bonaparte was of obscure Corsican origins, but the revolution and its wars allowed him to rise as a military and political genius. Concentrating power in his own hands, Napoleon crowned himself emperor of the French in 1804.

- The symbolism of this act, of putting the crown on his own head, was vast. In earlier ages, when monarchs claimed to rule by divine right, a pope would have crowned the emperor. But at this ceremony, the pope was relegated to the sidelines. Napoleon was announcing his own power.

- Unlike George Washington, who was marked by restraint, Napoleon's ego and military ambition were total. Moreover, he was able to exploit an innovation of the French revolutionaries: the *levée en masse*. If sovereignty belonged to the people or the nation, then everyone must be involved in war, whether soldier or civilian.

- The French armies that were sent into the field were huge (the largest ever seen in Europe) and actively motivated by patriotic ideology, not by passive obedience to kings or princes. In these new armies, promotion was based on merit, not aristocratic background, allowing men of genius, such as Napoleon, to rise through the ranks.

- The French revolutionaries invaded neighboring kingdoms to spread their ideas and claimed they came as liberators. But these conquests, like the ones of Napoleon that followed, touched off a chain reaction of nationalist resistance against the French.

- In the German lands, Spain, and Russia, nationalist volunteers rallied to fight guerrilla warfare against their supposed liberators. The wars of nations were bloodier than the wars of kings. With the impact of ideology, war was becoming more total, involving entire societies, not just professional soldiers.

- Napoleon's wars cost some six million lives, until he was finally defeated at Waterloo in 1815 by the duke of Wellington.

Revolutions as Turning Points

- Both the American and the French revolutions offered alluring ideas, as well as cautionary lessons and contrasts: a model that sought balance through separation of powers versus a vigorous impulse to centralize and concentrate authority.

- Both revolutions also shaped modern politics. They both challenged monarchies, and their claims to establish the sovereignty of the people were a milestone, opening the door to a new kind of ideological politics.

  o Whereas absolute kings had claimed authority from God, almost all regimes since these revolutions have tried to argue that they represent the people. Even tyrannies have to make this claim.

  o As a result of the emphasis on the people as the source of authority and sovereignty, entire modern ideologies came into being, whose proponents argued that their belief systems served the people best. It has been said that ideologies in the modern age take the place of religious worldviews of the past, offering comprehensive explanations and giving meaning to life.

- But the French Revolution also established a recurring tragic pattern of radical revolt leading to anarchy and tyranny. This was the pattern in the Russian Revolution of 1917 and in Germany between the two World Wars.

- A more immediate impact of the French revolutionary ideas came in the New World, with the great slave uprising in Haiti in 1791, led by Toussaint Louverture, who claimed for his people the rights of man and citizen. Challenged to live up to its ideals, the National Assembly in Paris abolished slavery in all French territory in 1794.

Suggested Reading

Himmelfarb, *The Roads to Modernity*.

Winik, *The Great Upheaval*.

Questions to Consider

1. What factors made the French Revolution as violent as it proved to be?

2. Was Napoleon's seizure of power inevitable? If not, what other scenarios can you imagine for the ending of the French Revolution?

1789—The French Revolution
Lecture 10—Transcript

In this lecture, we consider the French Revolution, which began in 1789. It started with high hopes for restructuring the state and reforming society, but then plunged into a Reign of Terror, which consumed both those who were judged to be enemies of the people, as well as many former revolutionaries themselves. Then, when the extreme violence had finally burned itself out, a new dictator appeared such as the world had never seen before: a new-made man of the Revolution, Napoleon Bonaparte, who seized power and turned what had been the French Republic into the French Empire, and then set out to conquer Europe, and perhaps the world.

A key legacy of the French Revolution would be the increasing intensity of warfare. First the wars of the French radicals as they sought to export their revolutionary ideology, and then Napoleon's compulsive campaigns of conquest moved the modern world towards ever more total warfare that would involve civilians and entire societies.

How had it come to this? How had a movement for liberation from the *ancien régime*, the old way of doing things, and from arbitrary royal authority, gone so wrong, producing a trajectory that led finally to a despotism bigger and bloodier than the one that had come before?

In our previous lecture, we considered events that had taken place just before: the building of a revolutionary United States, and those compromises that went into constructing a durable model for a constitutional republic, all of this cemented by George Washington. What a contrast this was to events in France! In this lecture, we'll see how these revolutions, both of them aiming for the new and modern political model of a republic with popular sovereignty, actually diverged radically, setting up different trajectories for political modernity that still resonate today.

Yet there was so much that linked these events on opposite sides of the Atlantic. To begin with, ironically, French intervention in the American war for independence to help the colonists also helped to bring on the crisis in

France that unleashed revolution there. That Revolution would be far more radical and more violent.

In essence, France was increasingly caught in a systemic crisis of the state. That state was headed by a monarch, King Louis XVI, who in theory was absolute, but who was actually ruling over a state that was in the process of seizing up, and a society that was seething. France had been almost constantly at war for over a century, and military expenses consumed three-quarters of the budget.

The expenses especially of intervention in the American conflict contributed to this financial emergency, which was added on to the losses of the Seven Years' War, that world war that had been started by George Washington in 1754 around what is now Pittsburgh. The royal debt had doubled in the reign of Louis XVI. Yet in this old regime system, the aristocracy paid no taxes, and the burden fell on the classes below them.

At the same time, society was in intense ferment, with traditional authority subjected to ever more corrosive criticism, since the time of Diderot. A popular underground press was hurriedly producing a whole torrent of pamphlets that denounced the King, his court, and what they judged to be its profligacy at a time of economic crisis.

Such anger especially focused on the Queen, Marie Antoinette, who was denounced as a foreigner (she was actually an Austrian Hapsburg). She was judged to be a luxurious and lustful hypocrite, and she was depicted in the most pornographic terms. Here was the medium of the printing press showing its power to destroy, to corrode authority, and to inflame passions, rather than always necessarily leading to reasoned debate and enlightenment.

In desperation at this crisis, King Louis XVI summoned a so-called Estates-General in 1789 to approve new taxation. This was a representative body that had not met since 1614 (that is a break of 175 years), but now, once it had been called, it developed a momentum of its own. Representatives of the common orders gained new confidence politically, and started making new demands. Soon, the non-aristocratic representatives of the Estates-General declared themselves to be representatives not just of their class but of the people at large, and resolved to write a constitution. Their slogan was "liberty, equality, and fraternity."

King Louis XVI was either too irresolute, too tired, or perhaps too unwilling to shed blood to shut down the Estates-General, so he resorted to a half measure, ordering that the meeting hall in the Versailles palace complex where the Estates-General were debating should simply be locked. When the delegates turned up and discovered that their meeting hall was locked, they simply went next door to a nearby indoor tennis court, and there—angry at the clumsy royal gesture—they took what came to be called the Tennis Court Oath. (By the way, this is what I love about history—you just couldn't make this kind of stuff up—the notion of a world historical political event taking place on a tennis court!)

The representatives vowed that they would remain together until they had written a new constitution, whether the king approved or not. This was a pivotal moment in the larger turning point of the French Revolution. It turned out that the king's weakness was provocative. Now that the National Assembly had challenged traditional royal authority outright, the king gave in. Everything was in flux; everything seemed possible now. The National Assembly was joined by some likeminded aristocrats, including the marquis de Lafayette, who had returned from America years before, and now would be hailed as the "Hero of Two Worlds," and of two revolutions.

Yet these days of revolutionary change were also haunted by a strain of fear that would run throughout these events. When rumors spread that the King was massing troops to put down the Revolution, the Paris mob intervened by storming the Bastille fortress on July 14, 1789, bringing royal authority down.

The Bastille prison, long feared, now only housed a handful of prisoners, and there were actually plans for tearing the prison down. But its symbolic status as a representation of despotism and absolute rule made it a target. The armed crowd gathered around the prison, and fighting broke out. The commander of the Bastille, the marquis de Launay, tried to surrender, but now passions ran high.

When the fortress was overrun by the Paris mob, de Launay and his surviving men were disarmed and taken prisoner, then paraded through the streets of Paris, and then hacked to pieces with swords and knives and bayonets before being shot. The crowds dragged their mutilated bodies through the streets, singing, and the head of the marquis de Launay was carried on spear above the crowd.

Much worse would follow, in the so-called Reign of Terror, as the revolutionary dynamic deepened. But it has to be said: That elemental, furious violence was there from the beginning, acid hatred directed against the old regime and those who were viewed as the privileged classes. Now, authority was up for grabs. In the countryside, manor houses and mansions were burned, as peasants laid claim to the land.

At the National Assembly, however, hopes ran high. In August 1789, in one memorable night, that body abolished feudalism on August 4, and the privileges of the old regime. On August 26, it issued the Declaration of the Rights of Man and Citizen. Its text had been proposed at first by the marquis de Lafayette. It was to a large extent modeled on the American Declaration of Independence and Bills of Rights of American states.

But even so, there were contrasts in *which* ideals were emphasized, *which* would take the central pride of place in the new authority under construction. The Enlightenment inspiration which informed the French Revolution came most from a contributor to Diderot's encyclopedia, the *philosophe* Jean-Jacques Rousseau.

Rousseau was a Swiss from Geneva, of lower-class origins, and a thinker who took the Enlightenment in new and more radical directions. Rousseau was a deeply strange man. He was a lover of mankind in the abstract, while sending his children to orphanages so that they wouldn't interfere with his work.

In his 1762 book *The Social Contract*, Rousseau argued for popular sovereignty, embodied in what he called the general will, in which individuals find their highest fulfillment and are subsumed. Indeed, in a chilling phrase,

Rousseau argued, if individuals disagreed with the general will, and what was best for them, they might have to be "forced to be free."

So the French Declaration of Rights announced, "Law is the expression of the general will." The new state was being established, and Lafayette, as a prominent figure and hero, was put in charge of the National Guard. But shortly, he was to experience worrying doubts.

Just two months later, the Paris mob was on the move again. They marched the 12 miles from Paris to nearby Versailles, where the royal palace lay, and they surrounded the royal family. Lafayette arrived with troops; he feared violence, and he hoped to shield the king and his family. The mob, however, marched the king, queen, and their children to Paris—at one and the same time the king was to be a head of state, and a hostage of the revolutionaries.

The revolutionaries also turned on the Church. This policy was another significant contrast to what had taken place in America, where free exercise of religion was enshrined in the Constitution. In France, at a stroke, all Church property and land was taken away by the government, and priests were also subordinated to the state, turned into civil servants.

The effects of this nationalization were explosive. Because most clerics refused this new measure, a civil war was in the offing. The state was centralizing its authority, perhaps unconsciously imitating the royal absolutism that it had replaced.

Internationally, reactions to the French Revolution were mixed. Some praised it as the beginning of a new age of mankind; for example, English writer William Wordsworth described his enthusiasm: "Bliss was it in that dawn to be alive, but to be young was very heaven!" Some American revolutionaries were proud of a movement that they felt was following the American example. Thomas Paine, earlier active in the American Revolution, actually moved to France to be a part of all of these exciting events.

The British parliamentarian Edmund Burke, however, had darker premonitions about what he feared might happen next. These he published in 1790, in a book entitled *Reflections on the Revolution in France*. He predicted that this Revolution, with its abstract rationalist ideals and total determination to tear down what came before, would end in cataclysmic disorder, and that this anarchy would soon be followed by a dictator who would step in to pick up the pieces and impose control.

On the night of June 20, 1791, the French royal family had finally had enough and made a break for it, in disguise. This was the head of state trying to escape his own country, but the king was actually recognized the next day as they were escaping, and the family was arrested. The king turned out in an odd way to actually be a victim of the printing press—the fact that prints showed portraits of the king meant that he was recognizable far away from Paris, out in the remote provinces. In the past, this would not have been the case—a king would have been a remote and vague unrecognizable figure to most people in the rest of the country. Now the royal family was brought back to Paris in disgrace. A new Constitution of 1791 was enacted, creating a constitutional monarchy, but unrest was accelerating fast.

Revolutionary France now went to war with the other monarchies of Europe in 1792 because of fears that they might try to restore the French monarchy. Fears grew that the foreign armies were winning and would restore the old regime, so, on August 10, 1792, the Paris mob stormed the Tuileries Palace in Paris.

In the palace, the royal bodyguards, the famous Swiss Guard, were massacred, torn to pieces, beaten to death, their bodies dismembered and spiked onto poles that were carried through the streets, and finally burned in bonfires. Their red uniforms were carried aloft by the crowds as bloody red banners of revolution. The king and queen and their family were kept alive, for now.

In September 1792, France was declared a republic; the monarchy was abolished. This was also the month of the September Massacres, when prisoners who were already held in the overcrowded jails of France, especially priests, were killed, forced to run the gauntlet of men wielding swords, bayonets, knives, and axes. This was not just a swift execution: Cheering crowds looked on, exultant as torture prolonged the torments of the doomed prisoners who were judged to be traitors. The crowds showed a fury and hatred that really resembles the later genocides of the modern age. Then, as if this were not enough, the violence really got going and became systematic, in what came to be called the Reign of Terror, lasting 10 months, from 1793 to 1794, and costing tens of thousands of lives.

The revolutionaries executed the king, then the queen. A Committee of Public Safety now ruled France. It was dominated by Maximilien Robespierre, known as The Incorruptible. Under his stern guidance, the Committee advocated what it called revolutionary terror, which it defined as defined as prompt and total justice, that would produce a "Republic of Virtue." Radical revolutionaries very proudly accepted the label of "terrorists." They saw it as a good thing.

Thousands were sent to their deaths on the guillotine, a killing machine that was praised as humane and really a kind of embodiment of Enlightenment utility. It was actually asserted that the condemned only felt kind of a rush of air on the back of the neck, and then nothing, so a humane tool of execution, allegedly.

In areas which revolted against the revolutionaries, like the city of Lyons or the Vendée region, the mass murder that followed was ruthless and energetic as these revolts were put down. It was on a scale far bigger than the individual guillotine. Grapeshot from cannon were used to mow down crowds of prisoners, who then fell into freshly dug mass graves. Barges full of men, women, and children were sunk in rivers in what the radicals jokingly called revolutionary baptisms. Chemists were even consulted on how it might eventually be possible to produce mass death by the use of poison gas, anticipating later genocidal horrors.

Even revolutionaries came to be suspected. Lafayette, increasingly aware that he was distrusted by the Committee for Public Safety, escaped the country, going into exile. The international revolutionary Thomas Paine was actually arrested by the state, perhaps because he had humanely pleaded that the king should not be executed but simply sent into exile.

All this was in the service of obliterating the old regime and creating a new, purified modern society. The revolutionaries sought to dechristianize France, replacing religion with a Cult of Reason, as they called it. The cathedral of Notre Dame in Paris had its altar deconstructed and was ceremonially consecrated as a temple to reason. A new revolutionary calendar, starting with the year in which the republic was declared, and abolishing Christian holidays, expressed this sense of a historical break that the revolutionaries were seeking. This was to be a definitive modernity, a decisive advance in human history that left tradition and earlier belief far behind.

At long last, the Terror burned itself out. The ringleader Robespierre was actually betrayed by his own associates who had started to be afraid of him, and he was executed in turn in 1794. Very aptly, the revolutionary Saint-Just famously called revolution "a mother who devours her children."

Thomas Paine, as it turns out, escaped that fate, but only barely: He had perhaps been only hours away from being guillotined when the Terror finally ended. The republic itself was ended in 1799, when a young general who posed as the defender of the new regime instead declared his own military dictatorship.

That was Napoleon Bonaparte. He wasn't French—he was of obscure Corsican origins, but the Revolution and its wars allowed him to rise, as a military and political genius. Concentrating power in his own hands, Napoleon in 1804 crowned himself the Emperor of the French. The symbolism of this act, of Napoleon actually putting the crown on his own head in a grand ceremony in Notre Dame Cathedral, was vast. In earlier ages, when monarchs claimed to rule by divine right, a pope would have been the one to crown the emperor. Now by contrast, at this ceremony, the pope was relegated to the sidelines; he sat off to the side looking on resentfully.

Napoleon was announcing in this way the power of the individual, or at least of *this* individual, himself. Napoleon was literally a self-made emperor. He rode the Revolution to power, surfing on the tides of history. Sometimes Napoleon called himself a son of the Revolution; at other times he simply stated, "I am the Revolution."

Napoleon's power lay in his military success, and he could never get enough of that success. Unlike Washington, who was marked by restraint, Napoleon's ego and ambition were total. Napoleon moreover was able to exploit a military revolution that was taking place at the same time, which had been inaugurated by nearly constant warfare. From 1792, when the French revolutionaries declared war on the monarchs of Europe, until 1815, when Napoleon was final defeated, Europe was all but constantly at war for almost a quarter of a century. This must have seemed like another Thirty Years' War, almost.

The French revolutionaries had done something new in military terms. In 1793, the Committee of Public Safety declared what it called the universal mobilization of the French nation, the *levée en masse*. Everyone was to be drafted. Men were to do battle, women were to produce for the war effort, and even old men were supposed to stand in public places giving patriotic speeches. If sovereignty belonged to the people or the nation now, then everyone was involved in the war, whether a soldier or a civilian.

Moreover, if the nation had sovereignty, it could make demands on ordinary people that far exceeded what monarchies had required in the past. The French armies that were sent into the field were huge (the largest seen in Europe until that time), and they were actively motivated by patriotic ideology, not just passive obedience to kings or princes, as in the past. In these new armies, promotion would be based on merit, not on whether you had aristocratic background, and it was this promotion by merit that would allow men of genius like Napoleon to shoot up through the ranks.

This new power was vividly demonstrated in a famous event, the cannonade, or artillery battle, of Valmy. For four hours, dedicated but often inexperienced French soldiers rained shells down on a professional army, made up of royal forces from Germany, that was advancing against them to restore the monarchy in France. As the French fired their cannon, they sang their fierce national anthem, the Marseillaise, and shouted, "*Vive le nation!*" ("Long live the nation.")

The French won this battle, defeating some of the best professional soldiers in the world. The French had fought with conviction—their enemy aristocrats said they fought like cannibals. The great German poet Johann Wolfgang von Goethe was actually at Valmy and witnessed this famous cannonade. He concluded: "Here and now a new era of world history is beginning." Old authority was defeated by a new, revolutionary authority.

The French revolutionaries also invaded neighboring kingdoms to spread their ideas and claimed that they came as liberators. Their slogan was, "War with all kings, peace with all peoples!" But these conquests, like the later ones of Napoleon, actually touched off a chain reaction of nationalist resistance against the French, so that in the German lands, in Spain, and in Russia, nationalist volunteers rallied to fight guerrilla warfare against their supposed French liberators. The wars of nations turned out to be far bloodier than the wars of kings, and this was a sign of things to come. With the impact of ideology, war was becoming more total, increasingly involving entire societies, not just professional soldiers. Napoleon's wars cost some six million lives, until he was finally defeated at Waterloo in 1815 by the Duke of Wellington. Interestingly enough, the Duke of Wellington had started his career as an officer in the British East India Company's private army.

As we have seen in this and the previous lecture, these revolutionary events, the American and the French upheavals, were both linked and contrasting events. Why were they turning points in modern world history? Their significance is such that it is still felt today. They offered both alluring ideals as well as cautionary lessons and contrasts. On the one hand, a model that sought balance through separation of powers. On the other hand, a vigorous impulse to centralize and concentrate authority. These revolutions changed modern politics. As they both challenged monarchies, their claims to establish the sovereignty of the people were a milestone, and really opened the way to a new kind of modern ideological politics.

Whereas absolute kings had claimed their authority from God, almost all regimes since these revolutions have tried to argue that they represent the people. Even tyrannies have to make this claim, to present themselves as somehow not totally illegitimate, claiming that they de facto rule in the name of the people. Certainly, Nazi Germany and the Soviet Union claimed to do so.

As a result of this emphasis on the people as the source of authority and sovereignty, entire modern ideologies came into being, whose proponents argued that their belief systems would serve the people best. It has been said that ideologies in the modern age have taken the place of religious worldviews of the past, offering comprehensive explanations, and a meaning to life.

Among these modern ideologies, liberalism emphasized individual freedoms, economically and politically. Nationalism, the claim of belonging to a national community (which was powerfully championed by both American and French revolutions), would be very potent in the 19th and 20th centuries, and in spite of repeated prophecies that nationalism is in decline, it seems to be going very strong now. Karl Marx, harkening back to the French Revolution as what he saw as a necessary historical stage, crafted socialism and communism, presenting these as scientific programs for future progress.

As we already saw, reacting against the French Revolution, Edmund Burke launched modern conservatism. On the other side of the political divide, the energies and dynamism of the French Revolution have made it a kind of template for radicals, to explore the possibilities of upheaval.

But the French Revolution also established a recurring tragic pattern: radical revolt, leading to anarchy, leading to tyranny. This turned out to be the pattern of the Russian Revolution of 1917: When the Russian emperor's rule was overthrown, democratic forces couldn't consolidate a new system, and Lenin and Stalin and their comrades were able to take power for their Bolshevik (or communist) regime.

Similarly, in Germany between the two World Wars, the German emperor's throne was toppled, but the German attempt at democracy was undermined by economic collapse and a loss of confidence, until the Nazis managed to come to power. As this model suggests, in times of crisis, there are often would-be men of destiny like Napoleon waiting in the wings.

One famous anecdote about the long-term consequences of the French Revolution deserves some mention. This story goes like this: In 1972, when

U.S. President Richard Nixon made his famous visit to communist China, he asked the Chinese prime minister, Zhou Enlai, what he thought of the French Revolution. Allegedly, Zhou famously replied, "It is too early to tell."

This story became famous, because it seemed to illustrate the long-range thinking and visionary quality which great political leaders and thinkers are supposed to have. Unfortunately, the story is untrue, because actually what was going on was a misunderstanding: It seems the Chinese premier was referring to the quite recent French student demonstrations in Paris of 1968, so only a few years in the past, not all the way back to 1789.

But in spite of this, the story took on a life of its own, and it actually captures an important insight. The reverberations of those revolutionary claims to the authority of popular sovereignty are with us still, and continue to work themselves out in the politics of our world!

A more immediate impact of the French revolutionary ideas came in the New World, with the great slave uprising in Haiti in 1791, led by Toussaint Louverture, who claimed for his people the rights of man and citizen, influenced by French revolutionary ideas. The National Assembly in Paris, challenged to actually live up to its own ideals, abolished slavery in all French territory in 1794 (Napoleon would later reinstate slavery). These facts point to another global movement for liberation, the abolition of slavery, which we'll consider in our next lecture.

1838—The British Slavery Abolition Act
Lecture 11

Other turning points we have examined so far involved scientific change, geographic discovery, technological innovation, and political transformation. But the abolition of slavery in the British Empire was a different kind of turning point: a change of heart. For centuries before 1838, many people saw slavery not as an abomination and a crime but as a seemingly permanent feature of human society. The change came through a movement of quite ordinary people that began in the late 18th century. It did not succeed quickly or all at once. Rather, success came gradually, pushed by social protest over several lifetimes. This was a turning point in the dawning recognition of human rights, universal to us all.

Slavery in Premodern and Modern Times

- Before the modern age, slavery, in many different forms and under different names, had been an almost universal phenomenon. In classical times, even Aristotle divided humanity into two great categories, slave and free. The monotheistic religions of Judaism, Christianity, and Islam, even as they preached a new religious message, did not call for the abolition of this institution.

- In medieval Europe, traffic in human beings was practiced in the growing towns. Often, these were young men and women from Eastern Europe. From 1200 to 1500, the Italian cities of Venice and Genoa did a brisk trade in slaves from the Caucasus mountain region through the Black Sea, sold in the slave markets of Cairo.

- When Constantinople fell, remaining Christians were sold into slavery by the Turkish conquerors, and Christian Europe took Muslims as slaves in turn. Later in the Middle Ages, slavery as such mostly disappeared in northwestern Europe, but serfs and peasants were subject to conditions of harsh servitude. This pattern lingered for centuries more in Eastern Europe, where serfs were bought and sold as unfree labor.

- Slavery came to the fore again with the expansion of colonial empires, especially after the encounter with the American continents in the years following 1492.

- When native Americans were decimated by the diseases of the Columbian exchange, the Spanish brought slaves from Africa to Hispaniola around 1501, and this set a new pattern of Atlantic slavery: Slaves from Africa were forcibly taken to the plantations of the Americas. This pattern endured for 350 years on the vast plantations in the New World.

- The numbers here are so vast as to defy comprehension. From 1500 to 1820, it is estimated that up to 15 million Africans were torn from their homes and shipped across the Atlantic. Of that number, an estimated 4 to 6 million slaves did not survive the crossing.

The Atlantic Slave Trade

- In the 1600s, the Portuguese dominated the slave trade, but other competitors moved in. The Dutch dominated for a while and then the British. As we saw in our lecture on the great trading companies, these were large ventures with multiple investors.

- The pattern of shipping undertaken by these companies came to be called the "triangle trade." Slave ships carried goods from England and Europe to West Africa; loaded up there with human cargo; moved across the Atlantic, disgorging those who survived; loaded up again with sugar, tobacco, and coffee; and sailed for northwestern Europe to begin the triangular cycle again.

- European ports grew rich on slavery, and a vast economy was built around the trade, including those who made the goods that were traded for human beings, those who built and outfitted ships, those who forged shackles for the prisoners, and those who resold the colonial commodities that came back from the Americas.

- The slave ships headed to the coasts of West Africa, from what is Senegal to Nigeria. Slaves were usually brought to the coast by

- The ships waited for weeks to be fully loaded. Then began the horrors of the Atlantic crossing. Aboard crowded ships, slaves were given only about four square feet of space. Chained together to hamper revolt, it was hard for the Africans to move about, and the decks were marked by horrible conditions that bred disease.

- The trip typically took a month from Africa to Brazil or two months from Africa to the Caribbean or North America. On average, 15 percent of the slaves died en route, often many more. Slave ship crews also experienced high mortality rates due to yellow fever and malaria. Some desperate slaves tried to resist; more than 300 mutinies took place on the slave ships.

- Those who survived were put to work in the plantations of the colonies, especially the sugar plantations. Almost half of all Africans shipped across the Atlantic were sent to the Caribbean, Barbados, Jamaica, or Saint-Domingue, now known as Haiti. Of the rest of the slave trade, about 40 percent of the slaves were shipped to Brazil; North America received some 5 percent.

Mobilization against Slavery

- Up to this point, there had been isolated criticisms of slavery among Enlightenment thinkers, but this criticism had been inconsistent. It was religion that finally produced the beginnings of a mass mobilization against slavery.

- In particular, this movement involved the Quakers. Members of this group believed in the fundamental equality of all people because of the immediate relationship each person could have with the divine.

- From these beliefs, the Quakers, both in England and in the American colonies, spoke out against slavery. As early as 1688, Quakers in Germantown, Pennsylvania, condemned slavery and the slave trade. By the 1760s, Quakers in Britain and America refused to accept slave traders into their communities. In Philadelphia in 1775, they founded the world's first antislavery society.

- Around the same time, in England, Quakers cooperated with Evangelicals within the Church of England, Methodists, and Baptists to work against the slave trade. In 1772, a legal case had prohibited slavery in the British Isles, so there were no slaves in Britain, but these activists were not content.

- The result of this movement was a powerful partnership that included Thomas Clarkson, a tireless organizer; the politician William Wilberforce in Parliament; and the African Olaudah Equiano, a former slave who had bought his freedom and published a best-selling autobiography.

- The group decided to concentrate first on the slave trade rather than working on banning slavery, even though that goal was what almost all of them ultimately sought. Slavery itself seemed too socially and economically entrenched to be overthrown all at once, so their hope was that ending the trade would lead to the gradual extinction of the practice as a whole.

- Clarkson traveled the country, collecting information and gathering witnesses to testify in parliamentary investigations. The movement's political voice was Wilberforce, who advanced the legal cause in Parliament.

- Because many of the members of the movement were Quakers, and in turn, many of the Quakers were merchants, the movement was very businesslike—efficient and inventive in its tactics. Activists printed masses of pamphlets and pioneered the use of fundraising letters. Women also played a role in the movement, speaking at public meetings, gathering signatures in petition drives, and organizing a boycott of sugar in 1791.

Ending the Slave Trade

- Soon, society was inflamed with the cause. The message appeared in debates, newspapers, and even poems. In Parliament, Wilberforce pushed the cause, and parliamentary committees investigated the details of the slave trade in hearings.

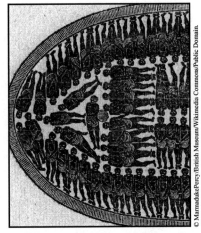

- In Parliament, proslavery forces, organized as the West Indian lobby, advanced ludicrous arguments in favor of the institution. Proposed bills banning the slave trade failed repeatedly.

A shocking diagram of the interior of the Brookes, a slave ship owned by a Liverpool family, actually showed fewer slaves than were sometimes transported and remains one of the most reproduced political images ever.

© Marmaduke Percy/British Museum/Wikimedia Commons/Public Domain.

- Finally, in 1807, Parliament passed a ban, declaring the slave trade a form of piracy. The legislation damaged the British economy, but the moral argument trumped financial considerations.

- Soon after, the United States, the Netherlands, and France also prohibited the importation of slaves, but it would take another quarter century until the goal of freeing slaves was achieved. In the meantime, the British government took action. In the decades after 1807, even during the war against Napoleon, royal navy ships patrolled slave ship routes to stop the trade.

Abolition at Last

- The British movement against slavery slowed down in the next decades, running out of energy and content to be "gradualist" in its hopes, until a new generation of women activists rose up to reenergize the movement and demand immediate abolition of slavery everywhere in the British Empire.

- Slave uprisings in Haiti and Jamaica helped convince many that emancipation had to come.
  - In 1833, Parliament passed legislation freeing some 800,000 slaves in the British Empire, mainly in the Caribbean islands. That emancipation came in stages, and owners were promised compensation, even though ex-slaves got none.

  - At long last, on August 1, 1838, the slaves were finally free. At the ground level, even if economic exploitation continued, experiencing the moral difference in status from slave to free was profound.

  - Of course, this did not end the story or the crime of slavery all at once. Ex-slaves continued to labor in hard conditions but at least without the old shackles. And slavery continued elsewhere in the Americas.

- American abolitionists, including William Lloyd Garrison and the former slave Frederick Douglass, traveled to Britain and cooperated in a transatlantic movement for abolition. But it would take the U.S. Civil War, which exacted some 750,000 lives, to free the slaves in the United States.

- The last open slave market in the Americas, in Havana, Cuba, was shut down in 1869. Cuba stopped exporting slaves in 1870, as a result of naval interdiction by the United States and Britain, and abolished slavery in 1886. Finally, in 1888, slavery was abolished in Brazil.

- Unfortunately, it is not possible to conclude there. Slavery continues today in many forms of involuntary labor, on many continents, and under new names. It is estimated that more than 20 million people are in servitude today worldwide; the anguish continues.

- But in the fight against this injustice, the legal abolition of the slave trade and slavery was a powerful turning point. That August night in 1838 brought great joy and comfort to the liberated Africans and left a lasting legacy. It created a new model for social mobilization, with key tactics and tools invented by the abolitionists, which are used by movements spearheaded by ordinary people even today for countless causes.

Suggested Reading

Bernstein, *A Splendid Exchange*.

Hochschild, *Bury the Chains*.

Questions to Consider

1. What later social movements (perhaps even of the present day) do you see as having adopted tactics similar to those of the abolitionist movement?

2. What was unique about the role of women in the movement to abolish slavery?

1838—The British Slavery Abolition Act
Lecture 11—Transcript

Imagine a worldwide celebration, on hearing of the end of a great injustice. It's nearing midnight, and in a few moments it will finally be August 1, 1838. By law, this will mark the end of slavery in the British Empire. In Jamaica, a British sugar-growing colony, through the warm night, a Baptist congregation has been waiting expectantly.

The clock ticks down to midnight, and at that precise moment, in the little church, the tumult is indescribable. Jubilant, the worshippers go outside, and there they bury a coffin symbolizing centuries of slavery. At just that moment as well, black congregations in Cincinnati and Philadelphia, and mass meetings in New York and cities in Britain all erupt in the same joy as well. For millions, this was the turning point of their lives. But how was it that the monster of slavery was finally killed?

Other turning points we've examined in this course involve scientific change, geographic discovery, technological innovation, and political transformations. This one is even deeper, a different kind of turning point: a change of heart. For centuries before 1838, indeed only decades before, many people saw slavery not as an abomination and a crime, but simply as part of the way things had always been, a seemingly permanent feature of human society.

This change came through a movement of quite ordinary people, not the high and mighty of the earth. It included slaves themselves who struggled against the condition that had been imposed upon them. It included British and American abolitionists. It included many acting out of religious convictions, and it even included a former slave trader.

This remarkable movement, unprecedented and thus a key turning point of modern history, began in the late 18th century, at a time when an estimated three-quarters of the world population lived under some form of servitude or involuntary labor, slavery, or serfdom. This movement did not succeed quickly, or all at once. Rather, success came in gradual steps, pushed along by social protest, and unfolding over several lifetimes.

A wonderful history, Adam Hochschild's *Bury the Chains*, makes a compelling argument that this was in a sense the mother of all citizens' movements, into our own times, inventing crucial tools for mobilizing public opinion, and turning it into a powerful force. Hochschild calls this "the greatest of all human rights movements." This, we'll argue, was a turning point in the dawning recognition of human rights, universal to us all. Historically, what needs explaining is not the cruel fact of slavery itself, but instead how it came to be seen as a crime, rather than normal. It had earlier been seen not as a fate one would wish for oneself, but simply in the order of things. How could one change such a state of mind? The movement to abolish the slave trade and then slavery itself had to be international, as we'll see in this lecture.

The slave trade was tied into the expansion of European colonial world empires, and linked with that emerging global economy based on commodities like sugar, tobacco, tea and coffee, so it was global in extent. Fighting this global phenomenon globally must have seemed daunting if not impossible, and yet, the movement endured, and then finally triumphed, but it would prove to be a long, long process.

It is tragic but true that slavery, before the modern age, in many different forms and under different names, has been an almost universal phenomenon. Few premodern societies did not have some form of slavery or forced labor. In classical times, even Aristotle divided humanity into two great categories, slave and free. The monotheistic religions of Judaism, Christianity, and Islam, even as they were preaching a new religious message, did not call for the abolition of this institution.

In medieval Europe, traffic in human beings was practiced in the growing towns. Often these were young men and women from Eastern Europe who were enslaved. Indeed, the word "slave" in English originally comes from the name "Slav," the major family of peoples in Eastern Europe. From 1200 to 1500, the trading empires of the great Italian cities of Venice and Genoa did a brisk trade in slaves taken from the Caucasus mountain region through the Black Sea, and then sold them in the slave markets of Cairo in Egypt.

At the start of our course, when Constantinople fell in 1453, the remaining Christians were sold into slavery by the Turkish conquerors, and Christian Europe took Muslims as slaves in turn. Later in the Middle Ages, slavery as such mostly disappeared in northwestern Europe, but serfs and peasants were subject to conditions of harsh servitude, and this was a pattern that lingered for centuries longer in Eastern Europe, where serfs were bought and sold, as un-free labor (in fact, serfdom was only abolished in Russia in 1861).

Slavery came to the fore again as a phenomenon with the expansion of colonial empires, especially after the encounter with the American continents after 1492. We'll remember that this began almost immediately. Remember our lecture on Columbus, how he seized Native Americans whom he met, to bring them back to Spain to show off to his royal patrons. Then, when Native Americans were decimated by the diseases that were part of the Columbian exchange, the Spanish began to bring slaves from Africa to Hispaniola around 1501, and this established a new pattern of Atlantic slavery: Slaves from Africa were forcibly taken to the plantations of the Americas. This pattern endured for 350 years, on the vast plantations in the new world, where sugar, tobacco, cotton, and coffee were grown, as global commodities, by slaves.

The numbers involved are so vast as to defy comprehension. The estimates are still debated to this day. From 1500 to 1820, it's estimated that between 12 and 15 million Africans were torn from their homes and shipped across the Atlantic. Such numbers mean that the movement of Africans easily outdistanced the number of European immigrants coming across the sea until the mid-19th century. Moreover, of that larger number, it's estimated that between two to six million slaves did not survive the crossing itself.

How was such a vast commerce organized? First, in the 1600s, the Portuguese dominated this trade, but then other competitors moved in. The Dutch dominated for a while, and then the British, while Dutch, Danish, and Swedes continued to participate. As we saw in our earlier lecture on the great trading companies of the earlier modern age, these were big ventures with multiple investors. In the British case, it was the Royal African

Company which had received a royal charter for this trade, and slaves in fact bore the brand mark "R.A.C." on their very skins.

Although no one country was able to totally monopolize the Atlantic slave trade, eventually the British predominated. From 1640 onwards, the British carried some 40 percent of the total slaves. The French were next, with some 20 percent. At the peak, British ships were carrying 40,000 slaves every year.

This vast pattern of shipping came to be called the triangle trade, or triangular trade. Slave ships carried goods from England and Europe to West Africa, loaded up with a human cargo there, and then moved across the Atlantic, disgorging those who survived, and then loaded up there with the great commodities of sugar, tobacco, and coffee, and sailed for northwestern Europe, to begin the triangular cycle again. This pattern was also further aided by the clockwise sea currents of the North Atlantic.

European ports grew rich on slavery, including the booming port cities of Liverpool and Bristol in England, or Nantes in France. A vast economy was built up around the slave trade, including those who made the goods which were traded for human beings, those who built and outfitted the ships that transported slaves, those who forged shackles for the prisoners, and those who resold the colonial commodities that came back from the Americas. Most of those who invested in the slave voyages and grew rich from them never actually set foot in Africa or the plantations to which the slaves were shipped.

The slave ships headed to the coasts of West Africa, from what is Senegal to Nigeria today. Slaves were usually brought to the coast by African middlemen, and then offered to the slavers. Such prisoners were usually captives of wars, or had been reduced to slavery because they were unable to pay their debts.

European traders mostly bought them with cloth (especially cloth from India was desirable, because it was lighter than English woolens—here we see another emerging global trade tie). Also desirable were bars of iron, glass beads, manufactured goods like pots and pans, alcohol and guns and gunpowder. A very elaborate pattern of trade in human beings developed along the African coasts.

Europeans were usually unable to go into interior themselves, as they proved very vulnerable to the tropical diseases. This was a marked contrast to what we described earlier, the experience of the Columbian exchange: Now the shoe was on the other foot, in terms of infection. The trade was a debilitating one for the Europeans in general (only 1 in 10 employees of the Royal African Company who traveled to Africa actually managed to retire alive).

For weeks, the ships waited at the coast, until they were loaded, or as the terrible expression went, "fully slaved." Then began the horrors of the Atlantic crossing, what was called the Middle Passage. Aboard crowded ships, slaves were given only about four square feet of space. Chained together so that it was harder for them to revolt, it was difficult for the Africans to move about, and the decks were marked by horrible conditions that bred epidemic disease. The trip typically took about a month from Africa to Brazil, or two months from Africa to the Caribbean or North America. It's estimated that an average of 15 percent of the slaves died en route, often many more. Slave ship crews also experienced very high mortality rates, due to yellow fever and malaria. Repeatedly, desperate slaves tried to resist: Over 300 mutinies took place on the slave ships.

Those who survived the passage were put to work in the plantations of the colonies, especially the sugar plantations. These had really taken off economically, from around 1650, in the Caribbean Islands, and they generated a huge industry to feed the sweet tooth of the modern world. Almost half of all Africans shipped across the Atlantic were sent to the Caribbean, to Barbados, Jamaica, or Saint-Domingue, now known as Haiti.

Sugar proved to be a deadly industry. Work conditions were backbreaking and dangerous: the cutting of the cane, then the fast turnaround time needed to process the cut cane into sugar, the furious heat of the so-called boiling houses where the sugar was processed. Most slaves were simply worked to death, often in about 10 years, and then replaced with new human cargo from Africa.

Of the rest of the slave trade, about 40 percent of the slaves were shipped to Brazil. North America actually received only some 5 percent of the total traffic, and actually saw a natural increase in the African population, which was unusual. As terrible as the conditions of slavery were in North America, the ones in the Caribbean were even worse, and fatal. All of this reached its peak in the 1790s.

Up to this point, there had been isolated criticisms of slavery, but a general condemnation of slavery is a recent sentiment, in relative terms. The Enlightenment, for instance, criticized many ancient institutions, including slavery. Often, these institutions were faulted for their irrationality and lack of utility. But Enlightenment criticism had not been consistent. The English philosopher John Locke, for instance, wrote powerfully about inalienable natural rights, and voluntarily social contracts, but he also was an investor in the Royal African Company.

But many thinkers did speak out against slavery along Enlightenment lines. To remember an earlier lecture, where we considered Diderot's *Encyclopédie*, that text condemned slavery as a violation of natural law, and it said if slavery was not a crime, then anything at all could be justified. The British Enlightenment economist Adam Smith saw slavery as less efficient, less profitable than free labor and free trade. The American Enlightenment *philosophe* Benjamin Franklin had also been an abolitionist.

It was, however, religion that produced the beginnings of a truly mass mobilization against slavery. In particular, this involved the Quakers, the Religious Society of Friends, as they called themselves. This group, which had been a persecuted minority in England, broke with the institutionalized churches to gather in meetings of their own. The Quakers saw a fundamental equality in all people because of the immediate relationship that each could have with the Divine, in a priesthood of all believers. It was from these beliefs that the Quakers, both in England and in the American colonies where many of them immigrated for a greater exercise of religious freedom, they spoke out against slavery. As early as 1688, Quakers in Germantown,

Pennsylvania, condemned slavery and the slave trade. By the 1760s, Quakers in Britain and in America were refusing to accept slave traders into their own faith communities. In Philadelphia in 1775, Quakers founded the world's first antislavery society.

It was around the same time in England that Quakers began to cooperate with Evangelicals within the Church of England, with Methodists and with Baptists, to together work against the slave trade. In 1772, a legal case in Britain had prohibited slavery in the British Isles, so there were no slaves in Britain at the time, but these activists were not content and had a global outlook. The result of this movement was a powerful partnership. It included Thomas Clarkson, a tireless organizer; the politician William Wilberforce in Parliament; and the African Olaudah Equiano, a former slave who had bought his freedom and had published a bestselling searing autobiography about his experiences.

The first meetings of this group, which called itself The Society for Effecting the Abolition of the Slave Trade, took place in a printing shop and bookstore in London in 1787 (this again underlines what we've seen before: the effect of printing as a means of spreading the message). This group decided to concentrate first on the slave trade, rather than working on banning all slavery at once, even though ultimately this is what most of them wanted to see. In Britain, "abolition" referred to the ending of the slave trade. This makes the British usage a little bit different from how we use the word "abolition" in American English to mean the abolition of slavery. Slavery itself seemed to these activists too socially and economically entrenched to be overthrown all at once, so their hope was that by ending the trade, this would lead to the gradual extinction of the practice as a whole.

The key organizer, Thomas Clarkson, had won an essay prize at University of Cambridge on the question of whether slavery was lawful. This had been just a theoretical, rhetorical exercise, but when he'd written his essay, he became obsessed with this question. Increasingly he felt that that someone should do something about this.

Then with a shock, he realized he was the one. His friends called him a "moral steam engine." Clarkson tirelessly travelled the country, collecting information on the slave trade, gathering witnesses to testify in parliamentary investigations. The movement's political voice was William Wilberforce, a man who was tiny physically, but who had a matchless, compelling voice and rhetoric. He was a real political insider who had become converted to Evangelical faith and now advanced the legal cause of abolition in Parliament.

There was also an unlikely recruit to the movement: a former slave captain, John Newton, who after four slave voyages had experienced a religious change of heart, and became a minister, and then a famous preacher. In 1772, Newton wrote the most famous Christian hymn in English, "Amazing Grace," which praises the power of repentance. But it actually took him many more years afterwards to finally denounce his past as a slaver. He noted the moral effects on those who engaged in the trade; quite apart from its sinfulness, he noted a dreadful hardening of hearts on the part of those who participated in the trade.

Because many of the members of this movement were Quakers, and because many Quakers in turn were merchants, this movement was itself very businesslike, efficient, and innovative in its tactics. Activists worked to gather the dreadful facts of the slave trade, and let those facts speak for themselves. They printed masses of pamphlets in many languages, to convince an international audience. In France, the marquis de Lafayette, for instance, helped start a society there for the same aims, entitled the "Society of the Friends of the Blacks."

They pioneered fundraising letters by direct appeal. The abolitionists also made great use of visual argument. Here is the key example: One activist was the manufacturer of china, Josiah Wedgwood, who became official Potter to the Queen. His Wedgwood china, with its innovative product lines and marketing, remains famous and desired today, and the firm, that was founded in 1759, is still active today. For the cause, Wedgwood used his talents to create an image for a medallion that became an icon. It showed a kneeling African in chains, asking the question, "Am I not a man and a brother?" This image was soon everywhere—on pottery, on bracelets, on hairpins, on cufflinks, on snuffboxes. Benjamin Franklin actually praised this image as equal to the best pamphlet in the world in terms of changing minds.

Another key winning tactic was using the role of women. Women spoke up in public meetings on the topic, which was unusual at the time. Women were also key activists in monster petition drives, huge petitions that were organized to appeal to Parliament. The act of signing a petition was, in a subtle way, very democratizing, because people were urged to sign up regardless of what their class was, regardless of whether they were men or women, and regardless of whether they currently had the right to vote or not (remember at this stage, even very few British men had the right to vote).

Women also organized the powerful boycott of sugar from 1791, to protest the slave origins of this commodity, the largest British import. The name "boycott" would actually be invented later, but this was an effective early example. It's estimated that in Britain, half a million people took part, and women, as the organizers of their households, are the ones who made it happen.

Soon society at large was inflamed with this cause. The message appeared in debates, newspapers, and even in poems. In Parliament, Wilberforce pushed the cause. His first speech against the trade was given in 1789, and Edmund Burke, the parliamentarian, called it one of the greatest speeches of all time. Parliamentary committees investigated the details of the slave trade in hearings, putting powerful facts on record.

The facts were damning, and in particular one image, which you've probably seen, because it's reproduced in almost every history textbook about slavery. It is a print of the inside of one ship, a ship called the *Brookes*, owned by a Liverpool family with that same last name. It was a slave ship that transported people from the Gold Coast in Africa to Jamaica. This famous diagram gave front, side, and top cutaway views of the inside, showing the inhuman crowding on the ship. In their care not to be accused of exaggerating, the committee that prepared this document even showed fewer slaves in their illustration than were sometimes carried by the ship. They showed 482 people crammed in the hold, not the over 700 who sometimes were forced into it. That diagram had an electric effect, and to this day, it's one of the most reproduced political images ever.

In Parliament, pro-slavery forces, organized as the West Indian Lobby, rallied and advanced some really ludicrous arguments in favor of continuing the institution. But in spite of all of the moral engagement, the proposed bills failed again and again; legislation was blocked by the House of Lords.

But consciences in society had been mobilized, and at long last Parliament did pass, in the year 1807, a ban on the slave trade, which was declared a form of piracy. This legislation did damage to the British economy, and some historians have even called it an act of "econocide,"—that's to say, doing damage to oneself, and one's economic resources—but the moral argument trumped these economic considerations. Soon after, the United States, the Netherlands, and France also prohibited the importation of slaves, but it would take another quarter century until the goal of freeing of slaves was achieved.

In the meantime, the British government took action. This action intersected with a crucial political fact of the times: the supremacy of the Royal Navy. At this point, Britain truly ruled the waves as the superpower of its day, and it saw its role as an international policeman to ensure the world order that came after the quarter century of war with revolutionary France and with Napoleon. For the next decades after 1807, even during those years when Britain was at war against Napoleon, Royal Navy ships patrolled the slave ship routes to stop the trade. At one point, a third of British Navy ships were involved in this exercise. They captured many, but not all slave ships. Some slave ships, when they were pursued by the British Navy, would actually throw their captives overboard as a way of destroying the evidence. The Royal Navy did manage to release some 116,000 slaves, but this was only part of the continuing slave trade; even after 1807, some three million more Africans were shipped, mostly from Africa to Cuba and Brazil. Many liberated slaves were set down in Sierra Leone, which became a British colony in Africa.

The British movement against slavery actually slowed down in the next decades; it seemed to run out of energy, and some activists became content to be gradualist in their hopes, until a new generation of women activists rose up to reenergize the movement and to demand immediate abolition of slavery everywhere in the British Empire.

Slave uprisings in Haiti and Jamaica also helped convince many that emancipation had to come. This finally led to the legislation in Parliament in 1833, which decreed the freeing of some 800,000 slaves in the British Empire, mainly in the Caribbean islands. That emancipation came in stages, and the owners of slaves were promised compensation, even though ex-slaves got none. But at long last, on August 1, 1838, the slaves were finally free. At the ground level, even if economic exploitation still continued, the former slaves must have experienced the moral difference in status, from slave to free; this must have felt profound.

It also needs to be noted that this does not end the story, or the crime of slavery indeed was not ended all at once. Ex-slaves continued to labor in hard conditions on plantations, but at least without the old shackles, without the legal status of slavery. Slavery however did continue elsewhere in the Americas. American abolitionists, black as well as white, often traveled to Britain and cooperated in a transatlantic movement for abolition. Figures included William Lloyd Garrison and the former slave Frederick Douglass. But it would take the U.S. Civil War, which exacted some 750,000 lives, to finally free the slaves in the United States. The last open slave market in the Americas, in Havana, Cuba, was finally shut down in 1869. Cuba stopped exporting slaves in 1870, due to naval interdiction by the United States and Britain, and abolished slavery in 1886. Finally, in 1888, slavery was also at last abolished in Brazil.

I wish that we could conclude right there, but that's not possible either. Slavery continues today, in many forms of involuntary labor, on many continents, and under new names. Today, for instance, we would speak of it as "trafficking," especially in women and children. It is estimated that more than 20 million people are in servitude today worldwide, so this anguish goes on.

But in the fight against this injustice, this legal abolition of the slave trade and then of slavery was a powerful turning point. That August night in 1838 brought great joy and comfort to the liberated Africans and left a lasting legacy. It created a new model for social mobilization, with key tactics and tools invented by the abolitionists, which could later be used by other movements, spearheaded by ordinary people, including today, whether for human rights, or environmentalist concerns, or countless other causes.

In this lecture, we examined the use of legal means and state power to eradicate an evil, but by a terrible irony, at almost the same time, legal means and state power were being used to promote a deadly drug trade, as a result of the British Opium War against the Chinese Empire, which we'll examine in our next lecture.

1839—The Opium War in China
Lecture 12

W hen we hear of a drug war, we usually think of a government fighting against smugglers or dealers in drugs, but can you imagine a world power fighting a war against another government in order to open it to the drug trade? That's what happened in the Opium War of 1839, when British forces assaulted the Chinese Empire, imposing the drug trade from outside. China, like so many other countries around the world, now confronted the full power of European imperialism. This was a traumatic reversal for China, which could no longer consider itself supreme or even sovereign. But it also proved to be a world turning point, revealing the destructive power of imperialism as an international force.

Tea Trade with China

- Tea first arrived in Britain from China around 1645. Initially, it was a luxury that only the richest in the royal court could afford, but by 1750, it was popular among the middle classes, and by 1800, it was a craze that extended throughout society.

- From 1700, the increasingly globalized economy was based on such commodities as sugar, cotton, coffee, and tea. By trading in large quantities of these, the British East India Company (EIC) had outcompeted its earlier rival, the Dutch East India Company and its spice monopolies.

- The EIC made huge profits by transporting large quantities of tea, and the royal treasury loved the trade, imposing a 100 percent import duty on tea. In the 1790s, the EIC was shipping 23 million pounds of tea every year to Britain from China.

- The EIC traded with China for tea through one open trading port, Canton. Foreign merchants were not allowed permanent residence but confined to the trading station, and they had to leave once the five-month trading season was completed, unable to return until the following year This policy spoke volumes about the structure of China under the Qing dynasty, a mighty empire of more than 300 million people.

- o From 1644, the Manchus from Manchuria had conquered China, displacing the Ming dynasty. But after conquering China, the Manchus found that China conquered them—they were absorbed into Chinese civilization.

- Under their dynamic rule, China expanded, adding Turkistan, Burma, and Tibet and moving into Nepal. The Manchu Qing dynasty limited foreign trade to the Portuguese station at Macau and to Canton, today known as Guangzhou. As in earlier ages, trade was understood as tribute from the far-flung parts of the less civilized world. As the EIC sought to trade with China to buy tea, a major problem arose. The British (and other Europeans) had little that China wanted. British products that were sent to impress the Chinese, such as carriages, cannon, and Wedgwood pottery, were rejected by the Manchu emperor. The EIC had no choice but to pay for tea with silver.

- Then it dawned on officials of the EIC that the company could supply one product that was in demand in China: opium, grown in the territories the EIC ruled in Bengal.

The Opium Trade in China
- The opium poppy had long been known in the classical world and was used as a remedy against pain and fever. If abused, it brought hallucinations and respiratory failure.

- Opium had also been known in China since the 8th century A.D. Unlike in Europe, however, by the 19th century, opium users in China were smoking it rather than taking it in smaller doses.

- The emperor declared the opium trade illegal in 1729, 1796, 1799, and again in 1800. Disregarding Chinese laws, the EIC, battling for its existence against calls to end royal monopolies, increased its trade in opium. On the China coast, the EIC sold opium to private

Clipper ships carried both tea and opium and were built for speed, with narrow hulls and huge sails.

dealers, who then sold it to local smugglers. American merchants were involved, as well.

- Eventually, the EIC sent new steamboats on its shipping routes from India, adding the power of the Industrial Revolution. On the receiving end, it is estimated that in China, half of men and a quarter of women were users of opium, although not all were addicted.

- As a result, the balance of trade with China reversed. Instead of silver flooding into China to pay for tea and silks, by the 1830s, Chinese silver was flooding out to pay for opium. At this point, in the late 1830s, more than 30,000 chests were brought in, each containing some 150 pounds of opium. This was a different kind of triangular trade, encompassing Britain, India, and China.

Call for Dynastic Reform
- The Chinese Empire, apparently monolithic and self-sufficient, was internally torn by tensions between the Manchu ruling class and

the masses of Chinese subjects, repeated revolts, and a governing apparatus beset with inefficiencies and corrupt officials.

- A reform movement touched off a crisis. A group of Confucian scholars, calling themselves the Spring Purification Circle, argued that renewal was needed, lest the Qing lose the mandate of heaven. Increasingly, opium seemed to be a symbol of things going wrong. It sapped the energy of the state, instilled lassitude and laziness, and drained away the vigor of a virtuous ruling elite.

- Emperor Daoguang, who had been an opium smoker himself, now acted. In 1839, he put Commissioner Lin Zexu in charge of Canton, where the Chinese traded with foreigners.
  - o Lin was a follower of the Spring Purification Circle and had a reputation for competence and dynamism.

  - o He announced a simple plan for fighting opium: execute the dealers and give users a one-year suspended death sentence so that they could kick the habit. If they did not, they were to be beheaded.

- Next, Commissioner Lin demanded that British merchants turn over their opium stores to him. But if these were confiscated, the dealers would be ruined.
  - o The British superintendent of trade in Canton was Captain Charles Elliot, a former royal navy officer. He was personally opposed to opium but also charged with protecting British economic interests.

  - o Elliot convinced the merchants to give 1,700 tons of opium to Lin, promising that they would be compensated. Lin had the opium destroyed. After more tension with the British mercantile community, Lin cut off their supplies of food and water.

  - o Elliot sent British ships with an ultimatum to Lin, and when it was refused, the British ships fired on Chinese war junks.

Gunboat Diplomacy

- The British government dispatched gunboats to Canton, including the *Nemesis*, the first oceangoing steam warship. Built by the EIC, it was 184 feet long, weighed 660 tons, was powered by two engines, and was heavily armed.

  o The role of the *Nemesis* points toward something dreadful that lay in the future: the destructive power of industrial warfare, to be fully revealed in the coming world wars.

  o The *Nemesis* blasted Chinese coastal forts at the Pearl River and sank Chinese war junks that were about half its size. This was the advent of what we still today call "gunboat diplomacy," in which technologically advanced firepower deployed by imperial powers would redraw the world map.

- Given the British advance, which eventually captured Shanghai, the emperor dismissed his reformist officials and acknowledged defeat. China signed the Treaty of Nanjing in 1842. The treaty did not mention opium, although the continued trade was the heart of the matter.

  o The treaty opened more "treaty ports" to Britain, allowed British and other merchants to live within Canton rather than being quarantined outside it, and ceded to the British the island of Hong Kong, which became a massive trading and military outpost of the British.

  o Crucially, the treaty also formalized the "extraterritoriality" of these bases: Foreigners were not to be subject to Chinese courts. Instead, they were subject to the jurisdiction of the imperialist powers. Other powers soon gained the same concessions.

  o Adding insult to injury, China was required to pay the costs of the war and to compensate for the opium destroyed by Commissioner Lin.

- To celebrate this victory, a Chinese war junk was brought to Britain for the Great Exhibition of 1851, although not everyone in

Britain was celebrating. Some condemned this war for an immoral trade, and others decried the hypocrisy of celebrating one's own sovereignty while denying that equality to other states.

The Second Opium War

- With the second Opium War, there would soon be more to question and condemn. British officials in the treaty ports had been looking for a pretext to revise the earlier agreements. They found it in the story of a ship named the *Arrow*, which was owned and run by Chinese smugglers and pirates but had been registered as British.

- Even though its registration had lapsed, it still flew the British flag when Chinese authorities seized it in 1856. The British government sent another expeditionary force, joined by a French force, and they quickly occupied Canton.

- The following treaty of 1858 legalized the import of opium, opened 10 more treaty ports, and allowed Europeans, including missionaries, to travel into the interior of China.

- When the emperor tried to back out of the treaty, an Anglo-French expedition battered its way to Beijing in October 1860 and burned the imperial Summer Palace. The Chinese emperor backed down, making further concessions and paying further indemnities to secure peace.

Crisis and Humiliation in China

- This was a time of crisis for China, in which the foreign depredations were but one part. An even greater challenge to the imperial throne came from the Taiping Rebellion, which raged from 1851 to 1864.

- Such crises were shattering to Chinese society and prompted young intellectuals to engage in what they called the "self-strengthening movement." The problem they would confront was the same as countless others among peoples subjected to imperialism: how to fight back and throw off outside control to achieve sovereignty.

- In 1874, in the wake of an uprising in India, the EIC was finally dissolved, but China's humiliations continued. In 1894, China was defeated by Japan in a war over Korea. When Chinese nationalists rose up against foreigners in the Boxer Rebellion in 1900, an international military force arrived in Beijing and crushed the movement with massive violence.

- The Opium Wars made clear the power of imperialism, especially when reinforced by the Industrial Revolution. By 1914, three-quarters of the globe had been seized by European powers, and the British Empire loomed above them all. These wars, and many others, swelled the self-confidence of European and other imperialist states but disguised for a time the great internal weaknesses of imperialism.

- From the perspective of China and other societies that bore the brunt of the violence, this turning point was psychologically devastating. An earlier sense of superiority and centrality in the world was replaced by a sense of weakness and humiliation, reactions that continue to echo in world politics to this day.

Suggested Reading

Bernstein, *A Splendid Exchange*.

Lawson, *The East India Company*.

Lovell, *The Opium War*.

Robins, *The Corporation That Changed the World*.

Questions to Consider

1. Did the Manchu emperors pursue the best policies to combat the opium trade, or should they have done something differently?

2. How could British society, while abolishing the slave trade, countenance these drug wars?

1839—The Opium War in China
Lecture 12—Transcript

In this lecture, we will examine a turning point involving an international drug war. When we hear of a drug war, we usually think of a government fighting against smugglers, dealers in drugs, or "narcoterrorism." But can you imagine the mightiest world power of its day fighting a war against another government in order to *open* it to the drug trade?

This is what happened in the Opium War of 1839, when British forces assaulted the Chinese Empire, imposing the drug trade from outside. Ironically, all this came just a year after the abolition of slavery in the British Empire. China, and then later Japan, like so many other countries around the world, were now confronted with the full power of European imperialism. For China, this was a true turning point.

Earlier, at the start of the modern period, China had seen itself as the central power of civilization, something which the voyages of Zheng He symbolically charted back in the 1430s. Now China found itself subjected. This was a hugely traumatic reversal. All at once, the self-understanding of being a universal empire was completely overthrown. Instead of being supreme, or even sovereign, China was humiliated by being forced to sign treaties that demonstrated its unequal status in international relations.

More than a century of turmoil followed. But this also proved to be a world turning point, because it showed the authority and destructive power of imperialism as an international force in the 19th century, a century which otherwise prided itself on its progress and civilization. How had it come to this?

It actually all started with tea, just like the American Revolution we discussed in a previous lecture. Tea, of course, is a much milder stimulant than opium, but it held Europeans, and especially the British, in thrall! Tea first arrived in Britain from China around 1645. Initially it was an unbelievable luxury that only the richest in the royal court could afford. A century later by 1750 it was tremendously popular among the middle classes. By 1800, it was a craze which extended throughout society. Think of all the tea culture that has evolved around the drink: the British afternoon tea ritual, the ever-present offer of a "cuppa."

Exotic Eastern drinks also deserved exotic Eastern dishes to be served out of, especially the famed thin, translucent and graceful china, that is to say, Chinese porcelain. In the Golden Age of the Dutch, Delftware, instantly recognizable for its blue and white colors, was a local homegrown substitute for the astronomically expensive porcelain that was imported from China. In England, the Wedgwood brand (still manufactured and sold today) had been founded in 1759 by Josiah Wedgwood, potter to the Queen, who you'll remember also was active in the abolition movement, and had produced its iconic image of a slave appealing for human rights. Wedgwood combined classical styles with the mechanized productivity of the new Industrial Revolution, and in the process he made what had once been a luxury available to ever-broader parts of society.

The oceans of tea that were drunk from such teacups were also sweetened with sugar from the plantations of Barbados and Jamaica, unless you were one of those abolitionists boycotting the sugar product. Here we observe already a global economy in action, bringing together in England tea from China with sweetener from the Americas. From 1700, the increasingly globalized economy was a traffic in commodities that had once been luxuries, but now had come to seem necessities. These included sugar, cotton, coffee, and especially tea. By trading in vast quantities of these, the British East India Company had out-competed its earlier rival, the Dutch East India Company and its earlier spice monopolies.

These commodities were hard, or in fact impossible to monopolize effectively. The EIC created special ships for their tea trade, great clippers that were built for speed, outfitted with custom-made chests that sealed in all of those fragrant tea leaves for the long sea journeys. Even as prices for tea dropped, the EIC was positioned to make huge profits by transporting ever-larger quantities, an economy of scale.

The British royal treasury loved it, imposing a 100 percent import duty on tea. As we saw in our lecture on the American Revolution, this sort of an import duty was a great incentive to smuggling, and it was attempts by the crown to crack down on the smuggling that led to the Boston Tea Party. In the 1790s, the EIC was doing a vast business: It was shipping 23 million pounds of tea every year to Britain from China.

The British East India Company traded with China for tea through the one open trading port, Canton. Foreign merchants were not allowed permanent residence, but they were confined to this one trading station, and then they had to leave it once the five-month trading season was completed, until next year! This policy, enforced on trade, spoke volumes about the structure of China under the Qing dynasty, a mighty empire of more than 300 million people.

From 1644, around the time of the Peace of Westphalia in Europe which we discussed in a previous lecture, the Manchus from Manchuria had conquered China. They displaced the Ming dynasty which had sponsored the voyages of Zheng He way back in the 1400s, at the start of our course. But after they conquered China, the Manchus found that China conquered them: Even though the Manchus were a distinct nomadic warrior people like the Mongols, they were soon absorbed into Chinese civilization.

Under their dynamic rule, China expanded, adding Turkestan, Burma, Tibet, and moving into Nepal. The Manchu Qing dynasty limited foreign trade to the Portuguese station at Macau and to Canton, today known as Guangzhou. As in earlier ages, trade was understood as a form of tribute from the far-flung parts of the less-civilized world converging on China.

As during the Ming dynasty, Chinese rulers claimed to hold the Mandate of Heaven, and the emperor was known as the "Son of Heaven." This exalted status was confirmed in diplomatic rituals, the kowtows or formal prostrations of foreign dignitaries who bowed to the emperor, and also in the tremendous cultivation of brilliant scholars, artists, and government officials.

As the EIC sought to trade with China to buy all of that tea, a major problem arose. The British (and other Europeans) it turns out, had little that China actually wanted. The Europeans had some success with selling clocks or music boxes as sort of exotic goods or curiosities, but you could only export so many of these.

In 1793, the British made an official request for a permanent trade representative to be based in Beijing, to increase trade. They also sent British products that they hoped would impress the emperor. This included carriages, cannon, a hot-air balloon, and even some Wedgwood china pottery. The Chinese response to this trade mission and its request was tremendously revealing.

The Manchu emperor replied in these terms: "Our Celestial Empire possesses all things in prolific abundance and lacks no product within its borders. There was therefore no need to import the manufactures of outside barbarians in exchange for our produce. But as the tea, silk and porcelain which the Celestial Empire produces are absolute necessities to European nations and to yourselves, we have permitted, as a signal mark of our favour, that foreign companies should be established at Canton, so that your wants may be supplied and your country thus participate in our beneficence." Thus, the EIC had no choice but to rely on paying with silver for tea. This was another one of those great global trade currents we've talked about: a vast flow of silver went from the mines of Mexico, into international trade, and thence to China to pay for tea.

It was at this point that it dawned on officials of the Honourable Company that actually there was one product that was in demand in China which they could supply. That was opium, grown in the territories that the EIC ruled in Bengal in India. The opium poppy, known by its Latin name as *Papaver somniferum*, the "sleep bringer," had long been known in the classical world: If cut, the buds of the poppy bled out tears of a narcotic substance, which congealed into cakes and made a powerful drug.

Opium was a remedy against pain and fever; it brought relief. It was chewed in India and drunk in liquid form in England, as laudanum. If abused (it was very addictive), it could bring dreams, visions, and respiratory failure. Due to this recognition of its power, someone like Karl Marx would later denounce religion as the "opiate of the masses," using this powerful image.

Opium's power attracted Romantic poets, like Samuel Taylor Coleridge, who fell into dreams of the Orient when under the influence of opium. These were dreams like those that had possessed Columbus back in 1492. He focused on the realms which Marco Polo had once travelled in. Under the influence, Coleridge composed an entire poem in 1797, probably the most famous drug-induced work of art. This poem began, "In Xanadu did Kubla Khan / A stately pleasure dome decree."

Coleridge's trance, however, as he was writing this poem, was interrupted by a knock at his door, and the poem's alleged perfection was shattered. But the poem contained mysterious and prophetic words. Coleridge wrote in his opiated dream that "Kubla heard from far / Ancestral voices prophesying war!" This turned out to be exactly true: Opium did lead to war.

Opium had been known long before in China, already in the 8th century A.D. Unlike in Europe, however, by the 19th century, Chinese opium users were smoking opium, rather than taking it in smaller doses. This practice of smoking opium is actually tied in with the Columbian exchange, which we discussed in an earlier lecture, especially the introduction of tobacco. Tobacco mixed with opium was probably first traded by the Dutch in Taiwan, where they had a trading post in the 1660s. Later, Chinese users shifted to simply smoking opium on its own, in special long pipes. This way of ingesting opium made it even more potent and addictive. The Chinese emperor declared the opium trade illegal in 1729, in 1796, in 1799, and then again in 1800. As you could see, it wasn't working.

Disregarding Chinese laws, the EIC increased its trade in opium because it felt that its very existence as a company was embattled. Back in Britain at this point, powerful voices like Adam Smith were calling for free trade, a maximum of capitalist activity without artificial barriers of import and export taxes, or of royal monopolies. Adam Smith promised that this would be a benefit to producers, merchants, and consumers alike. As such ideas gained steam, the EIC lost its monopoly on trade in India in 1813, but it still retained a monopoly on China trade, until 1833. For now, opium was a great boon to the EIC. The company grew opium in its Bengal plantations in India, then shipped it eastwards, but once it arrived in China, they disavowed it, to create a deniability, however weak.

Once on the China coast, the EIC ships sold the opium to private dealers, who then sold it in turn to local smugglers. Vast fortunes were made by dealers like Jardine, Matheson & Co., which is a firm still thriving today (but no longer dealing in opium). American merchants were involved as well. Clipper ships carried this trade, vessels built for tremendous speed, with narrow hulls and huge sails. Of these, the Cutty Sark, in dry dock in Greenwich, London, can still be viewed today. Eventually, the EIC sent new steamboats on these routes, adding the power of the Industrial Revolution to the process.

On the receiving end, it's estimated that in China, about half of men and a quarter of women were users of opium. Not all of them were addicted, but it still gives us a sense of the big scale of this traffic. As a result, the balance of trade with China actually reversed. Instead of silver flooding into China to pay for tea and silks and other exports, by the 1830s, Chinese silver was flooding out to pay for opium. At this point, in the late 1830s, more than 30,000 chests of opium were brought in, each containing some 150 pounds of the drug. This was a different kind of triangular trade, encompassing Britain, India, and China.

Back in 1433, when the Ming empire called off Admiral Zheng He's journeys, it was the outcome of a bureaucratic struggle within the state. That's what happened in this case too. The events that led to the Opium War involved bureaucratic infighting, and actually attempts at reform. The Chinese Empire, apparently monolithic and seemingly self-sufficient, was actually internally torn by tensions between the Manchu ruling class and the masses of Chinese subjects, repeated revolts, and a governing apparatus that really had lots of inefficiencies and corrupt officials.

To correct all this, a reform movement arose, which touched off a crisis. A group of Confucian scholars calling themselves by the poetic name, the Spring Purification Circle, argued that renewal was needed, because otherwise the Qing would lose the Mandate of Heaven. Increasingly, it was opium that seemed to be a central symbol of things that were going wrong in

China. It sapped the energy of the state. It produced lassitude and laziness, and it drained away the vigor of what should be a virtuous ruling elite. The emperor Daoguang, who actually had earlier been an opium smoker himself, now acted. In 1839, he put Commissioner Lin Zexu in charge of Canton, which was where the Chinese traded with foreigners.

Lin was a follower of the Spring Purification Circle and had a reputation as an official who was competent and dynamic. He now announced vast and simple plans for fighting opium: Execute the dealers. Give users a one-year suspended death sentence, so they could kick the habit in one year and if they did not, they'd have their heads cut off.

Lin also wrote a very brisk and businesslike letter to Queen Victoria, of Great Britain. In it, he upbraided her for the sheer hypocrisy of selling a drug in foreign lands which he said was illegal in her own kingdom (Lin was actually wrong about this—as we saw, it was legal and used in Great Britain). Lin finished his letter by ordering the Queen to acknowledge receipt and to report back to him on what she was doing to stop the opium trade. Given the Victorian sensibilities of Queen Victoria, it's probably just as well that she never got this forceful letter.

Next, Commissioner Lin demanded that the British merchants in China turn over their opium stores to him. If these were confiscated, the dealers understood they would lose fortunes; they would be ruined. The British superintendent of trade in Canton got involved. He was Captain Charles Elliot, a former Royal Navy officer, who actually earlier had been part of the West Africa squadron that patrolled those waters to stop the slave trade, as we saw in an earlier lecture. Elliot was personally opposed to the use of opium, and trade in opium, but he was also charged with protecting British economic interests. His next bureaucratic move was decisive.

Elliot convinced the British merchants to give the 1,700 tons of opium that they had to Lin, promising that the merchants would be compensated. Lin had all of this opium destroyed at the coast, in a dramatic scene as the drug was trampled underfoot in special trenches and then sluiced out into the sea, to cleanse China of this pollution. After tension grew with the British mercantile community, Lin soon cut off their supplies of food and water.

Elliot now had British ships sent in with an ultimatum to Lin, and when that ultimatum was refused, British ships fired on Chinese war junks. War had broken out.

The British government dispatched gunboats and British marines, all of which arrived at Canton. Among these was a tool of war which went on to demonstrate the power of European imperialism, especially when supercharged with the advances being made in the Industrial Revolution. In the Industrial Revolution, steam engines had multiplied the power of technology. This tool of war, fittingly, was a steamboat called the *Nemesis*. It was an iron steamboat, the first oceangoing steam warship, built by the EIC. It was 184 feet long; it weighed 660 tons; it was powered by two mighty engines; and it was heavily armed. Because of its shallow draft and engines, it could actually chug right up to the coastal cities and fortifications, even if the winds were blowing in the opposite direction. The role of this warship, the *Nemesis*, points toward something dreadful that lay in the future: the destructive power of industrial warfare, that would be fully revealed in World War I and World War II, when the force of industry and technology would completely overshadow the human element, no matter how heroic or determined.

In quick order, the *Nemesis* blasted the Chinese coastal forts at the Pearl River, and sank Chinese war junks that were about half its size. The Chinese had nothing comparable. This was the advent of what we still today call gunboat diplomacy, in which technologically advanced firepower deployed by imperialist powers could redraw the world map.

Given the British advance, which eventually captured Shanghai, the emperor dismissed his reformist officials and acknowledged defeat. China signed the Treaty of Nanjing in1842. Quite circumspectly, this treaty never actually mentioned opium, but everyone understood the continued trade in opium was really the heart of the matter. The treaty opened more treaty ports to Britain (Shanghai, Amoy, Foochow, and the island of Ningbo). It also allowed British and other merchants to live within Canton rather than being quarantined outside it, and also ceded to the British the island of Hong Kong at the mouth of the Pearl River, with a natural harbor that was wonderful for trade. Hong Kong grew into a massive trading and military outpost of the British, and was only returned to China in 1997.

Crucially, this treaty also formalized what was called the extraterritoriality of these bases: Foreigners were not to be subject to Chinese courts. Instead, they were to be subject to the jurisdiction of the imperialist powers. In a word, the sort of sovereignty that had been established increasingly through the Peace of Westphalia was to be denied to China. Other European powers soon gained the same concessions. Adding insult to injury, China was required to pay the costs of the war, and to compensate for all that opium that had been destroyed by Commissioner Lin.

To celebrate this victory, an entire Chinese war junk was brought to Britain for the Great Exhibition of 1851 to be shown off. This was ironic: It was brought as a spoil of war, but think back—if Zheng He's voyages of the 1430s had continued, that junk might have come as a conqueror.

It should be noted, as a testimony to Victorian reformist zeal, that not everybody in Britain celebrated this as a victory. Some condemned this war as an outcome of immoral trade. They decried the hypocrisy in celebrating your own sovereignty while denying that equality to other states. As one anti-opium crusader declared, "We stand convicted before the nations of the world, as well as before an Omniscient Deity … as a government and people actively and legally engaged in the perpetration of murder and desolation … We are all involved in the guilt, and participants, even by our silence, in a sin."

There would shortly be more to question and condemn, because there followed a second Opium War. British officials in the so-called treaty ports had in fact been looking for a long time for a pretext to revise the earlier agreements. They found the pretext in the story of a ship named *The Arrow*, which was owned and run by Chinese smugglers and pirates, but had been registered officially as a British ship. Even though its British registration had lapsed, it still flew the British flag when Chinese authorities seized it in 1856. The British government then sent another expeditionary force, and it was joined by a French force which had been sent because of the execution of a French missionary. This force quickly occupied Canton.

The following treaty of 1858 officially legalized the import of opium. It opened 10 more treaty ports and allowed Europeans, especially missionaries, to travel into the interior of China, which they hadn't been allowed before. When Emperor Xianfeng had second thoughts and tried to back out of the treaty he'd just signed, an Anglo-French expedition actually battered its way into Beijing in October 1860, and just to teach the emperor a lesson, burned his stately pleasure dome, the imperial Summer Palace.

Along with the artworks and furnishings that they looted, British officers also grabbed an imperial Pekinese dog, and gave that dog to Queen Victoria of Britain as a present. The dog was given the apt name "Looty," as in loot and pillage. Battered, the Chinese emperor backed down, and made further concessions and further indemnities were paid, to secure peace.

This was clearly a time of crisis for China, in which the foreign depredations were just one part of a larger emergency situation. An even greater challenge to the imperial throne came from the Taiping Rebellion, which raged from 1851 to 1864. The Taiping Rebellion was a massive revolt against Manchu rule, led by a religious visionary who claimed that he was Jesus Christ's younger brother, and called upon to reform society. This revolt was finally suppressed in 1864, and the staggering death toll is estimated at 20 million or more, completely surpassing the bloody losses of the American Civil War at the same time.

Such crises were shattering to Chinese society, and prompted young Chinese intellectuals to engage in what they called the self-strengthening movement. The problem they would confront was the same as countless others among peoples subjected to Western imperialism: how to fight back and throw off outside control—how to achieve sovereignty.

The greatest signal success in this challenging task came in Japan. Between the two Opium Wars in China, it seemed at first that Japan would be subjected to the same treatment as China had received. Instead, Japan created its own modernity, borrowing Western technology and ideas. In a coming lecture, we'll trace how Japanese success was another global turning point.

Another symptom of the inner stresses and latent weaknesses within imperialism came from the heart of the British Empire in India, in 1857. There, local troops recruited by the EIC in India, the so-called sepoys, rose up in massive revolt, which started to grow into a larger uprising throughout the country. This has been called the Indian Mutiny, or by some, The First War of Indian Independence. British control was restored only with difficulty and massive bloodshed. One conclusion that was drawn from this experience was that Indian territories that had been run by the EIC now had to come under direct British government control. Thus, 258 years of Company rule in India were ended. The company itself was finally dissolved in 1874. Think about it: The East India Company had existed for 274 years; that's longer than many other states or kingdoms.

But even if the East India Company was gone, China's humiliations continued. In 1894, China was defeated by Japan, in a war over Korea. When Chinese nationalists rose up against foreigners in the so-called Boxer Rebellion in 1900, an international military force arrived in Beijing, including Britain, France, Japan, Russia, Italy, Austria-Hungary, Germany, and the United States. This expeditionary force crushed the Chinese movement with massive violence. This proved that even if the imperialist powers competed against one another, they could cooperate to repress resistance.

What were the long-term consequences of this turning point? The Opium Wars made vividly clear the massive power of imperialism, especially when reinforced by the Industrial Revolution. By 1914, three-quarters of the globe were seized by European powers, and the British Empire loomed above them all, an "empire on which the sun never set," with a quarter of the world's people and land. These wars, and many others, swelled the self-confidence of European and other imperialist states, but disguised for a time the great internal weaknesses of imperialism.

From the perspective of China and other societies that had to bear the brunt of this violence, this turning point was psychologically devastating. An earlier civilizational sense of superiority and centrality in the world was with abrupt speed replaced by a sense of weakness and humiliation. These reactions continue to echo in world politics down to the present day, a consequence of imperialism.

But at just this time, the confident 19th century of progress, there arose another challenge, an intellectual challenge: The ideas of Darwin probed the origins of the human race, what it meant to be human. This challenge we'll consider in our next lecture.

1859—Darwin and the *Origin of Species*
Lecture 13

A s a young man, Charles Darwin embarked on a scientific journey that would lead him, over the course of 20 years, to the discovery of the theory of evolution. Although this extended development might not seem a true turning point, Darwin's concepts completely revolutionized how humans saw their relation to the natural world. This lecture illustrates the idea that historical turning points are not always the first or last word! In this case, Darwin was preceded by others who had speculated on evolution, and later thinkers took his concept in different directions. This turning point also underlined two sources of authority that had been growing in importance through the modern period: the authority of science and of progress.

Early Thinking on Creation and Evolution

- At the start of our course, from the early 1400s, the authoritative word on the natural world and where it came from was Scripture. In the Christian world, this meant the account of creation given in the Bible was understood literally, rather than as a symbolic rendering.

- In this understanding, creation took place once and for all, with species and creatures "fixed," that is, set in ideal types, and unchanging. But quite a few in the following centuries questioned this account of a fixed creation.

- Some thinkers instead spoke of "transmutation," the arising of new species. By the 19th century, "natural philosophers" began to notice the fossil record, which showed extinctions. The word "dinosaur," for instance, meaning "great or terrible lizard," was coined in 1842. It seemed increasingly clear that the world was not fixed but changing.

- The question then arose: How does the world change? A school of so-called "catastrophists" argued that intermittently, the earth is shaken by disruptive events, such as the biblical flood, and these shaped our world. By contrast, other geologists were called "uniformitarians"; they argued that the world changed slowly, in a uniform manner.

- In Darwin's Victorian age, society placed great emphasis on progress, and this conviction created a receptiveness to some version of the idea of evolution.

The Life of Charles Darwin

- Darwin was born in 1809. His father was a noted doctor, and his grandfather, Erasmus Darwin, had been a noted natural philosopher. His mother came from the Wedgwood family.

- Darwin trained as a medical student at the University of Edinburgh, but he could not abide the sight of blood. He was then sent to Cambridge to train to be a clergyman. Instead, he became a keen observer of nature.

- A botany professor with whom Darwin had worked recommended him for the position of natural historian on a ship, the *Beagle*, that was headed for a cartographic mission to South America under Captain Robert Fitzroy.

- The trip first took them to Brazil, where Darwin was enchanted by the rain forest. It continued to Argentina and Chile and, in 1835, reached the Galapagos Islands, a volcanic archipelago in the Pacific, now part of Ecuador but in possession of the British at the time.
  - There, Darwin saw astonishing wildlife, including huge tortoises, and overheard an offhand comment made by the British governor that one could guess which island a tortoise was from.

  - Later, replaying the comment in his mind, Darwin realized that the many different finches on the islands must have had common ancestry but had adapted themselves to different ecological niches. The rest of his life would be devoted to thinking through the implications of this idea.

- The naval voyage went on to Tahiti, New Zealand, Australia, around the southern tip of Africa, back to South America, and then to England. When Darwin returned to Britain in 1836, after five years travel, he was a changed man. He had new confidence and returned with thousands of pages of notes and more than 5,000 specimens.

- The book he published about his trip became a great success. His constant, almost obsessive attention to observed detail links him to Leeuwenhoek. Darwin called the trip "the first real training or education of my mind." He pursued his ideas in a series of notebooks.

- On his return from his voyage, Darwin seemed to retire. He married his cousin, Emma Wedgwood, and they had 10 children. Emma was deeply religious and immensely patient in nursing her husband through his chronically bad health. Darwin professed himself to be an agnostic in religious terms, believing it impossible to know of the existence or nonexistence of divinity, but in spite of this difference, he and his wife remained close and loving.

"Darwin's Delay"
- Historians call the next 20 years of his life "Darwin's delay." Instead of announcing his theories, Darwin kept quiet. He worked in secret, gathering information to support his theory of natural selection—a vast set of data based on research on barnacles, peas, pigeons, and many other living things.

- By 1844, he had written out an essay with his ideas in largely complete form but still held back from publishing, despite his friends' urging. Darwin replied to his friends that arguing that species were not fixed but evolved seemed like confessing to murder!

- What finally jolted Darwin into publishing his ideas was competition. He got a letter from a younger scientist, Alfred Russel Wallace, in which Wallace described an idea that was essentially the same as Darwin's natural selection. Darwin's friends informed Wallace of the work Darwin had been doing in secret for many years, and with great grace, Wallace conceded that Darwin was first. After this scare, Darwin cranked out his book in 13 months of nonstop work.

- The *Origin of Species* finally appeared in November of 1859. Its first printing of 1,250 copies sold out on the first day.
  o Darwin laid out his ideas in clear, accessible prose. The key principle is that nature produces more than can survive, and there are variations in traits in populations, which are then selected from, with the unfit destined not to survive. A species is a group of animals that can mate and reproduce.

  o Significantly, Darwin did not make humans the central question or even a special case. In fact, there was only one mention of humans in the book, the cryptic note: "Light will be thrown on the origin of man and his history."

Reaction to Darwin's Work

- Like Copernicus, whose theory displaced the earth from the center of the universe, Darwin dislodged man's status. But Darwin insisted that his worldview actually was richer. He declared, "There is a grandeur in this view of life… from so simple a beginning endless forms most beautiful and most wonderful have been and are being evolved."

- Natural selection did not imply a "teleology," or internally preordained plan, or the notion that there is a direction to evolution, but Darwin himself seemed ambiguous on this point. He sometimes spoke of "improvement," "higher forms," and "favoured races." In 1869, he accepted an earlier formulation by the philosopher Herbert Spencer and subtitled his core chapter "The Survival of the Fittest."

- To many people, "fittest" here suggested best. They congratulated themselves on being the end product that millennia of evolution had worked to produce, in the great onward sweep of progress .

- Epic controversy ensued; some eagerly accepted what they understood to be Darwin's message, while others were scandalized. The scientific theory spread quickly in this literate society with a mass audience and mass media. Religious figures devoted to a literal reading of Scripture denounced Darwin, while other religious thinkers argued that his message was compatible with divinity.

- Younger scientists rallied to Darwin's theory of evolution, even though not all of them accepted natural selection. Among his champions was the biologist Thomas Huxley, who came to be called "Darwin's bulldog," a role he played for 30 years.

Perhaps no age has believed so confidently in progress as the Victorian age, named after the British queen who ruled for most of the 19th century, from 1837 until 1901.

- Over time, Darwin's model of evolution gained wider acceptance, in part because it meshed so well with the Victorian confidence in progress. In 1871, he published *The Descent of Man*, in which he concluded that humans were descended from an ancestor that was also the ancestor of monkeys.

The Neo-Darwinian Synthesis

- Darwin died in 1882, at the age of 73. In a gesture of honor, he was buried in Westminster Abbey. Darwin's idea of natural selection was only vindicated decades later, as scientists created what is called the "Neo-Darwinian synthesis."

- Unknown to Darwin, while his fame was growing, a priest-scientist in Germany named Father Gregor Mendel researched hybrids in pea plants and followed the transmission of traits, laying the basis for genetics, yet his work remained obscure until around 1900. Then, in the 1920s, experts in population genetics put together Mendelian insights with Darwin.

Lecture 13: 1859—Darwin and the *Origin of Species*

© Photos.com/Thinkstock.

- The discovery of DNA followed. In 1953, James D. Watson and Francis Crick modeled the double helix. This forms the basis for our understanding of evolution today. In our own time, the sequencing of the human genome in 2003 is opening the way for diagnoses of illness and early preventive care.

The Impact of Darwin's Theories

- Darwin's theories had an impact that continued long after his death and still echo today. His ideas were so provocative that they were taken up by many different thinkers of many different political stripes and orientations, often quite removed from science and veering into politics.

- Objections to Darwinism on religious grounds by biblical literalists have continued, grouped under the heading "creationism." The famous 1925 Scopes "Monkey Trial" in Tennessee saw a schoolteacher convicted for teaching evolution. This confrontation continues into our times.

- Others avidly took up what they understood to be Darwin's message and sought to apply evolution to human society. This was so-called "social Darwinism," and many of its forms would have horrified Darwin.
  - The flip side of evolution's promise of progress was fear of what would happen if natural laws were distorted: "degeneracy" and social decline.

  - The opposite of survival of the fittest was the peril of extinction. To many, the international arena in this age of imperialism looked like a struggle for survival among nations, empires, and races.

  - Some thinkers argued that society should privilege the best human specimens and trample down the weak or poor as unfit. Darwin's own cousin, Francis Galton, invented the term "eugenics," meaning "good birth," to encourage policies to improve the human population and to discourage the reproduction of those judged less fit.

o   Eugenics gained popularity around 1900 and was later put into terrible practice by the Nazis. Ultimately, millions of human lives were lost or destroyed by those who professed an allegedly "scientific" racism.

•   Anxieties remain today about what it all means—the brave new world of genetic manipulation and human intervention in such processes as evolution. Consider headlines from our own times about cloning or genetically modified food. The turning point launched by Darwin is one we are still working through today.

Suggested Reading

Bowler, *Charles Darwin*.

Stott, *Darwin's Ghosts*.

Questions to Consider

1.   Which parts of Darwin's theories were attractive to many in the Victorian age and which were most shocking?

2.   If Darwin's ill health in part was due to his deep anxieties about how his work would be received, what might he have feared most in this regard?

1859—Darwin and the *Origin of Species*
Lecture 13—Transcript

Imagine a world historical turning point that began with an idea that needed more than 20 years to mature! As a young man, the pathbreaking scientist Charles Darwin was on a round-the-globe scientific journey that would lead him to the discovery of the theory of evolution.

In the Galapagos Islands, in 1835, Darwin heard a British colonial administrator say something that haunted him afterwards. That official said that you could actually tell which island a tortoise came from by the shape of its shell, as they were different. Darwin asked himself, why should this be so? Only afterwards did Darwin also realize that this was true of the finches that he had collected. Darwin's trip did not have one flash of discovery that made everything clear, but rather left him with a set of intuitions and suspicions that would take 20 years to ripen. This was the slow course of a thinker of bold, wildly ambitious, and controversial ideas: the theory of evolution and the concept of natural selection.

How was this a true turning point? Some have called Darwin the most controversial scientific thinker ever. His concepts completely overturned how humans saw their relation to the natural world, embedded in it, inextricably part of it. Also, as we will see with special clarity in this lecture, historical turning points are often not the first word or the last word on a subject. In this case, Darwin was actually preceded by many other thinkers who had speculated on evolution, that is to say, change over time by creatures that adapt to their environments. After Darwin introduced his ideas, many others took that concept in directions that he would not have endorsed.

Darwin's turning point underlined and reinforced two sources of authority that had been growing in importance throughout the modern period. These were the authority of science, and the authority of progress. We've already encountered them in our previous lectures on Leeuwenhoek and the broader scientific movement of which he was a part, and in the lecture on the *Encyclopédie* and the *philosophes*, who saw reason, utility, and progress as the moving spirit of a new enlightened age.

Probably no age has believed so confidently in progress as the Victorian age, named after the British queen Victoria who ruled for most of the 19th century, from 1837 until 1901. It's precisely in this period that people who had been called natural philosophers now came to be called scientists. The authority of science replaced of the earlier authority of a literal reading of revealed holy texts, or theology, in explanation of the material world.

We observe one other fascinating attribute of Darwin's turning point. It actually came in two episodes, like a rocket with two sections. In his excellent study of Darwin, Peter Bowler concludes, "The Darwinian revolution falls into two distinct stages; the conversion of the Victorian world to evolutionism, and the revival of the selection theory in modern times."

Many of Darwin's contemporaries eagerly accepted the idea that evolution was a form of progress, because it confirmed their status as those beings which all creation had worked to achieve! But Darwin's idea of natural selection to a great extent actually accented randomness and chance, not some predetermined working out of a preordained blueprint for progress—it would take roughly half a century more for scholars to really absorb this insight and create what we today call the modern Darwinian synthesis, or modern genetics.

At the start of our course, from the early 1400s, the authoritative word on the natural world and where it came from was scripture. In the Christian world, this meant the account of creation given in the Bible, understood literally, rather than as a symbolic rendering. In Genesis, God creates everything in six days: heavens and earth, day and night, skies, seas, and land, all the creatures, and then man and woman. In fact, one bishop, in 1650 worked out the date of creation—the precise date—by counting backwards from the time spans listed in Scripture, and pinned down the precise date. It was, he announced, just before Sunday, on October 23, 4004 B.C. In this understanding, creation had taken place once and for all, with species and creatures "fixed" as it were, set in ideal types, and unchanging.

But quite a few thinkers in the following centuries questioned this account of a fixed creation. Such thinkers instead spoke of "transmutation," the arising of new species. Indeed, Darwin's book *Origin of the Species* in later editions actually included an appendix which listed those before him who had thought along similar lines (by the fourth edition of his book, there were 38 men on that list). Not least among them was Darwin's own grandfather, who had written in 1794 of all animals developing from common origins, and over time winning new characteristics, and continuing to improve down to the present day.

Another precursor was the French zoologist Jean-Baptiste Lamarck, who announced his theory in 1815. Lamarck argued that offspring could inherit improvements that had been willed and achieved by their parents. The most famous example of this concerned giraffes, which Lamarck theorized had, generation by generation, stretched their necks out ever further and further to reach remote leaves on trees, and these characteristics had been passed along.

To show that many had actually thought about evolution as a theme before Darwin, let's (purely at random) choose an example of someone we discussed in an earlier lecture: the French *philosophe* Denis Diderot, the editor of the *Encyclopédie*. If you'll recall, we mentioned that one of the messages of the *Encyclopédie* as a project was that all knowledge was interconnected. Diderot, in his personal philosophy, went further and underlined how much all the world was interrelated.

According to Diderot, what we see about us now is not a permanent state of things, but just a snapshot of a world that's constantly in flux and constantly changing, emerging from formless origins, rising up and flourishing or going extinct, across vast uncountable oceans of time. This is a process, according to Diderot, continuing of its own volition, without a creator or an original maker. Species, like individuals, have their birth, maturity, and then die out, to be succeeded by new species. This for Diderot included human beings, who in millions of years might become something unrecognizably new.

These ideas, very dangerous for the time, found a rather guarded and oblique expression in the *Encyclopédie*; for example, the entry in that work for "Animal" in the first volume stated, "Nature advances by nuanced and often imperceptible degrees." More practically, natural philosophers, or scientists as we would call them today, were starting to notice the fossil record, which showed extinctions: creatures in other words that no longer existed. The name "dinosaur," for instance, meaning "great lizard" or "terrible lizard," was coined in 1842, so it seemed increasingly clear to thinkers that the world was not fixed, but constantly changing.

Then the question arose: How does it change? One school of thought, the so-called catastrophists, argued that intermittently, the earth is shaken by huge disruptive events, like the biblical flood, and that these in essence shape our world. By contrast, other geologists were called uniformitarians, because they argued that the world changed slowly, in a uniform, constant manner.

This debate raged! Here's a suggestion: The next time you are at a cocktail party, to break the ice, turn to a fellow guest and ask, "Are you a catastrophist, or a uniformitarian?" Clearly, this was a stage of thought where thinkers were increasingly debating the changing nature of the natural world. Also, we need to keep the cultural context in mind, just as we did with Leeuwenhoek and his discoveries of the smallest world during the Dutch Golden Age. In Darwin's Victorian Age, society placed a tremendous emphasis on progress, and this conviction created a receptiveness in society at large to some version of the idea of evolution.

The Victorian age was especially attracted to the idea of progress that could be achieved by personal individual effort. Indeed, one of the bestsellers of this time was Samuel Smiles's book, *Self-Help*, published in 1859, the same year as Darwin's book, and in fact it outsold Darwin's book many times over in their lifetimes! What Darwin did was to propose a powerful insight into what it was that propelled evolution. This was natural selection, the notion that nature selects particular qualities that adapt for survival. Darwin in essence provided the how and why of evolution.

Charles Darwin was born in 1809. His father was a noted doctor, whose father in turn, Erasmus Darwin, had been a noted natural philosopher. Science was in Darwin's own family tree on his father's side. His mother, however, also came from a notable family. In fact, it's a notable family we have already encountered in our lectures. This was the Wedgwood family, the makers of Wedgwood pottery and china. Recall that Josiah Wedgwood, who became potter to the Queen of England and founder of the Wedgwood brand, was in his day an active abolitionist and gave the anti-slavery movement its quintessential iconic image, the kneeling slave who's asking, "Am I not a man and a brother?" But in addition to his social activism, Wedgwood also had another set of interests, in science, because of its practical uses: Advances in chemistry could help him in making his pottery glazes and clays.

Yet Darwin's early career began not very promisingly. First, he trained as a medical student at Edinburgh University, but he could actually not abide the sight of blood and whenever he saw it would grow faint. So at the age of 18, he was sent to Cambridge, to train to be a clergyman. Instead, however, he discovered within himself a fascination for nature, and he became an especially fanatical collector of beetles. How fanatical? Once, he had captured a beetle in one hand and a beetle in the other hand when he spotted an even more desirable specimen, so he had to put one of them in his mouth in order to free his hand for the new one he was about to collect.

At this early juncture, Darwin had a life-changing experience: a journey around the world that lasted five years. A botany professor who had worked with Darwin recommended him for a job that had suddenly become available: to be the natural historian on a ship, the *Beagle*, which was headed for a cartographic mission under Captain Robert Fitzroy. Fitzroy was a young 26-year-old captain, and his mission was to chart the coast of South America. Darwin was 23, and this mission would be the making of the man. As this voyage began in 1831, we note here an intersection with a key global phenomenon of the 19th century; that was British sea power. British sea power had won dominance of trade in the activities of the East India Company, and Britain took on a role as the world's policeman (remember the role of the British Navy for instance in quelling the slave trade).

Once aboard the ship, Darwin enjoyed a good scientific library, and a full set of *Encyclopedia Britannica*. What Darwin could have done without was the nearly constant experience of epic seasickness. Yet remarkably, whenever the *Beagle* reached land, Darwin recovered instantly, and in his scientific fervor, set about explorations and investigations.

The trip first took them to South America, to Brazil, where Darwin was enchanted by the rainforest, and was constantly collecting and sending specimens back to Britain. It was also in Brazil that he witnessed slavery, which was still legal there, and he was profoundly disgusted by its cruelties.

The trip continued to Argentina, Chile, and in 1835, the expedition reached the Galapagos Islands, a volcanic archipelago in the Pacific, now part of Ecuador, but then a British possession. This was an area with astonishing wildlife, including those huge tortoises. It was there that Darwin heard that offhand comment made by the British governor, that one could guess which island a tortoise was from by its appearance.

Later, replaying the comment in his mind, Darwin realized that the many different finches on the islands that he had collected must also have had at one time a common ancestry, but then adapted themselves to particular, unique ecological niches. The rest of Darwin's life would be devoted to thinking through the implications of this discovery.

The naval voyage went on to Tahiti, New Zealand, Australia, around the southern tip of Africa, back to South America, and then to England. When Darwin returned to Britain in 1836, after five years of travel, he was a changed man. He had about himself a new confidence, and he returned with thousands of pages of notes, and over 5,000 specimens he had collected.

The book that he published about this trip became a great success. His constant, almost obsessive attention to the minutest observed detail links him to Leeuwenhoek. Darwin called this trip "the first real training or education of my mind." Darwin pursued his ideas in a series of notebooks where he laid down his evolving thinking, like the notebook in which he first sketched a tree (remarkably like Diderot's tree of human knowledge from the *Encyclopédie*), a tree in Darwin's version that was meant to show the branching off of species. In Darwin's original idea, natural selection involved the survival of those specimens which had traits best suited to their environment.

On his return from this epic voyage, Darwin however seemed almost to retire. He married his cousin, Emma Wedgwood (again from the famous

Wedgwood family), and they had 10 children. Emma was deeply religious, and immensely patient in constantly nursing her husband through his chronically bad health. Darwin, by contrast, professed himself to be agnostic in religious terms, believing that it was impossible to know of the existence or nonexistence of divinity, but in spite of this difference between man and wife, they remained close and loving. They lived in what was then the countryside, but today our London suburbs.

In this retirement, there now followed 20 years which historians call "Darwin's delay." Instead of announcing his theories, Darwin kept quiet. He had chronic ill health, and this was perhaps a combination of physical and emotional factors. His woes especially focused on his stomach, and resembled what today we would call panic attacks. In fact, Darwin kept a pot in his study at home for vomiting as he worked on his research.

He was hard at work, in a secret project that in many ways resembles the secrecy that Gutenberg had maintained as he engaged in his clandestine work of the books. Darwin gathered information to support his theory. He gathered a vast set of data, based on research on barnacles, peas, pigeons, and many other living things, and often he was working with a simple microscope, of the kind pioneered by Leeuwenhoek. By 1844, Darwin had written out an essay with his ideas in largely complete form, but he still held back from publishing it. His closest friends so insisted that he had to publish it now, but Darwin replied that arguing in public that species were not fixed but evolved, seemed to him like confessing to murder!

What finally jolted Darwin into publishing his ideas was competition. He received a letter out of the blue from a younger scientist, by the name of Alfred Russel Wallace, in which Wallace described an idea which was essentially that of natural selection. Darwin's friends intervened and informed Wallace that Darwin had been doing this work in secret for many years, and with great, perhaps even unique grace, Wallace conceded that Darwin was first. After this bad scare, Darwin cranked out the book, in which he stated his ideas, in 13 months of nonstop work. So, finally in our turning point, Darwin's *Origin of Species* appeared in November of 1859. Its full title was *On the Origin of Species by means of Natural Selection, or the*

Preservation of Favoured Races in the Struggle for Life. Its first print run of 1,250 copies sold out immediately, in the very first day.

In this book Darwin laid out his ideas in accessible and clear prose. The key principle is that nature produces more than can survive, and there are in all creatures variations in traits in the larger population, which then are selected from, with the unfit destined not to survive. A species is a group of animals that can mate and reproduce. Significantly, Darwin did not make humans the central question or even a special case in this book. In fact there was only one mention of humans in the book, the cryptic note that Darwin provided that, "Light will be thrown on the origin of man and his history."

Like Copernicus, whose theory displaced the Earth from the center of the universe, Darwin dislodged man's status in this subtle way. But Darwin insisted that his worldview was actually richer than the traditional one it replaced. Darwin declared, "There is a grandeur in this view of life ... from so simple a beginning endless forms most beautiful and most wonderful have been and are being evolved."

Now natural selection did not imply a "teleology," that's to say an internally preordained plan, or the notion that there's a set direction to evolution, but Darwin himself actually seemed ambiguous on this point sometimes: He sometimes spoke of "improvement," or of "higher forms," or of "favoured races." Also, in 1869, Darwin accepted a formulation by the philosopher Herbert Spencer (from 1864), the notion of the "Survival of the Fittest," and gave that title to his core chapter.

To many people, this suggested that the "fittest" was also in some sense the best. They congratulated themselves on being the end point that millennia of evolution had worked to produce, in the great onward sweep of progress.

Epic controversy ensued, as some in this Victorian age very eagerly accepted what they understood to be Darwin's message, while others were deeply scandalized. The scientific theory spread quickly in this literate society with a mass audience and mass media. Some religious figures devoted to a literal reading of scripture denounced Darwin, while other religious figures argued that his message was compatible with a divinity steering evolution.

Younger scientists rallied to Darwin's theory of evolution, even though not all of them accepted natural selection. Among his champions was the biologist Thomas Huxley, who came to be called Darwin's bulldog, a role that he played for 30 years, championing his ideas.

Huxley was one of the speakers at the famous, or infamous, 1860 debate of Darwin's ideas at Oxford University. Huxley defended Darwin (who was not present) against his critic, Bishop Samuel Wilberforce. The name Wilberforce should ring a bell and be familiar from an earlier lecture. This bishop was the son of William Wilberforce, that great anti-slavery crusader of a generation before.

The debate was heated, but not very edifying. Wilberforce ended by asking whether Huxley claimed to be descended from monkeys on his maternal or paternal side, and Huxley replied that he would prefer that lineage to one that included a bishop who misused his intelligence.

Over time, Darwin's model of evolution gained wider acceptance because it meshed so well with that Victorian confidence in progress. In 1871, Darwin published his book *The Descent of Man*, in which he concluded that humans were descended from an ancestor who was also the ancestor of monkeys.

Darwin died in 1882 at the age of 73, and he was working up until his last days. In a signal gesture of honor, Darwin was buried in Westminster Abbey. His idea of natural selection was only vindicated decades later, as scientists created what is called today the modern or Neo-Darwinian synthesis.

Unknown to Darwin, while his fame was growing, a priest scientist in Germany named Father Gregor Mendel was researching hybrids in pea plants and following the transmission of particular traits. This laid the basis for genetics, yet his work remained obscure until around 1900. Then, in the 1920s, experts in population genetics put together Mendelian insights with Darwin.

The discovery of DNA followed: In 1953, James D. Watson and Francis Crick modeled the double helix. This forms the basis for our understanding of evolution today. In our time, the sequencing of the human genome in 2003 is opening the way for early diagnosis of illness and early preventive care.

Darwin's theories had an impact that continued long after his death and still echoes today. His ideas were so provocative that they were taken up by many different thinkers of very many different political stripes and orientations, often quite removed from science and veering into politics. Objections to Darwinism on religious grounds by biblical literalists continue to the present, and came to be called creationism. The famous 1925 Scopes "Monkey Trial" in Tennessee saw a schoolteacher convicted for teaching evolution. This confrontation continues.

Others fervently took up what they understood to be Darwin's message and sought to apply evolution to human society and fellow humans. This was the so-called social Darwinism, and many of its forms would have horrified Darwin. For such thinkers of social Darwinism, the flipside of evolution promising progress was the fear of what would happen if natural laws were distorted: The result might be "degeneracy" as they called it, and social decline. The opposite of survival of the fittest was then the threat of extinction. To many, the international arena in this age of imperialism looked a lot like a struggle for survival between nations, empires, and races.

For instance, after the Opium Wars we discussed in our last lecture, some young Chinese reformers used the vocabulary of social Darwinism to argue that China had to pull itself together, strengthen itself, or face extinction. In imperialist societies, some racists argued that evolution proved the superiority of their race over others, claiming an allegedly scientific basis for their hatreds.

Worldwide, some thinkers argued that society should privilege the best human specimens (they usually had themselves in mind) and that society should trample down the weak or the poor as unfit. Darwin's own cousin, Francis Galton, invented the term and movement of "eugenics," meaning the good or true birth, to encourage social policies to improve the human population (and to discourage the reproduction of those judged less fit).

Eugenics gained worldwide but not universal popularity around 1900. The United States was in the forefront, with more than 100,000 forced sterilizations in hospitals, institutions, and prisons. From the 1930s, the Nazis in Germany fused racism and eugenic thinking and put it into terrible practice, as part of their ferocious determination to build a new and pure kind of racial state.

Once in power, the Nazis sterilized half a million Germans. They then moved on to kill some 200,000 Germans by euthanasia (meaning the "good death"), first children, and then adults. The Nazis' most determined killing campaign would be their genocide against the Jews, the Holocaust. When trains full of people arrived at the ramps at the death camp of Auschwitz, doctors supervised a selection of the prisoners, some to be gassed at once, others to be worked to death. Ultimately, millions of humans were destroyed by those who professed an allegedly scientific racism. Clearly, Darwin is not to blame for the Nazis, but it is a frightening instance of ideas being hijacked for terrible purposes.

Indeed, anxieties remain today about what it all means, the brave new world of genetic manipulation and human intervention in processes like evolution. Consider headlines from our own times, about cloning or genetically modified food.

It's striking how writers of science fiction have captured so many of these anxieties. That's especially the case with a novel from 1895 by H.G. Wells, entitled *The Time Machine*. This massively prolific British writer was a pioneer of what we call science fiction (then it was called speculative fiction), and he was often a prophet of things to come. He was fascinated by science and had studied biology under none other than Thomas Huxley, Darwin's bulldog.

In his famous novel *The Time Machine*, an inventor from the Victorian age crafts a vehicle that can zoom him forward to the year 802,701 in the future. He discovers that human society has been split by evolution into two new species: the beautiful, frivolous, childlike Eloi who live and play in the sunlight, and Morlocks, a technological working class, living in darkness underground and eating their cousin species.

The inventor finally escapes this future world by journeying 30 million years into the future, to find mankind extinct and the world dying. H.G. Wells presented an unforgettable thought experiment on the long-range trajectories of evolution. It's striking that he was already not so sure about the blessings of progress, and wondered about where science with its new authority would take us next. That's very much part of the turning point that we're still working through now!

At the same time, technology was also relentlessly surging ahead, and by 1869 was showing that it could cut across continents or pull them together. That will be the turning point we consider in our next lecture.

1869—Binding Continents
Lecture 14

In May 1869, the last spike was driven into the transcontinental railroad in Utah, connecting the East and West Coasts of North America. In November of that same year, half a world away, an international fleet did something that earlier had been physically impossible, sailing directly from the Mediterranean Sea to the Red Sea along the new Suez Canal in Egypt. These engineering accomplishments accelerated global communication and movement, raised the authority of science and technology to the status earlier held by religious revelation, and reconfigured world political power. This process had begun before and continues in the present, but 1869 was a pivotal year, showcasing the power and authority of technology.

The Dream of a Canal
- Of the two projects that culminated in 1869, the Suez Canal was started earlier and took longer. From the agreement to build the canal to its completion took 15 years, but it had a long prehistory. The idea of a canal that would cut across Egypt, linking the Mediterranean and Red seas, was very old. Even the ancient Egyptian pharaohs had worked on canal projects, although on a smaller scale.
  - Napoleon, when he invaded Egypt, ordered planning for a great canal to open new routes for French power, but the plan was shelved when an engineer researching the project mistakenly predicted that cutting a channel could lead to epic flooding.

  - A group of French utopian socialists called the Saint-Simonians attempted to interest the Egyptian authorities in a canal project in the 1830s, but their dream of reuniting East and West came to nothing.

- The man who would finally realize the dream was a figure who embodied public relations brilliance, the Frenchman Ferdinand de

Lesseps. In 1854, Lesseps got the new ruler of Egypt, Sa'īd Pasha, to agree to the project.

- A new company was founded to undertake construction, with international investors. It would run the canal for 99 years, collecting fees from shipping. There are echoes here of the age of the great commercial corporations, the British and Dutch East India companies we surveyed in our earlier lectures.

- Lesseps's project could revolutionize world travel and shipping: The route from East Asia to Europe would be shortened, from 11,000 miles around the Cape of Good Hope in southern Africa to only 6,000 miles. It could cut the time to move between Britain and India in half.

- The canal itself had its own turning point in 1864. Before then, the work was done by massive use of human labor. After 1864, giant dredging machines were brought in. Their steam engines put the construction on a new technical basis.

- From the perspective of the Egyptian rulers, the canal project was a gamble. They hoped to use European technology to modernize Egypt and stave off further European influence. Using European know-how to resist the West was an approach that we will see later taken in Japan with great success. But in this case, the gamble failed, and increased foreign influence followed.

- The 100-mile-long canal was at last completed, and a grand opening was orchestrated for November 1869. European nobles arrived in their own yachts to be part of a great ceremonial fleet to sail through the newly opened canal. Hundreds of dignitaries attended the ceremony and heard speeches proclaiming that the two worlds, East and West, had been united in a "great festival for all of humanity."

The Scramble for Africa

- Earlier, the British had been hostile to the canal idea; it would stand between them and India. But once it was built, they could not tolerate any other nation possessing it. When the next Egyptian ruler ran into a financial crisis and needed to sell his shares in the canal company, British Prime Minister Benjamin Disraeli snapped them up in 1875, gaining a controlling bloc of shares in the company.

- It was a great coup, but it set off an imperialist chain reaction. In 1882, Britain took advantage of a coup in Egypt to take over the country. The canal was too precious for Britain to allow any other nation to control it. This "temporary occupation" lasted for four decades.

- Similarly, the British were drawn into conquering Sudan, to the south of Egypt, again from the imperative to hold this key geopolitical juncture. Outraged French leaders reacted by grabbing other territories in Africa, and the "Scramble for Africa" ensued.
  o This was the high imperialism of the 1880s and 1890s: The mostly Western imperialist powers raced to seize the world's remaining territories as colonies.

  o By 1914, these powers held three-quarters of the world's land. In 1875, European colonies were less than 10 percent of Africa, but by 1895, they were more than 90 percent.

- In 1898, Anglo-French animosity almost led to the early outbreak of a new world war over the Fashoda crisis, when British and French colonial forces blundered into each other in the wilds of south Sudan. Fortunately, the crisis was resolved peacefully.

- Given the importance that the Suez Canal had in launching high imperialism, there is kind of a perfect symmetry to the fact that the canal later played a role in decolonization in the 20th century.
  o In 1956, in the Suez Crisis, an Egyptian nationalist regime nationalized the canal and then faced intervention from Britain, France, and Israel.

o   This intervention failed when both the United States and the Soviet Union, although Cold War rivals, insisted that this imperialist intervention stop—and it did. The era of European colonial power and gunboat diplomacy was ending.

The Transcontinental Railroad

- Six months before the Suez Canal opened, the first transcontinental railroad in the United States was completed. Earlier, an intrepid Yankee bound for California would need to make a six-month-long journey around South America, enduring the rough seas to round Cape Horn. Alternatively, he could cross Panama by land, braving the dangers of tropical diseases, then boarding a ship to head north.

- The uniting of North America by railroad was the dream of a young engineer who did not live to see the project completed. He was Theodore Judah, so set on the vision that he was nicknamed "Crazy Judah."

- Some contemporaries said that building this railroad would

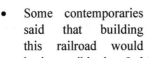

Lincoln believed that establishing a railway route to California would tie the West more firmly to the Union.

be impossible, but Judah was undaunted and mapped out a route through the formidable Sierra Nevada mountains. He sold the idea to Abraham Lincoln, who signed the Pacific Railway Act in 1862.

- What followed was a race—an economic and engineering competition in earnest—between rival yet cooperating companies. From the west, the Central Pacific Railroad Company worked eastward, while from the Missouri River, the Union Pacific Railroad

Company worked westward. The law promised payment for miles of track and gave public land along both sides of the railway to the companies.

- The construction faced huge obstacles: treacherous terrain, heavy snows in the Sierras, and raids by native American tribes to defend their land. Vast numbers of men worked on the railroad, including Civil War veterans from both sides, Irish immigrants, African Americans, and increasingly, Chinese immigrants, who were subjected to dreadful and often fatal mistreatment.
  - The crews worked seven days a week, often 14 hours every day, making their way across the continent. Surveyors worked far ahead, mapping the route. Graders moved behind them to level obstacles and prepare for the laying of rails. Chinese workers were given the dangerous job of handling nitroglycerine to blast barriers. Then, the track layers set the iron road in place.

  - Following the workers were herds of cattle and cooks, as well as dormitories on wheels for sleeping. Unsurprisingly, rough and wild settlements sprang up along the route to cater to the appetites and lusts of the workers.

- A bitter rivalry arose between the two companies, but after much wrangling and an ultimatum from President Grant, they agreed to meet up at Promontory Summit, Utah. A golden spike was driven to unite the two tracks, engraved with the words: "May God continue the unity of our country as this Railroad unites the two Great Oceans of the world."

Changing Perceptions of Space and Time

- Before the first steam trains of the early 19th century were developed in Britain, people were limited to movement as fast as a horse could carry them. The fact that trains accelerated this movement stirred considerable anxieties. Was railroad travel at such speeds healthy or proper? Accidents were not uncommon and could be horrific. But others celebrated the railroad as a vector of civilization and progress.

- Other effects of train travel and changed perceptions of time and space are with us still. One innovation in the United States and other countries was the triumph of "railroad time"—the standardization of what had been inaccurate or varying local timekeeping to conform to the schedules of the trains.

- Physically, the train station became a temple to the power of railroads. Entire cityscapes in modern cities were torn down and rebuilt to make way for the rail lines and their glorious terminus. And for millions worldwide, trains offered the chance of long-distance travel.

- Worldwide, railroads became a key means of binding together space into unities.
  - British India was connected with railroads, funded with British investment, as a way of securing Britain's hold on the subcontinent. By 1872, India had more than 5,000 miles of track.

  - Other states rushed to build such projects, as well. Russia built the Trans-Siberian Railroad from the 1890s to link its European west with its Asian east. Germany sought to fund and dominate a project for a railroad from Berlin to Baghdad, which made the British anxious and poisoned the international atmosphere leading up to World War I.

- When the U.S. transcontinental railroad was linked up, it was accompanied by a parallel line of telegraph wires for instant communication. Underwater cables also connected the world around this same time; a submarine cable was run from Britain to India in 1865 and from Britain to the United States in 1866.

- These trends of binding the world together inspired a bestseller about the global changes that were taking place: Jules Verne's adventure *Around the World in Eighty Days*. This feat could now be accomplished, but only two decades earlier, it is estimated that the same trip would have taken 11 months to complete!

- The year 1869 was a pivotal one, connecting the world in new ways. As we saw in earlier lectures, there certainly had been commercial globalization before, drawing the world closer in trade and exchange. This, however, was an astonishing acceleration of communication and movement. It changed how ordinary people perceived the very categories of space and time, and it made heroes of engineers and their technological know-how.

Suggested Reading

Ambrose, *Nothing Like It in the World*.

Cadbury, *Dreams of Iron and Steel*.

Headrick, *Tools of Empire*.

Jensen, *The American Heritage History of Railroads in America*.

Karabell, *Parting the Desert*.

Questions to Consider

1. Railroads bound together continents in the 19th century, but what takes that role today?

2. If Britain had not come to control the Suez Canal, how might that have changed subsequent history?

1869—Binding Continents
Lecture 14—Transcript

In 1869, several months apart, two events took place that marked a key turning point: the binding up of the world by modern technology, which now would assume vast significance as a source of authority, especially in the person of the engineer, the figure who could make all this happen, who could master nature!

In May 1869, the last spike was driven into the transcontinental railroad, in Utah. This marked the connecting of the North American East and West Coasts by an overland route of train travel! Six months later, in November of that same year, half a world away, a splendid international fleet did something which earlier had been physically impossible. For the first time, this fleet sailed directly from the Mediterranean Sea to the Red Sea, along the new Suez Canal in Egypt. The canal actually embodied a paradox—by cutting through continents, where Asia meets Africa, this engineering feat helped bind the world together by communications. It made the world one as it never had been before.

In what ways was this a turning point? First, these engineering accomplishments tied the globe together in new ways, speeding communication and movement. In the process, accelerating technology did something profound: it changed how humans saw the world around them by altering how they perceived categories as basic as space and distance.

Second, these engineering marvels also increased the authority of science and technology, raising them to the status earlier held by religious revelation! This would yield wonderful advances, but also came with perils, which we feel into our own time.

Third, the transcontinental railroad and the Suez Canal reconfigured world political power in new ways. Taken all together, in 1869, the world map was redrawn by the power of technology. This process had begun before, and would continue to the present, but 1869 was a pivotal year, showcasing the power and authority of technology.

Let's begin with the Suez Canal. Of the two projects that culminated in 1869, it was started earlier and took longer to bring about. From the agreement to build the canal to its completion took 15 years, but it also had a long prehistory. The idea of a canal that would cut across Egypt, linking the Mediterranean and Red Seas, was very old. The ancient Egyptian pharaohs had worked on canal projects, but on a much smaller scale.

Napoleon, when he invaded Egypt, had ordered planning for a grand canal to open new routes for French power (perhaps even access to British-controlled India), but the engineer who was researching the project for Napoleon made a crucial mistake: He calculated that the Red Sea was more than 30 feet higher than the Mediterranean waters were. This created a fearful prospect: If you cut the channel, it might lead to an epic flooding catastrophe, so Napoleon's plan was shelved.

But the dream continued, and in this case involved some pretty strange dreamers. They were from a French group of utopian socialists called the Saint-Simonians. The movement was inspired by and took its name from Claude Henri, the Count of Saint-Simon, one of the founders of sociology. Saint-Simon and his followers believed that if only older forms of authority, especially tradition and religion, were replaced by a deliberately constructed new society, a harmonious human race might finally achieve true equality and progress.

The Saint-Simonians worshipped progress and the new. In doing so, they built on the Enlightenment's dreams of perfectibility (recall our earlier lecture on the *Encyclopédie* as a quintessential Enlightenment project). The Saint-Simonians aimed to put this into practice. Saint-Simon himself preached, "The Golden Age is not behind us; it is ahead; it is the perfection of the social order." Other utopian socialists shared these millennial hopes: One, by the name of Charles Fourier, actually expected that in a future age of harmony the seas would turn to lemonade. It doesn't get any more utopian than that!

After Saint-Simon's death, his followers continued to dream about projects to advance their faith, and they found such an enterprise in the idea of a canal across Egypt. The linking of the seas, they felt, would have philosophical and world-historical meaning! Saint-Simonians declared that this canal would unite East and West, the feminine and the masculine, achieving a new harmony.

But attempts to interest the Egyptian authorities in the 1830s by the Saint-Simonians came to nothing. But the dream still lived on, and the man who would finally realize it was a figure who embodied public relations brilliance, the Frenchman Ferdinand de Lesseps.

In 1854, de Lesseps got the new ruler of Egypt, Sa'īd Pasha, an old friend of his, to agree to the project. First, de Lesseps hired engineers who recalculated the actual ocean levels, and they confirmed that no flood would ensue from this project. Then a new company was founded to undertake the project, with international investors. The company would run the canal for 99 years, and would collect fees from the shipping that passed through. There are echoes here of the age of the great commercial corporations, the British and the Dutch East India Companies that we surveyed in some of our earlier lectures.

De Lesseps's project would revolutionize world travel and shipping—the route from East Asia to Europe would be dramatically shortened, from 11,000 miles around the Cape of Good Hope in southern Africa, to only 6,000 miles. It would essentially cut the time to move between Britain and India in half.

The Canal Company itself was founded in 1858 and in the next year started work from the south, at Port Sa'īd. De Lesseps now hurried to get investors worldwide for this project. Most financing came from France—de Lesseps was the cousin of the Empress Eugénie, wife of the Emperor Napoleon III, and he used these social connections to the hilt.

The canal itself had its own turning point, in 1864. Before 1864, the work was done much like the ancient Pyramids had been built, by the massive use of human labor. But after 1864, giant dredging machines were brought in. Their steam engines put the construction on an entirely new technical basis. At this point, it was the largest gathering together of mechanical energy up until that point in history.

From the perspective of the rulers of Egypt, the entire canal project was a gamble. They hoped to use European technology to modernize Egypt, to stave off further European influence, to prevent the kind of humiliation that China experienced in the Opium Wars! Using European know-how to resist the West was an approach that we will see later taken in Japan with great success. In the case of Egypt, the gamble failed, and increasing foreign influence followed. But that still lay in the future.

The 100-mile-long canal was at last completed in August of 1869. The last sand between the seas was breached (and fortunately, no global flood ensued). To celebrate, a grand opening was orchestrated for November of 1869. The French empress Eugénie and many other European nobles, including the Emperor of Austria, the Crown Prince of Prussia, and the Grand Duke of Russia arrived in their own yachts to be part of a great ceremonial fleet that would sail through the newly opened canal. The Italian composer Giuseppe Verdi was commissioned to write a great opera, *Aida*, on a subject from Ancient Egypt. Its later premier performance in Cairo was part of this celebration of a great historical event.

At the same time, a young French sculptor by the name of Frédéric Auguste Bartholdi had an idea that he suggested. That was to build a 90-foot statue of an Egyptian woman holding a torch, and this statue would be called *Egypt Bringing Light to Asia*. Even an impresario like de Lesseps found this too much and politely declined the offer. But Bartholdi later produced on the basis of a similar idea a statue that you know, called *Liberty Enlightening the World*, and it was set up in New York in 1886—we know it as the Statue of Liberty.

At the ceremony in Egypt, a thousand dignitaries were in attendance, and they heard speeches proclaiming that two worlds, the East and West, had been united, in what they called a great festival for all humanity. De Lesseps was hailed as a new Christopher Columbus! In fact, he took this celebrity to heart, and decades later tried to build another canal in Panama, yet this later project ended for him in disappointment.

Let us instead focus for now on his moment of triumph: In 1869, the flotilla passed through the canal (there were actually some anxious moments because in fact, further work would still be needed to deepen the canal and to perfect it). But still, after 10 years of building, the canal was finally open. What happened after this opening made clear the project's truly global significance.

The key here was British attitudes. At first, Britain was hostile to the idea of a canal—the canal would stand between Britain and its jewel in the crown, India, which had been won earlier by the British East India Company, as we discussed in an earlier lecture.

If the canal was built, it would become a revolutionary fact—contemporaries called it a second Bosporus, comparing it to the Turkish Straits between Europe and Asia which made Constantinople such a geopolitical prize, as we saw in a lecture right at the start of our course. However, once the canal was actually built, the British found they could not tolerate anyone else possessing it. It now became vital to them. Remember, the canal would cut the time to move between Britain and India in half.

So, when the next Egyptian ruler, Ismail, son of Sa'īd, ran into a financial crisis, he needed to sell his shares in the Canal Company, and the British prime minister Benjamin Disraeli snapped them up in 1875, and thus gained a controlling block of shares in the company. This proved to be a great coup. But it also set off an imperialist chain reaction. For instance, when there was a coup against the Egyptian Khedive, Britain took over the country of Egypt in 1882. Now the entire country around the canal was too precious for Britain to allow anyone else to rule. This was declared to be a "temporary occupation," but the British in spite of this avowal held onto Egypt for four decades.

Similarly, as a result, the British were also drawn into conquering Sudan, to the south of Egypt, once again from the imperative of holding on to the key geopolitical juncture of the Suez Canal. All of this left French leaders outraged, as one might expect. The French reacted by grabbing other territories in Africa, and the so-called Scramble for Africa of imperialist powers ensued.

This was the high imperialism of the 1880s and 1890s: the mostly Western imperialist powers racing to seize the world's remaining territories as colonies. By 1914, they held three quarters of the world's land. Back in 1875, considering the continent of Africa, European colonies were less than 10 percent of Africa, but by 1895 they were more than 90 percent of Africa. In just 20 years, Africa was carved up.

Anglo-French animosity also almost led to the early outbreak of a new world war, over the so-called Fashoda crisis (now forgotten), which had taken place in 1898 in Sudan. There, British and French colonial forces blundered into one another out in the wilds of southern Sudan. Imagine how world history would have changed if the First World War had been fought not in the trenches of Europe between the Central Powers and the Allies, but between Britain and France! Cooler heads prevailed, and the Fashoda crisis was resolved peacefully.

Given the importance that the Suez Canal had in launching high imperialism, there's a kind of almost perfect symmetry to the fact that the canal later played a role in decolonization in the 20th century. In 1956 in the Suez Crisis, an Egyptian nationalist regime nationalized the canal, and then faced intervention from Britain, France, and Israel. This intervention failed when both the United States and the Soviet Union, even though they were Cold War rivals, insisted that this imperialism had to stop—and it did. The era of European colonial power and gunboat diplomacy was ending. But all that lay far in the future, and our later lectures will examine the trend of decolonization more fully.

Back in 1869, six months before the Suez Canal was opened, came the completion of the first transcontinental railroad in the United States. It bound together the North American continent in unprecedented ways. Before, an intrepid Yankee who wanted to go to California would need to make a journey lasting six months around South America, enduring the rough seas to be found at Cape Horn. Or, he could take a shortcut by crossing Panama by land, but then he'd have to brave the dangers of tropical diseases before once again getting on a ship to head northwards.

The dream that became a reality, of uniting North America by railroad, was launched by a young engineer who unfortunately did not live to see it completed. He was Theodore Judah, so set on the vision that possessed him that he was nicknamed "Crazy Judah." Some contemporaries said that building this transcontinental railroad would be impossible, like trying to "build a railway to the moon." But Judah was undaunted, and he mapped out a route through the formidable Sierra Nevada mountains, and then sold the idea to President Abraham Lincoln, even as the American Civil War was raging. Or perhaps we should say that he was able to sell it precisely because the Civil War was raging. Establishing this route to California would tie the West more firmly to the Union, and Lincoln signed the Pacific Railroad Act in 1862.

What followed was a race, an economic and engineering competition in earnest, between rival and yet cooperating companies. From the West, the Central Pacific Railroad Company worked eastwards, while from the Missouri River, the Union Pacific Railroad Company worked westwards. The law promised payment to the companies for miles of track they'd laid, and also gave public land along both sides of the railway to the companies, each of which naturally tried to maximize their share by speed and any means possible.

This construction faced huge obstacles: treacherous terrain, the heavy snows of the Sierras, raids by Native American tribes whose lands the railroaders were entering. The visionary engineer Judah died of disease while his project was underway, and was never to see his dream fulfilled.

Nonetheless, vast numbers of men continued to work on the railroad, many tens of thousands, and they were very diverse. They included Civil War veterans from both sides, Irish immigrants, African Americans, and increasingly multitudes of Chinese immigrants, who were subjected to dreadful and often fatal mistreatment (in fact, we're still not sure how many died in the project, because the records that were kept on this score were very slapdash).

The workers worked seven days a week, often 14 hours every day, in a pattern that moved its way across the continent. First, surveyors worked far ahead, mapping out the route. Graders moved behind them to level obstacles and to prepare for the laying of rails. Then the Chinese workers were often given the dangerous job of handling nitroglycerine to blast the barriers that were in place. Then the layers of track would move up and set the iron road on its course. The pace of work was backbreaking—at the end, a record was actually set for the laying of 10 miles and 56 feet of track in only 12 hours.

Following the workers were herds of cattle and cooks, as well as dormitories on wheels for sleeping. Unsurprisingly, some pretty rough and wild settlements sprang up along the route to cater to the appetites and lusts of those workers. These towns were nicknamed "Hell on Wheels," an expression we still use today, and included places like North Platte and Julesburg, Nebraska.

Some sense of the bitter rivalry between the companies headed in opposite directions is given by the fact that when their advance parties finally met, they actually passed one another, because neither side wanted to give up on the incentives of more mileage! There are in fact persistent stories that some of the units actually fought against one another.

Finally, after much wrangling and an ultimatum from President Grant to make this work, the companies agreed to meet up at Promontory Summit, Utah. On May 10, 1869, the occasion of the joining of the railroad took place and it was wild and very revealing. One dignitary who had to come from the east, a pretty slippery financier named Dr. Durant, was actually late to the occasion at first because some of his own employees had held him hostage for a few days in a labor dispute. When he finally arrived, mighty locomotives were drawn up on either side as the last spike was to be driven in. This was a solid gold spike engraved with the ringing words, "May God continue the unity of our country as this Railroad unites the two Great Oceans of the world."

The man given the honor of driving the spike in was California's former Governor Leland Stanford (incidentally, the founder with his wife of Stanford University). Stanford swung ... and missed, allegedly. Durant now stepped up, swung mightily ... and also is alleged to have missed. Somehow, somebody finally managed to get the spike in.

I should at this point mention one other detail so that nobody gets up right now after hearing this lecture and races out to Promontory Summit—that gold spike was immediately wrenched out and replaced with an iron one (the gold spike is preserved at Stanford University to this day). One other detail is suggestive: The spike and hammer were wired up to a telegraph line, which—when contact was finally made—with lighting speed conveyed worldwide the news of the uniting of the continent!

Let me take a moment to suggest how these two elements, trains and telegraphs, changed perceptions of space and time. Before the first steam trains of the early 19th century in Britain were developed and improved, people were really limited to movement as fast as a horse could carry them. Now by contrast, human beings accelerated, achieving ever greater speeds of movement!

This was a fact actually which stirred considerable anxieties—was railroad travel at great speeds even healthy or proper? Railroad accidents were not uncommon, and they could be horrific—the great writer Charles Dickens was involved in one, but survived. But even without these derailments, anxieties still spread about the effects of modern speed on the human being. Medical experts diagnosed a condition they called Railway Spine, which involved neural damage from the jolting and jarring of a railcar. There were anxieties about what train travel would do to nerves.

But others by contrast celebrated the railroad as a vector of civilization and progress. The American printmakers Currier and Ives had a famous print entitled "Across the Continent," which showed the relentless forward motion of the train, out of an urban setting into lands that were wilderness, but would not remain so for long!

Other effects of train travel and changed perceptions of time and space are with us still. One innovation in the United States as in other countries worldwide was the triumph of "railroad time" as it was called—the standardization of what earlier had been very many different patterns of local timekeeping to one time for all, to conform to the schedules of the trains.

Physically, the train station became a veritable temple to the power of railroads. Entire cityscapes of urban centers were torn down and rebuilt to make way for the rail lines and their glorious terminals, often a cathedral-like structure of glass and iron. Finally, for millions worldwide, the train offered the chance of long-distance travel.

Worldwide, railroads became a key means of binding together space into unities. British India, for instance, was connected with railroads funded by British investment as a way of securing Britain's hold on the subcontinent. By 1872, India had more than 5,000 miles of track.

Other states now also rushed to build such vast projects as well. Russia built the Trans-Siberian Railroad from the 1890s as the longest railway in the world, to link its European west with its Asian east. Germany sought to fund and dominate a project for a railroad from Berlin to Baghdad, which made the British very anxious, and ultimately poisoned the international atmosphere leading up to World War I.

I also want to briefly mention the telegraph. When the United States transcontinental railroad was linked up, it was accompanied by a parallel line of telegraph wires for instant communication. This replaced earlier telegraph lines that had been strung across the continent. The legendary Pony Express, famously, was put out of business in an instant!

The telegraph made worldwide communication possible almost instantaneously. Think all the way back to our second lecture in this course, on the fall of Constantinople. When that city fell in 1453, news of its capture by the Turks only reached Rome in Italy more than a month later! By contrast, when the transcontinental railroad was completed, the news reached Washington DC in mere moments.

Underwater telegraph cables also linked up the world, on the eve of the construction of the Suez Canal and the transcontinental railroad. A submarine cable was run from Britain all the way to India in 1865, and from Britain to the United States in 1866. The instantaneous nature of the telegraph made it in a real sense the precursor of the Internet of today, a topic that we'll take up at the very end of our course.

These trends, of binding the world together, all came together in a bestselling novel inspired by the global changes that were taking place. This was Jules Verne's adventure, *Around the World in Eighty Days*. This book perfectly, marvelously captured the spirit of its age! Verne has been called the father of science fiction, but in this popular classic, published in 1873, he certainly reveled in science, but without having to resort to the obviously fantastic. In a sense, what was sensational about this novel was that its story was quite plausible.

In this story, the British gentleman Phileas Fogg of London and his manservant set out to circle the globe on the basis of a bet agreed on at Fogg's club. They make the journey with many adventures on the way, using the Suez Canal, then across British India, through Hong Kong, and then on the Transcontinental Railroad across North America. At the end, and here I hope I'm not ruining the story for anyone, they think upon their return to London that they've lost the bet, they've arrived too late, but at the last moment they realize that in their travels, they actually gained a day in journeying across time zones, so there's a happy ending.

This feat could actually be done! But consider, only two decades before, around 1850 (that's before the Suez Canal and before the transcontinental railroad, before the technologies of improved train travel that we've discussed), this same trip, it is estimated, would have taken not 80 days, but rather 11 months to complete!

To sum up, 1869 was a pivotal year, binding the world together in new ways. As we saw in earlier lectures, there certainly had been a commercial globalization taking place before, that was beginning to draw the world closer in trade and exchange. This, however, was an astonishing acceleration of communication and movement. It changed how ordinary people perceived the very categories of space and time. The heroes of this venture were engineers, and their technological know-how.

Engineers were celebrated, worshipped, lionized. Little wonder that mothers at this time hoped that their sons would become engineers. If there are any engineers listening to this course, please stand up and take a bow!

Technology and engineers were redrawing the world map in ways that were both promising and dangerous, as we see increased competition to dominate this new world.

Socially, this swiftly changing globe was about to experience another enormous change: the first enfranchisement of women, at long last, starting in New Zealand, in a turning point that we'll consider in our next lecture.

1893—First Women Voters in New Zealand
Lecture 15

A prominent badge of the condition of being modern has also been the acceptance of a political and social voice for the individual, whether male or female. Yet for most of human history, half of the human race was mostly excluded from political power and participation. In fact, it was only in 1893 that the first national state, New Zealand, legally recognized women's right to vote. Other countries followed this first step, years and decades later. In this lecture, we trace how women's votes were achieved. In essence, two global trends, the demand for women's political voice and the growth of settler societies, intersected to create this crucial turning point, which spread from New Zealand worldwide.

Enlightenment Beginnings of the Suffrage Movement

- The international movement for women's votes can be seen as beginning in earnest with the Enlightenment ideas that emphasized individual freedom and personal sovereignty. In spite of this core idea and its universality, few male Enlightenment thinkers championed women's rights, so it would often be the role of remarkable women to argue vigorously for this cause.

- An example was Mary Wollstonecraft in England, who in 1792, published *A Vindication of the Rights of Woman* and has been seen as one of the founders of the feminist movement.

- In 1776, Abigail Adams warned her husband, John Adams, that if "the ladies" were not taken into consideration by the Continental Congress, they would "foment a rebellion."

- Women were active on both sides of the French Revolution. Olympia de Gouges, for instance, was both a royalist and an activist for women's rights. Such active spirits were disappointed by the constitution of 1791, which made women merely "passive citizens."

The Suffrage Movement in America

- The suffrage movement revived in earnest around 1840 in America. Elizabeth Cady Stanton and Lucretia Mott, two American women, had met at the World's Anti-Slavery Convention in London, but they were refused the right to participate in the convention because they were women. The experience galvanized them.

- On their return to the United States, Stanton and Mott helped organize the 1848 Seneca Falls Convention in New York, with 300 participants. The convention adopted a "Declaration of Sentiments," which adapted the original words of the Declaration of Independence for the cause of women's rights.

- In the following decades, Stanton worked with Susan B. Anthony to advance the cause. In 1866, Stanton stood for Congress and received 24 votes out of 12,000. In 1872, Anthony was arrested for voting in the presidential election. Together, these women founded the National Woman Suffrage Association.

- Successes finally came at the local level in the American West. In the Wyoming Territory, women's votes were recognized from 1869. When Wyoming became a state in 1890, its leaders insisted that it enter the Union with women's votes. Other western states also recognized women's right to vote, including Utah, Colorado, and Idaho.

The Suffrage Movement in Britain

- A mass movement for women's votes was also evolving in Britain. A Quaker, Anne Knight, published the first women's suffrage pamphlet in 1847. In 1851, the first suffrage society was founded in Britain. A following generation of women activists founded the Women's Social and Political Union and engaged in dramatic, militant action.

- Led by Christabel Pankhurst, the "suffragettes" as they came to be called, scuffled with police. Two militants smashed the windows of the prime minister's house. In 1912, the suffragettes organized a campaign of breaking windows, chaining themselves to fences, and setting fire to mailboxes to call attention to their cause. Then, they bombed the house of the Chancellor of the Exchequer. In prison, their hunger strikes gained further publicity and sympathy.

- In 1913, a young activist named Emily Davison attended the famous Epsom Derby horserace. Timing her action exactly, she stepped in front of the horse owned by the British king; she died of her injuries a few days later. Two thousand women activists marched in her funeral procession through the streets of London.

- Anti-suffrage movements arose, as well, in both Britain and the United States. Participants were convinced that allowing women's votes would be a violation of the "natural order" and social cohesion, which they saw as relegating women to an entirely domestic sphere.

The Settler Society of New Zealand
- Off in the South Pacific, New Zealand literally seemed to European imperialists the end of the earth. The original settlers there were the Maori people. Dutch traders encountered these islands in 1642, and eventually, British colonists settled there.
  - Colonial governors sought to balance the needs of incoming settlers with the rights of the Maori.

  - New Zealand was a settler society, like Canada and the United States, where envisioning society in new ways was not only possible but necessary!

- Women's votes were achieved in New Zealand in ways that both resembled and diverged from the more familiar pattern that was later seen in the United States and Britain, where large movements were organized for the struggle. In New Zealand, women achieved the vote after eight years of organizational work and did so much sooner.

- This had much to do with the social context. In this frontier setting, women and women's work were seen as vital to the establishment of the new society. As a result, women's education took on a prominence and sense of normalcy that were quite unusual for the times elsewhere in the world. By 1893, more than half of the university students in New Zealand were women.

- New Zealand women became famous for their independence and their ability to carve out a new way of life for themselves. Many entered the professions or became educators themselves.

The Suffrage Movement in New Zealand

- The key organizer of the women's movement was Kate Sheppard of Christchurch. Born in Liverpool in 1848 and raised in Scotland, she had emigrated to New Zealand with her family. She was marked by good humor, strength, winning charm, and great reserves of calm determination.

- Sheppard and other women first became active in the temperance movement, working against the abuse of alcohol, another common feature of many settler societies. Inspired by a visiting American temperance activist, New Zealand women founded a national Women's Christian Temperance Union in 1885. This organization was the first in the country led by women for women.

- As they set about drafting a reform program, it occurred to many of the women members of the Temperance Union that the best way of making their voices heard, on this as well as other issues, was to secure what had been denied them before: the right to vote. Kate Sheppard was put in charge of the committee on the franchise, and the struggle ensued.

- The organization borrowed from tactics we already saw pioneered in the abolitionist movement against slavery. The women wrote tracts and published pamphlets, spoke at meetings, and used their informal influence in society. Their public meetings drew women of different classes together. They also used mass petitions to great effect.

- Opposition to women's suffrage also organized at this point. Some of this opposition was sponsored and funded by the alcohol industry and tavern-keepers, who were anxious about the mobilization that had grown out of the temperance cause.

- Interestingly, many New Zealand men, including established political leaders of different backgrounds, supported women's right to vote. Some believed it would advance the fortunes of their particular political party, liberal or conservative.

- On September 8, 1893, the New Zealand Parliament finally enfranchised women over the age of 21, and the franchise became law 11 days later, so that women could vote in the upcoming parliamentary elections. In the election, more than 80 percent of women eligible to vote did so, eagerly taking up the right that they had been so long denied.

Effects of the Franchise

- This turning point in New Zealand had worldwide effects. When New Zealand women gained the vote, telegrams were sent to women's suffrage movements internationally to share the good news. Later, Sheppard would travel to England, Canada, and the United States, lecturing on how this success had been achieved.

- The heavy voting by women in the parliamentary elections refuted an argument that had been advanced by opponents of women's suffrage: the claim that most women did not want the vote. Many New Zealanders, both men and women, were proud of being identified with this new equal status for women.

- This turning point did not, however, overturn everything at once. In 1893, New Zealand women had won the vote, but the first woman was not elected to Parliament until 40 years later, in 1933.

- Even with the example of New Zealand, elsewhere around the world, women's votes were slow to come. Only four countries enfranchised women before World War I broke out in 1914. First

MANIFESTATIONS DES SUFFRAGETTES A LONDRES
Une sortie de prison triomphale

© Photos.com/Thinkstock

Some opponents of women's suffrage claimed that most women did not want the vote; it was only a loud and clamorous minority that was pressing the demand.

was New Zealand in 1893, then Australia in 1902, Finland in 1906, and Norway in 1913.

o   In many countries, the First World War would have a catalytic effect, transforming world views in a way that the suffrage movement's principled arguments had not been able to do.

o   The First World War would be a true total war, in which entire societies mobilized, in which industrial warfare made factory production as important as the movement of soldiers on the battlefield, and in which the lines between the war front and the home front blurred. Women on the home fronts took on new roles, as munitions workers, drivers, and clerical workers.

o This total war made vividly clear women's crucial role on the home front. In many countries, after the role they had played, the vote could no longer be denied them.

o In the United States, women gained the vote in 1920, but elsewhere, the process took longer. French women gained the vote in 1944, and Switzerland only allowed women to vote in federal elections in 1971. In Saudi Arabia, women are still not allowed to vote.

• Even though the completion of this turning point has not been fully reached, its effect has been tremendous. We have examined in our lectures how each of the turning points relates to what is seen as the legitimate and authentic principle of authority, and in this case, the authority of equal rights for women was a historic and profound step, changing how women and men viewed their world.

Suggested Reading

Fischer, *Fairness and Freedom.*

Grimshaw, *Women's Suffrage in New Zealand.*

Questions to Consider

1. Why did some settler societies, as in South America, not grant women the vote earlier?

2. Compare the movement for women's suffrage with the movement to abolish the slave trade: What are the main similarities and contrasts?

1893—First Women Voters in New Zealand
Lecture 15—Transcript

In the late 19th century and the early 20th century, determined women demanded the right to vote, which had been always been denied them before. They demanded it in ways that were more dramatic and forceful than before. In Britain, the suffragettes, as these most militant activists were called, engaged in increasingly dramatic clashes with authority.

They threw eggs at politicians; they chained themselves to fences and lampposts in protest; they smashed the windows of fancy downtown stores, and started fires on public trains. Once jailed, they went on hunger strikes. All of this to call attention to their cause. Yet, the real breakthrough came by less dramatic means: Women first gained the vote in New Zealand in 1893 by a sophisticated campaign of argument. How did this turning point happen as it did?

In thinking about that often-elusive term "modernity," a prominent badge of what it means to be modern has also been the acceptance of a political and social voice for the individual, whether that individual is male or female. Yet the self-evident and crucial step of recognizing women's right to vote actually came remarkably late, long after the revolutionary developments like the American Revolution or the French Revolution, which we considered in previous lectures. For most of human history, half of the human race was mostly excluded from political power and participation. In fact, it was only in 1893 that the first national state, New Zealand, legally recognized women's right to vote. Other countries followed this first step, years or decades later.

In this lecture, we trace how women's votes were achieved. Women's votes have also been called women's suffrage or franchise, which simply means the ability to participate politically in representative systems of government. Today we might take for granted that this makes perfect sense, but how did it come to pass at long last?

In essence, two global trends, the demand for women's political voice, and the growth of settler societies, intersected to create this crucial turning point, which spread from New Zealand worldwide. Let's examine these trends in turn and ask how and why they came together in 1893.

The international movement for women's votes can be seen as beginning in earnest with the Enlightenment ideas, which emphasized individual freedom and personal sovereignty. In spite of this core idea and its universality, actually few male Enlightenment thinkers championed women's rights, so it often would be the role of remarkable women to argue vigorously for this cause.

One example was Mary Wollstonecraft in England, who in 1792 published *A Vindication of the Rights of Woman* and has been seen as one of the founders of the feminist movement. In later decades, many activists for women's rights also drew inspiration from the anti-slavery movement which we discussed in an earlier lecture, as well as other reform movements active at the same time.

As the American Revolution was unfolding and a new American state was being created in 1776, Abigail Adams wrote to her husband, John Adams, then a member of the Continental Congress in Philadelphia, with the request: "I desire that you would remember the ladies, and be more generous and favorable to them than your ancestors," she wrote. If this did not happen, she warned of dire consequences: "If particular care and attention are not paid to the ladies, we are determined to foment a rebellion, and will not hold ourselves bound to obey any laws in which we have no voice or representation."

Unfortunately, Abigail Adams's request was disregarded, and the cause would have to be advanced in other ways. For a time, from 1776 to 1807, women had the right to vote in the state of New Jersey, but even these concessions were eroded over time.

At about the same era, as we've seen in an earlier lecture, the French Revolution pursued a trajectory that seemed to many to be full of radical possibilities for remaking society. Just as before the outbreak of the Revolution women had hosted the salons where Enlightenment ideas were actively discussed and where men and women could mix, so the revolutionary events saw the establishment of women's clubs and discussion groups, like the Society of Republican Revolutionary Women.

Women were also active on the opposite side of the growing radicalism of the revolutionaries. Olympia de Gouges, for instance, was both a royalist opposed to the radical revolutionaries, and an activist for women's rights. Such spirits were disappointed by the constitution of 1791, which made women merely "passive citizens."

Olympia de Gouges was critical of the "Declaration of the Rights of Man and Citizen," a founding document of the early stages of the French revolt in August 1789, so she wrote her own impassioned counterargument, entitled the "Declaration of the Rights of Woman and Female Citizen." In her text she argued, "Woman is born free and lives equal to man in her rights"; "The principle of all sovereignty rests essentially with the nation, which is nothing but the union of woman and man"; and she went on to state, "Liberty and justice consist of restoring all that belongs to others; thus, the only limits on the exercise of the natural rights of women are perpetual male tyranny; these limits are to be reformed by the laws of nature and reason." The very outspokenness of Olympia de Gouges and her independence of mind ended up alarming the fanatical revolutionaries, and de Gouges was sent to the guillotine in 1793.

The movement for women's rights revived in earnest around 1840 in America. Elizabeth Cady Stanton and Lucretia Mott, a Quaker from Philadelphia, had met actually in the context of a different movement. They had met at the World's Anti-Slavery Convention in London, which was part of a continuing worldwide struggle of abolitionists even after the abolition of slavery in the British Empire. So it was surprising that it was in this reformist context that the two women experienced something brutal that galvanized them. They were both refused the right to participate in the Congress as members because they were women.

It was this experience that propelled them to further activism when they returned to the United States, and they helped organize the famous Seneca Falls Convention in New York in 1848, with three hundred participants, men and women. There, a ringing resolution was passed: "It is the duty of the women of this country to secure to themselves the sacred right to the elective franchise."

The convention also adopted a Declaration of Rights and Sentiments, which took the original words of the Declaration of Independence and adapted them for their cause, like this: "We hold these truths to be self-evident: that all men and women are created equal ... the history of mankind is a history of repeated injuries and usurpations on the part of man toward woman, having in direct object the establishment of an absolute tyranny over her."

The cause that was championed at Seneca Falls also came at a time when women were active in the movement for the abolition of slavery in America. In 1851, Sojourner Truth, an African-American who had successfully escaped slavery, delivered a famous speech in Akron, Ohio at a women's conference. The speech was entitled "Ain't I a Woman?" This should ring a bell for us, because it was a deliberate echo of the famous motto of the British anti-slavery movement, "Am I Not a Man and a Brother?"

There are different versions of Sojourner Truth's speech, which was extemporaneous, but in the best-known version, Truth asked the question, "Ain't I a Woman?" as a refrain, while pointing out that this was an age in which there was much discussion of rights, whether for those in slavery in the South or women in the North. She pointed out that she had done the same hard labor as men; she had suffered as much or more than men while in slavery; and she concluded with a religious overture, that Christ had come from a woman and that "if the first woman God ever made was strong enough to turn the world upside down all alone, these women together ought to be able to turn it back, and get it right side up again! And now ... the men better let them."

In the decades that followed, Elizabeth Cady Stanton worked together with Susan B. Anthony to advance the cause. In 1866, Stanton stood for Congress, and received 24 votes out of 12,000. In 1872, Anthony was actually arrested for voting in the presidential election. Together, these women founded the National Woman Suffrage Association.

Successes finally came at the local level in the American western territories. In the Wyoming Territory, women's votes were recognized from 1869, the first modern legislature to allow it. When Wyoming became a state in 1890, its leaders insisted that when it entered the union it must do so with women's votes. To this day, Wyoming's nickname is the "Equality State." Other western states also recognized women's right to vote: Utah followed Wyoming by two months, Colorado in 1893, and Idaho in 1896.

Why was the frontier West first in this regard? The fact that these were areas of new settlement seems to have been crucial, because there, out in the West, social roles were more fluid, institutions inevitably less fixed and set in place, and experimentation was often viewed positively. These frontier states already had women playing very active and indeed indispensable roles in settlement and the building up of new institutions, especially educational institutions, so it's not surprising that women's education was also seen as vital in this regard.

Similarly, a mass movement for women's votes was also evolving in Britain in dramatic ways. A Quaker, Anne Knight, published the first women's suffrage pamphlet in 1847. In 1851, the first suffrage society was founded in Britain. A following generation of women's activists founded the Women's Social and Political Union and set out to engage in dramatic, militant action.

They were led by Christabel Pankhurst, and they were known as the "suffragettes" (this was first a term of abuse, but one that soon gained respect). They scuffled with the police from 1905. Let me give a few examples. Two militants actually smashed the windows on the house of Britain's prime minister. In 1912, the suffragettes organized a spectacular nationwide campaign of window breaking. They chained themselves to fences. They set fire to mailboxes to call attention to their cause. Then they bombed the house of the Chancellor of the Exchequer. Once in prison, suffragettes engaged in hunger strikes which gained further publicity, and eventually sympathy.

Most dramatically and tragically, in 1913, a young activist named Emily Davison came to the famous Epsom Derby horse race. She timed her action exactly, and stepped in front of the horse that was owned by none other than the British king George V. Davison was hit with tremendous speed by the startled racehorse and thrown to the ground. She died of her injuries several days later. Her funeral procession through London, with 2,000 women activists, was testimony to the determination of these activists.

In reaction, anti-suffrage movements rose up as well, both in the United States and in Britain. These protagonists (including both men and women) were convinced that allowing women's votes would be a violation of natural order and of social cohesion, which they saw as necessarily relegating women to an entirely domestic sphere. For instance, in 1889, over a hundred American women signed a so-called Appeal Against Female Suffrage, which argued that in fact, men who might have engaged in abuses in the past were actually really getting much much better, remarkably so (today we would say that they were "evolving"), and it promised that men would correct any abuses without changes in the law on voting.

In sum then, the continuing debate on women's vote was a key social issue in the later 19th century. It came to a climax in what for most people was really a stunningly remote place: the settler society of New Zealand, in 1893. Off in the South Pacific, New Zealand literally seemed to European imperialists the end of the earth. The original settlers of these lands were the Maori people. Dutch traders encountered these islands in 1642 and that's why they bear a Dutch name, "New Zealand." Eventually, British colonists moved in.

Colonial governors sent by London sought to balance the needs of new incoming settlement with the treaty rights of the Maori. Astonishingly, we've actually met one of these British governors of New Zealand in a previous lecture! That was Robert Fitzroy, who had been the captain of the survey ship the HMS *Beagle*, on which Charles Darwin sailed in the 1830s. Overall, New Zealand was an example of a settler society (like Canada and the United States), where envisioning society in new ways was not just possible, but often seemed existentially necessary!

Women's votes were achieved in New Zealand in ways that both resembled and diverged from the more familiar pattern that was seen later in the United States or Britain, where large movements were organized for the struggle. In New Zealand, women achieved the vote after eight years of hard organizational work, and did so much sooner than in the United States or Britain.

This had to do with the social context. In this frontier setting, women and women's work were seen as vital to the establishment of the new society. As a result, women's education took on a prominence and a sense of normalcy that were really quite unusual for the times elsewhere in the world.

Some key examples: In 1871, the first girls' high school opened in Dunedin, New Zealand. Soon young women were applying to New Zealand's new universities. One, Kate Edger, in 1877 became the first woman in the entire British Empire to earn an undergraduate degree. Helen Connon did so too and then went on to earn her master's degree. Others soon followed and by 1893, over half the university students in New Zealand were women!

Many New Zealanders were in fact proud of the achievements of these young women. New Zealand women became famous internationally for their independence and carving out a new way of life for themselves. Many after receiving education entered the professions or became educators themselves. Many also excelled at athletic pursuits, and what worldwide at the time was still regarded as a shocking sight, that of the female bicyclist wearing not a dress, but bloomer trousers while riding her bicycle, was increasingly quite ordinary in New Zealand. In 1891 it was even announced that in New Zealand a women's rugby team was being organized.

The key person who organized the women's movement was Kate Sheppard of Christchurch. She had been born in Liverpool in 1848 and then raised in Scotland, and had emigrated to New Zealand with her family. Sheppard was marked by good humor, strength, winning charm, and, beneath it all, tremendous reserves of calm determination. For instance, she was among those pioneering female bicyclists of New Zealand.

Moreover, Sheppard was motivated to action by tremendous and deeply felt moral conviction. She declared: "All that separates, whether of race, class, creed, or sex is inhuman, and must be overcome." She and other women first became active in New Zealand's temperance movement, to do something about the abuse of alcohol which was another common feature of many settler societies worldwide, wreaking damage on families and society at large.

They were inspired by a visiting American temperance activist, and they founded the National Women's Christian Temperance Union of New Zealand in 1885. Many activists were Congregationalists, Baptists, and Methodists, but what was really key here was that there was no doctrinal requirement to join and work in the organization, so ultimately it drew together women of different backgrounds and convictions for a common cause. The main historian of women's suffrage in New Zealand, historian Patricia Grimshaw, argues that the work of temperance was for New Zealand women kind of a vital "apprenticeship in the art of political agitation." The Temperance Union, with some 600 women members, was a first for the country: It was an organization led by women and a force for women.

As they set about drafting a reform program with temperance in mind, it occurred to many of these women that the best way of making their voices heard, on as the issue of temperance as well as other issues, was to secure what had been denied them before: the right to vote. Kate Sheppard was put in charge of the Temperance Union's committee on the franchise and legislation, and now the struggle ensued.

The organization borrowed from tactics we've already seen earlier pioneered in the abolitionist movement against slavery. These women wrote tracts and published pamphlets; they spoke at public meetings, and used their informal influence in society as well. Their meetings were drawing together women of different classes in a really remarkable alliance.

A tactic that had been most powerful for the abolitionists against slavery was also used to great effect by the women activists: the mass petition. Consider, here as in the case of abolition, even if one did not yet have the vote, the very act of signing a petition demanding reform was already a form of having a political voice. The suffrage activists organized a series of petition drives, the petitions to be signed by New Zealand women. In 1891, the first petition had 10,000 signers. Keep in mind this is from a smaller population. In 1892, the second petition already had double that number—20,000 signers. Then, the petition of 1893 had 31,871 signers, which was a quarter of all the adult women in the entire country! This was the largest petition ever submitted to the Parliament. When it was brought in to the New Zealand Parliament and unrolled, it was over 300 yards long, a visually impressive act! Another tactic by contrast was not one borrowed from earlier movements; it was new: Telegrams were sent. They were sent to wavering parliamentarians to bombard them with women's demands using this new technology.

However at the same time, opposition to women's suffrage also was being organized. Some were alarmed by the increasing support shown for this measure. Some of the opposition was actually sponsored and funded secretly by the alcohol industry and tavern keepers in New Zealand, called in general "the drink trade." They were anxious, with pretty good reason, about the mobilization that had grown out of the temperance cause. They wanted to quell it.

These critics asserted that the natural division of society was in danger of being violated or transgressed—that if this measure went through, women and men would become, as they called it "unsexed" and "degenerate" (these are social Darwinist terms) and society would collapse. As one magazine jibed, "When women's rights have come to stay, Oh, who will rock the cradle? When wives are at the polls all day, Oh who will rock the cradle?"

Similarly, a politician's speech in Parliament avowed, "Woman's Parliament is her home, and it is within that sphere that her function lies for making laws for our peace, order, and good government. I believe that, if you transfer her from that sphere to this, you spoil her for both." Some critics claimed that women would vote only as their ministers or priests told them to. The anti-suffrage organizations tried to organize a counter-petition of their own, but it was ultimately not very convincing, especially when news spread that free drinks were being offered to those who would sign such a petition.

In fact, many New Zealand men, including established political leaders of very different political backgrounds, supported women's right to vote. Some in fact thought that it would advance the fortunes of their own political party: Liberals expected women to vote liberal, while conservatives felt that women's votes would be helpfully conservative. One sees here that opinions on the subject cut across party lines and made for unusual alliances on both sides of the debate.

Then, on September 8, 1893, the New Zealand Parliament finally enfranchised women over the age of 21, and this became law 11 days later, so that women could vote in the upcoming parliamentary elections. And did they ever vote! Even before the registration offices were open, women were standing in long lines to register to vote long before. In the election that followed, more than 80 percent of the women who were eligible to vote did so. They were eagerly taking up a right that had been denied them so long, and they certainly felt that they were making history. As indeed they were.

The effects of the turning point in New Zealand were worldwide. When New Zealand women gained the vote, telegrams were sent to women's suffrage movements internationally from New Zealand to share the good news. Later, Kate Sheppard would travel around England, Canada, and the United States, lecturing about how this success had been achieved. Moreover, those first parliamentary elections of 1893 when women for the first time could cast their ballots also had a crucial effect: The very fact of the heavy voting by women refuted a longstanding argument that had been advanced by opponents of women's suffrage. That claim was that most women in fact didn't want the vote, were indifferent to it, and that allegedly it was only a loud and clamorous minority which was pressing this demand forward. Worldwide, many people saw New Zealand as a splendid experiment, as an example of progress taking place before their very eyes.

Many New Zealanders, men and women, were actually tremendously proud of being identified with a new equal status for women. The Prime Minister of New Zealand, Joseph Ward, explained, "The main argument ... which weighed with us was that of right, abstract right. If the foundation of the government is the consent of the governed, it appears monstrously unfair that one half of the population should not be represented or have any share in it." We see here, the trend towards popular sovereignty increasingly was recognized to include men and women.

This turning point however, let's be clear, did not overturn everything at once. In 1893, New Zealand women had won the vote, but the first woman in New Zealand was only elected to Parliament 40 years later, in 1933. Nor did all women all vote in the same way as a uniform block, but then it was precisely the ability to choose for oneself politically that had been at stake since the beginning. Kate Sheppard, who had been a prime mover of the cause (and today is to be seen on the New Zealand ten-dollar bill), reflected afterwards on what they had accomplished. She said, "Things have not been turned upside down. The country has not been brought to dire destruction, nor have all wrongs been righted. There has simply been an evolution."

Even with the example of New Zealand, elsewhere around the world women's votes were slow to come. Only four countries enfranchised women before the First World War broke out in 1914. First was New Zealand in 1893, then neighboring Australia in 1902, Finland in 1906, and Norway in 1913. In many countries, the experience of the First World War would have a catalytic effect, because it transformed views in a way that the suffrage movement's principled arguments had not been able to do (although their activism had certainly paved the way).

The First World War would be a true total war, in which entire societies were mobilized for total victory, and to stave off total defeat. It was a war in which industrial warfare made factory production as important as the movement of soldiers on the battlefield, and increasingly, the lines between the war front and home front blurred. Women on the home fronts took on new roles, as munitions workers, drivers, and clerical workers.

This total war made vividly clear women's crucial role on the home front, and in many countries, the vote simply couldn't be denied to them any more after the role they had played. In the United States for example, President Woodrow Wilson, who had opposed women's votes earlier, later endorsed women's suffrage as a measure for victory. In this new context, the 19th Amendment to the U.S. Constitution, enfranchising women, became law in 1920.

Similarly, after the First World War, other countries did likewise, including Britain, Germany, the Netherlands, and the Baltic countries of Estonia,

Latvia, and Lithuania. Elsewhere, the process took longer. French women gained the vote in 1944. Switzerland only allowed women to vote in federal elections in 1971, and the last restrictions on women's votes at the local level in Switzerland were removed only in 1990. Women gained the vote in Kuwait as recently as 2005. In Saudi Arabia, by contrast, women are still not allowed to vote today.

Even as the completion of this turning point, the enfranchisement of half the human race, has not been fully reached yet, its effect has been tremendous. We've examined in our lectures how each of the turning points relates to what is seen as the legitimate and authentic principle of authority, and in this case the authority of equal rights for women was a historic and profound step, changing how women and men viewed their world and themselves.

Around the same time, a literal change in viewing the world came with tremendous force, with the invention of motion pictures and film. It is this which we'll consider in our next lecture.

1896—The Invention of Motion Pictures
Lecture 16

On April 23, 1896, an audience in New York viewed moving pictures for the first time. Movies mirrored reality and, as we'll see in this lecture, could also create their own reality. But how was the invention of moving pictures a true turning point in modern history? It had a major impact on how humans viewed themselves and the world around them. After the invention of polished-metal mirrors in antiquity, the development of motion pictures revolutionized how the living, moving human body and image were regarded. By documenting, creating artistic visions, and delivering persuasive statements, whether aesthetic or political, moving pictures took on an authority and effectiveness that transformed our social and public lives.

Early Photographs and Moving Pictures
- During the Dutch Golden Age, Johannes Vermeer apparently used optical equipment in his paintings, the so-called "camera obscura" ("dark chamber").
  - Known since classical times, the camera obscura was an optical device that could be used to project an upside-down image of a scene onto a screen, where it could be traced with perfect perspective and color.

  - The camera obscura was a precursor to photography. By the first half of the 19th century, chemical processes were used to fix and duplicate those projected images.

- Movies and cinema were anticipated in the work of the photographer Eadweard Muybridge, who from the 1870s, worked on "motion studies" of animals and people, using a series of exposures to capture and freeze movement.

- Other inventors were also working on systems to capture motion. The Lumière brothers, Louis and Auguste, fused the process of filming and projecting film in early 1895. In films lasting about a minute, they captured scenes of everyday life and showed them to small audiences in Paris cafes.

- In the United States, Thomas Edison bought and improved a projector created by the inventors Thomas Armat and Charles Francis Jenkins. Edison renamed the projector the Vitascope, and his studio was soon turning out a wide range of short movies that appealed to a broad public.

The Life of Edison
- Edison is a fascinating and elusive character: a genius without much in the way of formal education, a charismatic but remote man, and an entrepreneur capable of considerable brutality in competition. But above all, Edison was the man who invented the inventor as a cultural ideal.

- Edison was born in Ohio in 1847 and raised in Port Huron, Michigan. As a youth, when he wasn't blowing up his parents' house with chemical experiments, he was reading Thomas Paine's *Age of Reason*, which he later recalled as a decisive moment of enlightenment in his life.

- Edison struggled with deafness that grew worse as he grew older, but he overcame it remarkably. Starting as a telegrapher, he moved on to becoming a fulltime tinkerer with technology. He produced a cascade of inventions, including the electrical vote recorder, mimeograph machine, microphone, and phonograph to record the human voice.

- He also invented an improved stock ticker, improved typewriter, improved telegraph technology, improved telephone, and more. He often used earlier inventions in new ways, innovating on how technology was organized. By the end of his life, he held more than 1,000 patents.

- Most of all, Edison invented the research laboratory. He set up his famous workshop in 1876 in Menlo Park, New Jersey. It came to be called an invention factory, and Edison was nicknamed the "Wizard of Menlo Park."

- The invention by Edison of the archetype of the genius inventor represents a decisive moment in the arrival of newness as a desirable thing in modernity. Edison sealed the American obsession with technology and technical solutions.

- Under Edison's direction, films poured forth from the custom-built studio he maintained, including one of kittens boxing and another of a couple kissing. At first, such films were shown not to audiences but to individuals in Kinetoscope parlors or nickelodeons.

Early Theaters and Audiences
- The shift from individual to public viewing opened up an entirely new social sphere, even larger and more inclusive than the print culture that Gutenberg's printing press had opened. By 1908, there were more than 8,000 nickelodeons in the United States, with millions of people attending every day.

- These early theaters were lively, bustling places, with continuous showings of films and seats often not segregated by class or price, accessible to both poor and wealthy audiences. The formula was escapism, to lose oneself in the new stories told in this new medium.

- Some historians of American immigration see movies as a vital integrating medium for newcomers. This emerging public also affected what films were produced. There was a feedback loop in terms of public taste, as nickelodeon managers listened to what features evoked most enthusiasm and then tried to get more of them.

- Moreover, this revolutionary development was global. Because the films were silent, they were uniquely accessible. If words were needed in some explanatory slide that punctuated the drama, these could be spliced in using the local language. This was radical accessibility!

- Silent films had to create their own visual vocabulary that would be understood and accepted. Thus, cutting from one scene and then back again and the use of close-ups or "dissolves" as transitions between scenes were all new conventions. An employee of Edison's, Edwin Porter, established many of these techniques in *The Great Train Robbery* of 1903.

- The man who endowed film with a powerful narrative impulse around this time was Georges Méliès. Without him, the novelty of short features might have faded. But Méliès was entranced by this new medium and used it to tell magical stories.
  o Méliès started showing his own movies in 1896, marked by fantastical images and creativity. He is called the father of special effects.

  o His most famous film is the 1902 *A Trip to the Moon*, in which French astronomers fly to the moon, poke the man in the moon in the eye, and encounter moon creatures before making a spectacular escape back to earth.

- Reportedly, early audiences reacted with shock and confusion to some unfamiliar scenes. It is said that when films showed oncoming trains, audiences scattered or ducked down, screaming. But they quickly came to comprehend the new rules and conventions of this medium.

- It's important to note that silent films were not really silent. Sometimes, live actors lip-synched offstage, and many theaters had employees who made sound effects or provided musical accompaniment. In Japan, *benshi* were narrators who explained what was going on, speaking the parts and commenting on the film.

Influences of Movies on Society

- From the very first, movies raised anxieties about morality. People of different classes mingled in some theaters. Unchaperoned youths frequented the movies. Early blockbusters, such as D. W. Griffith's *Birth of a Nation*, had patently racist messages. Edison's film of the kiss was soon followed by much racier fare, and violence in movies was a staple from the first. Concerns about the powerful effects of movies are with us still.

- But films also expanded the mental horizons of the millions who were making them a part of their ordinary lives. The ability to see faraway places and notable people and events revolutionized modern people's view of their world, making it smaller and seemingly more familiar.

- Eventually, the film industry centered on the dream factory of Hollywood, and theaters became veritable temples of cinema. The film industry also created the modern cult of celebrity, a global level of fame unlike anything ever seen before.

Such early film stars as Mary Pickford, along with Buster Keaton, Bela Lugosi, and Charlie Chaplin, were recognizable to millions of people worldwide.

- Many comedies poked fun at authority, such as the Keystone Kops series. In 1936, Charlie Chaplin's *Modern Times* was a comic comment on modernity itself, as the "little guy" battled to survive in a technological and often inhuman modern society.

- To meet calls for censorship, in 1922, the studios establish their own controlling office, the Hays Office. Paradoxically, this self-policing meant that a good deal of vice could be put on display as long as it was punished at the end and virtue triumphed.

Changes in Technology and Industry

- After three and a half decades of silent films, recorded sound came to the movies, an innovation that was at first met with skepticism. Sound meant rewiring thousands of cinemas and losing the universality and international accessibility of the earlier silent films. Color arrived in the 1930s, the decade of such blockbusters as *Gone with the Wind* and *The Wizard of Oz*.

- The Depression created cravings for escapism. By 1930, 90 million Americans were watching a movie at least once a week. Genres that are still with us today proliferated, including comedy, social dramas, westerns, horror films, action pictures, animation, and science fiction.

- Movies were also powerful in the hands of modern dictatorships as propaganda tools. This use was illustrated by the Soviet and Nazi regimes in turn.

  o When the Bolsheviks took power in the ruins of the Russian Empire in 1917, their aim was to build a new, revolutionary society. Their leader, Vladimir Lenin announced, "Of all the arts, cinema is the most important for us." Film would convince illiterate masses and spread a revolutionary message. So-called "agitprop" trains toured Russia, showing revolutionary films to peasants and workers.

  o When Stalin came to power, he dictated a new formula that all artists had to follow, "socialist realism," which commanded artists to depict the perfect society into which the Soviet Union was allegedly evolving.

  o In Germany in the 1930s, the Nazis were keenly aware of the propaganda power of film. The director Leni Riefenstahl used her considerable artistic talents to produce movies celebrating the Nazi vision of a racially united Germany, including the wicked propaganda masterpiece of 1935 *Triumph of the Will* and a record of the Nazi Olympics in Berlin.

- Today, we face another transformation of the movies. The great movie palaces have faded, and films have gone digital. In 2012, people in America watched an estimated 3.4 billion movies online, not together in magnificent movie palaces but individually, recalling the nickelodeon boxes of the earliest days of film.

Suggested Reading

Baldwin, *Edison.*

Dixon and Foster, *A Short History of Film.*

Ellis and Wexman, *A History of Film.*

Questions to Consider

1. Do all new technologies involve shocking first impressions, as film did?

2. What film has made the greatest impression on you and why?

1896—The Invention of Motion Pictures
Lecture 16—Transcript

Let's start this lecture about motion pictures with two astonishing scenes, taking place at the same time, but one in New York and the other in Paris.

Scene 1: It is April 23, 1896. We're in bustling New York, in Manhattan. We're at a vaudeville theater, Koster and Bial's Music Hall (today by the way, this is where the new main Macy's store now sits). In the darkness, light is projected onto a screen set in a gold-colored frame, and to our astonishment, we see what looks like a painting, but is actually moving!

The movie projector is the Vitascope, produced by the great inventor Thomas Edison. As we watch with amazement, we see the most astonishing images, real as life: dancers, a comic boxing match, and a seaside scene. In that scene, great waves of water rise up and prepare to crash onto us, soaking us to the bone. The audience screams and pulls back, but then no water follows. It's all on the screen. Imagine what it felt to see those moving pictures for the very first time! Now fade out to …

Scene 2: It is still 1896. In Paris, a magician named Méliès, filming the life of the city, accidentally discovers special effects. This is how it happened: His camera jammed for awhile as he was filming a city scene, but then he got it going again. When he later developed the film, he was astonished by the magic he had accidentally created. In the film, a bus that was going by, drawn by a horse, all of a sudden turned into a hearse! While he had been struggling with his camera, the traffic had moved on, and created this astonishing transformation on screen. Méliès had accidentally discovered special effects, and would turn them into an art form that endures into our own day.

What these scenes from the birth of the movies show is the tremendous potential of motion pictures. Movies mirrored reality (like those waves in the New York film) and created dreams (as in the special effects magic of Méliès) and, as we'll see later, movies could also create their own reality, persuading audiences through propaganda.

How was this a true turning point in modern history? It had a huge impact on how humans viewed themselves and the world around them. After the invention of polished metal mirrors in antiquity, it was really the development of motion pictures that revolutionized once again how the living, moving human body and image has been regarded.

In addition, motion pictures gave a kind of immortality to the person captured on screen. By documenting, creating artistic visions, and delivering persuasive statements, whether aesthetic, or political, or commercial, the image took on an authority and effectiveness that has transformed our social and public life. Of course, ultimately, it was this turning point that allowed for the marvelous filmed lectures of professors speaking to you as part of *The Great Courses!*

Yet motion pictures are really in a kind of succession. They represent but one very late stage in an overall human urge to observe, and represent, and to create. That urge can be seen from cave paintings to the videos posted on YouTube in our own times. In the visual arts, artists over the centuries have sought ways to powerfully render the realities they perceived. The movement towards perspective that marked the Renaissance was a key moment in that quest, and painters sought to push that verisimilitude, that likeness to real life ever further.

During the Dutch Golden Age which we discussed in an earlier lecture, that great painter, Johannes Fermeer, apparently used optical equipment to produce just such precise detailed paintings. While his good friend Leuwenhoek was discovering microorganisms through the microscope, Fermeer used the so-called camera obscura, the "dark chamber." This was an invention that had been known since classical times, and later was described in Diderot's *Encyclopédie*. The camera obscura was an optical device that, when light passed through a small hole in its wall, projected an upside down image of a scene onto a screen. There, that image could be traced and copied, with perfect perspective and color.

As you can tell from the technical description (and the name "camera"), this was a precursor to photography. By the first half of the 19th century chemical processes were being used to fix and duplicate those images projected onto a screen. The photographic image was also a huge transformation in how we saw ourselves and our world, but moving pictures would be incomparably more so!

Yet, what we call moving pictures are not quite that. In fact, what we see is the mechanically produced illusion of movement. Images flashing by at sufficient speed seem to us to move; that's a trick of the eye. But how was that accomplished?

Movies and cinema were in fact anticipated in the famous work of the English-born American photographer Eadweard Muybridge, who from the 1870s worked on motion studies, as they were called, of animals and people, using a quick series of exposures to capture and freeze movement.

While he was working in Palo Alto, California, Muybridge was asked to settle a bet by someone we met in an earlier lecture. This was the former governor of California, Leland Stanford, who back in 1869 swung at the last spike of the transcontinental railroad and apparently missed (and who also later founded Stanford University at Palo Alto). At the time, most people thought that a horse as it galloped always had at least one foot on the ground, but Stanford offered Muybridge $25,000 to prove that it did not. Muybridge worked for years to get the shutter speed and technique just right to photograph a running horse. In the process, he created the technology for motion pictures, and helped win the bet.

At this time, other inventors were also working on systems to capture motion. The Lumière Brothers, Louis and Auguste, fused the process of filming and projecting of film in early 1895. In films of usually just a minute in length, they captured scenes of everyday life and showed these to small audiences in Paris cafes, a sort of a small entertainment. But the brothers perhaps did not really foresee the medium's full potential, because one of them called it "an invention without a future."

In America, the inventor Thomas Edison had a very different perspective. He saw this medium as one that had a future and one that would last. In the United States, Edison bought and improved a projector created by the inventors Thomas Armat and Charles Francis Jenkins. Edison renamed it the Vitascope. Soon Edison's studio was turning out a wide range of short movies that appealed to an ever-broader public.

Who was this man? Edison is a fascinating and yet ultimately elusive character. He was a genius, without much in the way of formal education. A charismatic, but remote man. An entrepreneur, capable, as it turns out, of considerable brutality when it came to competition. But above all, Edison was the man who invented the inventor as a cultural ideal.

Edison was born in Ohio in 1847, and raised in Port Huron, Michigan. As a youth, Edison largely educated himself after some disastrous experiences with formal schooling. When Edison wasn't blowing up his parents' house with chemical experiments, he was reading Thomas Paine's *Age of Reason*, which he later recalled as a decisive moment of enlightenment in his own life.

Edison struggled with deafness that grew worse as he grew older, but he overcame it in remarkable ways. Starting as a telegrapher, he moved on to becoming a fulltime tinkerer with technology. Edison produced a cascade of inventions, many around in new forms today, like the electrical vote recorder, the mimeograph machine, the microphone, and the phonograph to record the human voice.

Edison also invented (see if you can spot the pattern here) an improved stock ticker, an improved typewriter, improved telegraph technology (in fact he was so besotted with the telegraph that he nicknamed his children "Dot" and "Dash," after Morse code). He also invented an improved telephone, improved electrical networks, improved dynamos, and improved storage batteries.

This was classic Edison. He used earlier inventions of others in new ways, innovating how technology was organized. As Edison himself put it, "I start where the last man left off." By the end of his life, Edison held more than a thousand patents.

Most of all, Edison invented the research laboratory. He set up his famous workshop that never slept, as the phrase went, in 1876 in Menlo Park, New

Jersey (25 miles southwest of New York City). It was the first of its kind. It came to be called an invention factory. Edison came to be nicknamed the "Wizard of Menlo Park" or the "New Jersey Columbus."

In this laboratory, in 1879, Edison abolished centuries of nighttime darkness by perfecting the incandescent light bulb. At a stroke, his improved light bulb altered daily routines that earlier had been ruled by the sun, and in the process he overthrew the kingdom of night and its darkness.

Clearly, Edison was the very archetype of the genius inventor—there had been people who invented before, but Edison made it his calling. We should say that he invented his job of being a genius inventor! This is really a decisive moment for our course. It's the moment of the arrival of newness as a desirable thing in modernity, which we've traced throughout our lectures. Edison sealed the characteristic American obsession with technology and technical solutions or fixes.

Under Edison's direction, films poured forth from the custom-built studio that he maintained; it was one of the first of its kind. It wasn't much to look at—it was a black shack covered in tarpaper to keep out the light. But it had some innovations: It was mounted on a circular track, so it could be moved to follow the sunlight. Edison's group produced (among many other films) films of kittens in a boxing match (so when you see some unbearably cute YouTube video of something like this, you know now whom to blame for it), a film of a couple kissing (which was a really saucy sensation at the time), and the first filmed commercial, for Dewar's Scotch whiskey.

Throughout the country, and increasingly worldwide, these short films were shown, but at first not to audiences. Rather, people watched them individually. In so-called Kinetoscope parlors or nickelodeons, viewers actually stood over and craned into a kind of box, reminiscent of the Dutch trunks as in the early days of telescopes, telescopes were called. Inside these boxes, a film was running continuously, and the viewer who deposited some money would examine it through a magnifying glass (there are shades here of Leeuwenhoek and his simple microscopes).

But over time, audiences shifted from individual viewing to collective public viewing. This opened up an entirely new social sphere, even bigger and more inclusive than the print culture which Gutenberg's printing press had opened up with the print revolution. By 1908, there were more than 8,000 Nickelodeons in the United States and millions were attending them every day.

These early theaters were lively, bustling places, with continuous showing of films, with seats often not segregated by class or price, and accessible as a result to poor audiences as well as the wealthy, showing a huge variety of films. The overall formula was escapism, to lose oneself in the new stories being told in this new medium.

In fact, some historians of American immigration see movies as a vital integrating medium for newcomers newly arrived in the United States. This emerging public also affected what films were produced. There was kind of a feedback loop in terms of public taste, because nickelodeon managers would stand close by and listen to which features they were showing evoked most enthusiasm and then they'd go out to order more of those.

Moreover, this revolutionary development of movies was global, for a world audience. Because the films were silent at first, without spoken dialogue, they were uniquely accessible internationally. If words were needed for some explanatory slide that punctuated the drama—if you imported the film to another country—it could be easily accomplished to splice in a new slide in the local language. This was radical accessibility! Recall from an earlier lecture how Diderot's *Encyclopédie* had aimed to be useful and accessible. How delighted Diderot would have been by this medium, which was even more open for all than print!

At the same time, we might also say that cinema was developing a kind of language on the spot. Silent films had to create what amounted to a visual vocabulary that would be understood and accepted, and it was not identical to traditional theater on the stage. Let me give some examples. Thus, cutting back from one scene and then back to another, was new. The use of close-ups in camera angles for instance, or "dissolves" as a way of showing transitions between scenes were all new conventions. An employee of Edison's, Edwin Porter, created one of the most famous early films, the 12-minute classic *The Great Train Robbery* in 1903. It was actually his film that established many of these techniques we take for granted today.

The man who endowed film with a powerful narrative impulse around this time was the Frenchman Georges Méliès. Without him, the novelty of short features of some half a minute or less might have faded. By contrast, Méliès told magical stories. In fact originally, he had been a magician who had been entranced by this new medium of film. Méliès started showing his own movies in 1896, marked by fantastical images and outlandish creativity. He's called the father of special effects. His most famous film is the 1902 film *A Trip to the Moon*, in which French astronomers fly to the Moon, in the process poking the man in the Moon in the eye, and on the Moon they encounter Moon creatures before making a spectacular escape back to Earth.

What do we know about how these early films were received? The first audience reactions are a thing of legend, and it's possible that some exaggeration has been built up about how the audiences reacted. Reportedly, early audiences reacted with shock and confusion to some unfamiliar scenes. Recall from our opening scene at the start of this lecture in 1896 in Koster and Bial's Music Hall, how the public was astonished and fearful at crashing waves coming in from the sea! It's also said that when films showed oncoming trains, audiences tended to scatter or duck down, screaming. In *The Great Train Robbery* film, there is a scene which is really a non sequitur right at the very end where a cowboy appears, points his pistol at the audience, smiles, and shoots. It doesn't really play a role in the plot; it was apparently put in just for the thrill of it.

But consider how quickly audiences assimilated and comprehended the new rules and conventions of this medium! Films that were made just a few years later in fact actually invited sophisticated film audiences to laugh at those who were not familiar with the conventions! One example is the 1902 film made by Edison's group, entitled *Uncle Josh at the Moving Picture Show*. It was actually a remake of a British film that had borne the title *The Countryman's First Sight of the Animated Pictures*.

This is a film about film viewing. It shows a rustic country bumpkin fellow at a cinema who seriously misunderstands what movies are. He tries to dance with a dancer on the screen; he jumps out of the way of an oncoming train that is actually on screen; and finally, outraged by the depiction of improper behavior on screen, he smashes up the place in search of the wrongdoers. Clearly, the audience was being invited to feel proud about its own progress, being modern and up to date compared to the bumpkin for whom all this was new. The movies were the cutting edge of the modern.

Another important point to add is that contrary to the name "silent films" they were actually not silent. First of all, there were the collective reactions of the audience: "oooo's" and "aaaah's" or shrieks or laughs. Sometimes in addition, live actors lip-synched what was going on on the screen offstage. Theaters sometimes had employees who made sounds for special effects, like the clip-clop of horses riding along. Many theaters also featured musical accompaniment, not always successfully chosen. Sometimes an employee would play a piano, trying to improvise music to match the film that was being seen. Some people called these pianos instruments of torture. Sometimes the music was wildly inappropriate. There were complaints at one theater, for instance, when a scene of tragedy was accompanied by cheerful jazz music.

Globally, each society had its own conventions for how to view film. In Japan for instance, *benshi* were narrators who explained to the audience what was going on on-screen, speaking the parts, and sometimes offering comments on the film itself. In Brazil, a kind of hybrid form evolved where singers sang the parts of musicals that were silent from behind the screen.

From the very first, the movies raised anxieties about morality. After all, people of different classes mingled in some theaters. Un-chaperoned youths frequented the movies. Early blockbuster films like D. W. Griffith's *Birth of a Nation* had patently racist messages. Edison's film of the kiss that we mentioned was soon followed by much racier fare. In addition, violence in movies was a staple from the very first as well, and not just in the form of kittens in a boxing ring. Worries about the powerful effect that movies have on us are with us still.

But films also did tremendous things for the mental horizons of the millions and millions who were making the movies a part of their ordinary lives. Film showing faraway places and notable people and current events in newsreels revolutionized modern people's view of their world, making it smaller and seemingly more familiar.

Eventually, this industry came to center on the dream factory of Hollywood in southern California. The films Hollywood produced were screened around the country and exported around the world (as of course they still are today). When they were screened, they were often shown in veritable temples to cinema! The phrase "movie palace" has it exactly right, for those who can still remember what some of these beautiful theaters used to look like, created to resemble the Alhambra or Babylonian temples.

The film also created the modern cult of celebrity, a global level of fame unlike anything seen before. Stars like Mary Pickford, Buster Keaton, or Bela Lugosi were recognizable to millions worldwide. Recall all the way back in our lecture on the French Revolution how King Louis XVI was trying to escape the revolution, but was recognized by somebody, by a fluke, because that person had seen printed currency with the king's face. Well, the fame of a movie star was infinitely greater than that of the unfortunate king.

Probably the very best example of movie stardom is still Charlie Chaplin. Earlier he'd been a vaudeville actor in England, but Chaplin went on to completely master film and created his distinctive character, the Tramp, a disheveled and often anarchic character who makes a mockery of respectability and propriety and social status, while at the same time evoking a shared humanity that viewers related to with tremendous intensity. This celebration of the common man (which was also accompanied by some of the most astonishing pantomime and physical slapstick) showed that the movies could have a democratizing aspect.

Many comedies also poked fun at authority similarly, like the Keystone Kops series. In 1936, Charlie Chaplin's film *Modern Times* was a comic comment on modernity itself, as Chaplin portrayed the little guy who just battled to survive in a technological, accelerated, and often inhuman modern society. But Chaplin, even when he played the Tramp—especially when he was playing the Tramp—was a superstar. By 1918, he commanded a salary of a million dollars a year.

Innovations continued at breakneck speed, and they reconfigured the medium of film again and again. To meet calls for censorship, in 1922, the studios establish their own controlling office, the so-called Hays Office. Paradoxically, in this practice, what ended up happening was that the self-policing of the studios meant that quite a lot of vice could be put on display, as long as it was punished at the end, and virtue was triumphant.

Then, after three and a half decades of silent films, recorded sound came to the movies. It was met with skepticism at first. In 1909, an article in the magazine *Moving Picture World* declared, "The whole business is unnatural, and nothing that is unnatural will ever last long." Sound in practice meant rewiring thousands of cinemas, and it also meant losing the universality and international accessibility of the earlier silent films. But sound was here to stay after the 1927 film *The Jazz Singer*. Color then arrived in the 1930s, the decade of blockbusters like *Gone with the Wind* and *Wizard of Oz*.

The Depression created cravings for escapism. By 1930, 90 million Americans were watching a movie at least once a week. Genres that are still with us today proliferated: comedy, social dramas, Westerns, horror films, action pictures, animation. Especially interesting for our purposes are science fiction films, because they were really thought experiments about world historical turning points. These films used special effects to conjure up future worlds, whether they were fearful or attractive.

Let me discuss just one example, a film made from a book by an author we've actually encountered in these lectures already. That is the British writer H.G Wells, and his book was entitled *The Shape of Things to Come*. In his book, published in 1933, he recounted a "future world history" taking us up to the year 2105. Wells predicted a cataclysmic world war (this was a really good prediction because World War II broke out soon afterwards), and then he predicted the reconstruction of the world on a new basis, led by technical experts who will use a "dictatorship of the air," use airpower to impose a benevolent new world order.

Wells imagines a world government beyond the Westphalian model of sovereignty, a one-world administration. The film version of this book opened in 1936, directed by Cameron Menzies. Because of its powerful images, it's considered by some one of the ten greatest movies ever. Wells, by contrast, was just crushed. He felt that the movie oversimplified and dumbed down his message—and Wells is surely not the first or last author to feel this way about a film version of a book.

I must also include a cautionary note here as well. If Chaplin's comedies and others carried a democratizing message for the masses, if science fiction movies like Wells's invited us to speculate about new ways of living, movies also were powerful in the hands of modern dictatorships, as propaganda tools. This was illustrated by the Soviet and Nazi regimes.

When the Bolsheviks took power in the ruins of the Russian empire in 1917, their aim was to build a new, fundamentally unprecedented, revolutionary society. Their leader, Vladimir Lenin, announced, "Of all the arts, cinema is the most important for us." Why was this? Film would convince illiterate masses and spread a revolutionary message. Special so-called agitprop trains—agitation propaganda trains—rode around revolutionary Russia, showing films to peasants and workers with a radical message. When Stalin came to power, he dictated a new formula that all artists had to follow, including filmmakers, from 1934. This was called socialist realism, and it commanded artists to show not what the Soviet Union was really like now at the moment, but rather the perfect society it was allegedly evolving into. This led to films on the formula of "boy meets tractor, boy falls in love with tractor, boy and tractor build socialism together." Oddly, such films are not much watched today.

In Nazi Germany in the 1930s, the Nazis for their part were keenly aware of the propaganda power of film. The director Leni Riefenstahl used her considerable artistic talents to produce movies that celebrated the Nazi vision of a racially united Germany, including that wicked propaganda masterpiece of 1935, *Triumph of the Will*, as well as a record of the Nazi Olympics in Berlin. Like so many inventions we we've seen in this course, movies could be weaponized as it were for political purposes, and they would be.

Today, we face another transformation of movies. The great movie palaces have faded. Now movies have gone digital. In 2012, people in America watched an estimated 3.4 billion movies online, not together in magnificent movie palaces. Now in fact, people can and do watch films on their cell phones—it's almost as if we're coming back full circle to the nickelodeon boxes of the earliest days of film.

But movies as a thing of dreams are with us still. Of human dreams, the oldest has been to soar with the birds in the sky, and we'll examine that turning point in our next lecture.

1903—Kitty Hawk and Powered Flight
Lecture 17

The moment when two bicycle engineers broke the shackles of earth for the first time must have been exhilarating. Today, we have become so used to the routine of air travel that it is difficult to imagine our way back to an earlier time, to feel the wonder that clung to the very idea! Humans soaring like birds had been declared impossible yet was a permanent fantasy of the human race. The heavens were both alluring and forbidding, the realm of divinity. In this lecture, we'll look at the way in which the development of flight redrew the world and shaped the experience of modernity.

Flight in Earlier Centuries

- In the 15th and 16th centuries, the genius Leonardo da Vinci had a lifelong fascination with flight. He mused, "A bird is an instrument working according to mathematical law... which it is within the capacity of man to reproduce."

- Just before the French Revolution, the brothers Joseph and Étienne Montgolfier built the first hot-air balloon and demonstrated their invention for King Louis XVI.

- In Britain, the engineer George Cayley experimented with gliders throughout the first half of the 19th century. One of his great advances involved understanding the importance of streamlining.

- Jules Verne based a number of stories on the impulse to fly, using different imagined technologies. His first popular novel was the 1863 *Five Weeks in a Balloon*, and his famous 1873 novel *Around the World in Eighty Days* also featured a balloon journey as part of the global race.

- Experiments with lighter-than-air craft continued, using hydrogen gas to lift the vehicles. In 1900, the German Count von Zeppelin pioneered airships named after himself.

- The German engineer Otto Lilienthal, in the 1890s, further perfected gliders, producing graceful, birdlike forms from which the pilot dangled. One in a long line of aviation fatalities, Lilienthal died in a gliding accident in 1896.

The Wright Brothers

- Wilbur and Orville Wright grew up in Dayton, Ohio. Their father, Milton Wright, was a bishop of the United Brethren Church, and his responsibilities in the ministry meant that he was often away from home. Their mother, Susan, was from a German family of carriage makers. She was adept at mechanical challenges and passed this trait to her sons.

The Wright brothers' life work was inspired by a toy helicopter given to them as children by their father.

- The brothers had little formal schooling but were fired by a love of science. As they grew older, they set up a printing shop and a bicycle shop.

- News of Lilienthal's death in Germany in a glider accident galvanized them. They set about studying all that was known about flight, surveying the work of earlier pioneers. As they did so, they were shocked to discover errors in calculations of air resistance, prompting them to launch their own experiments.

- The brothers built their own wind tunnel for making measurements and arrived at the innovation of "wing warping" to stabilize flight. From 1900, they took their experiments to Kill Devil Hills, a site near Kitty Hawk, North Carolina. The area had sand dunes for soft landings, and the height of the dunes made them ideal for launching. But the environment could be cold and fiercely windy, and during summer, mosquitoes were a terrible plague.

- At Kitty Hawk, using a succession of gliders, the brothers worked out the challenges before them. Ultimately, they created a biplane glider design, with a rudder for steering and forward elevators to ascend or descend. To this, they added a 12-horsepower engine, which drove revolving propellers, essentially wings that spun around to propel flight.

- The Wright brothers had invited locals from miles around to see their experiment on December 17, 1903, but only five people showed up. After tossing a coin to decide who would begin, Orville made the first flight, which lasted 12 seconds. A flight by Wilbur lasted 59 seconds and covered 852 feet.

- Back in Ohio, the brothers continued improving their machine. They received a patent for their plane in 1906 and, later, successfully fought off disputes by competitors. In 1908, Wilbur Wright traveled to Europe to demonstrate the craft.

- In 1909, the Wright brothers founded a company to build and sell planes. Wilbur died in 1912, but Orville lived until 1948, having witnessed revolutionary improvements in his invention.

A Craze for Flight

- The result of the Wright brothers' invention was a flying craze. Huge crowds gathered to witness this amazing spectacle. Contemporaries marveled at what they felt was the dawn of a new age of human history: the "Air Age."

- The American writer Ida Tarbell reflected keenly on her experience of flying for the first time. Wearing a silk hood and goggles, she sat behind the pilot as they took off, accelerating to 50 miles per hour. When she looked down, she declared, "The surprise of it seemed to stun me. Not that I lost consciousness, but I was literally lost in amazement at the suddenness and ease of it."

- Contests, exhibitions, races, and barnstorming stunt shows became all the rage. Nations competed against each other, with the French surging ahead. By 1911, the world records for speed, altitude, and endurance were all held by French pilots. The French founded the first flight training schools and led the world in plane production before the First World War.

- Pilots were idolized as people who had mastered the soulless machines of the 19th century.
  - The American Charles Lindbergh, nicknamed the "Lone Eagle," was deified when he made his 1927 solo flight across the Atlantic, covering 3,600 miles from New York to Paris. On his return to New York, he was greeted by 4 million people and a ticker-tape parade. Even a popular dance was named after him, the "lindy hop."

  - The most famous female aviator was Amelia Earhart, the first woman to fly alone across the Atlantic. In 1937, Earhart set out to become the first woman to fly around the world, but her plane was lost in the Pacific, a mystery still unsolved to this day.

○ Love of flying also drove Bessie Coleman, the first female African American pilot, who overcame both gender and racial discrimination to earn her pilot's license in France in 1921.

- There was even a word that became popular at this time to suggest how flight was changing what was possible. This word was "air-mindedness," which suggested a modern willingness to do things in a new way, to explore what flight could do.

- The first major U.S. airlines, including TWA, American Airlines, United Airlines, and Northwest Airlines, originated as carriers of air mail. Later, they branched out to passenger service.

- In 1935, the first transpacific commercial flight took place, the "China Clipper" of Pan American Airlines. The name of this flying boat was intentionally reminiscent of those ships that had carried tea from China in the age of sail.

Military Applications of Flight

- Aviation threatened to upset the Westphalian order of territorial sovereignty launched in 1648. That order had established the authority of rule over land, but who would enforce sovereignty in the skies?

- No sooner had powered flight been invented than it was put to military uses, to rain death from the skies. This was not only the perversity of arms dealers and generals at work. In fact, the Wrights marketed their invention as a formidable tool of war and got the first contract in 1908 from the U.S. Army. An air arms race was on!

- The first use of the airplane in war came in 1911—only eight years after its invention—in the Italian-Turkish war over Libya. World War I saw both the celebrated fighter aces dueling in the skies and the beginnings of strategic bombing.

- More than anything else, air warfare ushered in the reality of total war. This term refers to industrialized warfare not of armies alone but of entire societies and home fronts, in which everyone, including civilians, is a participant and a potential target. Strategic bombing brought that home, terrifying political and military leaders and populations at large.

- Hitler's air force pioneered dive bombers equipped with sirens that wailed as they attacked to terrify those on the ground. In World War II, Nazi terror bombing of Warsaw, Rotterdam, and London was followed by round-the-clock bombing of Germany by Allied air forces and the obliteration of Hamburg and Dresden.

- Incredibly, one man had predicted this development in uncanny ways—the British writer H. G. Wells in his novel *The War in the Air*, published in 1908. The core thesis of the book was that the airplane alters the character of war. Just as war becomes more destructive, it becomes less decisive and more meaningless.

Flight in the Modern World
- Today, flight is a turning point so woven into our lives that many of us take it for granted. It is reported that in 2010, global air passengers topped 5 billion for the first time.

- Yet to fly and arrive hours later on a different continent still has its effects. Being that mobile can broaden your horizons intellectually and produce a different you, a you that would not have existed without human flight.

Suggested Reading

Kennett, *A History of Strategic Bombing.*

Wohl, *A Passion for Wings.*

1. What was the Wright brothers' key to success that led them to triumph where others had failed?

2. Could the militarization of flight have been avoided?

1903—Kitty Hawk and Powered Flight
Lecture 17—Transcript

The winds are blowing at Kitty Hawk, North Carolina. We're walking nearby at the lonely Kill Devil Hills, part of the Outer Banks barrier islands of North Carolina. The cold winds intensify, up to 21 miles per hour. Occasionally, sand from the beach swirls up around us.

It is the morning of December 17, 1903, at 10:35. Just ahead of us, we see a small cluster of seven people, standing by the side of a strange long contraption, a frame covered with muslin cloth. Two men are the focus of attention, both dressed with a certain odd formality in white shirts with dark ties and wearing dark suits. They shake hands, then one man lies down upon the structure, which vibrates with the pulse of a machine, and then starts to move along a track on the ground. The other man runs alongside the sliding object.

Then, suddenly, to our amazement, the structure lifts up into the air! This thing, which its inventors call the Wright Flyer, hovers up and up. For 12 seconds, it has been up in the air, and then smacks down into the sand, after having traversing 120 feet. Later flights last longer and go further.

We have just witnessed an exhilarating turning point in human history, as two bicycle engineers on a lonely beach have broken the shackles of Earth for the very first time, achieving the most ancient human dream of steered and powered human flight. How would you feel at having witnessed this sight?

Today, we've become so used to the routine of air travel that it's difficult to imagine our way back to the time before, to really feel the wonder that clung to the very idea of flying. Humans soaring like birds had been declared impossible many times, and yet this was always a permanent fantasy of the human race. The heavens were both alluring and forbidding; they were the realm of divinity, not of humans. From the earliest art, gods and angels and spirits were depicted with wings added to human-like forms, to show their power and transcendence, literally their ability to rise above.

Psalm 55 exclaims for instance, "Oh, that I had the wings of a dove. I would fly away."

The ancient Greek myth of Daedalus and his son Icarus depicted both the attraction and the dangers of flying. In this story, to escape imprisonment on the island of Crete, the inventor Daedalus built himself and his son wings of wax and feathers, and then they both took off for freedom, over the waters of the Mediterranean. In the process, Daedalus warned Icarus to take a middle course, flying above the waves but not too close to the sun, not too high, because that would melt the artificial wings. But his son Icarus, once he had begun flying, was just enraptured by the sheer joy of it, and flew too high, until the sun melted his wings and he fell to his death. So from the very beginnings, there was a cautionary note about the entrancing prospect of flying.

Over the centuries, in each age there were men who were driven by this dream to fly, who sought to recreate birdlike wings to get themselves aloft after jumping from heights. Predictably, many of these intrepid souls ended up killing themselves in the attempt.

In the 15th and 16th centuries, the genius inventor Leonardo da Vinci also had a lifelong fascination with flight, but fortunately he did not injure himself with such practical experiments. He mused, "A bird is an instrument working according to mathematical law … which it is within the capacity of man to reproduce." Showing very great prudence, Leonardo advised anyone who did want to experiment with flying to do so near a lake, in order to avoid injury.

Just before the epic events of the French Revolution that we surveyed in an earlier lecture, two brothers achieved something marvelous in France. These were the Montgolfier brothers, Joseph and Étienne, who had observed a fascinating fact: Lighting a fire under a bag would cause it to rise. This led the Montgolfiers to build the first hot-air balloons. At the palace at Versailles in September 1783, the Montgolfiers demonstrated their invention for the king of France, Louis XVI, in happier days. Their balloon did not take up human subjects, but instead, a sheep, a rooster, and a duck. The crowds were astonished (we have no record about how the involuntary animal travelers felt about this). Then in November of 1783, with the American scientist Benjamin Franklin watching, the Montgolfiers' balloon actually carried two men over Paris. Yet, steering such an aircraft remained a problem.

In Britain, the engineer George Cayley experimented with gliders throughout the first half of the 19th century. One of his great advances involved understanding the importance of streamlining to reduce air resistance. It is said that in 1853, Cayley built a glider and had his coachman fly it across a valley. The experiment was a success, but the coachman on returning to earth is said to have immediately quit his job, complaining to Cayley that he had been hired to drive, not to fly.

The dream endured, among the many engineering marvels of the 19th century. Jules Verne based a number of stories on this impulse, using different imagined technologies in his fiction. His first popular novel was the 1863 text *Five Weeks in a Balloon*, about English explorers charting Africa from the air. Then his 1886 novel *Robur the Conqueror* told of a heroic man who had conquered the heavens by constructing a heavier-than-air craft. Verne's famous 1873 novel *Around the World in Eighty Days* also featured a balloon journey as part of that epic global race.

Experiments with lighter-than-air craft continued, using hydrogen gas to lift the vehicles. In the year 1900, the German Count von Zeppelin pioneered airships named after himself. Vividly showing that the quest for flight also had a global reach, let me mention the Brazilian Alberto Santos-Dumont, who was heir to a coffee fortune, who was absolutely obsessed with flying. In fact, in his apartment in Paris he actually ate meals in the air on a specially designed table and chairs that were six feet high. The waiter would need to get a ladder in order to serve this budding flyer and his guests. In 1901, Santos-Dumont flew above and around the Eiffel Tower in a dirigible.

The German engineer Otto Lilienthal, in the 1890s, further perfected gliders. He produced graceful birdlike forms from which the pilot dangled. However, Lilienthal turned out to be one in a long line of aviation fatalities. He died in a gliding accident in 1896. It was Lilienthal's crash and his fate that inspired the Wright Brothers. Orville Wright remembered afterwards that, "Flight was generally looked upon as an impossibility." This did not deter the Wright brothers—it actually provoked them! As Wilbur Wright somewhat understatedly confessed, "For some years I have been afflicted with the belief that flight is possible to man."

So, who were these Wright brothers, who succeeded in the fateful leap where others crashed? The Wright brothers grew up in Dayton, Ohio. Wilbur and his younger brother Orville together formed a close partnership. Neither man married, but devoted all of their lives to their shared work. As Wilbur put it, they even "thought together" in a sense. Their father, Milton Wright, was a bishop of the United Brethren church, and his responsibilities in ministry meant that he was often away from home and his family. The Wrights' mother, Susan, was of German background from a family of carriage makers. She was very adept at mechanical challenges, and seems to have passed this trait along to her sons.

One day, their father, perhaps returning from one of his frequent travels, gave the boys a toy, a toy which launched their life's work. It was a toy helicopter, a fragile construct of cork and bamboo and rubber bands that twisted rotors that were attached to the toy. Coming into the house, their father threw it to them, and instead of it falling, it flew and buzzed about the room. As the brothers recalled later, the toy didn't last very long in the hands of energetic small boys, but the memory of that toy was abiding.

The brothers had little in the way of formal schooling, but were fired in their youth by a love of science, much like the youthful Thomas Edison. As they grew older, the Wrights set up a printing shop, following the invention of Gutenberg. In addition, they also set up a bicycle shop, to sell and repair bicycles, which in the 1890s were all the rage.

News of the death of the German inventor Lilienthal in a glider accident galvanized them. They set about studying all that was known about flying, surveying the work of earlier pioneers. As they did so, they discovered something that shocked them. They uncovered errors in calculations of air resistance, and this fact prompted them not to rely any longer on received wisdom or other people's earlier work, but to launch their own experiments.

The Wrights even built their own wind tunnel for measurements. A key innovation they arrived at was so-called wing warping, which was intended to stabilize flight. These inventions came not from a university or an extensive research institute, but from their own small workshop in Dayton, Ohio.

From 1900, the Wrights took their experiments to a site near Kitty Hawk, North Carolina. There they settled at the Kill Devil Hills in a rickety cabin. The area had sand dunes for soft landings (or at least softer than otherwise would have been the case), and the height of the dunes made them ideal for launching aircraft. But this environment was not mild or pleasant. It could be cold and fiercely windy, and during the summer mosquitoes were a terrible besetting plague.

Here, on a succession of gliders, the Wrights worked out practically the challenges before them. Ultimately, they created a biplane glider design, with a rudder for steering and forward elevators to ascend or descend. To all of this they added a 12 horsepower engine, which drove revolving propellers, which were essentially wings that spun round and round and round to propel the flight.

The brothers were men of few words. Inside, however, beneath that calm exterior, they oscillated between confidence and doubt. They were sure that they were making real progress on their own. Yet, in 1901, just two years before their triumphant moment, Wilbur had told a friend that he didn't really expect to see flight achieved in his lifetime.

Then, on December 17, 1903, there arrived the scene we started this lecture with. The Wright brothers invited locals from miles around to come see this experiment. Only five people took them up on this invitation, but those people witnessed world history. After tossing a coin to decide which of the brothers would begin, Orville won and made the first flight.

The fact that the Wrights had a lifeguard there to take a photograph with a camera on a tripod that they had set up in advance meant that the Wright brothers suspected they were going to succeed that day and wanted it recorded for history. In that first flight, lasting 12 seconds, Orville fulfilled the oldest dream. Then Wilbur his brother took a turn, covering 175 feet. Then Orville flew again, travelling 200 feet. Then, on Wilbur's second flight, they had the most success of that day. Wilbur now covered 852 feet. This time, Wilbur had been in the air for 59 seconds. The two brothers telegraphed their father with the news. The first word of the message they sent really said it all: "Success."

Both North Carolina (with its slogan "First in Flight") and Ohio (with its slogan "Birthplace of Aviation") claim to this day for themselves special status in the history of flying, and they are both right, because of the Wright brothers. Back in Ohio, the brothers continued improving their machine. They received a patent for their plane design in 1906, and later successfully fought off legal disputes by competitors. In 1908, Wilbur Wright took the show on the road as it were. He travelled to France to demonstrate the invention, and elsewhere in Europe.

The French, proud of the pioneering role of the Montgolfier brothers, were sure that their nation would achieve flight first. For this reason, the French often mocked the claims of the Wrights at first, but then actually seeing the demonstration meant believing. In 1909, the Wright brothers founded a company to build and sell their planes. Wilbur died in 1912, but Orville Wright lived until 1948. Imagine, by 1948, how much Orville had seen in the way of their invention being improved, revolutionized, and improved again.

The result of this invention was a veritable flying craze. Huge crowds gathered to witness this amazing spectacle. When Wilbur Wright flew over Manhattan in 1909, a million people watched him, enthralled. A French journalist who witnessed Wilbur's demonstration of flying in France put it very eloquently. He said, "Nothing can give an idea of the emotion experienced and the impression felt ... a flight of mastery, assurance and incomparable elegance." Contemporaries marveled at what they felt was really the beginning of a new age of human history. Some of them called it the "Air Age." In a word, to fly was to be modern!

What did it feel like for the first people who undertook flight? Pilots spoke of almost being drunk on the experience of flying, and yet they needed to be cautious: This was an undertaking that was full of danger. For instance, in the first half of the year 1911, thirty aviators were killed in accidents. We also have fascinating testimony from someone who was a passenger on an early flight, and reflected keenly and insightfully on her experience of flying for the first time. She was the American writer Ida Tarbell. Tarbell was one of the most famous muckraking journalists of the age. She wrote investigative exposés of the abuses of big corporations and industry.

In 1913, Tarbell wrote up her experiences of flying. Wearing a silk hood and goggles, she sat behind the pilot as they took off, accelerating to the fantastic speed of 50 miles per hour. When Tarbell looked down once aloft, she declared, "The surprise of it seemed to stun me. Not that I lost consciousness, but I was literally lost in amazement at the suddenness and ease of it." As she and the pilot flew on, she continued, "Then the whole thing began to go to my head and I wanted to laugh and shout. The sense of exhilaration is one that I have never known before. You seem to have gotten as far above physical fears as you are above the earth, and you have a curious sense of being part of the whole thing." Tarbell concluded with words that were prophetic. She said, "You will fly one of these days, I shall fly again—I hope. Possibly before we die we may both be traveling back and forth to business from country to city in an aeroplane!"

How right she proved to be. What she probably didn't expect in all that initial exhilaration was how routine and unexciting, sometimes even burdensome, flying would become for people. But here was the authority of personal, lived experience: Something that had been dreamed of and thought impossible, was now lived—the miracle of flight.

Contests, exhibitions, races, and so-called barnstorming stunt shows became all the rage. Nations also competed against one another in a race to master the air. The French surged ahead, so that by 1911, the world records for speed, altitude, and endurance were all held by French pilots. The French founded the first flight training schools and led the world in plane production before the First World War. It was a French pilot, Louis Blériot, who crossed the English Channel in July 1909 and won a rich prize from the *London Daily Mail* newspaper for achieving this feat.

Little wonder then that pilots were idolized, as people who had mastered the soulless technology of the 19th century, all those machine. Pilots became global celebrities, like film stars. The American Charles Lindbergh for instance, who was nicknamed "The Lone Eagle," was almost deified when he made his 1927 solo flight across the Atlantic, covering the 3,600 miles from New York all the way to Paris. When Lindbergh returned to New York, he was greeted by four million people in a massive ticker-tape parade. Even a popular dance was named after him, the "lindy hop."

Great charisma attached to these pilots, or as they were sometimes called, birdmen and birdwomen. The most famous of the birdwomen was Amelia Earhart. She was the first woman to fly alone across the Atlantic in 1932. In 1937, Earhart set out to become first woman to fly around the world, but her plane was lost in the Pacific, a mystery that's still unsolved to this very day. Love of flying also drove Bessie Coleman, the first female African American pilot, who overcame both gender and racial discrimination to earn her pilot's license in France in 1921.

There was even a word that became current at this time that suggests how flight seemed to many people to be changing what was possible. This term was "airmindedness." Airmindedness suggested a modern willingness to do things in a new way, to explore all of the potential of flight. There were any number of predictions, including the expectation that in the future there would be a family airplane in every garage.

Airmail, which we today take for granted (or simply ignore entirely due to the speed of the Internet), was at the time a thrilling concept. The first official airmail flight took place on May 15, 1918, from Washington DC to New York. The pilot, who was not very experienced, was simply given a map showing Union Station in DC and told to just follow the train tracks north to New York.

While President Wilson and a huge crowd looked on in downtown Washington, the pilot took off, circled around, and then headed south. This meant that the first airmail flight had actually taken off in the wrong direction, and shortly after that crash-landed, so that the mail actually had to go by train after all. The first major U.S. airlines actually originated as carriers of airmail. The earliest included TWA, American Airlines, United Airlines, and Northwest Airlines. Later they branched out into passenger service.

In 1935 there took place, to great excitement, the first transpacific commercial flight, the Pan American airline's flying boat, the *China Clipper*. The *China Clipper* actually flew through the Golden Gate in San Francisco as it headed for China. President Roosevelt's telegram with best wishes really said it best. He communicated, "I thrill to the wonder of it all."

As you probably guessed, the name of the flying boat, *China Clipper*, was intentionally reminiscent of those ships that had carried tea from China in the age of sail, and the hope was that American trade with Asia would surge again. In a real sense, aviation was redrawing the world, making it smaller and more accessible in modern technological ways.

But this modernity also brought peril. The political and military implications of flight were just as far-reaching. In a word, aviation threatened to upset the Westphalian order of territorial sovereignty that was launched at the Peace of Westphalia back in 1648. That Westphalian order had established the authority of rule over land or territory. But who would enforce sovereignty in the skies? When the first airplane flight took place in Europe, a British newspaper magnate announced that the real news that had taken place that day was that the English Channel had essentially disappeared. What he meant was Britain was no longer safe, from the air.

Because no sooner had powered flight been invented than it was put to military uses, to rain death down from the skies. This was not only a matter of the perversity of particular arms dealers and generals at work. In fact, the Wrights themselves marketed their invention as a formidable tool of war and got their first contract in 1908 from the U.S. Army. An air arms race was on!

The first use of the airplane for war came in 1911 in the Italian-Turkish War over Libya; airplanes were used for reconnaissance and then for bombing. Do the math on this: It took only eight years from the invention to its use for war. World War I saw both the celebrated fighter aces dueling in the skies as well as the first beginnings of strategic bombing.

More than anything else, it was air warfare that ushered in the reality of total war. When we speak of total war as a historical phenomenon, we mean industrialized warfare—not of armies alone on the battlefield, but of entire societies and home fronts, in which everyone, including civilians, is a participant and a potential target. Strategic bombing brought all of this home, and it terrified political and military leaders and populations at large. From those first tentative bombings of cities in World War I, contemporaries drew the terrifying lesson in the phrase of the time, that "the bomber always gets through."

It was Hitler's air force that pioneered dive-bombers equipped with sirens that wailed as they attacked targets, to terrify those who were on the ground. In World War II, Nazi terror bombing of Warsaw in Poland, Rotterdam in the Netherlands, and London was followed then by round-the-clock bombing of Germany by Allied air forces, and the obliteration of Hamburg and Dresden. Civil defense sirens, bunkers, crowds hunkered underground with gas masks at the ready: This is what modern total war looked like for much of the world.

Incredibly, one man actually predicted this development in really uncanny ways. This was a man we've met before, that prolific British writer H.G. Wells. What today we call science fiction, H.G. Wells preferred to call "fantasias of possibility," an opportunity to imagine and think through the consequences of turning points! H.G. Wells's novel *The War in the Air* was written in 1907, and then published as a book in 1908. The core thesis of the book was correct and prophetic. The airplane alters the character of war. With airplanes, war will no longer be fought on fronts, but everywhere, including behind the lines. No one is safe; no one is immune. Just as war is getting more destructive, Wells argued, it was also becoming less decisive and ever more meaningless.

Wells's novel follows a humble British bicycle mechanic who witnesses by accident world historical events: He sees a German air fleet attacking New York and smashing that city. He sees how Germany ultimately proves unable to master America even after this attack, because even as the government surrenders, the American people keep fighting below. He witnesses an Asian alliance of China and Japan in turn attacking the Europeans and defeating them. Finally, as governments and cities collapse, in this novel, civilization as a whole is destroyed.

Wells was in a real sense the prophet of air war. When the book was republished again during World War II, Wells said bitterly that when he died his tombstone should eventually bear the words, "I told you so. You *damned* fools." But paradoxically, Wells also hoped that airpower might be the answer as well as the problem. Elsewhere in his fiction, Wells speculated that a world government that ruled from the air with airpower could reconstruct all of human society. Wells was convinced that the solution was world government by scientifically minded intellectuals (like himself). Even this prophet, otherwise so insightful, proved touchingly naïve or innocent in his view of benevolent elites holding overwhelming power over others.

Where are we now, more than a century after this turning point? How airminded are we today? Flight is a turning point that's so woven into the lives of many people that we take it for granted. It's reported that in 2010 global air passengers topped five billion for the first time.

How routine flight has become! Yet, to fly and arrive hours later on a different continent still has its effects. Being that mobile can broaden horizons intellectually, and in essence, produce a different you, a you that would not have existed without human flight.

In this lecture, we saw the way in which flying redrew the world and really shaped the experience of modernity. Just a few years after the flight of the Wright Brothers, another event on the ground reconfigured world politics, when to the surprise of a global audience, Japan beat a European imperialist power, Russia, in a modern war in 1905. This surprise we consider in our next lecture.

1904—The Russo-Japanese War
Lecture 18

The Russo-Japanese War of 1904–1905 is without a doubt one of the turning points of modern world history, yet it is little remembered today. This war started the process of global decolonization that would last for the rest of the 20th century. Fought with new weaponry, it also revealed for the first time the destructiveness of modern industrial war. Finally, it set the stage for the First and Second World Wars. In fact, the Russo-Japanese War did so much to usher in the age of World War I and World War II that some historians have provocatively labeled it "World War Zero," the vital precursor.

Japan's Rise to Imperialism

- The island empire of Japan had largely closed itself off to outsiders and their influence, trade, and ideas after 1638.
  - From their isolation, Japanese leaders looked on with horror at what was happening elsewhere in Asia. In particular, they followed the British Opium Wars against China.

  - They saw European powers regularly and hypocritically infringing on the ideas of national sovereignty and equality of nations in a family of states that had grown out of the 1648 Peace of Westphalia.

- While debating how to avoid being the next victims of imperialism, Japan's leaders had their hand forced when American ships suddenly appeared off the coast in 1853.
  - The American naval force, led by Commodore Matthew Perry, "opened" Japan to the outside world after 200 years of self-containment.

  - The 1854 Treaty of Kanagawa gave trade concessions. As other European powers made demands, a regime of unequal treaties, similar to what was in place in China, was set up, humiliating the Japanese.

- A group of Japanese reformers took decisive action that altered what seemed the likely fate of Japan.
  - In 1868, they undertook a coup against the shogun, the warlord who had held true power and had sidelined the emperor for centuries. This event came to be celebrated as the Meiji Restoration.

  - A generation of young Japanese rallied to the 15-year-old emperor Mutsuhito as a symbol of a great national undertaking: to resist outside pressure by adapting Western successes.

- From the new capital of Tokyo, the reformers created an extensive blending of traditional Japanese culture with Western technology and ideas to reach for Great Power status. Schools were established using French models, and a German-style army and British-style navy were developed. A constitution was passed in 1889, and rapid industrial growth occurred.

- Young Japanese were proud of what they saw: a Japanese modernity—not merely wholesale adoption of the West. Ultimately, the point of this movement was to ensure survival in the age of imperialism by enabling the Japanese to become an imperial power themselves.

Encountering Russia

- In seeking imperial expansion, Japan ran up against its first European rival, Russia. While Britain and France expanded overseas, Russia had expanded eastward into Asia and the Pacific. In 1860, the Russian czar founded Vladivostok on the Pacific. Soon, Russia clashed with Japan in northeast Asia, especially where their interests collided, in Manchuria.

- When Japan won its war against China in 1895, Russia worked actively to rob Japan of the rewards of that victory. Japan had gained a large payment of an indemnity, the island of Taiwan, and the Liaotung Peninsula in Manchuria. Russia, along with France and Germany, pressured Japan into giving up that Manchurian holding.

- The Japanese were infuriated by the inequality with which their state was being treated in the imperialist competition and even more embittered when Russia pressured China to give it a 25-year lease on the same Liaotung Peninsula and Port Arthur (today Lüshun) as an ice-free naval base.
  o Southern Manchuria became almost a Russian colony, and the Japanese feared that Korea, which they saw as their area of influence, would be Russia's next target.

  o Russian diplomats scorned Japanese suggestions that each recognize the other's claims; thus, Japan signed an alliance with Britain in 1902 and prepared for war.

A Strange Conflict
- As war approached, it was clear that this would be a strange conflict. It would be fought by modern armies, equipped with industrial weapons, but not in Japan or Russia. Rather, it would be fought in northern China and Korea, in the territories of other nations. The Japanese estimated their chances of success at 50/50.

- The war began with a surprise attack on the Russian naval base at Port Arthur. On February 8, 1904, Japan's Admiral Tōgō pounced. Shock and surprise were total, as Japanese torpedoes hit two battleships, and Russian defenders pulled back.

- On the same day, another Japanese naval force attacked Russian positions at the Korean port of Chemulpo (today Inch'ŏn), sank two battleships, and landed a Japanese army. Two days after the dual surprise attacks, Japan declared war.

The Course of the War
- The Japanese army in Korea crossed the Yalu River and advanced into Manchuria. Soon, Port Arthur was under siege. The Japanese

mounted costly frontal assaults against the city, losing 20,000 soldiers in the first attack, but the city surrendered in January 1905.

- From February to March 1905, the Battle of Mukden was fought, which became the largest and longest battle in modern military history to that point. More than half a million men fought for weeks on end. Japanese frontal attacks ground down the Russian forces but at tremendous cost: Japanese casualties numbered 70,000.

- The climax of the war came on May 27, 1905, with the naval engagement at Tsushima. There, Japan's Admiral Tōgō sank the Russian Baltic Fleet in one of the greatest naval victories of all time. The fleets were evenly matched in strength, but the Japanese proved superior, with new British-built ships and better training.

Reactions to War
- In Korea and China, the war devastated the civilian population; both armies took food and resources and shot locals suspected of spying. The fighting created countless refugees.

- In Japan, the war was greeted with great enthusiasm. Girls wore kimonos printed with battle scenes, and more than 270 films were created about the war as it took place.

- In Russia, news of defeats brought depression and a longing for reform. On January 22, 1905, peaceful petitioners outside the Winter Palace in Saint Petersburg were shot by soldiers of the czar. This sparked the Russian Revolution of 1905, which almost brought down the empire.
  - Mass strikes broke out, illegal trade unions were set up, and unrest flared in the countryside. Civil order and the police melted away. Pogroms against the persecuted Jewish minority took place. News of the unrest leaked to troops in spite of censorship, and the battleship *Potemkin* in the Black Sea mutinied.

  - Russian revolutionaries, such as Lenin, eagerly awaited defeat, hoping it could be turned to a radical revolutionary force.

The Treaty of Portsmouth

- After the Battle of Tsushima and given the vast costs of the war, both sides were ready for peace.

- A treaty was signed on September 5, 1905, in Portsmouth, New Hampshire. Japan won control over Korea, which became a Japanese colony by 1910. It won Port Arthur and railroads the Russians had built in Manchuria and the southern half of Sakhalin Island. But Russia paid no indemnity, nor did it give up any Russian mainland territory.

President Theodore Roosevelt offered himself as mediator in the peace negotiations following the Battle of Tsushima and won the Nobel Prize for his efforts.

- In Japan, the treaty was met with outrage, and there were riots against the peace in the cities. Protestors were upset that Japan had not won more for its victory and often blamed America for shortchanging Japan. In spite of this, Japan's arrival as a Great Power was obvious to all.

Effects of the Turning Point

- The Russo-Japanese War lit the fuse for the longer-term process of decolonization, which has lasted into our own times. This was a body blow to the authority that imperialism had earlier commanded! This first Asian victory against a Great Power had tremendous psychological impact worldwide, inspiring Indian, Indonesian, Vietnamese, Iranian, and Polish nationalists.
  - Japan's victory also undermined racial stereotypes and alleged hierarchies of Western dominance. Some in Europe and America worried about what they called the "yellow peril," the vision of a resurgent Asia that would challenge Western predominance. Others in the West welcomed Japan to the family of imperialist powers.

○ Japan's equality with imperialist Great Powers also points to an irony: Japan had defeated an imperialist power and sparked a powerful movement for decolonization, but its real aim was to claim empire for itself. Japan annexed Korea in 1910, split Manchuria off from China in 1931 as a puppet state, and invaded China in 1937. The Great Pacific War of 1937–1945 followed and still has powerful reverberations in the region today.

• The second impact of the war involves the lessons that were learned, which, as it turned out, were all the wrong lessons. Large numbers of military observers from neutral countries were sent to observe this modern industrial war.
   ○ These observers admired the ferocity and spirit of Japanese frontal attacks as "human bullets" sent against enemy defenses, even against machine guns. The cost had been great, of course—Japan had lost more than 100,000 men in the war—but the observers noted that Japan had won.

   ○ This was part of a so-called "cult of the offensive," which argued that not weapons or firepower or equipment was decisive but willpower and morale and fighting spirit. In 1914, this approach was tried out on the western front of the First World War. Direct attacks, even by motivated troops, produced not victory but senseless deaths by the millions.

   ○ Further, the war created for many Japanese an image of their army and navy as invincible. The military's power in politics led to more imperialism, more war, and the gamble of Pearl Harbor.

• This points to the third great impact of the Russo-Japanese War: It set the stage for two world wars.
   ○ Defeat in the East turned Russia westward again, toward the Balkans, where the First World War erupted.

- Japan was determined to carve out an empire in East Asia and believed that a decisive blow could win a war in one stroke at the start. It would use this formula at Pearl Harbor in 1941.

- Finally, defeat in 1905 was an omen for Russia of worse tragedies to come. In the 1905 revolution, the Russian Empire had nearly collapsed, and when the First World War hit in 1914, it did. In the vacuum of authority, Lenin and his Bolsheviks established a new kind of state: one that aimed to abolish all other states in the name of a world revolution.

Suggested Reading

Goto-Jones, *Modern Japan.*

Jukes, *The Russo-Japanese War, 1904–1905.*

Kowner, ed., *The Impact of the Russo-Japanese War.*

Wells and Wilson, eds., *The Russo-Japanese War in Cultural Perspective, 1904–05.*

Questions to Consider

1. What political lessons did contemporaries draw from Japan's victory?

2. What lessons should have been drawn about the true nature of modern industrial war based on the Russo-Japanese conflict?

1904—The Russo-Japanese War

Lecture 18—Transcript

Moving with utmost secrecy, in the early morning hours, a Japanese naval force stealthily approaches its intended target, an important naval base. War has not yet been declared. Japan aims to catch its enemy by surprise and to strike a decisive, unexpected blow! The stillness is unbroken, as Japanese warships creep closer in, and then the attack begins, with salvos of heavy guns, the streak of torpedoes, and explosions that wake the unsuspecting garrison.

At first, this story actually sounds familiar. It sounds like December 7, 1941, when Japan attacked the United States without warning at Pearl Harbor, on a "date which will live in infamy," bringing the United States into World War II. But the story we started with is not Pearl Harbor. Rather, this event came 37 years earlier, on February 8, 1904. This was the Japanese attack on the Russian Empire's forces at Port Arthur in the Far East. It marked the beginning of the Russo-Japanese War of 1904–1905, which ended in Japanese victory.

This war was without a doubt one of the turning points of modern world history, as we will see shortly. Yet, it is little remembered today, in part because it gets so completely overshadowed by the First and Second World Wars that came soon after. In fact, this is one of those historical events that gets more important the further we move away from it in time. Let's consider why.

This war, in which a modernizing Japan beat a European colonial empire, was a turning point really for three reasons. First, the war started the process that would last the rest of the 20th century, global decolonization, as countries that had been taken over by imperialist powers shed outside control to achieve their own sovereignty and independence. Seeing Japan win inspired other non-Western nationalists. Second, this war, fought with new weaponry, revealed for the first time what modern industrial war was like and how destructive it would be, and yet in spite of great numbers of observers, the wrong lessons were drawn from this war. Third, this war set the stage for the First World War and Second World War, as well as preparing the way for the collapse of the Russian state and the establishment of an unprecedented communist government. In fact, the Russo-Japanese war did so much to usher in the age of World War I and World War II that some historians have very provocatively labeled it World War Zero, the vital precursor.

You will recall from our lecture on the Opium Wars in China that these ushered in the period of frantic European imperialism worldwide, the age of gunboat diplomacy. By 1914, when the First World War broke out, three-quarters of the globe had been seized by European imperialist powers. One after another non-Western society was simply overrun.

Yet many resisted fiercely. Some were quite dramatically successful in their resistance, as when the Ethiopians defeated an Italian expeditionary army in 1896 at the Battle of Adowa. But the most successful of all societies in fending off the imperial power of the West was Japan.

The island empire of Japan had closed itself off to outsiders and their influence, trade, and ideas after 1638. This isolation was not total. Some severely limited trade was still allowed at the port of Nagasaki with merchants of the Dutch East India Company, the VOC (I'll bet that you didn't think we were going to encounter the Dutch East India Company again in these lectures, but we did).

From their isolation, Japanese leaders looked on with a sense of horror at what was happening elsewhere in Asia. In particular, they followed the British Opium Wars against China, and drew strong conclusions. They saw European powers regularly and hypocritically infringing on the very ideas of national sovereignty and the equality of nations in a family of states that had grown out of the 1648 Peace of Westphalia.

While debating how to avoid becoming the next victims of imperialism, Japan's leaders actually had their hand forced, as American ships suddenly appeared off the Japanese coast in 1853. These were the awe-inspiring black ships as they were called, steam vessels built for war, belching black smoke as they moved. The American naval force led by Commodore Perry opened Japan to the outside world after 200 years of self-containment. The 1854 Treaty of Kanagawa gave trade concessions. As other European powers also made demands, a regime of unequal treaties like that in China was set up, humiliating to the Japanese.

At this point a group of bold Japanese reformers took decisive action that altered what seemed the likely impending fate of Japan. In 1868, they undertook a coup against the shogun, the warlord who had held true power and had sidelined the emperor for centuries before. This event came to be celebrated as the Meiji Restoration. "Meiji" means "enlightened rule," and a young generation of Japanese rallied to the 15-year-old Emperor Mutsuhito as a symbol of this great national undertaking, to resist outside pressure by adapting Western successes.

From the new capital of Tokyo, the reformers, by a remarkable act of collective will, created an extensive blending of traditional Japanese culture with Western technology and ideas to reach for Great Power status. Schools were established using French models. The army was built up on the German model. The navy was built up on the famed British model. In the armed forces, the earlier warrior class of samurai were assimilated into the officer class, and their warrior ethos of *Bushido* popularized as a form of general Japanese patriotism. A constitution was passed in 1889. Rapid industrial growth boomed.

Little wonder that young Japanese were very proud of what they saw: a Japanese modernity, not merely a wholesale adoption of the West. Their program was summed up in the slogan *fukoku-kyōhei:* "rich country, strong army." Ultimately, the point of this remarkable movement was to ensure survival in the age of imperialism, by becoming an imperialist power themselves.

Among the selective borrowings from the West was a very strong infusion of social Darwinist thinking, summed up in an apt description of international politics: Either you eat, or you will be eaten. The first demonstration of this attitude came with Japan's war against China, in 1894–1895, which Japan won with devastating and astonishing speed.

But in seeking its own imperial expansion, Japan ran up against its first European rival, Russia. While Britain and France were expanding overseas,

Russia had expanded eastwards into Asia and to the Pacific. In 1860, the Russian tsar had founded the city of Vladivostok on the Pacific, a town whose name literally meant "Ruler of the East." Soon Russia clashed with Japan in northeast Asia, especially where their interests collided, in northeastern China, Manchuria. At this time, Russia was the most conservative and autocratic of European empires (in fact, it was so conservative that it had only abolished serfdom in 1861), but like other European powers it saw its own superiority over non-Westerners as self-evident, and it meant to press its claims to expand in Asia.

A physical monument to this will to expand was the Trans-Siberian Railroad, the longest railroad in the world. Just as the transcontinental railroad was built in the U.S. in 1869, this Trans-Siberian line was meant to secure continental dominion, and it was also meant to be a competitor to the trade routes that ran through the Suez Canal. From 1890, the building of the Trans-Siberian surged ahead, from Vladivostok to link with Moscow and European Russia, running over 6,000 miles. By 1904, it was largely, but not totally, finished. It only had a single track, so movement even at the best of times could be quite slow.

When Japan won its war against China in 1895, Russia worked actively to rob Japan of the rewards of that victory. Japan had forced upon China a large payment of an indemnity, and also forced the cession of the island of Taiwan and the Liaotung Peninsula in Manchuria. At this point, Russia, along with France and Germany, pressured Japan into giving up that Manchurian holding.

Japanese were infuriated by what they saw, the way in which their state was not being treated as an equal in imperialist competition, and they were even more embittered when Russia turned around and then pressured China to give Russia a 25-year lease on that same Liaotung Peninsula and Port Arthur (today Lüshun) as an ice-free naval base for Russia. Southern Manchuria became almost a Russian colony, and Japan feared that Korea, which it saw as in its own area of influence, might be Russia's next target. Russian diplomats scorned repeated Japanese suggestions that each should politically recognize the other's claims in the area, so Japan instead signed an alliance with Britain in 1902 and prepared for war.

As the war approached, it was clear that it would be a strange conflict. It would be fought by modern armies, equipped with industrial weapons, but not in Japan or in Russia. Rather, it would be fought in northern China and Korea, on other people's territories.

The Japanese were not overconfident. The army itself estimated a 50/50 chance of success, and the navy actually planned on losing half of its ships in this war. To improve its chances, Japan planned the start of the war for winter, when they knew that bringing Russian reinforcements by the Trans-Siberian Railroad would be hardest.

So the war began with a surprise attack on the Russian naval base at Port Arthur. On February 8, 1904, Japan's Admiral Tōgō pounced. Shock and surprise were total, as Japanese torpedoes hit two battleships, and the Russian defenders pulled back.

On the same day, another Japanese naval force also attacked Russian positions at the Korean port of Chemulpo. They sank two battleships and landed a Japanese army. Incidentally, Chemulpo is the old name for Inch'ŏn, where the American landing took place during the Korean War in 1950. Two days later, after the dual surprise attacks, Japan declared war on Russia.

The Japanese army landed in Korea, crossed the Yalu River, and advanced into Manchuria. Soon Port Arthur itself was under siege. Russian efforts were plagued by a run of bad luck, as when the defending Russian admiral was drowned when his flagship hit a Japanese mine in the water. Japanese soldiers surrounded Port Arthur by land, and then mounted a series of costly frontal attacks against the city. In the first of these attacks, 20,000 Japanese soldiers were lost. In December of 1904, the Japanese finally managed to capture 203 Meter Hill as it was called, a crucial vantage point above Port Arthur. This was an attack that cost some 14,000 Japanese dead. In January of 1905, with the situation hopeless, Port Arthur finally surrendered.

Just after, the Battle of Mukden commenced, from February to March of 1905. It was a struggle for the capital city of the area (Mukden is today called Shenyang). The titanic battle turned out to be the largest and longest battle in modern military history up to this point, surpassing even the battles of the Napoleonic wars. Both armies had been reinforced, so now over half a million men did battle for weeks on end.

At the end, Japanese frontal attacks ground down the Russian forces, but at tremendous cost. Japanese casualties were 70,000 men, or a quarter of their entire army. Then the climax of the war came with the naval Battle of Tsushima.

After the attack on Port Arthur, Russia's Baltic Fleet had been ordered in October of 1904 to undertake an epic trek from the Baltic Sea to the Pacific Ocean, half a world away! The trip was going to be 17,800 miles long, and took seven and a half months. That trip could have been shortened by using the Suez Canal, but Japan's ally Britain controlled the canal and would not allow its use by the Russians.

The trip east turned into a disaster, starting with an incident off Dogger Bank off the coast of Britain that nearly started another war. Russian warships saw British fishing boats, and assumed that they were Japanese torpedo ships, and they fired on them, killing some fisherman. Perhaps vodka was involved in this story somewhere. Only subtle diplomacy and reparations smoothed over this crisis between Britain and Russia.

Then, when at last the Russian Baltic Fleet arrived off Korea on May 27, 1905, it met total disaster. Japan's Admiral Tōgō sank the Russian Baltic Fleet at Tsushima Strait, in one of the greatest naval victories of all time. The fleets were evenly matched in strength, but the Japanese proved superior with new British-built ships and better training for their men.

Two-thirds of the Russian fleet was sunk, along with almost 50,000 sailors. A young lieutenant who was with Admiral Tōgō that day, by the name of Yamamoto Isoruku, later would come up with the idea for the attack on Pearl Harbor. In Korea and China, the war devastated the civilian population, as both armies took food and resources and shot locals suspected of spying for the other side. The fighting created countless refugees.

Further away, the war was greeted differently in Japan and Russia themselves. Japan experienced great enthusiasm. Little girls wore kimonos with bore beautiful prints of battle scenes, cavalry charges, and naval combat. These images also recurred on fans, lanterns, and even cakes. The new medium of film, discussed in a previous lecture, celebrated the war.

In 1904–1905, eighty percent of Japanese films were about the war with Russia. They included such stirring titles as *Occupation in the Vicinity of _____ (Name Withheld for Reasons of National Security)*. Over 270 films were created in Japan about the war as it was going on. In Japanese theaters, the *benshi*, those narrators of silent films, actually told audiences when to shout "Banzai!" along with the charging infantry that they saw on the screen.

In Russia, the reception was grim. News of defeats brought depression and a longing for reform. But instead of reform, the Russian Empire got Bloody Sunday. On January 22, 1905, peaceful petitioners outside the beautiful Winter Palace in St. Petersburg were shot down by soldiers of the tsar. This sparked the Revolution of 1905 which almost brought the empire crashing down.

Mass strikes broke out in the Russian Empire. Illegal trade unions were set up. Unrest flared in the broad countryside with the burning of manor houses. It seemed that civil order—as well as the police—just melted away. *Pogroms*, or riots, against the persecuted Jewish minority also took place. News of all of this unrest back home leaked to Russian troops in the field in spite of censorship. Famously depicted in a classic film by Sergei Eisenstein, the battleship *Potemkin* in the Black Sea mutinied as a result of this discontent. Russian revolutionaries like Lenin eagerly awaited Russia's defeat, hoping that defeat could be turned to a revolutionary radical force.

After the battle of Tsushima, both sides were really ready for peace, given the vast costs of war on both sides. Japan had relied on many foreign loans to finance the war, and drafted some 20 percent of its male workforce. As we just saw, Russia was wracked with internal crisis. Peace was finally negotiated by the American president Theodore Roosevelt, who offered himself as mediator and later actually won the Nobel Peace Prize for his peacemaking.

On August 9, 1905, the talks began in Portsmouth, New Hampshire. Why Portsmouth? The town was as it turns out was much cooler than hot Washington DC, and it also had a naval base, with an underwater telegraph cable for speeding of international communications. After negotiations, the treaty was signed on September 5, 1905. Japan won control over Korea, which became an official Japanese colony by 1910. It won Port Arthur and the railroads that the Russians had built in Manchuria, as well as the southern half of Sakhalin Island. But Russia paid no indemnity, nor did it have to give up any Russian mainland territory.

In Japan, the treaty was not viewed as a success. It was met with outrage, and there were riots against the peace in the cities. Protestors were upset that Japan had not won more for its victory, and many of them blamed America for sabotaging victory, and shortchanging Japan in this conflict. In spite of this dissatisfaction, Japan's arrival as a Great Power due to its victory in this war was obvious to all.

So, if this was a true historical turning point, what were its effects? First, this event lit the fuse for the longer-term process of decolonization, which has lasted into our own times. In a word, this was a body blow to the authority that imperialism earlier had commanded! This first Asian victory against a great European power had tremendous psychological impact worldwide, and it really encouraged decolonization because it showed that it could be done.

This was one of the most actively observed wars in modern history. Real documentary films with footage of the fighting, as well as reenacted documentary films, were popular worldwide, not just in Japan. In fact, Thomas Edison's studios in 1904 produced a film reenactment of naval combat at Chemulpo Bay.

As you would expect, especially engaged observers came from subject peoples living under foreign rule, including many who later led independence movements in their own countries. The effect on Asians was electrifying.

One Indian poet wrote, "Japan! ... The proudest European Powers Thee now dread, Thou amazed all, all nations, thee the world adores."

During the war, the Chinese revolutionary Sun Yat-sen (later president of China), was travelling through the Suez Canal. At one point an Arab man rushed up to him to ask if he was Japanese, and he told him how proud he was to be an Asian, how joyful he was at Japan's victory. In India at this time, Jawaharlal Nehru, later prime minister of independent India, recalled that as a boy he'd been so excited about these events, that they "lessened the feeling of inferiority, from which most of us suffered," he said. Gandhi, at this point living in South Africa, was also excited and declared, "The people of the East seem to be waking up from their lethargy."

Japanese victory inspired Indonesian, Vietnamese, and Iranian nationalists. Not only Asians were affected. Within Russia, Finns and Poles admired the example of Japan (in fact, leaders of the Polish national movement actually came to Japan during the war to discuss cooperating against the common Russian foe).

Japan's victory obviously rattled all sorts of racial stereotypes and alleged hierarchies of Western superiority. An American missionary wrote that this really marked a new era in the world, because, "For now begins a readjustment of the balance of power among the nations, a readjustment which promises to halt the territorial expansion of white races and to check their racial pride."

Some in Europe and America worried about what they called the "yellow peril," the vision of a resurgent Asia, perhaps led by the Japanese, that would in the future challenge Western predominance. Others in the West on the contrary welcomed Japan to the family of imperialist powers. In a poem published in Britain, one Jane Oakley celebrated Japan in verse: "On *modern* lines Japan now wages war; 'Tis well that Europe should quite grasp this fact—And, duly *civilized* at every point, Consistent proves in every word and act."

Yet this, Japan's equality with imperialist Great Powers, actually points to a big irony. Japan had defeated an imperialist power and sparked a powerful movement for decolonization, but its real aim was to claim empire for itself. It was Korea and China that bore the brunt of this most quickly. Japan annexed Korea in 1910, split Manchuria off from China in 1931 as a puppet state, and then invaded China in 1937. The great Pacific War of 1937 to 1945 followed, and still has powerful reverberations in the region today, with continuing disputes over memories of modern history and over island territories.

The second historical impact involves the lessons that were learned. These were all the wrong lessons, as it turned out. Huge numbers of military observers were sent to the war by neutral countries to see firsthand what modern industrial war would look like. Among them was the young Douglas MacArthur, who didn't know at this point that he was seeing places he would later direct troops in decades afterwards.

Many European officers who were sent as observers would shortly be fighting one another in World War I, which here was essentially being rehearsed. Many elements were there: machine guns, trenches, barbed wire, massive firepower, soldiers' uniforms in drab colors to blend in. Airplanes were not used in this war, as they had been invented too recently.

Yet the observers saw what they wanted to see. They admired the ferocity and spirit of Japanese frontal attacks, as so-called human bullets were sent against the enemy defenses, even against machine guns. Observers recorded bayonet charges of latter-day samurai shouting "Banzai." But the cost had been great. Japan lost over 100,000 men in the war, but the observers focused on the face that Japan had won. A French observer recorded how Japanese officers jumped forward, swords flashing, and entire units of men went into a merciless hail of bullets. Entire units were shot to pieces, but others came up behind in a human wave that was pressing on to win!

This was part of a so-called cult of the offensive, current in the world at the time, which argued that not weapons or firepower or equipment was decisive, but willpower and morale and fighting spirit. In 1914, this approach was tried out on the western front of the First World War. Direct attacks, even by motivated troops, produced not victory, but senseless deaths by the millions.

For its part, the war created for many Japanese an image of their army and navy as invincible, true pillars of the nation along with the emperor. Until the end of World War II, the anniversary of Mukden was Army Day and the anniversary of Tsushima was Navy Day. Shrines were built, dedicated to General Nogi and Admiral Tōgō. The military's power in politics led to more imperialism, more war, and then the gamble of Pearl Harbor.

This points to the third great impact of the Russo-Japanese war. It set the stage for two world wars to come, more total and even more destructive. Defeat in the East ended up turning Russia westwards again, towards the Balkans, where the First World War would erupt. Japan for its part was launched on a course of carving out empire in East Asia. Japan had been left, as a result of that victory at Port Arthur, with the durable dream of being able to strike a decisive knockout blow that could win the war in one stroke right from the start!

Japan later used exactly this formula against Pearl Harbor in 1941. In fact, the commanding vessel in the attack on Pearl Harbor (the carrier *Akagi*) was actually flying Admiral Tōgō's old battle flag from his flagship at the attack on Port Arthur, the *Mikasa*. The attack on the United States was a huge gamble that willpower could compensate for inferiority in economic reserves and firepower. That gamble backfired, disastrously.

Finally, defeat in 1905 was a bad omen for Russia, an omen of worse tragedies to come. In the 1905 revolution, the Russian Empire had almost collapsed. The Tsar's subjects never again fully trusted him or his government, after troops had fired on peaceful civilians. But instead of using the interval of peace for reforms, the Romanov dynasty slumped into the grip of a mad smelly monk from Siberia, Grigori Rasputin.

When the First World War hit in 1914, the Russian Empire soon collapsed, and in the power vacuum, Lenin and his Bolsheviks established a new kind of state, following the formula of the French Revolution and its radical, violent trajectory. They created a state that aimed to abolish all other states in the name of a world revolution, and helped set the violent trajectory for much of the rest of the century.

So this conflict, the Russo-Japanese War of 1904–1905, set the stage for the devastating use of killing technology in two World Wars and a violent century in general. To balance off this dreadful legacy, we'll consider next a healing revolution, in the discovery of penicillin, in our next lecture.

1928—The Discovery of Penicillin
Lecture 19

The discovery of penicillin by Alexander Fleming in September of 1928 illustrates the power of serendipity, the phenomenon of finding something valuable while looking for something else. Yet it was not just chance at work here. Fortune favors those who are prepared, and in the case of Dr. Fleming, those who are attentive enough to observe carefully. Further, every discovery takes place in a larger context: Fleming's insight needed to be made practically accessible before it became the turning point that saved millions of lives and transformed medicine. In a real sense, the discovery of penicillin was a turning point within a larger turning point, taking place in the context of the development of germ theory.

The Four Humors
- As we saw in a previous lecture, the microscopic investigations of Leeuwenhoek had revealed microorganisms, but the importance of those bacteria for human beings was not understood.

- Over the previous centuries—from the time of the ancient Greeks—health and disease were most often understood in terms of the theory of humors, which postulated that four fluids operated within human beings: blood, phlegm, yellow bile, and black bile. Having an excess of one of these determined a person's temperament: sanguine, phlegmatic, choleric, or melancholic.
  - Illness, thus, was understood as a loss of internal balance. A high fever, for instance, meant that the patient had an excess of blood, and bleeding was called for.

  - People also believed that internal imbalances could be caused by bad air, or "miasmas."

Germ Theory
- In the decades before 1900, the authority of earlier concepts was overturned by medical pioneers who advanced germ theory, the

understanding that important diseases were caused by infection with microorganisms. This revolutionized pathology and surgery. The pioneers of germ theory included a series of great scientists who further interpreted the discoveries of Leeuwenhoek.

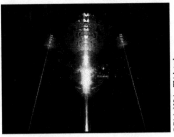

The Martians in H. G. Wells's 1898 novel *The War of the Worlds* were slain by the "disease bacteria against which their systems were unprepared."

- By the 1840s, a number of physicians noticed evidence for the spread of disease from person to person, not by miasmas. For example, Ignaz Semmelweis, a German-Hungarian doctor, discovered that doctors themselves were responsible for spreading puerperal ("childbed") fever at a hospital in Vienna.

- Another doctor, John Snow, traced deaths in London's cholera epidemic to one neighborhood water pump and showed that cholera was a waterborne disease. In 1865, Joseph Lister, a professor of surgery at the University of Glasgow, revolutionized antiseptic procedures in surgery, reducing infections markedly.

- The 19th century saw worldwide reform movements to create more hygienic urban environments, to inspect food production, and to instill ordinary means of ensuring public health. Something as basic as washing hands with soap was a revolution of its own.

- The great breakthrough came with the work of the French microbiologist Louis Pasteur.
    o Pasteur's experiments proved that the fermentation of wine and milk was caused by microbes. "Pasteurization" is the process of heating foodstuffs to delay the action of microbes.

- o Pasteur arrived at the conclusion that germs caused infectious disease. This was confirmed in his investigations of an anthrax epidemic affecting sheep and humans in 1879.

- At the same time, in Germany, Robert Koch was also studying anthrax and came to the same conclusion. In 1882–1883, he identified the bacteria that caused tuberculosis and cholera. As a result, he won the Nobel Prize in Medicine for 1905.

- From 1900, the hunt for bacteria and disease agents became an international and collective exercise. Significant advances in medical knowledge were made as a result of cooperation through medical journals and conferences worldwide. The microbes that caused typhoid, diphtheria, tetanus, plague, and rabies were identified.

A New Drug War
- Once vectors of disease were discovered, it might be possible to work methodically to prevent them (by vaccine) or cure them. Now, the front shifted to fighting diseases that already had established themselves. The stage was set for a new drug war—one to discover healing medicines.

- Impressive advances were made in Germany. The Nobel Prize–winning German-Jewish scientist Paul Ehrlich conducted work on the effects of chemicals on diseases, seeking what he memorably called the "magic bullet."

- In 1910, with a Japanese colleague, Ehrlich tested Salvarsan, an arsenic drug that helped destroy syphilis. Later, the German scientist Gerhard Domagk pioneered the first of the sulfonamide drugs. And a path-breaking advance came with the serendipitous discovery of penicillin by Alexander Fleming in 1928.

Fleming's Life
- Fleming was born in rural southwestern Scotland in 1881, the seventh of eight children. Like Darwin, his youth was spent close to nature, observing and exploring. This shaped his later life and career.

- When he was 14, Alexander was sent to London to school. For a while, he was employed at a shipping business, but that made clear to him that he did not want a commercial career. Eventually, he followed an older brother into the medical profession. From 1901, Fleming studied at St. Mary's Hospital Medical School in London and went on to spend the rest of his career there.

- He studied under the notable bacteriologist Almroth Wright, the discoverer of the typhoid vaccine. Once Fleming earned his degree, he went into private practice, treating syphilis with the Salvarsan that Ehrlich had invented.

- During the First World War, he worked in a military hospital in France, at a time when many soldiers died from infections of their wounds after they were evacuated from the trenches. Fleming experimented with different antiseptic procedures and found that strong chemical antiseptics did more harm than good, destroying tissue.

- On returning to St. Mary's after the war, Fleming continued his work with antiseptics. In 1921, he accidentally discovered lysosome, a natural human antibacterial enzyme found in bodily fluids.

- At this point, Fleming was an established and noted scholar, although his laboratory was marked by creative disorder rather than severe regimentation. The fact that he kept the door to the lab open to encourage air circulation resulted in his fateful discovery of penicillin.
  - The spores from a downstairs mycology lab, where experiments were conducted on fungi and molds, drifted into Fleming's rooms.

  - When the weather turned unseasonably warm, the mold spores reproduced where they had landed—in petri dishes containing staphylococci.

  - In looking at the petri dishes carefully, Fleming noticed that the mold was somehow inhibiting the growth of the bacteria. He identified the mold as *Penicillium notatum*.

Development and Application

- Of course, Fleming's observation was not the end of the matter. There was now the question of how to use this discovery, how to develop it as a practical healing tool that could be produced in a cost-effective way. Fleming continued to experiment with the new product. He found that even in small quantities, it was remarkably effective in stopping bacteria.

- When he first discovered this strange substance, Fleming called it "mold broth" or "mold juice," which were good descriptions of what it was but not as impressive as the new name he found for it: penicillin. Then, in 1932, Fleming largely gave up on active work on his discovery; his laboratory was not designed to produce purified penicillin on a substantial scale.

- After a lag of some years, Howard Florey, a professor of pathology at Oxford, read an article about Fleming's findings and decided to follow up on this research. In a large laboratory at Oxford, Florey, Ernst Chain, and others purified penicillin in large quantities and showed that they could cure mice injected with bacteria. In 1940, they tried out their product for the first time on a human, a policeman, who recovered from a serious infection.

- Research also extended to the United States. There, in 1942, the first person whose life was saved with penicillin was a native New Yorker, Anne Miller, who was battling a life-threatening streptococcal infection. After an injection of penicillin she recovered and lived another 57 years!

- The outbreak of the Second World War created the desperate need for mobilization to produce vast quantities of penicillin at breakneck speed. The British and American governments backed this effort. During the war and in the reconstruction afterward, penicillin saved millions of lives.

- After penicillin showed its potency during the war, other antibiotics were developed. In 1944, American researcher Selman Waksman developed streptomycin, which reduced and controlled tuberculosis.

- In the 1950s came the development of broad-spectrum antibiotics for a range of bacteria not covered by penicillin. These were heady days, when some thought that medicine's advance was so successful and relentless that soon all diseases might be wiped out by magic bullets. Progress continues, with the eradication of smallpox in 1980 and guinea worm disease likely also to be eradicated soon.

The Future of Antibiotics

- Already by 1946, Dr. Fleming warned that incorrect use of penicillin could backfire. If the doses were too small to truly wipe out an illness, eventually, bacteria would develop resistance to penicillin. This is precisely what is happening today.

- Doctors today are seeing more and more diseases that have developed resistance to generations of antibiotics. Tuberculosis is making a comeback. Illnesses that decades ago could be treated with penicillin pills now demand hospitalization and intensive care. Antibiotics have been extensively used in livestock agriculture, and experts also warn of the dangers of this use.

- The prospect before us is frightening and discouraging. The head of the World Health Organization has stated, "A post-antibiotic era means, in effect, an end to modern medicine as we know it... Things as common as strep throat or a child's scratched knee could once again kill."

- Paradoxically, some profound turning points are not permanent. They can be overtaken by other great forces, for good or ill. Yet improved understanding is always a source of hope. A new model of the human body as an ecosystem, complete with a "microbiome" of trillions of bacteria, may yield new strategies for maintaining health.

Suggested Reading

Brown, *Penicillin Man.*

Hobby, *Penicillin.*

Horvitz, *Eureka!*

Waller, *The Discovery of the Germ.*

Questions to Consider

1. How can one cultivate the alertness to chance that Dr. Alexander Fleming exhibited so well?

2. Given that Dr. Fleming and Leeuwenhoek both experienced serendipity, what were the main differences between the two men and their work?

1928—The Discovery of Penicillin
Lecture 19—Transcript

It is early September in 1928, in London. Fall is in the air, cooler days, and that feeling of a new beginning as one gets back to work. The Scottish biologist Alexander Fleming has just returned from vacation, and is now cleaning up his laboratory to prepare for a new season of research. Before going on his holiday in late summer, he had been working with experiments with staphylococci bacteria in small petri dishes.

So, on September 3, 1928, he started to clean up, placing a stack of contaminated dishes into antiseptic trays with antiseptic fluid. But some dishes were out of the reach of the antiseptic. In other words, this project was a mess—contaminated, unclean, with fuzzy growths, something that really was in dire need of cleaning up. Ordinarily, a laboratory assistant would have set to work then scrubbing and cleaning and getting everything ready for a fresh start.

Instead, and this made all the difference, Fleming took his time and looked closely, because to his trained eye, something unexpected and interesting was to be seen. He saw in one of the top dishes the greenish-yellow color of mold, and surrounding it, a kind of open area. The mold was somehow inhibiting the growth of the bacteria.

As Fleming investigated further, he discovered that the mold that had insinuated itself into his experiment was *Penicillium notatum*, a mold that under the microscope looks brush-like, hence its Latin name, *Penicillium* or "small brush." What was happening around the mold was that the cells of the bacteria were breaking down—something the mold was producing was working to destroy bacteria. This powerful substance Fleming dubbed "Penicillin." The antibiotic revolution was launched, giving mankind new tools in an eternal battle against disease.

This scene illustrates the power of serendipity, finding something while looking for something else. Yet, it was not just chance that was at work here. Fortune favors those who are prepared, and in the case of Dr. Fleming, those who are attentive enough to take the time to look and observe. Further, every discovery takes place in a larger context: Fleming's insight needed to be made practically accessible and useful before it became the turning point that saved millions of lives and transformed medicine into our own times.

In a real sense, the scene we witnessed and will explore further in this lecture was a turning point within a turning point, a revolution within a larger revolution. The advance of antibiotics took place in the larger context of the development of germ theory, which revealed how many diseases worked, to begin with.

Before effective therapies could be found, mechanisms of infection and disease needed to be understood. In just a few decades before 1900, germ theory overturned how we understood health and disease, and how we envisioned human beings in relation to their environment.

We saw in a previous lecture how the microscopic investigations of Leeuwenhoek had revealed microorganisms, that smallest invisible world. What was not understood was the importance of those bacteria, for good or for ill, for human beings. Over the previous centuries, indeed from the time of the ancient Greeks, health and disease were most often understood in terms of the theory of humors. The word "humor" comes from the Latin word for liquid or fluid. This theory of humors postulated that all human beings were creatures in whom four fluids mixed and operated. These fluids were blood, phlegm, yellow bile, and black bile. Having more of one of these determined a person's temperament: sanguine, phlegmatic, choleric, or melancholic.

Even in our own times, the terminology of this older theory is still with us. We speak of someone as having a sense of humor, and we still speak of people being marked by a temperament, whether sanguine, that is marked by blood, for someone who is lively and sociable, or phlegmatic for the understated and quiet among us.

Illness thus was understood as a loss of internal balance of these fluids. If a high fever occurred, for instance, this would be understood as an excess of blood, and bloodletting was called for. Such a therapy is familiar from novels and movies about the 18th and 19th centuries, and could involve the use of leeches to deplete an alleged excess of blood. These aquatic worms were fastened onto the skin to draw off blood and restore balance.

In addition, contemporaries also believed that internal imbalances could be caused by bad air, miasmas as they were called, as a source of infection. When we think of the theory of the humors, this older conception of the human body, this theory has sometimes been compared to a hydraulic system, the body as a finely tuned machine.

In the decades before 1900, the authority of these concepts was overturned by medical pioneers who instead advanced germ theory, the understanding that important diseases were caused by infection with microorganisms. This revolutionized pathology and surgery. The pioneers of germ theory included a series of great scientists. We already mentioned Leeuwenhoek, but now his discoveries needed further interpretation.

By the 1840s, a number of physicians were noticing evidence for the contagious nature of disease being spread from person to person, not being caused by miasmas or clouds of bad air. One discovery was made by Dr. Ignaz Semmelweis, and it was a horrifying discovery for doctors: He found that it had been doctors who had been spreading a deadly disease.

Semmelweis was a German-Hungarian doctor at work in Vienna, who noticed the high incidence of so-called childbed fever, or puerperal infection, among new mothers in maternity wards. He was astonished at two wards that he visited, which had mortality rates respectively of 29 percent and 3 percent. Seeking the reason for the difference, he discovered that in the ward with soaring mortality, medical students who did autopsies went right on in to deliver babies, and thus infected their patients. When he ordered all staff to wash their hands in chlorinated water, deaths from childbed fever simply plummeted.

Another doctor, John Snow, traced deaths in London's cholera epidemic to one neighborhood water pump, and showed that cholera was a waterborne disease. In 1865, Joseph Lister, a professor of surgery at Glasgow University, revolutionized antiseptic procedures in surgery, and infections were reduced markedly as a result of these sterilization procedures. Indeed, Listerine mouthwash was named after him, in tribute.

The 19th century saw worldwide reform movements to create more hygienic urban environments, to inspect food production, and to instill quite ordinary means of ensuring public health. Something as basic as washing one's hands with soap turned into a revolution of its own.

The great breakthrough came with the work of French microbiologist Louis Pasteur. Pasteur's experiments proved that fermentation of wine and milk going bad were caused by microbes. Pasteurization was the process of heating foodstuffs to delay the action of microbes. In other practical applications, Pasteur saved the wine industry in France (now that's really saying something!) and the silk industry (where a disease had struck the silkworms).

Pasteur arrived at the conclusion that germs caused infectious disease. This was confirmed in his investigations of an anthrax epidemic affecting sheep and humans in 1879. Pasteur developed a vaccine.

At the same time, in Germany, the German doctor Robert Koch was also studying anthrax and came to the same conclusions. He also identified the bacteria that caused tuberculosis in 1882 and cholera in 1883. As a result, Koch won the Nobel Prize in Medicine for 1905.

Along with his rival Pasteur, Koch was a founder of microbiology, and developed rules for identifying specific microbes that caused disease. These are called Koch's postulates, and they're still used as a guide today. They stated that you had to first identify the microorganism that was always linked to a particular disease, then isolate that microbe and grow it in the laboratory, then verify it caused disease in a healthy animal, and then be able to isolate it again in that new subject.

Here was the rigor of the scientific method applied to the new exciting hunt for microbes. In his lab, by the way, Koch also chose an especially successful material on which bacteria colonies could grow. This was an ordinary slice of the potato, that product of the Columbian exchange from the start of our course.

In the hands of Robert Koch, the potato contributed to the triumph of germ theory by around 1900. The message spread to ordinary people, who became newly attuned to the dangers of microorganisms and contagion, as well as to the reality Leeuwenhoek had long ago discovered: Germs are everywhere, not least on and in each human being.

I want to mention one splendid and eloquent piece of evidence for the new thinking in terms of germ theory around this time. This actually occurs in a novel by a figure we've encountered before in our course, the British writer of "speculative fiction" or "scientific romances," H.G. Wells.

In 1898, Wells published one of his most famous stories. This was entitled *The War of the Worlds* and later was turned into a frightening radio broadcast by Orson Welles. In this story, we see the Earth invaded by Martians. This technologically advanced race sets down in their rockets on the Earth and builds large tripod vehicles that are equipped with deadly heat rays to attack the cities of the humans. The Martians drain blood from the humans that they capture. London is nearly destroyed. Human weapons seem to be able to do little against the Martians. The Martian invasion lasts for 12 days, and then suddenly stops (should I add here a spoiler alert? I am about to reveal the surprise ending).

The narrator by the end of the story has lost all hope, and goes out just to die in fighting against the Martians, but instead discovers that all of them have suddenly fallen dead. The aliens had been killed, you guessed it, by germs. As Wells puts it, they were slain by the "disease bacteria against which their systems were unprepared ... slain, after all man's devices had failed, by the humblest things that God in his wisdom has put upon this earth."

So for Wells, as a committed Darwinist, evolution played a key role, along with germs. Humans, through natural selection, had acquired immunities which the Martians did not have. In a sense, this was the devastating epidemic dimension of the Columbian exchange from 1492 that we talked about, but in reverse. What Wells calls our microscopic allies in his story had saved humanity from aliens. At least for now.

From 1900 then, the hunt for bacteria and disease agents was an international and collective scientific enterprise. Big advances in medical knowledge were due to cooperation internationally through medical journals and worldwide conferences. It was a great fight. The microbes that caused typhoid, diphtheria, tetanus, plague, and rabies were identified.

Once vectors of disease were discovered, it might be possible then to work methodically to prevent them (by vaccine) or to cure them. Now the front shifted to fighting disease that already had established itself. The stage was set for a new kind of drug war. This drug war would not be like the Opium Wars we discussed in an earlier lecture for narcotics, but a drug war to discover healing medicines.

Impressive advances were made in Germany, which around 1900 was in its golden age of medical research. The Nobel Prize–winning German-Jewish scientist Paul Ehrlich conducted work on the effects of chemicals on diseases. He was always seeking what he memorably called the magic bullet or *Zauberkugel* that would solve a medical problem. In 1910, with a Japanese colleague, Ehrlich tested Salvarsan, an arsenic drug that helped destroy syphilis. The very name Salvarsan meant "saves through arsenic," a real but effective paradox of the healing powers of a poison. Later, the German scientist Gerhard Domagk pioneered the first of the sulfonamide drugs. Further advances seemed possible and real.

A pathbreaking advance then came with that surprising scene of serendipity from 1928 with which we began this lecture, the discovery of penicillin. Who was Dr. Alexander Fleming, and how did the discovery occur? Fleming was born in rural southwestern Scotland in 1881, into a large family, the seventh of eight children. Like Darwin, Fleming's youth was spent close to nature, observing and exploring. This shaped his later life and career.

When Fleming was 14, he was sent to London to school. For a while he was employed at a shipping business, but that only made clear to him that he did not want to spend the rest of his life on a commercial career. Eventually, he followed an older brother into the medical profession. From 1901, Fleming studied at St. Mary's medical school in London, and he later went on to spend the rest of his career there at St. Mary's.

He studied under the notable bacteriologist Almroth Wright, the discoverer of the typhoid vaccine. Once Fleming earned his degree, he went into private practice, treating syphilis with the Salvarsan which Ehrlich had invented. During the First World War, Dr. Fleming worked in a military hospital in France, at a time when many lives were being lost to soldiers being wounded in the trenches and then becoming infected as they were evacuated to the rear.

Fleming experimented with different antiseptic procedures in the military hospital, and found strong chemical antiseptics actually often did more harm than good because they destroyed tissue. On returning to St. Mary's after the war, he continued working on these antiseptic questions.

In 1921, Fleming made an accidental discovery that Leeuwenhoek would have much appreciated, and which really makes clear how good he was at using accidents. While experimenting with bacteria, Fleming, who at the time had a bad cold, saw that mucus from his nose fell into a petri dish. Instead of cleaning it, he left it there to see what would happen (do you see a pattern emerging here in his research?). Fleming discovered that the bacteria had been disrupted, and this revealed to him the existence of lysosome, a natural human antibacterial enzyme that's found in body fluids, including tears.

At this point, Fleming was already an established and noted scholar, a successful scientist. He was soft-spoken, shy, often a bit disheveled, and known for his eccentricities, not least the wearing of really dramatic bowties. His laboratory was marked by creative disorder, rather than severe, efficient regimentation. If anyone complains to you in the future about the messiness of your office, just refer them to the example of Dr. Fleming and his discoveries!

The entire building in which Fleming's laboratory was housed was not in the best of shape, either. In his lab, it was hard to open a window to get some air circulation, so Fleming kept the door open, which connected with the rest of the building. As it turns out, this was fateful, because down some stairs was a mycology lab, where experiments on fungus and molds were being done at the same time. It was from down there that spores of mold had drifted silently up and into Fleming's laboratory.

While Fleming was away for his late summer vacation, the weather turned unseasonably warm for London, and this allowed the mold spores to reproduce where they had landed. They were ready for him to notice on that fateful day, September 3, 1928. Fleming later declared, with becoming modesty: "Do not wait for fortune to smile on you; prepare yourself with knowledge." Overall, he was understated about what he had done, saying, "My only merit is that I did not neglect the observation."

But now that the observation had been made—and this is a really important point—that was not the end of the matter. It didn't finish there. Now the question arose of how to use this discovery, how to develop it as a healing tool practically and in cost-effective ways. For a time Fleming continued to experiment with this new product. He isolated it and diluted it, and was glad to find that even in small, small quantities it was really remarkably effective in stopping bacteria.

Fleming tried it out on mice and rabbits, without ill effects, and that was good news too as well. When he first discovered this strange substance, he called it mold broth or mold juice. Those were pretty good literal descriptions of what it was, but not as scientifically impressive as the new name that he found for it: penicillin. Then, in 1932, Fleming largely gave up active work on it.

Why? Fleming had made this individual discovery, but producing penicillin on a purified and substantial scale was not what his laboratory was designed for. His own interests in fact also tended much more towards noting new research findings, precisely what he'd done in this case, rather than finding practical uses.

After a lag of some years, however, in a collective effort, the discovery was utilized more effectively. This was done by Howard Florey and Ernst Chain at Oxford University. Florey was born 1898 in Australia, became a doctor, then went to Oxford as a professor of pathology. On reading an article of Fleming's about his findings, he decided to follow up on his research. In a large laboratory at Oxford, Florey worked together with Ernst Chain, a German-Jewish chemist who had fled Nazi Germany, as well as other technicians and scientists. It really was a large group undertaking, not a serendipitous venture by one man. Their work was also further supported by funding from the Rockefeller Foundation.

This large team purified penicillin in greater quantities than Fleming had been able to. They showed that they could cure mice injected with bacteria. In 1940, they tried out their product for the first time on a human being, a policeman, who recovered from a very serious infection as a result.

Research also extended to the United States. It was there in 1942 that the first person whose life was saved was to be found. This was a native New Yorker, Anne Miller. After a month at the New Haven Hospital, battling a streptococcal infection, she was at death's door. Her fever was soaring to 107, and she was often lapsing into unconsciousness and then reemerging. Nothing doctors could do seemed to help.

In the desperate situation, her doctors got a small sample, the very first, of penicillin being produced in New Jersey, and injected it into her as a final venture. Overnight the fever went down. By the next morning she was not delirious and soon was on the road to recovery. Mrs. Miller in fact lived another 57 years after that moment of medical history!

The next astonishing chapter in this story was how the arrival of the Second World War created the desperate need for and the mobilization to produce vast quantities of penicillin at breakneck speed. The American and British governments backed this effort. Howard Florey even went to the Soviet Union, the ally of the United States and Britain, to help them set up production as well.

When the invasion of France was launched with D-Day in 1944, vast quantities of penicillin were on hand to treat the wounded. During the war, and in the difficult reconstruction of a ruined world after the war, penicillin saved millions of lives that otherwise would have been lost.

In 1945, the Nobel Prize committee awarded a shared prize for penicillin to Alexander Fleming, Howard Florey, and Ernst Chain. This was highly merited praise, but the drama ever since of Fleming's accidental discovery has tended to overshadow the contributions of Florey, Chain, and other members of the teams that had developed penicillin for practical and extensive use.

After penicillin showed its potency during the war, other antibiotics were also developed, part of that much larger antibiotic revolution. In 1944, American researcher Selman Waksman developed streptomycin, against tuberculosis, an ancient scourge of mankind. Tuberculosis was not eradicated worldwide, but much reduced and controlled.

Then in the 1950s, came the development of so-called broad spectrum antibiotics, for a range of bacteria not covered by penicillin. These were exciting and heady days, at a time when it seemed reasonable to feel and think that medicine's advance was so successful and relentless that soon perhaps all diseases might be wiped out by medicines that function almost like magic bullets (like penicillin). In our own times, progress continues, with the eradication of smallpox in 1980, and guinea worm disease also likely to be eradicated soon. Efforts are continuing to wipe out polio.

How good and pleasant it would be to end the story right there, looking forward to the inevitable progress and improvement that continues. But the real story is actually much more complicated and threatening. Already by 1946, Fleming, taking on sort of a role as a talking head that he really felt himself into and enjoyed, Fleming warned that incorrect use of penicillin could actually backfire on humanity. If the doses of penicillin that were used were too small to absolutely really wipe out an illness, eventually he argued bacteria would evolve to develop resistance to penicillin. This was a warning taken right out of Darwin's teachings about natural selection that we considered as an earlier turning point, and it's precisely what has happened and is happening since.

The very confidence in the seemingly miraculous powers of antibiotics led to their overuse and misuse. Ordinary patients, feeling a certain improvement once they had started a regimen of antibiotics, would then discontinue taking their medicines. Other patients, craving the reassurance of being under good treatment with powerful medicine, insisted to their doctors that they prescribe them with antibiotics, even in cases when antibiotics were not going to be of any use, for instance against viruses.

As a result, like Fleming predicted, we're seeing more and more diseases that have developed resistance to entire generations of antibiotics. As a result in dire news, tuberculosis is making a comeback. Illnesses that decades ago could be treated with penicillin pills may now instead demand hospitalization and intensive care. Antibiotics also have been extensively used in livestock agriculture; indeed much more antibiotics go to animals than to humans (in fact, in the United States it's estimated that 80 percent goes to livestock), and experts are warning of the possible dangers of this use as well.

The prospect before us is in many ways a frightening and discouraging one. The head of the World Health Organization stated, "A post-antibiotic era means, in effect, an end to modern medicine as we know it ... Things as common as strep throat or a child's scratched knee could once again kill."

This is one other worry to add on to the anxieties of our present day, with the threat of global pandemics, or of the global transmission of diseases, monitored by the Centers for Disease Control. In a paradox, the ability of air travel that we discussed in an earlier lecture as a turning point, the ability of air travel to move increasing numbers of people around the world, with all the good that that can imply, also has inadvertently created another effective vector for the wide spread of disease.

A sobering observation to make here thus is that some profound historical turning points, paradoxically, are not always permanent. They function, they have their results, and then they can be overtaken by other great forces, for good or ill. Yet in a sense improved understanding is always a source of hope. This may be the case in new ways of understanding the very existence of a human being biologically.

Before the advent of germ theory, the human body was seen, as we discussed, as a hydraulic machine sloshing about with humors, those fluids that make us go and determine wellness or sickness. Today, a new model is coming to the fore. That is a new vision of the human being, in a sense, as an ecosystem, as an extensive environment. Each of us harbors some 100 trillion bacteria of hundreds of species, many of them crucial to our digestion, health, and life; collectively this is called the microbiome. Leeuwenhoek would nod in agreement. So one question we face now is how better understanding of our own interdependence with the larger microbiome might yield new strategies for health and fighting sickness.

At the same time as penicillin was coming into its own, during the storms of the Second World War, another turning point came with the unleashing of vast new power, through atomic energy. This we will consider in our next lecture.

1942—The Dawn of the Atom
Lecture 20

O n December 2, 1942, Enrico Fermi and a team at the University of Chicago produced and controlled a fission chain reaction for the first time in human history. This beginning was small—producing only enough energy to power a light bulb—but within three years, it led to the construction of the atomic bomb. The effects of this turning point were profound. The work in Chicago ushered in the nuclear age. The atom bomb and later generations of nuclear weapons made the modern phenomenon of total war absolute: For the first time, mankind possessed the technology by which it might destroy itself. Modernity is marked by this peril, produced by our own progress in technology and science.

Changing Theories in Classical Physics
- Until the start of the 20th century, the dominant model of physics had been classical mechanics—the physics shaped by Isaac Newton—which suggested a universe of regularity, predictability, and stability.

- Just before the turn of the century, new discoveries were made. The work of the French researchers Marie and Pierre Curie revealed that atoms were not stable, orderly units but could emit subatomic particles and energy.

- In 1900, the German physicist Max Planck produced quantum theory, which described what had been seen as solid matter as having qualities of waves and radiation as having qualities of particles. The new quantum mechanics on the atomic and subatomic scale dealt with probabilities, not the certainties of classical mechanics.

- In 1905, the German-born physicist Albert Einstein announced his special theory of relativity, which along with quantum mechanics is one of the bases of modern physics. In his famous equation, $E =$

mc^2, Einstein showed that matter was a form of energy. Mass can be converted into energy and vice versa.

- Ernest Rutherford, a British physicist, established the nuclear model of the atom, and in quick succession, different subatomic particles were identified: electrons, protons, and neutrons. This subatomic world acted according to the postulates of quantum mechanics.

- In 1927, the German physicist Werner Heisenberg proposed his famed "uncertainty principle," according to which the very act of measurement altered that which was being observed, further undermining the certainties promised by classical physics.

- The tremendous power latent in the atom was intuited by a figure we have encountered repeatedly in these lectures, the British writer H. G. Wells. In 1914, Wells published a novel entitled *The World Set Free*, in which he predicted the development of the atom bomb. Wells is fascinating for the purposes of our course, not as a hero or someone who was always right, but as someone who wrestled with questions of progress, modernity, and the human future.

Launch of the Manhattan Project

- New advances in atomic knowledge started cascading at a time of great international peril, the 1930s, with dictatorships on the march. In this decade, more than 100 noted scientists emigrated to Britain or the United States, and this "brain drain" would prove decisive. It included Einstein, Fermi, and Leo Szilard, Eugene Wigner, and Edward Teller.

- Initially, it seemed that Hitler's Germany had a lead. In 1938, German physicists conducted experiments in nuclear fission, splitting the atom. The news of the German advance frightened the refugee scientists. Nuclear fission could release significant power, which could be used to produce bombs.

- Other scientists asked Einstein to write a letter to President Roosevelt, warning him that recent scientific advances could result in the construction of a powerful bomb. In a sense, this letter launched American efforts to build a bomb in order to reach that goal before the Nazis.

- In 1941, Roosevelt ordered the founding of the Office of Scientific Research and Development, headed by Vannevar Bush, an engineer, inventor, dean at MIT, and later, head of the Carnegie Institution. Bush's job, simply put, was to mobilize science for total war. Indeed, he has been called the father of the military-industrial complex.

- The outcome of these efforts was the Manhattan Project. The military commander was General Leslie Groves. The physicist Robert Oppenheimer was put in charge of the research effort. Overall, the project, which began with a $6,000 budget, ended up costing $2 billion.

Progress of the Manhattan Project

- The Manhattan Project gathered an ever-expanding group of scientists and engineers, who often knew only their parts of the larger project. Some didn't find out what they had been working on until they heard the news of the bombing of Hiroshima on the radio.

- From the start, the scientists wrestled with the moral implications of their work—creating a weapon of mass destruction. All agreed that the Nazis must not build the bomb first. Many saw themselves as building a tool that would function as a deterrent. Whether this idea was realistic or not, the race continued at breakneck speed.

- The first step was to start and control a chain reaction, as was done in Chicago in December 1942. This first nuclear reactor was code-named CP1 for "Chicago Pile #1." The pile of almost 400 tons of graphite bricks and uranium and the control rods were assembled in secrecy from around mid-November.

- When the first test was run, no one knew for sure that the chain reaction would not run out of control or that no explosion would ensue. There was no shield or cooling system. A technician stood ready to insert a control rod that would stop the reaction, and others had buckets of cadmium and salt to throw onto the pile as a last resort.

- Fermi started the process, and the pile began to operate, building to criticality over the course of hours. At one point, Fermi called for a lunch break, but afterward, the experiment resumed and, by 3:25, was declared successful.

- With this door to atomic energy opened, the project to build a bomb took off in earnest. Different lines of research were pursued simultaneously at different sites: in Hanford, Washington; in the mountains of eastern Tennessee; and at Los Alamos in New Mexico, 34 miles north of Santa Fe.

- On July 16, 1945, the first atomic bomb was detonated at 5:29 am in New Mexico, at an air force base in Alamogordo, 120 miles south of Albuquerque. This was the Trinity test. The atomic explosive device was installed atop a steel tower. Some five and a half miles away, observers with scientific instruments crouched down in a bunker to experience the results.

- This test, too, was accompanied by uncertainty; some physicists argued about whether the explosion would cause the earth's atmosphere to catch fire, ending all humanity at once. First came a blinding flash, then a heat wave, followed by a shock wave. The explosion sent a mushroom cloud more than seven miles into the air and was heard in three states. The bomb was ready for use.

Hiroshima and Nagasaki

- After years of hard struggle, Hitler's Germany had been defeated in May of 1945, but the Second World War continued in the Pacific. What happened next marked the point where total war became absolute.

- In August 1945, the United States dropped two bombs on Japan at Hiroshima and Nagasaki. In Hiroshima, between 80,000 and 140,000 died at once, and many more succumbed afterwards. In Nagasaki, 24,000 were killed immediately. The blast, firestorm, and human suffering surpass words and imagination. This was truly ground zero for the revelation of the destructiveness of war.

- The decision to use the atomic bombs remains controversial today. That decision was made in the context of a war in which 60 million had been killed and when the extent of the bomb's destructive capabilities were not yet known.

© iStockphoto/Thinkstock.

The Atomic Bomb Dome still stands in Hiroshima, now serving as a memorial to those who were killed on August 6, 1945.

The Nuclear Legacy

- Nuclear weapons loomed over the decades that followed, especially in the escalating Cold War that began once the United States and the Soviet Union, former allies, confronted each other on a global scale.
  - By 1949, the Soviet Union had detonated its own atomic bomb, aided by both brilliant physicists and spies who had infiltrated the Manhattan Project. Both sides produced even more powerful hydrogen bombs in the 1950s.

  - The ruling logic of the Cold War was that of deterrence: threatening one's enemy with weapons of unthinkable power to stave off an attack. This doomsday scenario even acquired its own appropriately official-sounding bureaucratic acronym: MAD, meaning "mutually assured destruction."

- Throughout the atomic age, which we still live in today, some 128,000 nuclear weapons were built. More than 500 aboveground and more than 1,500 underground nuclear tests were conducted. The club of those states going nuclear also grew, with Britain joining in October 1952, France in 1960, and China in 1964. Since then, India, Pakistan, Israel, and North Korea have been added.

- Anxieties about the spread of nuclear weapons led to the Nuclear Test-Ban Treaty of 1963, then the Treaty on the Non-Proliferation of Nuclear Weapons in 1968. But fears grow today of what further proliferation might mean, with what we might ironically call a democratization of these weapons.

- A well-known peak moment of Cold War peril, when the confrontation might have turned hot, was the Cuban missile crisis of 1962, which was defused by negotiation. Almost unknown is that nuclear war might have broken out accidentally in 1983, when Soviet early-warning devices incorrectly reported an American missile launch.

- Even the peaceful use of nuclear energy has remained problematic in the eyes of many. Nuclear accidents at Chernobyl in the Soviet Union in 1986 and in Japan at Fukushima in 2011 further stoked concerns.

- The opening of the atomic age raised profound questions about the authority of progress through science.

Suggested Reading

DeGroot, *The Bomb*.

Rhodes, *The Making of the Atomic Bomb*.

1. If World War II had not broken out, how might atomic research have developed differently without military necessity to drive it?

2. Were the hopes of scientists that the atomic bomb would be used only as a deterrent basically naïve?

1942—The Dawn of the Atom
Lecture 20—Transcript

This lecture opens in my hometown, Chicago, and actually at my undergraduate alma mater, the University of Chicago, in Hyde Park, on the city's South Side. It's a bitterly cold Chicago winter morning. It's December 2, 1942. As the Second World War rages, scientists are in a race to employ atomic power to end the war. Here, a team of scientists are about to undertake an experiment that will open the door to new uses for atomic power, and create a decisive turning point—not just in modern history, but in all of human history.

The team assembled today includes 48 men and one woman, presided over by the brilliant Italian physicist Enrico Fermi. They have gathered under the stands of the university's football stadium, Stagg Field. (By the way, this harkens back to the days when the University of Chicago was a national football powerhouse. Those days are long gone). There, under the stands, during peacetime were the indoor courts for playing squash. Now, instead, an apparatus has been constructed here in the darkness. It consists of wood, graphite bricks, clumps of uranium, and cadmium control rods.

A great deal of uncertainty hovered over this experiment, which had never been done before. What if the experiment got out of control? What if it took on a life of its own, erupting in unpredictable ways that had not been anticipated, even by experts?

At 9:54 am, Fermi orders the control rods withdrawn, and everyone listens. Suddenly the neutron counters come alive, and their ticking grows in intensity. That ticking increases over the next hour, as the structure, known as a nuclear pile, approaches critical state. Going critical means producing a self-sustaining chain reaction. Then by 3:25 pm, the neutron counters are no longer clicking in separate clicks—the clicks are coming so fast that they're just buzzing. Enrico Fermi proudly announces, "The reaction is self-sustaining."

This was the first time in all of history that humans had produced and controlled a fission chain reaction. This beginning was small. Before the chain reaction was shut down, by reinserting the control rods that had been pulled out, the power produced had only been enough to power a light bulb. But it showed the way, and led within three short years of nonstop work to the building of the atomic bomb.

Some turning points are ones that build slowly in history, unfolding over time. This one, however, was a race. The effects of this turning point were profound. That Chicago pile ushered in the nuclear age, in which we live today. The atom bomb, and later generations of nuclear weapons, made the modern phenomenon of total war absolute: For the first time, mankind possessed the technology by which it might destroy itself in a comprehensive way.

Ever since then, we've lived in a world overshadowed by that reality, from which it seems there is no going back. However much one might desire it, there proved to be no way of uninventing the bomb, unknowing such knowledge after it had been acquired. Modernity is marked by this peril, produced by its own progress in technological and scientific directions.

This turning point was born of a broader change in the understanding of physics. The unsettling discoveries made by scientists only slowly percolated out to a broader audience. The earlier dominant model had been that of classical mechanics, the sort of physics shaped by Sir Isaac Newton and his laws, which together suggested a universe of regularity, predictability, and stability. This sort of worldview, sometimes called Newton's world machine, was now going to be challenged in fundamental.

Around the start of the 20th century, new discoveries were being made. The French researchers Marie Curie and Pierre Curie researched radioactivity (and she won two Nobel Prizes for her scientific work). This work revealed atoms as not just stable orderly units, but ones that could emit subatomic particles and energy.

In 1900, the German physicist Max Planck produced quantum theory, which described what had earlier been seen as solid matter as actually having qualities of waves, and radiation also having qualities of particles.

This new quantum mechanics on the atomic and subatomic scale dealt with probabilities, not with the seeming certainties of classical mechanics.

In 1905, the German-born physicist Albert Einstein announced his special theory of relativity, which along with quantum mechanics is one of the bases of modern physics. In his famous equation, $E=mc^2$, Einstein showed that matter was a form of energy. Mass and energy can be converted into one another.

Between the world wars, in the 1920s, came what has been called the heroic age of physics. By its end, with the bomb and nuclear power, unworldly scientists would be regarded with an awe that surpassed their earlier stature; increasingly they seemed arbiters of our world. Ernest Rutherford, a British physicist who had been born in New Zealand, established the nuclear model of the atom, and in quick succession different subatomic particles were also identified: electrons, protons, and neutrons. This subatomic world acted according to the postulates of quantum mechanics.

In 1927, German physicist Werner Heisenberg proposed his famed uncertainty principle, according to which the very act of measurement altered that which was being observed. This further undermined the certainties earlier promised by classical physics.

The tremendous power latent in the atom was intuited by a figure we've actually encountered repeatedly before in this course for his visionary insights. This was the British writer H.G. Wells. It rarely gets more visionary than this: Just before the outbreak of the First World War in 1914, Wells actually predicted the atom bomb. In fact, he's the one who coined the term "atom bomb." In 1914 he published a novel that was entitled *The World Set Free*. This was a future history, predicting events that had not yet come to pass.

Wells imagined in this book that by 1933, the atom had been split, generating boundless reserves of energy, what he called "worlds of limitless power." In fact, he postulated in his book that gold was a waste byproduct of this process which would instantly overturn worldwide finance). In his story, the nations of the world soon set about building atom bombs of devastating force. In Wells's imagination, atom bombs once dropped did not simply explode once, but continued to explode for years afterwards until exhausted, burrowing down into the earth. This was an aspect that he didn't get quite right. But by a dreadful paradox, Wells argued, war had finally become so efficient that it had become impossible to control.

Moreover, and here is Wells's diagnosis of modernity, the political arrangements and social organization of mankind was fatally lagging behind humanity's scientific and technical powers. In his story, by 1956, a general atomic war breaks out lasting for years, with over 200 cities bombed into oblivion, with countries one after another seeking to seize power, until finally civilization has been completely destroyed.

In the aftermath, in Wells's story, survivors recognize that what they need most of all is a change of heart that will usher in a new phase of human history. Individualism, Wells argues, needs to give way to science and service; humanity needs to be organized not into separate sovereign states (on the Westphalian model originated in 1648), but rather under one common world government, a World Republic ruled not by democracy, but regulation and administration by experts. Indeed, science would be the basis of an entire new social order of what Wells called "unity and collectivism." Continuous planning on a global scale was now needed, and in Wells's story, desperately desired by survivors. According to Wells, now at last humanity would face a bright future in which humanity itself could be shaped deliberately.

In a disturbing note at the end of Wells's story, the book suggests that the previous world had become so old, ill, and confused, that "nothing less than the violence" of the atomic bombs could finally release the world and set it free, hence the title of the book. Wells is fascinating for the purposes of our course not as a hero or as someone who was always right in his prophecies, but rather as someone who wrestled with questions of progress, modernity, and the human future. Yet this concept of progress through apocalypse is surely a deeply alarming one.

So how did Wells's predictions of an atom bomb and atomic warfare come true? New advances in atomic knowledge started cascading at a time of great international peril, the 1930s, a time when dictatorships were on the march. Hitler was coming to power in Nazi Germany, Benito Mussolini was ruling over Fascist Italy, and Stalin was presiding over the Soviet Union. In this decade, more than a hundred noted scientists emigrated to Britain or the United States, from Germany and Italy, and this brain drain would prove decisive. It included Albert Einstein from Germany, Enrico Fermi from Italy, and from Hungary Leo Szilard, Eugene Wigner, and Edward Teller.

But to begin with, it seemed that Hitler's Germany had a lead in the new physics. In 1938, German physicists conducted experiments in nuclear fission, splitting the atom. The news of this German advance scared refugee scientists. Leo Szilard was a refugee from Hungary who had come to the United States in 1937 and taught at Columbia. On hearing the news on what the Germans had accomplished he reported, suddenly, "All the things which H.G. Wells predicted appeared suddenly very real to me." Nuclear fission would release huge power, and this could be used to produce bombs.

Sharing these worries was Enrico Fermi. He was a brilliant Italian scientist, boundlessly energetic and famously charismatic. Fermi himself was not politically active, but he had grown disgusted by the anti-Semitic policies of Fascist Italy, especially as his wife was Jewish. Fermi won the Nobel Prize, and then promptly left for the United States in 1939, to teach at Columbia.

Fermi tried to warn officials in Washington of the advances the Germans were making, but got little hearing. Next, Szilard, Teller, and Wigner decided that they needed to send a special letter to President Roosevelt that would get attention, and so they went to see Albert Einstein to have the letter come from him, already a generally famed scientist on a global scale. Einstein signed the letter—he would not go on to build the bomb.

In a real sense, however, the building of the bomb was launched by this letter, dated August 2, 1939. The letter warned that "extremely powerful bombs of a new type" might be constructed as a result of the newest research. The urgency of this situation at last seemed to dawn on American officials: What if the Nazis built these new weapons first? They would have no compunction in their use.

A first research project was approved in the United States in 1940, with a budget of $6,000. In 1941, Roosevelt ordered the founding of the Office of Scientific Research and Development, headed by Vannevar Bush, who was an engineer, inventor, dean at MIT, and later head of the Carnegie Institution. Vannevar Bush's job, simply put, was to mobilize science for total war. Indeed, Vannevar Bush been called the father of the military-industrial complex as we know it.

The outcome of this mobilization was the so-called Manhattan Project. It got this codename because so much early work was done at Columbia University in Manhattan. In spite of the name however, work would indeed be done all over the United States. The military commander was the hard-driving General Leslie Groves. The physicist Robert Oppenheimer was put in charge of the research effort itself.

Overall, the project which began with a budget of $6,000 ended up costing two billion dollars, essentially equivalent to the value of the United States auto industry at the time. This was unprecedented, the largest national undertaking before the space missions that we'll consider in a future lecture.

Success was not assured. Indeed, there were those who had considerable doubts. One admiral said the project was "the biggest fool thing we have ever done. The bomb will never go off, and I speak as an expert in explosives."

The project gathered an ever-expanding group of scientists and engineers, who would often work only knowing their part of the larger project. Some indeed only found out what they'd been working on when they heard about the bombing of Hiroshima on the radio.

There were culture clashes aplenty between the military authorities and the scientists. When General Groves briefed his military staff about the project, he explained, "Your job won't be easy. At great expense we have gathered the largest collection of crackpots ever seen." Actually as it turned out, a critical mass of scientists and minds had been gathered into this larger research undertaking.

There was in a sense a direct line of descent from Thomas Edison's Menlo Park laboratory to this project. The venture was international, as Britain and Canada collaborated on the project. Also, as we already noted, many scientists were refugees from Europe. One popular joke at the time went that whenever Enrico Fermi the Italian left the room, the other physicists breathed a sigh of relief and lapsed back into their common native language, Hungarian.

From the start, scientists wrestled with the moral implications of this work, the job of creating a weapon of mass destruction. All agreed that the Nazis must not be allowed to build the bomb first. Many scientists saw themselves as building a tool that would function as a deterrent: If it were held in reserve, others might be reluctant to use this technology. Perhaps this would be a weapon so terrible that it made war impossible.

Whether or not this was realistic, the race continued at breakneck speed. At the same time as penicillin was being mass-produced as a healing invention, work was surging ahead on the building of this super weapon.

The first key step was the one that we started our lecture with: beginning and controlling a chain reaction, as was done for the first time in December 1942 in Chicago. This first nuclear reactor was codenamed CP1 for "Chicago Pile #1." The pile of almost 400 tons of graphite bricks and uranium and control rods was assembled in an arduous process in secrecy from mid-November. It was literally shrouded from view by a grey balloon stretched around the project. The Goodyear company provided that balloon, but could not be told what it was for. The sole woman on the team, Leona Woods, measured the pile as it was slowly put together.

Finally, it was ready to go. A lot of tension played in the air. Think about this: No one knew for sure that the chain reaction would not run out of control. No one knew that an explosion might not ensue, in one of the biggest cities of the world. There was no shield or cooling system for the procedure. Instead, for protection, a technician stood ready with an axe, to cut a rope that would insert one more control rod. In addition, some workers stood by with buckets of cadmium and salt to throw onto the pile if it went out of control as a last resort. Imagine that: an axe and some buckets against the first nuclear chain reaction.

Fermi started the process and the pile began to operate; over hours it built to criticality. Then Fermi called for a lunch break. Try for a moment to envision how his team must have felt at this historic moment, being forced to take a break. None of our other turning points of modern history have been interrupted by a lunch break.

Then after lunch, the experiment resumed, and by 3:25 pm was successful. From somewhere, someone pulled a bottle of Chianti to toast their success from paper cups. One of the physicists, Dean Arthur Compton of the University of Chicago, now had to report by phone to their military superiors that the experiment had been successful. But no code had been prearranged, so Compton had to improvise on the phone, and the words that leapt up for him are really telling. Compton spoke into the phone: "The Italian navigator has landed in the New World." Spontaneously, this turning point was linked to the encounter of Columbus with the Americas. Columbus's 1492 was linked to Enrico Fermi's 1942.

There is a persistent urban legend that all 49 participants in the experiment soon died of cancer, as if a kind of curse had hovered over the event. That is clearly not true—many lived much longer and died of many different causes (indeed, of 27 participants whose cause of death is known, 6 died of cancers, but ones that are said to have been unlikely to have been caused by radiation exposure).

With this fateful door to atomic energy opened, the project took off in earnest. So urgent did the goal seem that the Manhattan Project actually pursued several different courses of action simultaneously, to see which seemed most promising. So, for instance, since it was not clear whether Uranium-235 or plutonium would be the best material to use, both were worked on at the same time. When different bomb designs for triggering the explosion were in dispute, both were pursued.

The work also took place at different sites: Hanford, Washington, in the mountains of eastern Tennessee, and in the deserts of New Mexico, at Los Alamos, 34 miles north of Santa Fe. I actually teach just down the road from the Oak Ridge site, which is near Knoxville, Tennessee, in the foothills of the Smoky Mountains. This remote site was where uranium and plutonium were separated and produced for use in the bomb. This entire "Secret City" was enclosed and self-sufficient, behind barbed wire, with up to 70,000 men and women working 10-hour shifts around the clock to produce a weapon that might win the war—not possessing it might mean losing the war.

The work raced ahead, and was soon ready for a test. On July 16, 1945, the first atomic bomb was detonated at 5:29 am in New Mexico, at Alamogordo air force base, 120 miles south of Albuquerque. This was the so-called Trinity test. The atomic explosive device was installed atop a steel tower. Some five and a half miles away, observers with scientific instruments crouched down in a bunker to experience the results.

This test was also accompanied by uncertainty, and some physicists actually argued about whether the explosion might not cause the Earth's atmosphere to catch fire, ending all of humanity all at once. First came a blinding flash (a light greater than any before on earth, and one that could have been seen from other planets), then a heat wave, followed by a shock wave. The explosion sent a mushroom cloud seven and a half miles into the air. This was it: *the* symbol of the new atomic age in all of its fearsome potential.

At ground zero, the metal tower was vaporized, and the ground at the center of the explosion had been subjected to such heat that the desert sands had turned into glass. The successful experiment was to be kept secret, but obviously something like this was of course hard to hide. The explosion had been heard in three states. One laconic Westerner actually remarked to some of the workers afterwards: "You boys must have been up to something this morning. The sun came up in the west and went on down again."

The bomb was ready for use. After years of hard struggle, Hitler's Germany had been defeated in May of 1945, in part by a campaign of strategic bombing that killed 635,000 Germans on the ground, mostly civilians. Searching among the ruins afterwards, Allied officials discovered that Germany had in fact, after a promising head start, made little progress on an atom bomb.

Yet the Second World War continued in the Pacific, raging there with great intensity and ferocity. What happened next marked the point where total war became absolute. We've mentioned before in this course the modern phenomenon of total war, involving soldiers and civilians, for total victory or total defeat, blurring the lines between the home front and the battlefront. Now in a sense, total war reached critical mass as well.

In August 1945, the United States dropped two bombs on Japan, at Hiroshima and Nagasaki. In Hiroshima between 80,000 and 140,000 people died at once, with many more succumbing afterwards. In Nagasaki, 24,000 were killed immediately. The blast, firestorm, and human suffering surpass words and imagination. This was truly ground zero for the revelation of the destructiveness of war.

Survivors would ever after be marked by their memories. Among them was Tsutomu Yamaguchi, a man who survived the Hiroshima blast, and went to heal at Nagasaki, surviving that ordeal as well, who finally passed away in 2010.

The decision to use the atomic bombs remains controversial today. That decision was taken in the context of a war in which 60 million were killed, and when the knowledge we have, of what the bomb was truly like in practice, was not yet known. We know, because all history afterwards has been lived in the shadow of the bomb. This was a turning point that was obvious at the time, unlike some others in our course. People understood something fundamental had happened.

Nuclear weapons loomed over the decades that followed, especially in the escalating Cold War that commenced once the former Allies, the United States and the Soviet Union, confronted one another on a global scale. America's nuclear monopoly turned out to be vanishingly brief. By 1949 the Soviet Union had detonated its own atomic bomb, aided both by brilliant physicists as well as atomic espionage, spies who had been infiltrated into the Manhattan Project. Both sides produced even more powerful hydrogen bombs in the 1950s.

The ruling logic of the Cold War was that of deterrence: threatening one's enemy with weapons of unthinkable power to stave off an attack, by being in a position to massively retaliate against any first strike. This doomsday scenario even acquired its own appropriately official-sounding bureaucratic acronym, MAD. MAD stands for "Mutually Assured Destruction."

Throughout the atomic age, which we still live in today, some 128,000 nuclear weapons were built. More than 500 aboveground tests and more than 1,500 underground nuclear tests were held. The club of those states going nuclear also kept growing. Britain joined in October of 1952, France in 1960, and China in 1964. Since then, India, Pakistan, Israel, and North Korea were added.

Anxieties about the spread of nuclear weapons led to the Nuclear Test-Ban Treaty of 1963, then the Treaty on Non-Proliferation of Nuclear Weapons in 1968. But fears grow today of what further proliferation might mean, what one might ironically call a democratization of these weapons.

A well-known peak moment of Cold War peril, when the confrontation of the Cold War might have turned hot, was the Cuban missile crisis of 1962, which was fortunately defused by negotiation. Almost unknown however is that nuclear war might have broken out accidentally in 1983, when the Soviets' early warning devices reported (incorrectly) an American missile launch. A Soviet satellite mistook the sun reflecting off the tops of clouds over the North American continent for five American missiles in launch. A Russian officer, who was sitting at the controls, decided that this must be an error. He reasoned that any American attack would involve not five, but thousands of incoming missiles. By reporting this to his superiors as a false alarm, he may have saved millions of lives.

One might add that even the peaceful use of nuclear energy has remained problematic in the eyes of many. Nuclear accidents at Chernobyl in the Soviet Union in 1986 and in Japan at Fukushima in 2011 have further stoked such concerns.

The opening of the atomic age raised profound questions about the authority of progress through science. The Cold War in turn, produced another world historical first, the voyage to the moon, and it is to that topic that we turn in our next lecture.

1969—Walking on the Moon
Lecture 21

The first humans walked on the moon on July 20, 1969, during the Apollo *11* mission. Those steps on another world marked a new epoch in how humans viewed their own earth and potential. Yet since 1972, with the end of follow-up missions to the moon, humans have not returned, nor have they gone on manned expeditions to other planets. Is the moon landing, like the voyages of Zheng He in the 1430s or those of Columbus around 1492, a turning point that did not turn—an end—or a beginning of vast discoveries and exchanges?

Wonderment at the Moon

- Throughout much of history, mankind had wondered at the moon. Prehistoric astronomers aligned such monuments as Stonehenge with their reckoning of the positions of the moon and stars. In modern times, Galileo used his telescope to make more detailed surveys of lunar features.

- Repeatedly, people imagined what it would be like to journey to the moon. Jules Verne's popular 1865 novel, *From the Earth to the Moon*, predicted a moon launch from a site in Florida. In 1901, H. G. Wells published *The First Men in the Moon*, detailing a mission undertaken by a shady businessman and a scientist. A year after Wells's novel, the first master of film special effects, Georges Méliès, produced *A Trip to the Moon*.

- At the start of the 20th century, scientists were emboldened to think about how to turn these speculative stories into reality. Their answer was not a giant cannon but rockets, an old technology from China that offered new possibilities when built on a larger scale.
  - The Russian mathematician Konstantin Tsiolkovsky explored theoretical aspects of space flight—the use of rockets to reach out into the cosmos.

The names given to features of the moon—craters called Columbus, Leeuwenhoek, Darwin, Diderot, Edison, and Fermi—echo our turning points.

- o In the United States, Robert Hutchings Goddard was fascinated by rocketry. He worked on liquid-fueled rockets, launching the first in 1926.

- o The German rocket scientist Hermann Oberth was particularly inspired by Verne's *From the Earth to the Moon*. In Germany, enthusiasts formed rocket clubs.

Wartime Advances in Rocketry
- Ultimately, the space program grew out of the Second World War and the advances in rocketry during wartime. This phenomenon, of discovery following from war, is a reverse of the pattern we have

often seen in this course: inventions being weaponized. In this case, weapons were turned to more peaceful uses.

- In the aftermath of the Second World War, scientists discovered that the Nazis were not as far along in the development of the atomic bomb as had earlier been feared. They had, however, been at work on other superweapons. The young engineer Wernher von Braun had been put in charge of a research project into rockets, in particular, to produce the V-2 missile.

- As the defeat of Nazi Germany neared, the former Allies began to position themselves for the postwar world. This was the opening of the Cold War. American and Soviet intelligence officials fanned out to grab German rocket scientists and exploit their know-how. Most of the scientists surrendered to the Americans, but others opted to help the Soviet effort.

- In 1945, the Americans brought von Braun and the team that had built the V-2 to the United States. Their missiles were tested at White Sands, New Mexico. Von Braun became an effective spokesman for space exploration, infecting others with the dream that possessed him.

- On the Soviet side, the impetus passed to Sergey Korolyov, an aeronautical engineer. He had been arrested in 1937 by the Soviet secret police in the purges ordered by Stalin. During the war, he was put to work in a prison laboratory. Afterwards, Korolyov became a driving force of the Soviet space effort, but because of intense Soviet secrecy, he always remained hidden in obscurity.

The Space Race

- As the Cold War intensified, it became clear that satellites could be powerful tools for information gathering. The United States and the Soviet Union raced to put a satellite in orbit. The military dimension of this work was prominent; for instance, the rockets to launch satellites could also be used to deliver nuclear warheads.

- The Soviet Union amazed the world when, after intense secrecy, it launched Sputnik on October 4, 1957. The satellite was small and basic looking, a 23-inch-diameter sphere with four antennas, weighing 184 pounds.

- In response, the American media spread a mood of alarm, seeing the launch as proof of a Soviet technological leap that the United States could not yet match. Money poured in to scientific research projects and science education programs.

- In November of 1957, the Soviet Union launched the first animal into outer space, a dog, on Sputnik 2. After American failures to match the Soviet feat, von Braun's team of researchers finally succeeded with their own launch of Explorer 1 in January 1958.

- Research facilities were established. Although intense secrecy surrounded the Soviet effort, publicity accompanied the founding of NASA in 1958, and the organization grew to mammoth proportions. At its height during the Apollo program, 34,000 employees worked directly for NASA and hundreds of companies were involved in providing equipment and materials.

Human Spaceflight

- The Soviet Union again seemed to gain the lead in the race when it put the first human into space on April 12, 1961. The Soviet cosmonaut Yury Gagarin was lifted into orbital flight on the Vostok 1. After 108 minutes, he returned to earth.

- After Gagarin's flight, U.S. President John F. Kennedy was informed that the Soviets might soon be able to send larger spacecraft with more cosmonauts around the earth and even around the moon.

- In response, Kennedy charged his advisors with drafting a "space program which promises dramatic results." The strategic plan that followed concluded that the moon should be the object, because of the immense prestige that came from space exploration achievements as "part of the battle along the fluid front of the Cold War."

- On May 25, 1961, Kennedy announced to a joint session of Congress that the United States would land a man on the moon before the end of the decade. Winning the race to the moon was viewed as a necessary victory in the Cold War. The building of the Berlin Wall in 1961 and the Cuban missile crisis of October 1962 highlighted Cold War tensions.

Reaching the Moon

- Within three years of Kennedy's announcement, NASA's budget increased five times over. The costs of the program were five times greater than those of the Manhattan Project we discussed in the last lecture. Intense publicity surrounded the selection of a team of American astronauts, who became national heroes.

- The basis of the Apollo moon program was the Saturn V rocket. It was decided to mount the spacecraft on the rocket rather than assemble it in outer space. The Apollo spacecraft came in three parts: a command module, a service module, and the lunar module. A command post was established near Cape Canaveral in Florida.

- Meanwhile, the Soviet program was also racing forward. A Soviet cosmonaut, Aleksey Leonov, was the first to achieve a spacewalk. The new Soyuz spacecraft was launched in 1967, but on reentry, it slammed into the earth, and Vladimir Komarov became the first casualty of a space mission. The death of the engineer Korolyov in 1966 was a further setback for the Soviet efforts.

- The American effort also experienced a tragic setback: In January 1967, three American astronauts were killed during a fire while testing the Apollo command module. In spite of this, the first manned Apollo mission was put into orbit in October 1968.

- On December 24, 1968, American astronauts on Apollo *8* were the first to orbit the moon and send back photographs of the "earthrise" over the moon. No one had ever before seen the whole earth in all of its beauty and fragile perfection.

- Apollo *11* lifted off on July 16, 1969. On board were Neil Armstrong; Edwin "Buzz" Aldrin, Jr.; and Michael Collins. The search for a safe landing place on the moon used up almost all of the reserves of fuel, and a computer alarm caused by a software problem could have led to aborting the mission. But at 4:18 p.m. EST on July 20, Armstrong announced to Houston, "The Eagle has landed."

- Six and a half hours later, Armstrong stepped out of the craft and became the first man to walk on the moon. He and Aldrin gathered moon rock samples, planted an American flag on the surface, and left a plaque that reads, "We came in peace for all mankind." The men returned safely to earth on July 24, landing in the Pacific.

A Global Event

- The moon landing was, well and truly, a global event. More than half a billion people around the world watched the moment on live television, the most widely witnessed live media event until that time. Even in the Soviet space control station, cheering was reported to have broken out for this triumph.

- So epic were the proportions of this turning point that inevitably, contrarian voices arose. Conspiracy theories developed about this and later moon missions, claiming that they were the product of special effects in a studio. Some historians suggest that in the era of the Watergate scandal, this was a symptom of mistrust in government and authority.

- In all, 12 Americans on six Apollo missions walked on the moon from 1969 to 1972. After Apollo *17* in 1972, no humans have left the orbit of the earth. The Soviets never managed to make their rocket perform and canceled their program in 1974.

- While it lasted, the era of moon exploration gave a new conception of human capacity. Certainly, being able to explore space was more constructive and positive than being able to destroy the earth with nuclear weapons. A new mantra entered human consciousness: If we can put a man on the moon, why can't we...? This feat expanded our sense of the humanly possible, an attribute of modernity.

- Today, more than 40 years later, we ask: Is this turning point an end or a beginning? Has human capacity or will declined since the 1970s?
  - Some experts point out that new participants have begun space exploration. In 2003, China sent its first astronaut into orbit and plans more space activity to follow.

  - Currently, while NASA funding has been cut and space activity declines, commercial ventures have risen to new prominence. Does the future of space exploration lie with private enterprise?

  - Most basically, does humanity's future extend beyond the earth? The British physicist Stephen Hawking has declared that without space colonization, humanity is not likely to survive.

Suggested Reading

Cadbury, *Space Race.*

McDougall, *The Heavens and the Earth.*

Questions to Consider

1. Would the moon mission have taken place without the Cold War?

2. Do you think that manned space exploration is just beginning or largely over?

Lecture 21: 1969—Walking on the Moon

1969—Walking on the Moon
Lecture 21—Transcript

The first humans walked on the Moon on July 20, 1969, during the *Apollo 11* mission. Those steps on another world marked a new era in how humans viewed their own Earth and their own potential. The astronauts gazed up at the Earth, and gained an entirely new perspective on our shared home. Yet, since 1972, with the end of follow-up missions to the Moon, humans have not returned, nor have they gone on manned expeditions to further planets. As one astronaut has put it, with a kind of bitter astonishment, we have been marooned for 40 years now.

So here is a fascinating, perplexing question that confronts us. At present, we're still learning what this turning point actually means. In fact, in our entire course on modern turning points, we've discovered that the closer we get to the present, the harder it inevitably becomes to define in full what the real impact is of a turning point, because that turning point is still unfolding.

In this case, we should ask: Is the moon landing more like the voyages of Zheng He in the 1430s, or more like those of Columbus around 1492? In other words, does this mark a turning point that did not turn, an ending, or is it rather a beginning of vast discoveries and exchanges?

To make this turning point in 1969 happen, humans needed to do a lot of things. They needed to find a way to tear away from the Earth's gravitational pull. Then they had to cross nearly a quarter million miles. Then they faced the uncertainties of what for the human race was an entirely unprecedented environment, the airless and cold emptiness of space. Then they had to touch down on the Moon's unknown surface. All of these things were entirely new.

Yet mankind had actually spent all of its existence wondering at the Moon and observing it. Prehistoric astronomers aligned monuments like Stonehenge with their reckoning of the Moon and stars. In modern times, Galileo used his telescope to make ever more detailed surveys of lunar features. Astronomers mapped the lunar landscapes they could discern from the Earth. In fact, the names they gave to these features in fact actually echo turning points we've examined in over course. Consider some of the lunar craters named for people we're familiar: the Leeuwenhoek crater, the Darwin crater, Diderot crater, Edison crater, and Fermi crater, and the Colombo crater, named for Christopher Columbus.

Repeatedly, people imagined over centuries what it might be like to journey to the Moon. In a sense, literature and film anticipated this later historic step. Jules Verne presented a popular novel in 1865, entitled *From the Earth to the Moon*, which had some remarkable predictions to make. In that novel, American artillery experts who are idled by the end of the Civil War start to restlessly seek a new goal, and they find that goal in building a super cannon that will shoot a space capsule to the Moon. Incidentally, the super cannon they build is actually even modeled on the one which shattered the walls of Constantinople in 1453 at the start of our course.

The name given to Verne's super cannon also refers to another turning point. It is called a Columbiad, after Christopher Columbus. Most remarkably, Jules Verne set the launch site for this expedition in Florida, a remarkable prediction that turned out to be true. The further adventures of the crew, made up of two Americans and one Frenchman, are related in a sequel novel by Verne. They circle the Moon, they find it to be lifeless, and then are pulled back towards the Earth, where they finally land safely and are celebrated worldwide.

Then in 1901, a science fiction pioneer whom we've met repeatedly in this course, H.G. Wells, published his book entitled *The First Men in the Moon*. In this novel, a somewhat shady businessman and a scientist team up to undertake the mission. Whereas Jules Verne sought to suggest technically realistic means, or at least more realistic means, Wells started his story unrealistically. The scientist, Mr. Cavor, a kind of Thomas Edison figure of the abstracted genius inventor, discovers a new substance, which then promptly is named Cavorite, that actually counteracts gravity. It kind of shuts it off. Cavor designs a spherical capsule, covers it in Cavorite, and that allows the two men to climb inside and rise up to the Moon.

As they discover, the Moon turns out to be inhabited, underground, by a strange, intelligent insect-like race. The Moon is also, as it turns out, full of gold. Only the shady businessman is able to escape and return to Earth.

Eventually, when the truth about the Moon becomes known, it will unleash wars by humans to get at that gold, what Wells in his novel calls an inevitable "struggle for mastery." In fact this novel is in many ways an attack on Western imperialism and the greed it represented, and how often discovery turns to conquest.

A year after Wells's novel, the early medium of motion pictures took up the same story. That first master of special effects who we discussed in an earlier lectures, George Méliès, blended plotlines from Vernes and Wells, and created his most famous film, in fact the first science fiction film, the 1902 film *A Trip to the Moon*, in which French astronomers fly to the Moon, in the process poking the Man in the Moon in the eye, and then encounter Moon creatures before making a spectacular escape back to Earth.

After these fictional speculations at the start of the 20th century, scientists were emboldened to start thinking about how to turn such speculative stories into reality. Their answer was not a giant cannon, but rather rockets. Rockets were an old technology from China from about a thousand years ago, but now they offered new possibilities when built on a larger scale.

The Russian mathematician Konstantin Tsiolkovsky explored theoretical aspects of space flight, the use of rockets to reach out into the cosmos. In the United States, Robert Hutchings Goddard was fascinated by rocketry as well, in part from reading books like those of H.G. Wells. Later, as a physics professor, Goddard worked on liquid-fueled rockets, launching the first of these in 1926. The German rocket scientist Hermann Oberth also had been inspired by fiction, in particular Verne's *From the Earth to the Moon*. Following his example, in Germany, many enthusiasts formed rocket clubs, looking forward to the future.

These were the beginnings, but ultimately, the real space program grew out of the Second World War and the advances made in rocketry during wartime. This larger phenomenon of discovery following from war is actually a reverse of the pattern we've seen so often in this course. Often, we've seen inventions being weaponized (so, discovery leading to conquest, or the airplane used for war, or films used for propaganda, or the splitting of the atom leading to Hiroshima). In this case, by contrast, weapons were turned to more peaceful uses.

The Second World War itself represented a culmination of a modern trend towards perfected total war, a kind of war fueled by ideology and technology, that became steadily more destructive and all-encompassing. This phenomenon haunted the thinker H.G. Wells; he hoped against hope that the very destructiveness of total modern war would increasingly make it impossible.

Indeed, during the First World War, it was actually H.G. Wells who coined that well-known phrase that this was going to be the "war to end all war," precisely because Wells felt that it was becoming unsustainable. In 1913, just before the First World War broke out, Wells even published a book called *Little Wars*, which was a guidebook to war games, using toy soldiers and cannon, which he hoped might become a kind of proxy form of conflict that might replace actual warfare. Today, if you know people who play war games on a tabletop or a computer, they are indebted to Wells who started this trend.

How did the space program grow out of wartime? Remember from our lecture on the atom bomb the persistent fears that the Nazis were working on this project too. It later was learned that they were not as far along as had been initially feared, but in fact they had been at work on other superweapons that they hoped would help them win the war. In particular, the young German engineer Wernher von Braun, earlier a rocket club member in Germany, had been put in charge of a research project into the military uses of rockets, in particular, to produce the feared V-2 missile.

From 1944, V-2 missiles rained down on London and other Allied targets. These were actions to avenge, the Nazi regime said, the Allied bombings of Germany—indeed, the name of the missile itself meant *Vergeltungswaffe* in German, or the "Vengeance Weapon." Slave labor was used to produce these reasons, and many historians believe that von Braun actually knew more about this fact than he later admitted to. Von Braun generally was entranced by what this weapon could instead do for space flight, his original and true enthusiasm.

As the defeat of Nazi Germany neared, the former Allies began to pull apart—now the United States and its allies on the one hand, and Stalin's Soviet Union on the other, started to position themselves for the postwar world. This was in fact the opening stage of what came to be called the Cold War. As part of this, American and Soviet intelligence officials spread out across the ruined landscape of Germany to grab hold of the German rocket scientists and to exploit their knowhow for their side. Most of the scientists surrendered to the Americans, but others opted to help the Soviet effort.

In 1945, the Americans brought von Braun to the United States, along with his team who had built the V-2 rockets. At White Sands, New Mexico, their missiles were tested. In America, von Braun became a very effective spokesman for space exploration. Braun had style and charisma. He managed to infect others with the dream that possessed him personally. To one such audience, von Braun explained, "The first man who puts his foot on the Moon or another planet will be in much the same position as Columbus, when he discovered the New World. With mankind visiting and exploring other planets, the future history of our world is both unlimited and unpredictable."

On the Soviet side, after using the expertise of some German scientists as well, the real impetus passed to a Soviet aeronautical engineer, Sergey Korolyov. He had actually been arrested in 1937 by the Soviet secret police in the purges that Stalin ordered. During the war, Korolyov was put to work in a prison laboratory. Afterwards, this former prisoner became a driving force of the Soviet space effort, but because of intense Soviet secrecy, Korolyov always remained hidden in obscurity.

As the Cold War intensified, it became clear that satellites, in orbit around the globe, could be a powerful tool of information gathering. Satellites were able to fly above sovereign territory and peer down into it, at distances that were far safer than those of spy planes. The United States and the Soviets raced to be first to achieve these satellites. Always, the military dimension of this work was prominent. For instance, the rockets to launch satellites also could in wartime deliver nuclear warheads, as intercontinental ballistic missiles.

The Soviet Union amazed the world when after intense secrecy, it launched its satellite, called *Sputnik*, on October 4, 1957. *Sputnik* was small and very basic looking: It weighed 184 pounds; it was a 23-inch-diameter silver sphere with four antennas. As it coursed high overhead in the skies, it emitted a steady "beep beep beep" radio signal, as if taunting the opponents on Earth that it had left in the dust.

As a result, the American media spread a mood of alarm, seeing this as proof of a Soviet technological leap which the United States could not yet match. Soon, money poured into scientific research and science education (indeed, it's a good bet that some listeners to this course actually had their educations shaped by this infusion of resources into the sciences).

The next month, November, the Soviet Union followed by launching the first animal in outer space, the dog Laika, on *Sputnik 2*. After American failures with rockets to match the Soviet feat, von Braun's Army team of researchers now were cleared to try, and in January of 1958 they succeeded, with *Explorer 1*. The space race was truly on!

Incidentally, the drive in this Cold War competition in space led to what really has to be classed among the worst ideas of all time. This was the proposal to nuke the Moon. That is, some American planners suggested that a gesture that could show that the Soviets were not the only ones capable of achieving something dramatic might be to send a nuclear missile to the Moon, with its impact point plotted precisely so that there would be a spectacular explosion visible from the Earth! Obviously the scientific value of all this would be negligible, but the visuals would be outstanding and impressive, it was argued.

By the way, this idea also occurred to some Soviet experts around the same time, as a way of confirming that a lunar probe had actually successfully landed. In both cases, fortunately, cooler heads prevailed and the idea was shelved. Imagine what a way of encountering a new world that would have been—blasting it into smithereens!

More productively, research establishments were built up. While intense secrecy surrounded the Soviet effort, publicity that accompanied the founding in 1958 of NASA, or the National Aeronautics and Space Administration, was meant to excite the American people at large. This project grew to huge proportions. At its height during the Apollo program, 34,000 employees worked directly for NASA and hundreds of other companies were involved in providing equipment and materials for the project, with more than a third of a million contractors.

Then the Soviet Union stole a march again, seeming to widen its scientific lead. It put the first human into space, with a launch on April 12, 1961 from the Baikonur Cosmodrome in Kazakhstan. The Soviet cosmonaut Yury Gagarin was lifted into orbital flight on the *Vostok 1*, the new orbital spacecraft. After 108 minutes in space, he returned to Earth.

This first human spaceflight was full of perils and unknowns. How would weightlessness be dealt with? How would the isolation of space affect the psychology of a human being? Would the dangers of reentry into the Earth's atmosphere be managed successfully? As it turns out, the flight was a success, space sickness could be surmounted, and Gagarin's smiling face became famous globally. The 27-year-old cosmonaut became a world celebrity, the first to embody the cosmonaut (or astronaut) as a hero! In 1963, Valentina Tereshkova became the first woman in space on the *Vostok 6*. Within a decade of Gagarin's flight, humans were walking on the Moon. This was an astonishing pace of advance!

The impetus for this, like that of the voyages of Zheng He back in the 1400s, involved questions of prestige and authority, in a global Cold War context. After Gagarin's famous flight, the United States president John F. Kennedy was informed that experts like von Braun believed the Soviets might soon be able to send larger spacecraft with more cosmonauts around the Earth and even around the Moon.

Hearing this, Kennedy charged his advisors with drafting a "space program which promises dramatic results in which we could win." The resulting strategic plan concluded that the Moon should be the object, because of the immense prestige that came from space exploration achievements, as "part of the battle along the fluid front of the Cold War."

As a result, on May 25, 1961, Kennedy now announced publicly, to a joint session of Congress, that the United States would get to the Moon. Kennedy declared, "I believe this nation should commit itself to achieving the goal, before the decade is out, of landing a man on the Moon and returning him safely to the Earth. No single space project in this period will be more impressive to mankind, or more important for the long-range exploration of space, and none will be so difficult or expensive to accomplish."

As Kennedy later added, "We choose to go to the moon in this decade and do the other things, not because they are easy, but because they are hard. Because the challenge is one that we are willing to accept, one we are unwilling to postpone, and one which we intend to win." Here, the context was everything, and that context was the Cold War.

Later that same year, in August of 1961, Khrushchev and his East German clients started building the Berlin Wall. Then, the Cuban missile crisis of October 1962 highlighted just how much tension and peril and risk the Cold War really involved!

The American space effort leapt into high gear, at a breakneck speed that really reminds us of the building of the transcontinental railroad that we discussed in an earlier lecture. In the three years after Kennedy's announcement, NASA's budget increased five times over. In 1966, NASA was actually spending 4.4 percent of the entire federal budget. The costs of this program were five times more than those of the Manhattan Project to build the atomic bomb that we discussed in an earlier lecture. Intense publicity surrounded the selection of a team of American astronauts, who became national heroes. *Time* magazine compared them to Columbus and to the Wright Brothers.

The basis of the Apollo Moon program was the Saturn V rocket. It was decided to mount the spacecraft on the rocket rather than assemble it in outer space, as was an alternative proposal. The *Apollo* spacecraft came in three parts: a Command Module, a Service Module, and a Lunar Module. A big command post for this mission was established near Cape Canaveral in Florida, near where Jules Verne had set his fictional moonshot.

Meanwhile, the Soviet program was also racing forward. One of their cosmonauts, Aleksey Leonov, was the first to achieve a spacewalk. The new *Soyuz* spacecraft was launched in 1967, but on reentry it slammed into the Earth, and Vladimir Komarov became the first casualty of a space flight. The engineer Korolyov directed the Soviet effort, but when he died in 1966 (essentially from overwork), this was a huge setback for the Soviet program, as his successors were not as effective as he had been.

The American effort also met a tragic setback, when in January 1967, three American astronauts were killed during a fire while testing the *Apollo* Command Module. In spite of this, the first manned *Apollo* mission was put into orbit on October 1968.

On December 24 of 1968, American astronauts on *Apollo 8* were the first to orbit the Moon and send back photographs of the "earthrise" over the Moon. No one before had seen the whole Earth itself in all its beauty and fragile perfection. You could say that a new planetary consciousness would follow from this act!

The stage was now set for the Moon mission itself. *Apollo 11* lifted off on July 16, 1969. On board were Neil Armstrong, Edwin "Buzz" Aldrin, Jr., and Michael Collins. When they covered the distance to orbit the Moon, Collins was posted to the orbiting Command Module, while Armstrong steered the Lunar Module, with Aldrin aboard.

The craft that would touch down on the Moon's surface was nicknamed the "Eagle." The landing was tricky, needing to avoid boulders, and to find a spot to touch down on the open plain, the Sea of Tranquility. This was nerve-racking, as searching for a safe landing space used up almost all the reserves of fuel, and a computer alarm caused by a software problem could have led to aborting of the entire mission. But instead the astronauts continued, and touched down at 4:17 pm eastern daylight time. Armstrong announced to Houston, "The Eagle has landed."

Then, after six and a half hours, the moment arrived to leave the module. Armstrong stepped out, and he announced, "That's one small step for man, one giant leap for mankind." Armstrong had intended to say "one small step for a man"—either he passed over the word "a" in his excitement, or the radio transmission cut out that word.

For two and a half hours, Armstrong, joined by Aldrin, moved about on the surface of the Moon. They planted an American flag, and they also placed a plaque which stated, "We came in peace for all mankind." They continued to gather Moon rock samples as well. Then, they again took off, and met up with the Command Module in orbit. The astronauts returned safely to the Earth on July 24, landing in the Pacific.

It's quite poignant to know as we do now that a press release had actually been drafted in advance for the American president to read in case the mission ended in failure. This press release lauded the heroism of real-life epic heroes. Fortunately, that text was not needed. When the astronauts returned, they were placed in quarantine. This was an insight from the Columbian exchange that we discussed in an early lecture. NASA wanted to ensure that no bacteria or viruses had accompanied the men from their encounter back to the Earth.

This had been, well and truly, a global event. More than half a billion people around the world had watched live television capturing this moment in human history. It was the most widely witnessed live media event up until then. At the moment of the Moon landing, even in the Soviet space control station, where you would probably have expected glum silence and a sense of defeat and dismay at having been beaten to the Moon, the reaction was actually deeply touching. Reportedly, in the Soviet command station, cheering broke out for this triumph, which now seemed to be part of the property of mankind in general!

Indeed, so epic were the proportions of this turning point that inevitably, contrarian voices arose. Conspiracy theories developed about this and later Moon missions, claiming that they weren't real, but rather were the product of special effects in a Hollywood studio. Some historians argue that in the era of the Watergate scandal, this was a symptom of mistrust in general of government and authority.

In reality, 12 Americans on six *Apollo* missions walked on the Moon's surface from 1969 to 1972, or rode about in a Moon rover on the last missions. The very last mission was *Apollo 17* in 1972. After that point, no humans left the orbit of the Earth. For their part, the Soviets never managed to make their N1 rocket perform, and they cancelled their program in 1974.

While it lasted, the era of Moon exploration gave us a new conception of human capacity, what humans could achieve. Certainly, being able to explore space was much more constructive and positive than being able to destroy the Earth with nuclear weapons. As a result of the Moon landing, a new mantra entered human consciousness. Now people would often ask, "If we're able to put men on the moon, why can't we _____?" and then fill in the blank, whatever project it is they had in mind. This feat of the Moon landing expanded our sense of what was humanly possible, and as we've seen before, this is a key attribute of the condition of modernity.

But where does this all leave us today, more than 40 years after these events? Is this turning point an end, or only a beginning? Has human capacity or willpower declined since the 1970s? Some experts point out that new participants have actually entered this process. In 2003, China sent its first astronaut into orbit and plans more space activity to follow. Currently, while NASA funding has been cut and space activity declines, commercial ventures have risen to a new prominence. Does the future of space exploration perhaps lie with private companies, harkening back to the private enterprise of companies like the many East India Companies of centuries past that we saw in our course?

Most basically, does humanity's future extend beyond the Earth? The British physicist Stephen Hawking has declared that without space colonization, humanity likely will not survive, probably falling prey to biological dangers.

In the very longest term, how this turning point we've examined in this lecture turns out is existentially important. Meanwhile, back on Earth, world politics were about to be reconfigured by China's return to the world stage, vividly clear in 1972. It is to this turning point that we turn in our next lecture.

1972—China Enters the World Balance
Lecture 22

O n February 21, 1972, an hour-long meeting took place in China between U.S. President Richard Nixon and Chairman Mao Zedong of the People's Republic of China. What made this meeting a turning point was both the fact of the conversation itself and the massive international realignment of world politics that followed. This turning point revealed a key moment in a more extended process: that of China seeking its own modernity and place in the modern world. After deadly and destructive internal convulsions, it set China on the course it continues to follow today. Further, it redrew world politics, shifting the balance of the Cold War and producing an international transformation with global consequences that are still unfolding today.

China's Role in the Modern World

- As we saw at the start of our course, successive dynasties and emperors had understood China as occupying a central place of importance in the world. They had seen their realm as self-sufficient. The voyages of Zheng He had been about manifesting that authority far and wide.

- This self-understanding and concept of authority were shattered in the Opium Wars.
    - The onslaught of the British East India Company and its drug trade revealed the full power of Western imperialism when united to the energies of the Industrial Revolution.

    - The emperor was forced to sign unequal treaties that gave special trade privileges to foreigners and set up treaty ports. Moreover, these foreigners were not subject to Chinese legal authority but enjoyed so-called extraterritoriality.

    - For the Chinese, this was nothing less than a civilizational crisis. China suddenly appeared weaker than the foreigners it had earlier belittled. Further, China was not even sovereign, not the ruler of its own house.

- For the next century, Chinese political leaders and thinkers struggled with the implications of this crisis. How could China best find its place in the new world? What sort of modernity could it craft for itself? Should it imitate Western models or seek to renew its old values, such as Confucianism, for the present? Several generations tried all of these paths in succession.

The People's Republic
- In 1912, the Manchu dynasty was overthrown by Chinese nationalists and the Chinese republic was proclaimed. The revolutionary movement was led by Sun Yat-sen, who founded the new nationalist revolutionary party to modernize China. The aims of the party were to promote national independence, progress, and science.

- Still, unequal treaties with foreign powers remained in force, and China's continuing inferior status was made bitterly clear in the aftermath of the First World War. China had entered the war against Germany on the side of the Allied powers, but at the Treaty of Versailles in 1919, Germany's holdings in China were awarded to Japan.

- This shocking news provoked a huge demonstration on May 4, 1919. Thousands of students from the university in Beijing massed at Tiananmen Square in protest. Those few hours of dissent gave birth to the May Fourth Movement, sometimes known as the New Culture Movement, marking a break with Confucian values in favor of new ideas imported from the West.

- Amidst this turmoil, some radicals from the university founded the Chinese Communist Party in 1921. Among them was a young assistant at the university library, Mao.
    o The Communists saw the answer to China's problems in terms of another ideology imported from the West: Marxism and its program of "scientific socialism." These would, it was

promised, eliminate class exploitation by establishing the dictatorship of the working class.

o The Chinese Communists looked above all to the new Soviet Union, which had been established by Lenin and the Bolsheviks in the wreckage of the Russian Empire.

Mao was born in 1893 in Hunan province, the son of a peasant landlord; at the time of the May Fourth Movement, he was an assistant at the university library in Peking.

- In addition to this internal conflict between the nationalist government and the Communists, China now also was confronted with the invasion of Japanese imperialism. From 1937 to 1945, a Japanese-Chinese war raged.

- When this war ended, the civil war between the nationalist forces and the Communists under Mao resumed in full force. This conflict finally ended by 1949, with the nationalist forces retreating to Taiwan. Meanwhile, on October 1, 1949, Mao proclaimed the establishment of the People's Republic of China. The building of a new China on the communist model of modernity had begun, at what would be tremendous human cost.

China under Mao's Leadership

- Under Mao's leadership, China was shaped by some of his core convictions. Whereas Confucian thought valued order, harmony, and stability, Mao praised turmoil and revolution. Disorder promised him access to power, which he could use to create the modern China he envisioned. Revolution would not only remake China but place it at the center of the world again.

- The costs of Mao's policies were harrowing. Attempts from 1958 to 1962 to industrialize the country through the creation of huge communes for collectivized agriculture were called the Great Leap Forward. These efforts led to a horrific famine that left an estimated 40 million dead.

- Then, Mao launched a further campaign against the old China with the Cultural Revolution of 1966 to 1976. This campaign attacked the Communist Party and the government, which were accused of having strayed from a true revolutionary path.
  - Mao's concern was that the forward momentum of the revolution had slowed, winding down when it needed to be accelerated.

  - Thus, the young generation, organized into Red Guard units, was encouraged to attack the older generation, their teachers, local authorities, and even parents. Soon, there were several million Red Guards.

- At the same time, millions of Chinese were purged, arrested, killed, or sent to reeducation camps. Senior party officials were accused of being spies and counterrevolutionaries, eerily echoing the French Revolution, which also had consumed many of its own creators during the Reign of Terror. Indeed, the Red Guards proudly espoused what they called "Red Terror."

- Public campaigns aimed to erase foreign influence and traces of the past, especially the rich Confucian culture. One slogan condemned the "Four Olds": "old ideas, old culture, old customs, old habits of the exploiting classes."

- China also seemed to shut itself off from the world: Chinese ambassadors were recalled from those countries where China was diplomatically recognized to be examined for their political loyalties and, perhaps, purged.

- In the midst of this upheaval, Mao and his comrades began to fear China's increasing isolation and the threat of their former ally, the Soviet Union. Relations between the two powers had cooled, then grew poisonous. By 1969, Soviet and Chinese troops were clashing at the Amur River, at China's northern border. Would this unofficial conflict turn into full-scale war? Mao decided that China needed to find new relationships internationally and began to wind down the internal fury of the Cultural Revolution.

China and the United States

- The time was ripe for a mutual approach between China and the United States, which had not had a relationship for decades. Indeed, up to this point, the United States did not recognize Communist China, favoring instead the Kuomintang government in Taiwan as the legitimate China.

- Now, however, President Richard Nixon saw a chance for a profound change in international affairs. He was convinced that crafting a new relationship with China would put pressure on America's rival in the Cold War, the Soviet Union. He also hoped that China might help end the Vietnam War, which was dragging on inconclusively and devastating public opinion in America. In the end, his aim was an overarching stability worldwide.

- In secret, Secretary of State Henry Kissinger and the Chinese foreign minister Zhou Enlai planned a visit. To Nixon, the visit seemed politically risky, even if his anticommunist reputation gave him cover. But in the end, he counted the trip a great success.

- The shift in the Cold War balance that resulted from the visit gave the United States more leverage in dealing with the Soviet Union. Nixon was able to draw the Vietnam War to a close. The normalization of relations between the United States and China marked a new stage in their relationship, quite different from the previous frosty silence.

- In spite of this success, Nixon's presidency imploded soon afterward with the Watergate cover-up and his resignation in 1974. But to this day, "Nixon goes to China" is synonymous with a surprising event. Indeed, ironically it was Nixon's anticommunist record that allowed him to make this approach.

The Opening of China

- The new relationship with the United States was only part of a larger entry of China onto the world stage as a sovereign state, part of the Westphalian international system. China was no longer subject to what had been called a "century of humiliation."

- With the opening of 1972, the regime in China underwent surprising, even shocking changes. After Mao's death in 1976, a fierce leadership struggle took place, at the end of which Deng Xiaoping became leader.
  - A more pragmatic leader who had been purged by the radicals, Deng set a new course that introduced a reform era from 1978. Without repudiating Mao explicitly, Deng altered many of the earlier leader's principles radically.

  - His policy pressed the so-called "Four Modernizations": agriculture, industry, military, and science. In a profound reversal from Marxist ideology, Deng also endorsed the slogan "It is glorious to get rich."

- Deng sought to unleash China's economic potential by promoting private enterprise while retaining political control for the Communist Party.
  - The huge collective farms that had been the essence of Mao's policies were dismantled in stages, and farmers were allowed to sell some of their produce on the market.

  - Small businesses were permitted, and by 1985, there were about 12 million of them. As a result, during the 1980s, per capita income roughly doubled.

- o Deng also created four Special Economic Zones with low tax rates to encourage foreign investment.

- Economic development in China surged ahead. For three decades, the Chinese economy has boomed, and in the first years of the 21st century, Chinese annual growth rates were around 10 percent. In 2011, China overtook Japan as the world's second largest economy, and some predict that it may be the world's largest by 2025.

- But these changes perhaps have produced what Marx would have called internal contradictions. After the Communist Party endorsed private enterprise, where does that leave its ideological legitimacy, its authority?
  - o In 1978, a dissident named Wei Jingsheng called for a "Fifth Modernization" to add to Deng's Four: democracy. Wei announced, "Democracy, freedom, and happiness are the only goals of modernization. Without this fifth modernization, the four others are nothing more than a new-fangled lie."

  - o For his statements about what modernization really means, Wei was arrested and sentenced to 15 years in jail.

Suggested Reading

Lovell, *The Opium War*.

MacMillan, *Nixon and Mao*.

Mitter, *Modern China*.

Ropp, *China in World History*.

Spence, *Mao Zedong*.

1. In this turning point, were the personalities of the leaders (Nixon and Mao) incidental to the outcome or vitally important?

2. If China had remained in international isolation for several more decades, how would our world be different today?

1972—China Enters the World Balance
Lecture 22—Transcript

On February 21, 1972, a fateful meeting took place in China. It had been prepared months in advance, in secret. The meeting unfolded in the exclusive Communist Party leadership compound called the Zhongnanhai in Beijing. The Zhongnanhai was a private walled community where the Communist officials and their families lived in splendid villas, a kind of modern Forbidden City like the Chinese emperors had once occupied, away from the masses of ordinary people.

A limousine drove into the compound, carrying special foreign guests. These were the United States president Richard Nixon and his National Security Advisor Henry Kissinger. They had just flown into China, and on arrival, both had actually been very nervous. In spite of the many careful and clandestine preparations that had preceded this visit, the Chinese officials had never confirmed whether the American president would actually meet with Chairman Mao Zedong, the leader of this vast country. Without such a meeting, their entire trip might prove an embarrassing failure.

But then, suddenly, soon after they had settled into their guest rooms, they were summoned for the meeting with Mao. Once inside the Zhongnanhai compound, they were ushered into Mao's study. The elderly Mao was in very bad health, wracked with congestive heart failure. He was so weak that for days before he had been practicing the simple act of sitting down and rising up again, in advance of just this meeting. The discussion that ensued took place through a Chinese government translator, a young woman who had lived in Brooklyn as a little girl.

The meeting lasted just over an hour, and it was vague, polite, and noncommital, full of mutual compliments and self-deprecating humor and jokes. Mao, for instance, claimed that he had voted for Nixon in the last election! Even as the very earnest Nixon sought to draw Mao into a profound discussion of world politics, Mao said that those topics should really be handled by their officials and subordinates. Mao announced that he only discussed philosophical questions. Soon the meeting was over.

Nixon assumed that surely they would meet again while he was on his historic visit to China, the first ever by an American president, but they did not meet again. That hour was it for this visit.

The historian Margaret Macmillan has written a marvelous historical account of this meeting, which she entitled *Nixon and Mao: The Week That Changed the World*. In her book, Macmillan calls this hour-long chat "curiously inconclusive." So we really need to ask, how could a "curiously inconclusive" and vague chat be one of the turning points of modern history?

In fact, it was not the words that were exchanged that were crucial, nor even the dramatic and striking personalities of the people involved. What makes this a key turning point was the mere fact of the conversation itself (coming as it did after decades of diplomatic silence between the United States and China, and estrangement). It also was a turning point due to the massive international realignment of world politics that followed from the visit and changed the Chinese and American relationship. This turning point revealed a key moment in a much longer and extended process, that of China seeking its own form of modernity and its own place in the modern world. First, after deadly and destructive convulsions within China, this event set China on the course it continues to follow today. Second, as a result, this meeting also redrew world politics, shifting the balance of the Cold War that was then going on. But beyond even that, the international transformation that followed produced global consequences that are still unfolding as we speak.

In essence, the larger drama in which this turning point is set is China seeking to resolve how to relate to the modern world at large. As we saw from the start of our course on modern turning points, successive dynasties and Chinese emperors had understood China as the Middle Kingdom, occupying the central place of importance in the world. They had seen their realm as self-sufficient, not needing anything from the peripheries. The voyages of Zheng He from 1405–1433 had been all about manifesting that authority far and wide.

This self-understanding, and this concept of authority, was shattered in the Opium Wars of 1839–1842 and of 1856–1860, which we discussed in an earlier lecture. We saw how the onslaught of the British East India Company and its drug trade revealed the full power of Western imperialism when united to the energies of the Industrial Revolution that was going on at the same time. The Chinese emperor was forced to sign unequal treaties that gave special trade privileges to foreigners and set up special treaty ports. Moreover, these foreigners in China were not subject to Chinese legal authority, but instead had so-called extraterritoriality.

One really has to work hard to imagine the depth and impact of this on the Chinese as they considered what it all meant. In essence, this was nothing less than a civilizational crisis for China. Contrary to earlier understanding, China suddenly appeared not as central, but weaker than the foreigners it earlier had belittled. Even more, China was revealed to be not even an equal, not even sovereign, not the ruler in its own house. Think back to our lecture on the Peace of Westphalia back in 1648, and how out of that peace settlement there evolved a system of sovereign states interacting with one another in a dynamic balance of power. Sovereignty meant internal self-rule without an outside, overarching authority, but China in the late 19th century didn't even possess that, as unequal treaties and extraterritoriality made vividly clear.

For the next century, Chinese political leaders and thinkers struggled with the implications of this crisis. How could China best find its place in the new world? What sort of modernity should it craft for itself? Should it imitate Western models, or should it seek to renew its own old values, like Confucianism, adapted for the present? Several generations tried many of these paths in succession.

For young Chinese in the later 19th century, the message of nationalism had great potency. We've seen in this course how nationalism grew out of the American and French revolutions, and how by a kind of chain reaction, nationalism spread further and further afield, to the non-Western world as well. In a Westphalian international system of sovereign states, the nation-state seemed to many the most effective and desirable way to organize a people for sovereignty and the exercise of self-rule. Another Western set of ideas that appealed was social Darwinism, drawing on the ideas about evolution and the struggle for survival which we discussed in an earlier lecture. If nations and societies were really entities that flourished or became extinct like natural species, then threatened societies like China needed to revitalize themselves and engage in the struggle, or simply go under. Young Chinese who planned a so-called Self-Strengthening Movement for China felt a tremendous urgency to modernize their country for survival.

In this quest, Japan obviously was a model for selective adaptation of Western technology and organization, while allied to one's own cultural values. But as it turns out Japan was a difficult role model for China to accept. In earlier centuries, Japan had always been seen as a recipient of Chinese culture. Now, in an added difficulty, Japan was actually one of the imperialist powers that threatened to carve up China. It had already taken over Taiwan as a colony. So Japan was at one and the same time admired and resented.

In 1912, the Manchu (or Qing) dynasty was overthrown by Chinese nationalists, and the Chinese republic was proclaimed. The revolutionary movement was led by Sun Yat-sen, who founded the new Kuomintang nationalist revolutionary party to modernize China. The aims of this party were to promote national independence, progress, and science. Yet, even in the republic, unequal treaties with foreign powers remained in force, and China's continuing inferior status internationally was made bitterly clear in the aftermath of the First World War. During that war China had entered the war against Germany on the side of the Allied Powers, but then, when the Treaty of Versailles took place in 1919, instead of Germany's colonial holdings in China being returned to China, those holdings were awarded to Japan.

This truly shocking news provoked a huge Chinese demonstration on May 4, 1919. Thousands of students from Beijing University gathered in masses at the Tiananmen Square to protest and denounce this international treatment of their country. Those few hours of protest actually gave birth to a larger movement that called itself the May Fourth Movement, and also sometimes also went by the name of New Culture. That name New Culture is enormously significant, because of what it meant ideologically—it urged a break with the old Confucian culture and with traditional values, in favor of adopting new imported Western ideas. These ideas were given the names "Mr. Science" and "Mr. Democracy," as the two core values of modernization that this young generation envisioned.

Amidst all this turmoil, some radicals from Beijing University founded the Chinese Communist Party in 1921. Among them was a young assistant at the university library, Mao. He was born 1893 in Hunan province, the son of a peasant landlord. In his youth, Mao admired Napoleon (in retrospect this kind of sounds an ominous note, given what we know of how Napoleon used a revolution to establish a personal dictatorship). The Communists saw the answer to China's problems in terms of another ideology that was imported from the West. This was Marxism, and its program of so-called scientific socialism, which would, it was promised, eliminate class exploitation by establishing the ultimate dictatorship of the working class. The Chinese Communists looked above all to the new Soviet Union which had been established by Lenin and the Bolsheviks in the wreckage of the Russian empire.

In addition to the internal conflict between the nationalist government and the Communists, China in this period also now confronted the terrible invasion of Japanese imperialism. From 1937 to 1945, the Japanese-Chinese war raged, with mass atrocities against civilians in places like Nanjing. This was one of the starting points of the Second World War. Estimates of Chinese deaths in this war range between 15 to 35 million.

Yet even when this war ended in 1945, peace did not come for China. Instead, civil war between the nationalist forces and the Communists under Mao resumed in full force. That conflict finally ended by 1949, when the nationalist forces retreated to Taiwan, where they claimed (and still claim) that they were the legitimate rulers of all of mainland China. Meanwhile, on October 1, 1949, Mao stood above the Tiananmen Square in Beijing and proclaimed the establishment of the People's Republic of China. Mao announced, "We, the 475 million Chinese people have stood up and our future is infinitely bright." At this point, the building of a new China on the

Communist model of modernity commenced, and as it turns out, did so at tremendous human cost.

Under Mao's leadership, China would also be shaped by some of his core convictions. Whereas Confucian thought and its traditions valued order and harmony and stability, Mao by contrast praised turmoil and revolution. In one of his earliest writings, Mao stated, "A long period of peace, pure peace without any disorder of any kind, would be unbearable." Disorder promised Mao access to power, which he could use to create a modern China as he envisioned. Mao called China "a clean sheet of paper … [on which] the newest and most beautiful words can be written." Revolution would not only remake China, but he was sure would set it at the center of the world again. There's an irony here: After breaking with the past totally, Communist China would once again—it was promised—find itself in a place of centrality, as it had had in the days of Zheng He. Mao declared, "The Chinese revolution is the key factor in the world situation, and its victory is heartily anticipated by the people of every country."

Mao launched Communist China into this transformation, increasingly determined to overtake the capitalists, and China's former ally, the Soviet Union. The costs of Mao's policies were harrowing. His attempts to industrialize the country through the creation of huge communes for collectivized agriculture were called the "Great Leap Forward" of 1958 to 1962. These led to a horrific manmade famine that left an estimated 40 million dead. In China today, only in the last decade is this traumatic event being studied and more openly discussed.

Then, Mao launched a further campaign against the old China in the name of the future modern China. This was the "Cultural Revolution" of 1966 to 1976. This campaign attacked even the Communist Party and the government itself, because they were accused of having strayed from the true revolutionary path. Mao's concern was that in some sense the forward momentum of the revolution had slowed, winding down at a point when he felt it should be accelerated. So, the young generation of Chinese, organized into Red Guard units, were encouraged to attack the older generation, their teachers, local authorities, even their parents. Soon there were several million Red Guards, dressed in Mao suits and waving Mao's

Little Red Book with his sayings and aphorisms. A huge cult of personality was built up around Mao, and 2.2 billion badges with Mao's picture on them were produced.

At the same time, millions of Chinese were purged, arrested, killed, or sent to reeducation camps called *laogai*. When senior party officials were accused of being spies or counterrevolutionaries, one could almost discern eerie echoes of the days of the French Revolution, a time when many who had been makers of that revolution had been consumed by that revolution during the Reign of Terror. Indeed, looking back to those earlier events, the Red Guards proudly espoused what they called "Red Terror" in action.

Public campaigns aimed to erase foreign influence, and traces of the past. This affected especially the rich Confucian culture, in architecture, libraries, schools, and temples, increasingly destroyed. One slogan condemned the so-called Four Olds: old ideas, old culture, old customs, old habits of the exploiting classes. In this course on turning points, we've explored how modernity is marked by breaks with the past. In this utopian and totalitarian vision of what modernity should look like, the break was supposed to be total and complete. China also at this time seemed to shut itself off from the world: Chinese ambassadors were recalled from those countries where China was diplomatically recognized, brought back to Beijing to be examined for their political loyalties, and perhaps purged.

Yet in the midst of all this upheaval, another sudden fear struck Mao and his comrades. They began to fear China's increasing isolation, and the threat of their former ally, the Soviet Union. Because the Soviet Union and China both claimed for themselves the position of being in the vanguard of international revolution, relations between the two powers had cooled, and then had grown poisonous. By 1969, Soviet and Chinese troops were actually clashing at the Amur River, at China's northern border. The question emerged, would this unofficial conflict turn into an all-out war? Soviet diplomats at this time were even asking their Western counterparts how they might react if the Soviet Union undertook a preemptive strike on China. By 1970, the Chinese leadership was gripped by a war scare. Mao decided that China needed to find new relationships internationally, and also to begin to wind down the internal fury of the Cultural Revolution.

The time was felt ripe for a mutual approach between China and the United States, but they had not spoken to one another for decades. Indeed, up to this point the United States didn't recognize Communist China, favoring instead the nationalist Kuomintang government in Taiwan as the legitimate China.

Now, however, President Richard Nixon saw a chance for a profound change in international affairs. He was convinced that crafting a new relationship with China would put pressure on America's rival in the Cold War, the Soviet Union. Nixon also hoped that China might help end the Vietnam War that was dragging on inconclusively for the Americans, and devastating public opinion in America itself. In the end, Nixon's aim was a new overarching stability worldwide.

President Nixon was a complex, even strange man and political actor. He blended many qualities: ambition, self-pity, paranoia, a deep isolation and a lack of friendships, but he also had political sophistication and strategic vision. Together with his controversial National Security Advisor and later Secretary of State, Henry Kissinger, Nixon set about a dramatic diplomatic reversal. One of Nixon's favorite movies was *Around the World in Eighty Days*, the Jules Verne story which had charted a worldwide trajectory, as we saw in an earlier lecture. Nixon's aim was worldwide and global, and in the pursuit of that goal, the man who had made his name politically in his early career through fierce anti-communism now reached out to "Red China."

In secret, Henry Kissinger and the Chinese foreign minister Zhou Enlai had planned the visit. Zhou, you may recall, allegedly said that it was "too soon to know" the real results of the French Revolution. A first sign of these thawing relations was the oddly named phenomenon of "ping pong diplomacy," when an American sports team visited China and was welcomed there. Nixon's planned visit seemed to him a leap into the unknown, and politically risky at home as well, even though his reputation as a fierce anti-communist gave him cover. Indeed, the bloody course of internal struggle and persecution during the Great Leap Forward and its famine, and then the intensity of the Cultural Revolution, remained largely unknown to the Westerners. As Nixon cast about for some comparison to describe the venture he was undertaking, he fell back on a recent turning point from our course. Nixon repeatedly compared his trip to the Moon mission of three years previous. He said, "A trip to China is like going to the Moon." He added that his motto for his trip, like the plaque that the astronauts had left on the Moon, should read, "We came in peace for all mankind."

Overall, Nixon counted his trip a great success. He spoke of it as the "week that changed the world." Indeed, many people worldwide watched televised images of the trip, and Gallup polling in the United States showed more public awareness (at 98 percent) of this event than any other in the history of their polling. The shift in the Cold War balance that resulted gave the United States more leverage in dealing with the Soviet Union. Nixon was able to draw the Vietnam War to a close. The normalization of relations between the United States and China marked a new stage in their relationship, which was quite different from the previous frosty silence of the past.

In spite of this success, Nixon's presidency soon afterwards imploded with the Watergate cover-up and his resignation in 1974. But to this day, the phrase "Nixon goes to China" is synonymous with a politically surprising event. Indeed ironically, it was Nixon's very fervent anti-communist record that allowed him to make this approach to the Chinese Communists. So—the next time someone criticizes you for doing something that seems out of character or strange, just turn to them and astonish and baffle them by answering, "Only Nixon could go to China." It could be the perfect alibi!

Even more important, however, was what this turning point meant for China and for world politics at large. Indeed, the consequences are still reverberating now, as China races to a leading economic position in the world.

The new relationship with the United States was only part of a larger opening to the world and Chinese entry onto the world stage, as a sovereign state, part of the Westphalian international system. Part of the worldwide trend toward decolonization we've surveyed in this course also was to be seen here. China was no longer subject to what had been called a century of humiliation.

The opening to the wider world, rather than being in a state of isolation, was the beginning of a process that led to China growing into the position of great economic and exporting power it holds today. Let me suggest this: The next time you see the words "Made in China" on a product, think of 1972 and this turning point.

With the opening of 1972, the regime in China underwent surprising, even shocking changes. After Mao's death in 1976 there was a fierce leadership struggle, and at its end Deng Xiaoping became leader of China. He was a more pragmatic leader who in fact had been purged by radicals during the Cultural Revolution. Deng set a new course which introduced a so-called reform era from 1978. Without repudiating Mao explicitly, Deng altered many of the earlier leader's principles in radical ways. Deng's policy pressed the so-called Four Modernizations: modernization in agriculture, industry, military, and science. Deng also endorsed the slogan "It is glorious to get rich," in really a profound reversal of earlier Marxist ideology. In place of the Maoist slogan "serve the people," a new slogan declared, "create wealth for the people." That meant a market economy.

Deng sought to unleash China's economic potential by promoting private enterprise all while retaining political control for the Communist Party. The huge collective farms that had been at the core of Mao's policies were now dismantled in stages. Farmers were allowed to sell ever more of their produce on the market. Their free enterprise in small garden plots was not just tolerated, but encouraged. Small businesses were permitted, and by 1985, there were about 12 million of them. As a result, during the 1980s, per capita income roughly doubled in China.

China also opened for foreign investment, as Deng created four Special Economic Zones, as they were called, on the Chinese coast to encourage investment, to entice people from abroad with special low tax rates. was Actually there's a terrific irony here, as it was these coastal locations where the treaty ports during the time of the unequal treaties had been located, but now this trade was desired. Deng also travelled to the United States and even wore a cowboy hat at a Texas rodeo, all part of his campaign to pursue trade opportunities wherever they could be found.

Economic development in China surged ahead. For three decades the Chinese economy has boomed, and in the first decade of the 21st century, Chinese annual growth rates were at around 10 percent, astonishing. Chinese exports flowed out in vast quantities. China ran huge trade surpluses as a result. In 2011, China overtook Japan as the world's second-largest economy, and some experts predict that it may be the world's largest economy by 2025, overtaking the United States. At the same time, a human flow of Chinese students studying abroad commenced as well. Hundreds of thousands studied and are studying now in the United States and Europe, engaging with new ideas and experiences. These were changes that flowed from the turning point of 1972, could not have happened without it, and are still unfolding today.

But these changes perhaps have produced internal contradictions, as Marx would have called them. After the Communist Party endorsed private enterprise which earlier had been taboo, where does that leave Communist ideological legitimacy, or the authority of the government?

Deng had announced that the changes to government policy were to achieve the Four Modernizations. But then in 1978, a dissident named Wei Jingsheng plastered a poster in Beijing at at a spot called the Democracy Wall, where others were also pasting up their ideas. Wei's poster called for the "Fifth Modernization: Democracy," and he scorned Deng's program. Wei announced, "Democracy, freedom, and happiness are the only goals of modernization. Without this fifth modernization, the four others are nothing more than a newfangled lie." For this statement, for engaging in a debate about what modernization really means, Wei was arrested and sentenced to 15 years in jail.

So it is to that topic, dissent for democracy as modernization, which led to the fall of the Berlin Wall in 1989 and the crushing of Chinese protests in Tiananmen Square, that we will turn in our next lecture.

1989—The Fall of the Berlin Wall
Lecture 23

In this lecture, we consider a relatively recent turning point that already has become history: the largely peaceful collapse of communist dictatorships as a result of the social mobilization of ordinary people for nonviolent protest. With amazing speed and little warning, the collapse of communist regimes in Central and Eastern Europe ended the Cold War that had defined world politics for half a century and pushed forward a global phenomenon we have traced already, decolonization. This revolution was striking for the grassroots mobilization that made it happen: It resulted from the convictions of millions of ordinary people who shed their fear of authority and power.

Modernization under Stalin
- Ever since its founding by Lenin after the 1917 Bolshevik revolution, the Soviet Union was a radical new kind of state. The Marxist ideology of this communist project looked forward to launching a new stage of human history, a final modernization.

- Marx projected a final revolution that would eliminate all inequalities, all private property, and all classes but the working class. He and his followers claimed that theirs was a scientific socialism that had discerned the direction of history and its iron laws.

- This conviction of certainty gave vast confidence to the revolutionaries. But it also could be used to justify great crimes. Stalin proved a master of just such atrocities in the name of modernization, with a death toll in the millions.

- In this course, we have discussed different paths to modernization. Like Mao, Stalin pressed a compulsory version of modernization that involved subordination to a plan that was synonymous with the will of the leader. It also involved an assault on existing society in the form of a collectivization drive and famine, as well as purges, mass arrests, and executions. All this was in favor of a future planned society.

Berlin Crises

- After the Allied victory in World War II, Stalin expanded his personal rule. The Soviet Union absorbed the Baltic states and parts of Poland and set up allied regimes in Poland, Czechoslovakia, Hungary, Romania, and Bulgaria. Stalinist political systems were imposed on these countries, and a sustained assault took place on these societies to bring them under state control.

- As the Cold War escalated, Germany became ground zero. The country was divided into separate zones of military occupation, and Berlin itself, the capital, was also divided, even though it was inside the Soviet zone. Eventually, a Federal Republic of Germany under American sponsorship was established in the west and the German Democratic Republic under Soviet sponsorship was established in the east.

- For years, the existence of West Berlin inside the Soviet area of control was an irritant to Stalin and his successor, Khrushchev. The result was a series of Berlin crises, making the city a hotspot where the Cold War might potentially tip over into World War III.

- Stalin tried blockading West Berlin in 1948, but the Americans and British used a dramatic airlift to supply the civilian population for 11 months, and Stalin was forced to call off the attempt. After Stalin died in 1953, East Berlin was the scene of the Arbeiteraufstand, the Workers' Uprising, when striking workers had begun calling for free elections. Soviet tanks crushed the workers but left in tatters the ideological claim of the East German communists to represent the working classes.

- Because Berlin was a city under shared control, one could travel to Berlin, cross over to the western part of the city, and then travel on to western Germany, where citizenship was automatic to Germans.

The East German government termed the wall the "Anti-Fascist Protection Barrier."

From 1949 to 1961, some 2.5 million people fled from East to West Germany, and communist leaders became determined to stop the exodus.

- Without warning but with the approval of Khrushchev and the Soviet Union, East German police erected the Berlin Wall on August 13, 1961. Police set up blockades and barbed-wire fences. The new barrier provoked panic and desperation on the part of East Germans who still wanted to leave; escaping the republic became a crime.

- Eventually, the wall inside Berlin ran for 28 miles through the city center, and another wall surrounded the rest of West Berlin for 75 miles. The border between East and West Germany was likewise separated by walls, electrified fences, and "death strips" with raked sand that would reveal the footprints of escapees.

Disintegration of the Soviet Empire
- After Stalin's death, the combination of fear and ideological fervor that had propelled communism was increasingly replaced by conformity, a loss of momentum, and less resort to mass violence, although uprisings in Poland, Hungary, and Czechoslovakia were brutally crushed.

- As the promises of outpacing the Western capitalist countries and the United States were dropped, a sort of malaise set in. This is hard to quantify or pinpoint, but in aggregate, it was a major

421

transformation, especially in the psychology of the ruling elites of the party.

- Indeed, even the existence of party elites, with special privileges and access to goods and travel for themselves and their families not allowed to ordinary people, made a mockery of the ideological promise of equality.

- These factors conspired to engender cynicism and a loss of confidence. But confidence and certainty had been key attributes for Lenin and Stalin, who praised a certain hardness of ideological confidence based on inevitable historical victory. When that historical certainty was eroded, the confidence of the ruling class went, as well.

- On the western side, the wall was mocked and covered in graffiti. Presidents John F. Kennedy and Ronald Reagan came to Berlin and denounced it. A peace activist from Seattle, John Runnings, conducted a series of one-man protests against the wall.

- In the East, a generation of dissidents urged themselves and others to "live in truth," whatever the price, rather than repeat the party line. They counseled, "act as if you are free." If one could do this, fear would no longer rule. The modernity many dissidents envisioned was one of a healthy civil society of free individuals, not pervasive control by the state.

The Reforms of Gorbachev

- In 1985, Mikhail Gorbachev was appointed general secretary of the Soviet Union. A committed Leninist, Gorbachev aimed to introduce a reform program to inject new confidence into the Soviet system and make it work.

- Among Gorbachev's reforms was a policy of openness in public expression, intended to produce constructive criticism. Soon, however, this reform escaped Gorbachev's control, unleashing criticism of the ruling regime.

- To reduce the crushing costs of military spending and commitments to its satellite states in Eastern Europe, Gorbachev allowed those states to go their own way. Public demonstrations for free elections led to noncommunist governments in Poland and Hungary.

- East Germany did not liberalize and found itself increasingly isolated. Peaceful demonstrations in Leipzig grew, testimony to an increasing loss of fear by ordinary people.
  - In a kind of domino effect, the liberalization in Hungary undermined East German authority, and an increasing stream of East Germans used Hungary as a way of making their way west.

  - In desperation, the East German communist elite dropped the hardline leader who was urging a violent crackdown and promised reforms, to buy time.

The Wall Comes Down
- In the fall of 1989, new rules for freer travel abroad were being worked out by the communist government—to be enacted sometime in the future. But then, on November 9, 1989, a member of the Politburo prematurely announced these new rules to the press and stated that they were effective immediately.

- Astonished East Berliners went to the border crossings to see what was really going on. The border guards, who were themselves confused, stood aside. Soon, crowds were passing freely into West Berlin, climbing on the wall, and smashing at it with hammers and chisels.

- Less than a year after the Berlin Wall was brought down, Germany was reunited, on October 3, 1990. Today, the wall is completely gone, no longer standing even as ruins.

Collapse of the Soviet Union
- Similar waves of nonviolent protest also brought down the Soviet Union and other communist regimes in Eastern Europe. The Baltic states declared their independence from the Soviet Union in a

process that spread. Ironically, eventually even Russia declared its independence.

- In early 1991, Gorbachev turned toward repression. In Lithuania, Soviet special forces and their tanks killed civilian protestors but could not halt the drive toward freedom. In August 1991, some of Gorbachev's associates sought to take power in a coup and clamp down. But the coup soon folded, and by the end of the year, the Soviet Union was dissolved.

- As independent republics emerged from the wreckage of the Soviet Union, another stage of world decolonization had been achieved, with the end of the ideological empire Stalin had constructed.

- The countries of Central and Eastern Europe have since worked to build democracies on the basis of the sovereignty they were earlier denied and to reintegrate themselves into a Europe from which they had been split.

Tiananmen Square

- China also experienced protests and crisis in 1989, but there, the outcome was not so positive.

- For seven weeks in the spring of 1989, thousands of Chinese students gathered in Beijing's Tiananmen Square, peacefully raising demands for change and democracy. But on June 4, tanks and soldiers moved in and killed hundreds of the protestors.

- Some historians suggest that memories of the Cultural Revolution and fear of disorder stopped the democracy movement from spreading throughout China as a whole. Clearly, a key difference here—compared with East Berlin—is that the party leaders did have the confidence to use violence.

- In the aftermath, the government focused on nationalism as a rallying point and source of legitimacy. A program of "patriotic education" cultivated memories of the Japanese invasion of the

1930s and the Opium Wars. The question remains open today for China's 1.4 billion people: Does such nationalism and economic growth effectively mute calls for democratic change, or are those demands merely postponed to a later day?

Results of the Year of Revolution

- The fall of the Berlin Wall and the collapse of the Soviet Union's ideological empire showed the power and ultimate resilience of civil society, the voluntary interaction of individuals seeking freedom and refusing to fear. In spite of the communist model that had worked to absorb society into the state, civil society revived.

- The newly independent countries of Central and Eastern Europe regained their sovereignty. In spite of predictions that nationalism and ethnic divisions would lead to endless wars, for the most part, these countries have taken a democratic and peaceful road. Now, many of them are part of the European Union.

- Without the democratic revolutions of 1989, only a Europe in the West could have been organized, and that would have been achingly incomplete. Now the question arises: What sort of Europe will emerge or is emerging today?

Suggested Reading

Hitchcock, *The Struggle for Europe*.

Kenney, *1989*.

Taylor, *The Berlin Wall*.

Questions to Consider

1. If, as planned, a perfectly automated border wall had been achieved by the East German regime, how might these events have evolved differently?

2. Was the Berlin Wall, in the end, self-defeating?

1989—The Fall of the Berlin Wall
Lecture 23—Transcript

The year is 1989, and the fall of a wall will herald the end of an empire. If you think back to the start of our course, you'll recall that we witnessed something in some ways similar, and yet very different. That earlier scene came in 1453, with the fall of Constantinople and the collapse of the Eastern Roman Empire. We heard the sound of the approaching end, the booming of monster cannon that smashed the ancient ramparts on which we were standing. But now, over five centuries later, let's revisit the question of how a modern empire falls.

It is the night of November 9, and we are in Berlin, Germany, in the center of this metropolis. Once again, we are standing atop a wall. It's not a thousand years old as the walls of Constantinople were, but only 28 years old, made of concrete, and festooned with barbed wire. As we listen to this turning point, this is what we hear: laughter, singing, shouts of joy and wonder, champagne corks popping, and a steady noise of hammering.

That hammering is not the great booming sound of monster cannon like at besieged Constantinople, but rather the small sound of countless sledgehammers, picks, and chisels that people are using to break down the wall itself. The infamous Berlin Wall we are standing on will in short order be gone, deconstructed by the efforts of quite ordinary people. In a way, there is a perfect justice to that, because this wall was not built to keep invaders out, like the walls of Constantinople. Rather, it had been built to keep ordinary people in, subjects in a vast political and social experiment in forced modernization.

In this lecture, we consider a comparatively recent turning point that already has become part of history, the year of revolutions, 1989. Today, we often take for granted what was a huge surprise: the largely peaceful collapse of communist dictatorships as a result of the social mobilization of millions of ordinary people for nonviolent protest. We will see how these elements made this a turning point of huge and continuing significance.

First, with amazing speed and little warning, the collapse of Communist regimes in Central and Eastern Europe ended the half-century-long Cold War which had defined world politics and also pushed forward a global phenomenon that we've traced already in our course: decolonization. Second, this revolution was striking for the grassroots mobilization which made it happen. It resulted most of all from the convictions of millions of ordinary people who had shed their fear of authority and power. Third, and this is something that we're enormously grateful for (or should be), the revolution was generally peaceful, not marked by mass bloodshed or war, as had essentially been the rule in the past. Let's explore these astonishing dimensions to that year of miracles, 1989.

The empire whose collapse we will observe was built up by Joseph Stalin, leader of the Soviet Union. Ever since its founding by Lenin after the 1917 Bolshevik revolution, the Soviet Union was a radical new kind of state. The Marxist ideology of this communist project looked forward to launching a new stage of human history, a final modernization.

Marx projected a coming great final revolution which would eliminate all inequalities, and all private property, all classes but the working class. He and his followers claimed that theirs was a scientific socialism that had discerned the direction of history and history's iron laws. This conviction of certainty which they gained as a result gave vast confidence to revolutionaries, like Lenin and Stalin. But it could also be used to justify great crimes, imposing final solutions to the problems of modernity. Stalin proved a great master of just such atrocities in the name of modernization, with a death toll in the many many millions.

In this course, we've discussed modernity as a process, and we've different concepts of how to modernize. Like China's Mao (who was discussed in an earlier lecture), Stalin had pressed a compulsory version of modernization that involved subordinating everything to a plan, allegedly scientific, a plan that was synonymous with the will of the infallible leader. It also involved an assault on existing society. In the case of the Soviet Union, this came in the form of a collectivization drive and a famine like that which later took place under Mao, as well as waves of purges, mass arrests, and executions. All this was done in favor of a future planned society.

In fact, the lure of planned societies extended very far in the 20th century. The British science fiction author and visionary H.G. Wells, among many others, saw liberal democracy as messy and not really up to the task of building a rational, ordered future. When Wells actually met Stalin in Moscow, Wells proved disappointed (mostly because Stalin wouldn't accept his advice about how to govern), but Wells kept returning nonetheless in his writings and in his musings on the future to the idea of a dictatorship of elite experts who would scientifically plan and regiment society and individuals, all in the name of progress. Even at the time, these hopes were really willfully naïve.

After the Allied victory in the Second World War, Stalin expanded his personal rule. The Soviet Union absorbed the Baltic States, parts of Poland, and set up allied regimes in Poland, Czechoslovakia, Hungary, Romania, and Bulgaria. Stalinist political systems were imposed on these countries, and a sustained assault took place on their societies to bring those societies under state control.

The real aim was to eliminate civil society. Civil society is that zone between the individual and the state or government—that zone where voluntary relations and interactions take place: a zone of organizations, churches, clubs, even friendships. Across Central and Eastern Europe, where the victorious Red Army was stationed, the Soviet takeover was experienced as colonialism—not overseas imperialism, but in Europe itself.

As the Cold War escalated, with the former allies, the United States and the Soviet Union, squaring off against one another, it was the defeated and occupied land of Germany that was ground zero. Germany was divided into separate zones of military occupation, and its capital, Berlin, likewise was divided into zones even though it was inside the Soviet zone itself. Eventually, a Federal Republic of Germany under American sponsorship was established in the West, and the German Democratic Republic under Soviet sponsorship in the East. Both claimed to be the one, true, legitimate Germany.

For years, for Stalin and then for his successor Khrushchev, the existence of West Berlin inside their area of control was an irritant and really an offense. The result was a series of Berlin crises, which made the city a hotspot where the Cold War might potentially tip over into World War III (in which case we would likely not be having this lecture today).

Stalin tried blockading West Berlin in 1948, but the Americans and the British used a dramatic airlift to supply the civilian population for 11 months, and Stalin was forced to call off his attempt to throttle West Berlin. After Stalin died in 1953, East Berlin was the scene of the Arbeiteraufstand, the Workers' Uprising, when striking workers had begun calling for free elections. Soviet tanks crushed the workers, but as a result, they left in tatters the ideological claim of the East German communists to represent the working classes at large.

Through these years, an ominous thing was happening moreover, from the perspective of the East German leaders and their Soviet patrons. The very best and most talented people, especially from the younger generation, were draining out of East Germany. Because Berlin was a city with shared control by the victors of World War II, one could travel from East Germany to Berlin, cross over into the western part of the city, and then travel safely onwards to West Germany, where citizenship was automatic to Germans.

Thus, from 1949 to 1961, some two and a half million Germans fled from East Germany to West Germany. These were the cream of the crop—the skilled, the venturesome—and the communist leaders were determined to stop this. Without any advance warning, but with the approval of Khrushchev and the Soviet Union, East German police put up the Berlin Wall on August 13, 1961, on what should have been a quiet and peaceful Sunday morning. East German police set up blockades and barbed wire fences. This surprise move, by the way, actually intersected with another one of our turning points, with the space race that we discussed in an earlier lecture. The Soviets deliberately scheduled the flight of one of their cosmonauts to coincide with the building of the wall to emphasize the superiority of their ideology on Earth and in space!

This new barrier provoked panic and desperation on the part of East Germans who still wanted to leave. On one particular street in downtown Berlin, the *Bernauer Strasse*, where windows on buildings of that street faced west, people actually jumped from them to get to freedom. An ordinary

East German soldier, who had been ordered to guard the barbed wire fence, decided in a moment of personal resolve, on the spur of the moment, that he would defect, and he leapt across himself.

While just before all this, East German government propaganda had declared that "no one has the intention of building a wall," now propaganda turned on a dime and celebrated what the East German government called the new Anti-Fascist Protection Barrier. For East German citizens, it now became a crime to try to escape the republic; in German this was known as *Republikflucht* as a crime.

This threat was revealed as deadly earnest when the first victim was shot by border guards at the wall, a week and a half after it had been set up. This was a young worker trying to get to the West, a 24-year-old tailor named Günter Litfin. The United States and other Western powers protested against the wall, but did not move to prevent its construction.

In the years that followed, amazing ingenuity and daring were on display as people escaped from East Berlin by tunnels, or were smuggled out in hidden compartments of cars, or even sought to escape by hot-air balloons. But increasingly the wall took on permanence. That earlier improvised construction of cinderblocks and barbed wire was steadily replaced by tall concrete walls up to 15 feet high. Watchtowers were erected. The wall inside Berlin between East and West ran for 28 miles through the city center, and then another wall ran around the rest of West Berlin for 75 miles.

The border between East and West Germany likewise was separated by walls, electrified fences, and so-called death strips, where raked sand would reveal the footprints of those trying to escape. Mines and automatic machine guns triggered might be triggered by people fleeing, and would bring instant death. At the Berlin Wall in Berlin, an estimated 5,000 people actually made it over the wall. The same number, it's estimated, were captured in trying to get across. An estimated 191 people were killed as they tried to escape.

Behind the wall, in East Germany, most had no choice but to conform and to accommodate themselves to the plans of the state. To keep people in line and under observation, an extraordinary secret police institution was set up in East Germany, the Ministry for State Security, informally known as the Stasi. Stasi officers and legions of secret informers kept people under watch. Indeed, East Germany has been called the most comprehensively spied-on society of the modern age.

All of this took place behind the wall. Just before the wall fell, East German leaders predicted that the wall would stand for centuries longer, and they sought to make it indeed into a perfect automated barrier by the year 2000. Yet ultimately, perhaps the Wall was truly self-defeating in the long run. Building it proved that the planned and centrally controlled communist society ultimately needed to rely on compulsion and force, not the consent of the governed.

This admission, over the long haul and in ways that were visible only to very very keen observers, would ultimately lead to the disintegration of the East German state and the Soviet Empire as a whole. After Stalin's death, the combination of fear and ideological fervor that had propelled communism was increasingly replaced by a kind of dull conformity, a loss of momentum, and less resort to mass violence (although uprisings in Hungary and Czechoslovakia were crushed very brutally).

As the promises of outpacing the Western capitalist countries and the United States in industrial production, and quality consumer goods, or even in the space race that we discussed were dropped, a sort of malaise set in. This is really hard to quantify or really to pinpoint exactly, but in aggregate it was a big transformation, especially in the psychology of the ruling elites of the Community Party.

Even the very existence of party elites—with special privileges, and access to goods or travel abroad for themselves and their families that weren't allowed to ordinary people—really made a mockery of the ideological promise of equality. Ordinary people stood in long lines to buy scarce and often shoddy goods; they could not dream of travel abroad; and often were reduced to making an art of speaking one way in public, and inside thinking | something different.

These factors conspired to create a certain general cynicism and loss of confidence. Here let me inject some personal experience. I was able to make a trip to the Soviet Union in the 1970s and then another one in 1989, the year of our turning point. A mood of malaise was palpable. It also produced brilliant political jokes as a genre.

For instance, ordinary people joked, "We pretend to work, and the government pretends to pay us." Another anecdote described the history of the Soviet Union as a train. Stalin had the engineer arrested as an enemy of the people and shot. His successor, Khrushchev, rehabilitated the dead engineer, but the train still didn't move. The next leader, Brezhnev, had everyone pull down the shades, rock from side to side and make "choo-choo" noises, to pretend that the train was actually speeding along.

When I was engaged in Russian language study, my Russian teacher announced to us a deep truth. She said, "To speak Russian, you must have confidence." Actually what she said was, "To speak Russian, you must have confidence." Likewise, confidence and certainty were key attributes for Lenin and Stalin, who praised a certain hardness of ideological conviction, based on the trust in inevitable historical victory. When that historical certainty was eroded, the confidence of the ruling class would go as well.

From the Western side of the wall, the wall was mocked. President John F. Kennedy and President Ronald Reagan came to Berlin and denounced the wall. Everyone has probably seen the pictures of the graffiti-covered concrete of the Berlin Wall. All those drawings and declarations were on the Western side, not on the Eastern side.

In addition, one man, a man who was an eccentric on a truly heroic scale, found a way of illuminating the madness of the wall. His name was John Runnings. He was a peace activist from Seattle, a man from Quaker background, who crusaded (among other things) against the very idea of borders and passports. You might even consider him a rebel against the entire Westphalian international system that we've discussed. In 1986, he actually climbed up onto the wall (at the age of 68) and ran atop it until he was finally wrestled to the ground by border guards. After being released, John Runnings went back to the wall, and got arrested again, and so on and so on and so on.

Eventually, Runnings even went after the wall with a homemade battering ram, and he urged others to join him in a great "pee-in" to urinate on the structure to show disgust. These antics revealed the greater absurdity of the wall itself. In a way, Runnings reminds me of Walking Stewart, that famous eccentric ex-employee of the East India Company who walked home from India to London to protest policies he didn't agree with. Both men showed something really impressive in their personal determination.

In Eastern Europe, an entire generation of dissidents was showing even greater personal determination, at high personal cost, including imprisonment and brutalization by the secret police. Such dissidents urged themselves and society at large to, as they put it, "live in truth," whatever the price, rather than simply repeating the party line, or the orthodoxy. These dissidents counseled, "Act as if you are free." If one could do this, fear would no longer rule. The modernity which many dissidents envisioned and set against the modernity that communism postulated was a modernity of a healthy civil society of free individuals, not pervasive control by the state.

In 1985, a younger Communist leader was appointed general secretary of the Soviet Union, Mikhail Sergeiyevich Gorbachev. A committed Leninist, Gorbachev aimed to introduce a reform program to inject new confidence into the Soviet system and to fundamentally make it work. As has often been the case in history, the moment when a regime tries to reform itself can prove fatal, because the fundamental principles of the entire ruling system may come under question at just that moment.

Among Gorbachev's reforms was a policy of openness in public expression. He intended that openness would produce useful constructive criticism. Soon however, that openness unleashed criticism of the ruling regime itself, and its record. Gorbachev's reforms soon escaped his control, like the story of the sorcerer's apprentice who loses control of spells.

To reduce the crushing costs of military spending in the Cold War, and the commitments of the Soviet Union to its outer empire of satellite states in Eastern Europe, Gorbachev allowed those states to go their own way. Public demonstrations demanding free elections led to the creation of non-communist governments in Poland and Hungary, a remarkable sight.

Meanwhile, while these countries liberalized, East Germany did not liberalize, and as a result found itself increasingly isolated even in the Eastern Bloc. Peaceful demonstrations in Leipzig grew, testimony to an increasing loss of fear by ordinary people. Then in a kind of domino effect, the liberalization of Hungary ended up undermining East German authority, because Hungary opened its borders to Austria to allow free travel, and an increasing stream of East Germans traveled to Hungary to use it as a way of making their way west. In fact, bizarrely, some East Berliners actually travelled hundreds of miles through Hungary and Austria to go to the west to end up in West Berlin, blocks away from where their odyssey had begun. In desperation, the East German communist elite dropped the hard-line leader who at the time was urging a violent crackdown against the protesters, and instead they promised reforms as a way of buying time.

At this point, accident intervened as a force in history. How much of our lives and history is ruled by accident. In this case it was a bureaucratic blunder. New rules allowing freer travel abroad were being worked out by the East German communist government, and they were to be enacted sometime in the future. The draft of the legislation had not been worked out fully, but then on the night of November 9, 1989, a member of the ruling elite, the Politburo, gave a disorganized press conference, in which he read the press release to reporters. On hearing of this new freedom of travel, a reporter shouted out, "When does this come into effect?" The flustered spokesman, who didn't really know, improvised on the spot and said, "Immediately."

At this point, astonished East Berliners, who had just seen this exchange on television, went out to the border crossings to see what was really going on. There, confusion reigned. The border guards, some of whom had been listening as well, had heard the same words, so who knew what the party line was? Fatefully, the confused guards stood aside. Soon crowds were passing freely into West Berlin. They were soon climbing on the wall, and smashing at it with hammers or whatever else was near to hand. Popular protest for fundamental change grew within East Germany, and a dynamic that was unstoppable had developed.

Thus, less than a year after the Berlin Wall was brought down, Germany was reunited, on October 3, 1990. In 1990, I was actually able to visit the wall and I was able to rent a sledgehammer from an entrepreneur on the street for five minutes at the cost of a few Deutschmarks. I was able smash away at the wall myself. I can tell you this was a deeply satisfying experience. Indeed, so many people did just that that the wall no longer stands today even as ruins. You really have to make a special effort in Berlin to trace where the wall once ran.

Similar waves of nonviolent protest then also in a chain reaction brought down the Soviet Union and other communist regimes in Eastern Europe. Within the Soviet Union, the Baltic states declared their independence from the Soviet Union, in a process that soon spread. Ironically, eventually even Russia had declared its independence from the Soviet Union. In early 1991, Gorbachev turned towards repression. In Lithuania, Soviet special forces and their tanks killed civilian protestors, but even this could not halt the dynamic.

Finally, in August of 1991, some of Gorbachev's associates sought to take matters into their own hands, take power in a coup and clamp down. But this is where the role of confidence in a ruling elite showed itself: At the press conference that the plotters held, some of them appeared with shaking hands. Others appeared to be drunk. The coup soon folded, and by the end of the year, the Soviet Union was officially dissolved. As independent republics emerged from the wreckage of the Soviet Union, another stage of that longer process of world decolonization had been achieved, with the end of the ideological empire that Stalin had built up.

Among the marvels of this process unleashed in 1989, the greatest was the restraint of the protestors, who did not turn to violence when they easily might have. Since then, the countries of Central and Eastern Europe have worked hard to build democracies on the basis of the sovereignty that earlier had been denied to them in an empire, and they're working to reintegrate themselves into a Europe that they had earlier been split off from for decades.

However, we need to be clear about this: A happy outcome was never foreordained or inevitable. That's made clear by events in the same year, 1989, in China. China had also experienced protests and crisis. For seven weeks, crowds of thousands of Chinese students had gathered in Beijing's

435

famous Tiananmen Square, peacefully raising demands for change and democracy.

But in stark contrast to the liberation experienced at the Berlin Wall, the Chinese communists ruthlessly crushed the movement. On June 4, tanks and soldiers were moved in and killed hundreds of the protestors. Even the bravery of an unknown man in famous photographs standing in the way of a column of tanks could not prevent the outcome. Some historians suggest that it was memories of the Cultural Revolution and fear of general disorder that really stopped the democracy movement spreading from the cities throughout China as a whole. Clearly, a key difference here (compared with East Berlin) is that in the Chinese case party leaders did have the confidence to use violence.

In the aftermath of these events, the Chinese government focused on nationalism as a rallying point and a source of legitimacy to replace their earlier Communist ideology. Thus, a program of "patriotic education" worked to cultivate memories of the Japanese invasion of the 1930s, along with commemoration of the Opium Wars in a new generation. The question remains open today for China's 1.4 billion people: Does such nationalism and booming economic growth effectively mute calls for democratic change? Or are those demands merely deferred to a later day? What will happen in an economic slowdown, or in another crisis? The question remains open.

So, what were the ultimate results of this turning point? The fall of the Berlin Wall and the collapse of the Soviet Union's entire structure of ideological empire showed the power and ultimate resilience of civil society, that voluntary interaction of individuals seeking freedom and refusing to fear. In spite of the communist model which had worked to absorb society into the state in its plans, civil society revived.

The newly independent countries of Central and Eastern Europe regained their sovereignty, that key element of the Westphalian system. In spite of many predictions that nationalism and ethnic divisions would lead to endless wars, for the most part, these countries have taken a democratic and peaceful road. Now many of them are part of the project of the European Union, pooling their national sovereignty. But without 1989, only a Europe in the

West could have been organized on a federal basis, and still would have been achingly incomplete. Now the question arises: What sort of Europe will emerge or is emerging today?

In this lecture, we followed a remarkable and vast social mobilization in 1989. New technologies, called social media, were about to supercharge just such interactions, and so we'll consider those in our next lecture.

2004—The Rise of Social Media
Lecture 24

In the last few years, social media and the Internet have changed patterns of how we relate to one another; they have also supercharged key developments that we have discussed earlier in this course: print culture, encyclopedic knowledge, global reach, and the elaboration of civil society. But are our connections through social media making us more global or more insular, locked into niche societies? Is the Internet changing our relationships, our politics, our self-understanding? In this lecture, we examine these questions and further ask whether we are heading toward a turning point of turning points—a profound transformation that we cannot yet even predict.

Facebook and the World Brain

- In 2004, a sophomore computer science major, Mark Zuckerberg, launched a project that he called "thefacebook" from his dorm room. This platform allowed individuals to post information about themselves, along with photographs. Facebook quickly expanded to universities and colleges across America and overseas. In the summer of 2012, it was approaching 100 million users worldwide.

- An earlier dreamer who had envisioned a world connected by scientific knowledge was H. G. Wells. In 1938, he published a book called *World Brain*, in which he argued that we could achieve world peace if everyone were given the same frame of reference so that science might rule the world. That frame of reference was what he called a "World Encyclopedia."

- Another important scientific figure also weighed concepts that foreshadowed the Internet. This was Vannevar Bush, a scientist and one of the administrators of the Manhattan Project. In 1945, he proposed what he called a "memex" ("memory extender") machine as a new kind of encyclopedia. It would be a desk with built-in access to a collection of fully indexed microfilms containing all the contents of a full library.

The Birth of Modern Computers and the Internet

- The first electronic general computer is often considered the ENIAC machine of 1946. It was developed at the University of Pennsylvania for use in computing artillery firing tables for the U.S. Army. In 1950, at Princeton's Institute for Advanced Study, an all-purpose computer was built for the calculations needed to construct a hydrogen bomb.

- In 1969, the ARPANET was developed by the Advanced Research Projects Agency of the U.S. Department of Defense. This network linked a number of West Coast universities where government-supported research took place.
  - Then, through a program called Internetting, other research networks were linked to the ARPANET, using standardized protocols for communication. The National Science Foundation also worked on spreading access more widely.

  - After 1993, commercial users, who earlier had not been allowed to participate in what was meant to be a purely research undertaking, were included, and expansion accelerated.

- From the late 1980s, the Internet doubled every year. This growth, in turn, set the stage for the World Wide Web, an Internet application that allows users to survey documents connected by hypertext or hyperlinks.
  - This development began with Tim Berners-Lee, a British engineer and computer scientist, and his coworkers at CERN, a scientific facility in Geneva, Switzerland. They developed a protocol for standardized communication and a browser by 1992.

  - Building on this work, the Mosaic browser was developed at the University of Illinois and made available in 1993, followed by the Netscape Navigator system in 1994. The use of the web became increasingly popular and, indeed, taken for granted.

- In these early stages, not all were enthusiastic. *Time* magazine concluded in 1994 that the Internet "was not designed for doing commerce," and *Newsweek* called it a "trendy and oversold community."

- Others, however, were entranced by the seemingly unlimited potential of the Internet. Investors and speculators poured in money and enthusiasm, producing the dot-com bubble, which lasted from 1995 to the fall of 2001. The fallout from the bursting of the bubble, paradoxically, allowed the growth of a new set of approaches to the Internet, known as Web 2.0.

Social Media
- The term "Web 2.0" describes patterns, practices, and programs for the Internet that are interactive, collaborative, and focused on empowering the user and harnessing "collective intelligence." Part of this iteration of the Internet is social media, in which the user is not a passive absorber of content but a creator, sharer, shaper, and exchanger of content.

- From its origins in a Harvard dorm room in 2004, Zuckerberg's enterprise grew to fantastic and still-expanding proportions. In 2011, Facebook had earned $3.7 billion and reportedly became the first website to receive a trillion page views in one month.

- Like Edison, Zuckerberg was adept at integrating earlier inventions and developments in a new way. He has repeatedly described Facebook as a "utility," echoing Diderot's emphasis on usefulness and utility in the *Encyclopédie*.

- In the spring of 2012, Facebook's initial public offering was the largest Internet stock market launch in history. At first, it did not do well, but the future remains to be seen. The key issue lies in

Every month, some 30 billion pieces of information are posted on Facebook by users: photos, links, and messages.

developing a revenue model out of the promise of knowing more about consumers so that advertising can be targeted as never before.

- The impact of Facebook and other social media on current events is already beyond question. In 2008, activists in Colombia used Facebook to rally massive demonstrations against the FARC guerrilla movement and its kidnapping of civilians. In 2009, the youthful Green Movement in Iran used Facebook and Twitter to protest against what they charged were fraudulent elections.
  - o Some thinkers see this as part of a broader democratization that is being forced worldwide by the Internet. University of

Tennessee law professor Glenn Reynolds calls this the spread of "horizontal knowledge."

o   If earlier media focused on one authoritative voice speaking down to the many—vertically—this new technology encourages a more diffuse, participatory, horizontal communication. Decentralized and self-motivated individuals aggregate and challenge an earlier model of centralized authority.

New Media and Modernity

- What can we say about the promise and perils of the new media as a part of our modernity? Is being connected to social media giving us richer social lives, or is the Internet inviting us to become more insular, locked into niche societies? Internet use also can lead to compulsive overuse or addiction, and some worry that social media foster exhibitionism and narcissism.

- Some commentators speak of an "Internet paradox," noting that Internet usage correlates with reports of feeling lonely. Is the virtual world of "online" displacing what has been, until now, the norm of interaction offline?

- At an even more basic level of concern, some ask whether use of the Internet and digital technology is rewiring our brains. Numerous news reports speak of changes in reading habits, which had been declining even before the Internet.

- Many workers today complain of being overwhelmed by the flood of data, and it has been estimated that that flood will expand 40 times over by 2020. Optimists propose that we are already seeing human adaptation to such challenges.

- It's also true that if the Internet empowers, it can empower the destructive and dangerous—criminals, terrorists, and small-scale thugs alike. Identity theft and deception online are everyday events. Governments warn of the dangers of cyberattacks and cyberwar.

- There is also danger from within. What does the new technology imply in terms of the power of governments to keep people under surveillance or to control their access to information?
  - Some critics speak of China's intensifying efforts to block access to certain websites as a "Great Firewall of China," but such efforts have also been called the "dictator's dilemma."

  - If a ruler shuts off access to the Internet and, thus, the world, the country suffers economically and may experience greater discontent and revolt.

- Throughout this course, we have asked how our turning points redefined authority. In the case of the Internet and digital media, it may be too early to say. But earlier formulas seem up for grabs.
  - Does the Westphalian system of territorial sovereignty that grew up around 1648 still apply in cyberspace as the Internet abolishes borders?

  - Are individuals empowered enough in this new world to escape another, later wave of technological change devoted to their regimentation and suppression?

The Turning Point of Turning Points
- In many ways, the Internet and social media have supercharged key developments that we have looked at throughout these lectures: print culture, encyclopedic knowledge, global reach, and the elaboration of civil society.
  - At a far slower pace, Gutenberg's printing press and motion pictures worked to diffuse knowledge.

  - The impulse to encyclopedic, comprehensive, and useful knowledge was present in Diderot's *Encyclopédie* and the research of Leeuwenhoek and Alexander Fleming.

  - Global reach is a theme we have encountered from the beginning, in the voyages of Zheng He and Columbus, the trading travel of the East India companies, and powered flight.

- o Globalization was present as imperialism in the Opium Wars and appeared as a global challenge to imperialism from the Russo-Japanese War. The perils of the atomic weapon and the great achievement of humans on the moon likewise were global in impact.

- o We have repeatedly seen issues of how to build a civil society: in the 1648 Peace of Westphalia, the American Revolution, the French Revolution, the abolitionist movement, women's suffrage, and the fall of the Berlin Wall.

- Some thinkers have proposed that we are now at the turning point of turning points—the "singularity"—which they claim is rapidly approaching.
  - o What is meant by the singularity is a transformation and progress in technology so profound that we cannot even begin to predict what will happen after this unique moment.

  - o Will technology be embedded in human bodies with the result of creating something beyond the human? What follows on the manipulation of the human genome or artificial intelligence, and to what ends? Will the Internet and its proliferating connections grow into the kind of World Brain that H. G. Wells envisioned?

- We can perhaps conclude our course on the turning points of modern history on an optimistic note.
  - o As all these turning points have appeared and left our world transformed, a constant has been the deeply creative response that humans have found to meet those changes or to push them further. That creative response to the unending challenge of the new is in part what being "modern" means to us today.

  - o The ancient Greek philosopher Heraclitus uttered a thought that is as true today as it was 25 centuries ago: "The only thing that is constant is… change." Thus, achieving creative synthesis of what is abiding, time-tested, and valuable with that which is new, exciting, dynamic, and promising—that is how we will survive and thrive.

Suggested Reading

Kirkpatrick, *The Facebook Effect*.

Mandiberg, *The Social Media Reader*.

Reynolds, *An Army of Davids*.

Shirky, *Here Comes Everybody*.

Questions to Consider

1. What is the one greatest impact of the Internet on your own life?

2. Are social media and Internet usage drawing us closer together or isolating users?

2004—The Rise of Social Media
Lecture 24—Transcript

At Harvard's Kirkland House dormitory, on an autumn afternoon in 2004, a sophomore computer science major named Mark Zuckerberg is tapping away at his computer. He was born in 1984, in New York. In his dorm room, he is working on one of his many software projects. In those days some colleges produced little booklets with the photographs of incoming freshmen, as a way for people to get to know one another, to start recognizing people one had classes with or perhaps passed in the quads. These booklets were called facebooks.

The semester previous, in October 2003, Zuckerberg had aggregated these photographs, sometimes by hacking into dorm systems, and had created a website, called Facemash, which invited Harvard undergraduates to vote on who was most attractive. Harvard shut that project down, responding to complaints, including issues of privacy—those photographs had not been taken for this project; they hadn't been volunteered by students. They'd simply been taken. But one other fact was especially striking: the intensity of usage of this website. Apparently, students who started clicking through in the program would not stop—the activity somehow had a compelling and almost entrancing aspect.

Let off with a relatively light censure, Zuckerberg now launched a new project, initially called "thefacebook." (Later "the" was dropped so I'll refer to it here as Facebook.) All this from his dorm room. On Wednesday, February 4, 2004, in the afternoon, it was active. It was a platform with a minimalist appearance, which allowed individuals to post information about themselves, and a photograph (later, many photographs). Using their real names, users chose what to post about themselves, and then established links with others (called friending) with whom they would share content. The element of flirtation was there too, of course: Users "poked" friends. No one knew exactly what that poke signified, which of course made it all that more exciting.

At first limited to Harvard, Facebook soon expanded to other Ivy League schools, then to universities and colleges across America, and then overseas.

Soon Zuckerberg left Harvard, moving to Palo Alto in Silicon Valley, to work on the company full time. Its growth was phenomenal, unprecedented. One collaborator in Facebook described its early aims: Not to get rich, but motivated by the idea, "Let's build something that has lasting cultural value and try to take over the world."

In the summer of 2012, Facebook was approaching 100 million users worldwide. It's now an integral part of a new, digitally linked modernity that we inhabit today. Today, 2 billion people are online. E-commerce sales now are at 8 trillion dollars a year. But only a few decades ago, this world would have seemed improbable, almost magical in some of its capacities. Yet in fact there had been some who had dreamed of a world like this, in dim outline. Those dreamers were librarians and creators of encyclopedias.

In some sense, the dream of making information accessible is as old as libraries. Think of the tremendous aggregation of knowledge that the ancient Library of Alexandria represented. It was this impulse also that was the motivating concept for the project of Diderot's *Encyclopédie*, which we discussed in an earlier lecture: to demonstrate and make useful to everyone the interrelatedness of all knowledge.

Even closer to our own times, another figure elaborated on this dream. This was H.G. Wells, that prolific and visionary British author of scientific romances, whom we've met in many earlier lectures in this course. We encountered him wrestling with the problem of human evolution, and warning of the destructive impact of human flight when turned to air war; we saw him anticipating the fearful outlines of atomic weapons, and also looking forward to humans reaching the Moon!

So it should hardly surprise anyone to hear that Wells also projected an idea that anticipated the Internet. In 1938, H.G. Wells published a book called *World Brain*, in which he argued that we would have world peace if everyone were given the same frame of reference, so that science might rule the world. That frame of reference was to be provided by what he called a "World Encyclopedia," as a new global institution.

Wells quite deliberately referenced Diderot's *Encyclopédie* as his inspiration for this idea, but he wanted to push it further, to make it something far larger and more extensive. His project would gather up all the most up-to-date and authoritative knowledge of experts and make it available, perhaps by the new technology (for those days) of microfilm, so that it be as he said, "the mental background of every intelligent man in the world," an "undogmatic Bible to a world culture." We might even call it a planetary consciousness. Universities and research laboratories would constantly work on updating this World Brain, or World Encyclopedia. The World Encyclopedia would, he promised, end up holding "the world together mentally."

The result of such a new institution would be virtually a network of nerves that spread worldwide, a World Brain. As the storm clouds of the Second World War gathered, before the world had even recovered from the first total war, Wells undertook a lecture tour, including to the United States, all as an effort to stir up general enthusiasm for the World Encyclopedia, but he actually found very little response.

Shortly afterwards however, another important scientific figure, even though he's largely unknown today, also weighed concepts that foreshadowed the Internet. This was a person we briefly encountered before in a previous lecture: Vannevar Bush, a scientist and one of the administrators of the Manhattan Project to build the atomic bomb. In a sense, Vannevar Bush was right at that crucial intersection of science and policy.

In 1945, while the Second World War was still raging, Vannevar Bush published an article in *Atlantic* magazine, in which he proposed what he called a "memex" machine, as a new kind of encyclopedia. ("Memex" stood for "memory extender.") A memex would be a desk with a built-in microfilm reader and a collection of a fully indexed set of microfilms containing all the contents of a full research library. Following links and establishing connections between pages of different texts, the memex would in a sense become a browseable auxiliary mind.

The hardware that made such shadowy anticipations of the Internet a practical reality obviously was the modern computer. Computers likewise had their origins in World War II. The first electronic general computer is often considered the ENIAC machine of 1946. This acronym stood for the "Electronic Numerical Integrator and Computer." It was developed at the University of Pennsylvania's engineering school for the U.S. Army Ballistic Research Laboratory for use in computing artillery firing tables.

Originally, at the start of the Second World War, a "computer" was not a thing but a person, someone who did these complicated mathematical calculations himself, or very often, herself. Now this task could be automated. Then in 1950, at Princeton's Institute for Advanced Study, the next step was taken, with the building of an all-purpose computer for the calculations that were needed to build a hydrogen bomb. Thus, as the historian of science George Dyson concludes, "The digital universe and the hydrogen bomb were brought into existence at the same time."

Building on this growing work on computers, the stage was set for the Internet. It is sometimes called the "network of networks," a way of connecting up computer networks. In 1969 in the United States, the ARPANET was developed by ARPA (or Advanced Research Projects Agency) of the U.S. Department of Defense.

The ARPANET linked a number of West Coast universities where government-supported research was taking place. Then, through a program called Internetting, other research networks were linked up to the ARPANET, using standardized protocols for communication. The National Science Foundation also worked on spreading access more widely. After 1993, commercial users, who earlier had not been allowed to participate in what was meant to be really a purely research undertaking, were included, and expansion now accelerated.

Let me now state what almost rings like understatement: The Internet has revolutionized how information is accessed and used. It truly merits the label of an information revolution. The Internet enables e-mail, newsgroups, digital libraries, and has transformed commerce, spawning "e-businesses." From the late 1980s, the Internet was doubling every year, first concentrated in the United States and Europe, and then spreading worldwide.

This in turn set the stage for the World Wide Web, known informally as the "web." This is an Internet application which gives web users the chance to survey documents connected by hypertext or hyperlinks. To begin with, the British engineer and computer scientist Tim Berners-Lee and his coworkers at CERN, a laboratory in Geneva, Switzerland, developed a protocol for standardized communication and a browser by 1992.

Building on this work, the Mosaic browser was developed at the University of Illinois and made available in 1993, and this was followed by the Netscape Navigator system in 1994. The use of the web became increasingly popular, and indeed, taken for granted. We can sense just how ubiquitous and common the Internet had become by mentioning a famous cartoon in the July 1993 issue of *The New Yorker*. In this famous cartoon, by Peter Steiner, two dogs are sitting in front of a computer terminal, and one dog is explaining to the other: "On the Internet, nobody knows you're a dog."

This has actually become the most reprinted cartoon from that magazine, because it says something about the fluidity of online activities and online personality. But it was also a key cultural moment oddly enough because of what was not said (the dog that did not bark, in other words). No explanation was provided in that cartoon, or needed, for what the Internet was. It had now become common cultural property.

In these early stages, not everybody was enthusiastic. Dubious reactions included the comment that was made in 2001 by that great American philosopher Homer Simpson, who asked, "The Internet? Is that thing still around?" Back in 1994, Time Magazine concluded that that the Internet "was not designed for doing commerce" and Newsweek called it a "trendy and oversold community." Others declared that the Internet would really be "the CB radio of the 1990s," a fad, not something really lasting an durable.

But others were entranced by the seemingly unlimited potential they saw. Enlivened with an almost utopian sense of the possibilities and the commercial potential of the Internet, investors and speculators poured in money and enthusiasm and drove up what afterwards was known as the dot-com bubble or Internet bubble from 1995 to the fall of 2001, when it burst. This shakeout, paradoxically, allowed the rise of a new set of approaches to the Internet, what's been called the Web 2.0, a new version of the phenomenon.

The term was popularized by Internet entrepreneur Tim O'Reilly to describe patterns, practices, and programs for the Internet that were interactive, collaborative, focused on empowering the user, and as O'Reilly puts it, "to harness collective intelligence." Part of this includes so-called social media, in which the user is not a passive absorber of content that's, but a creator, a sharer, a shaper, and an exchanger of content. This includes a wide and ever-expanding range of technical approaches: e-mail, instant-messaging, text messaging, photo sharing, blogging, and social networking sites like Twitter. Or Facebook.

From its origins that afternoon in a Harvard dorm room in 2004, Zuckerberg's enterprise grew to fantastic and today still-expanding proportions. In the summer of 2012, Facebook was approaching 100 million users. In 2011, it had earned 3.7 billion dollars. In 2011 as well, Facebook reportedly became the first website to receive a trillion page views in one month.

The intensity of usage is striking. Over half of the users of Facebook log on daily. In a book by the same name, David Kirkpatrick calls this the "Facebook effect." He considers it "a fundamentally new form of communication" with "fundamentally new interpersonal and social effects," as information becomes viral and moves swiftly across networks.

Individuals now can take on the role of publishers, initiators of new ideas and messages. Consider this: Each man or woman is potentially his or her own Gutenberg! Every month, some 30 billion pieces of information are posted by users: photos, links, messages. All this was directed by a young man who taught himself to be a CEO while sticking to his trademark style of aggressively informal dress—t-shirts, hooded sweatshirts, and rubber flip-flops.

Like Thomas Edison, whom we discussed in an earlier lecture, Zuckerberg was adept at integrating earlier inventions and earlier developments in a new way (in fact, there were lawsuits alleging that the idea for Facebook was originated by others, but these were settled). As his company grew, Mark Zuckerberg refused repeated offers to be bought out.

Why? His ambitions apparently ran—and run—in a different direction. On his own Facebook page, Zuckerberg describes himself and his aims: "openness, breaking things, revolutions, information flow, minimalism, making things, eliminating desire for all that really doesn't matter." Striving to express what is distinctive and new about Facebook, Zuckerberg repeatedly has described it as a "utility." There is an echo there of the way in which Diderot's *Encyclopédie* had stressed utility and usefulness in its project to diffuse information as well. But Facebook breaks new ground. It is perhaps the fastest-growing company of any kind in history. It is also resolutely global, with about three-quarters of its users outside the United States, using a multitude of different languages.

In spring of 2012, Facebook's initial public offering was the largest Internet stock market launch in history. At first it did not do well, but the future remains to be seen. The key question really is what revenue model can be developed out of the promise of knowing more about consumers so that advertising can be targeted as it never has been before.

But the impact that Facebook and other social media have already had in current events is just beyond question. A few examples: In 2008, activists in Colombia used Facebook to rally massive demonstrations against the FARC guerrilla movement and its kidnapping of civilians. In 2009, the youthful Green Movement in Iran used Facebook and Twitter to protest against what they charged were fraudulent elections. Also in Iran, a movement called the One Million Signatures Campaign seeks to collect signatures for a petition for women's equality in legislation, using both personal contacts (face-to-face) and the Internet.

Social media also played a role in the uprisings in Arab countries since December of 2010. I can make a confident prediction: If you read or listen to the news today, you will find your own examples of this ongoing impact. As the examples indicate, not every movement using this media succeeds, but its use has become vital.

Some thinkers see this as part of a broader democratization that's being forced worldwide by the Internet. University of Tennessee law professor Glenn Reynolds, who blogs as "Instapundit," calls this the spread of "horizontal knowledge." What he means is this: If earlier media focused on one authoritative voice speaking down to the many, vertically, this new technology encourages a more diffuse, participatory, horizontal mode of communication. Reynolds sees this as part of a new dynamic of the 21st century, in which an "army of Davids" confronts Goliath, or centralized authority. Decentralized and self-motivated individuals aggregate, and they can challenge an earlier model of centralized authority.

While it is too early to make definitive statements, what can we say of the promise and perils of this new media as a part of our modernity? We need to in our discussion treat both the hopes and fears in tandem, because often they're actually linked. What is the Internet doing to us? Is being connected to social media making us more global and connected, with richer social lives and constant contact? Or is the Internet actually inviting us to become more insular, locked into small niche societies, and not interacting with those who are different from us, however that difference is defined?

Internet use also can lead, as has been recognized, to compulsive overuse, or addiction. Just recall the trancelike states that some of the first users of Facebook experienced, clicking through again and again, unable to get enough of the experience.

Others worry that social media fosters exhibitionism and narcissism. Certainly there is a lot of both offline, but online, will we soon be drowning in a sea of blogs that nobody reads, with individuals revealing more and more of themselves to less and less effect, without an audience? Is Internet use making us lonely, with illusory relationships rather than deep real bonds?

Some commentators speak of an "Internet paradox," noting that Internet usage correlates with reports of feeling lonely. Is the virtual world of being online displacing what has been throughout history until now the norm of interaction offline? Some authors speak, with a tinge of irony, of there being cyberspace, and then "meatspace." By "meatspace" they mean the opposite of cyberspace, the flesh-and-blood world of physical reality.

At an even more basic level of concern, some ask whether and how use of the Internet and digital technology might actually be rewiring our brains. As one article asks quite bluntly, "Is Google Making Us Stupid?" Numerous news reports speak of changes in reading habits, which had already been declining even before the Internet, but now these reading habits are being recast again: lessened attention spans, scanning rather than deeply engaging with ideas as we read.

Might we say that Gutenberg's invention of the printed word is dying? Are e-books, instantly downloadable, replacing Gutenberg's original invention? In 2012 for instance, there were over a hundred million e-readers and tablets being used in the United States, and e-books generated more sales than traditional adult hardcover books. Or might we say that a revival of reading is being pressed forward in this way?

In studies, many workers today complain of simply being swamped by a flood of data, overwhelmed by information. That flood apparently will not stop. In fact, it was estimated in 2011 that by 2020, data will expand 40 times over. Some optimists propose that we're actually already seeing human adaptation to these challenges. They speak of the younger generations as "digital natives," who are really in their element, because a digital world is the only one they've ever known.

Indeed, those with young children can probably testify how readily and fearlessly they take to the media. All of the rest of us, the older ones, are called "digital immigrants," who may adjust more or less successfully, but never completely, to the new digital environment. Some experts argue that education will have to be fundamentally remade to speak to the digital natives.

But if the Internet empowers, it can also empower the destructive and the dangerous—criminals and terrorists and small-scale thugs alike. We read reports of cyberbullying. Identity theft and deception online are everyday events—remember the Peter Steiner cartoon about how nobody knows who (or what) you are on the Internet. Governments warn of the dangers of cyberattacks and cyberwar.

These are not merely potential. In fact, in 2007 and 2008, Estonia and Georgia both experienced attacks from Russian computers during international disputes. Then there is the danger within. What does the new technology imply in terms of the power of governments to keep people under surveillance? Or to control their access to information?

In this context, some critics speak of China's intensifying efforts to block access to websites it does not want Chinese people to visit. Some call this the "Great Firewall of China." But it's also part of what has sometimes been called the "dictator's dilemma." If a modern ruler shuts off access to the Internet, and thus the world at large, the country will suffer economically and the dictator may provoke even bigger discontent and revolt as a consequence, because now, to be modern is to be online.

Throughout this course, we have asked how the turning points we examined have redefined authority. In the case of the Internet and digital media, it may be too early to say. But certainly, earlier formulas seem up for grabs. For instance, does the Westphalian system of territorial sovereignty that grew up after 1648 and which we discussed in an earlier lecture, does all that still apply in cyberspace? The Internet is abolishing borders. Also, are individuals empowered enough in this new world to escape later waves of technological change that might be devoted to regimenting and suppressing individuals?

All of this is new, and yet, we've also seen aspects of it before. In many ways, the Internet and social media essentially supercharge key earlier developments we saw in this course, including print culture and media, encyclopedic knowledge, an increasing global reach, and the elaboration of civil societies. At a far slower pace, Gutenberg's printing press and then motion pictures worked to diffuse knowledge in their day as well.

The impulse to be encyclopedic, comprehensive, and to diffuse useful knowledge was the core idea of Diderot's *Encyclopédie*, and of the research of Leeuwenhoek and the discovery of penicillin. The theme of global reach is one that we've encountered from the beginning of our course, even if at first it was achingly slow and uncertain: the voyages of Zheng He and Columbus, the trading travel of the East India Companies, and then later, powered flight. Globalization as a phenomenon was also there in a negative way, during the

Opium Wars, and as imperialism spread, and it also appeared as a global challenge to imperialism during the Russo-Japanese War. The perils of the atomic weapon, and then the great achievement of humans walking on the Moon likewise were global and planetary in impact.

Issues of how to build a civil society for modernity we also saw repeatedly: at the 1648 Peace of Westphalia, in the American Revolution, the French Revolution, and in the abolitionist movement, the movement for women's suffrage, and in the fall of the Berlin Wall. What is new is the intensity of interconnectedness and its speed. But we see that interconnectedness as such is not new or unique to our times.

Yet, let me here introduce a radical alternative that some thinkers have proposed: What if we're actually now at the turning point of turning points today, in our own lives? Some thinkers have called this the singularity, and they claim that the singularity is approaching—fast.

What they mean by "singularity" is a transformation and progress in technology so profound that at present, we cannot even begin to predict what happens after this unique moment in the future. Will technology for instance be embedded in human bodies, with the result of creating something beyond the human? What follows on the manipulation of the human genome, or the creation of artificial intelligence? To what ends? Does the Internet and its proliferating connections eventually grow into the kind of World Brain that H.G. Wells envisioned? What happens next?

As we end our course on the turning points of modern history, we should ask what it all means for us, who are so busy being modern in our everyday lives. In this course we traced old turning points, and ones that continue to unfold around us today. We can conclude—I hope—on ultimately an optimistic note. As all these turning points have appeared and left our world transformed, a constant has been the deeply creative response that humans have found to meet those changes, or even to push them further.

That creative response to the unending challenge of the new is in great part what being modern means to us today. We need thus to be creative and attentive, as we ask urgent questions: Is a turning point building in our world at this very moment? Are we living through a turning point right now?

The ancient Greek philosopher Heraclitus uttered a thought which is as true today as it was 25 centuries ago: "The only thing that is constant … is change." Thus, achieving a kind of creative synthesis of what is abiding, time-tested, and valuable, with that which is new, exciting, dynamic, and promising—that is how we will survive and thrive.

Thank you for being a part of this course, and let me wish everyone the very best turning points (and creative responses to those turning points) for the future!

Timeline

1405 .... Start of the voyages of
Admiral Zheng He

1433 .... End of the voyages of
Admiral Zheng He

1453.. Constantinople falls, end of
the Eastern Roman Empire

1455.. Gutenberg's invention of
the printing press

1475.. First book published in English

1492.. Columbus encounters America

1494.. Treaty of Tordesillas divides
newly discovered lands between
Spain and Portugal

1507.. Waldseemüller map names "America"

1517.. Martin Luther launches the Reformation

1543.. Copernicus's heliocentric
theory published

1570–1720....................................... Dutch Golden Age

1600.. Founding of English (later British)
East India Company (EIC)

1602.. Founding of Dutch East
                                                   India Company (VOC)

1618.. Thirty Years' War breaks out

1623.. Amboyna Massacre

1631.. Publishing of the Wicked
                                                   Bible, with its crucial typo

1648.. Treaty of Westphalia

1676.. Antonie van Leeuwenhoek
                                                   discovers bacteria

1751.. Start of the publishing of
                                                   the *Encyclopédie*

1756–1763....................................... Seven Years' War between
                                                   Britain and France

1757.. Battle of Plassey in India; EIC
                                                   wins control of Bengal

1759 .... Founding of the Wedgwood company

1773.. Boston Tea Party

1776.. Paine's *Common Sense* published;
                                                   American independence declared

1783.. Treaty of Paris: Britain recognizes
                                                   American independence

1787.. American Constitution drafted

1789.. American Constitution ratified

Timeline

461

1961	Soviet cosmonaut Gagarin is the first human in space
1961	Berlin Wall erected
1966–1976	Mao's Cultural Revolution
1969	Apollo *11* mission and U.S. astronauts walk on the moon
1969	ARPANET developed in the United States
1972	Nixon travels to China, marking China's entry into the world balance
1972	Last manned moon mission to date
1978	Deng's reform era launched in China
1989	Fall of the Berlin Wall; Tiananmen Square massacre
1991	Collapse of the Soviet Union; Cold War ends
1997	Hong Kong returned to China
2003	Sequencing of the human genome
2003	First Chinese astronaut sent into orbit
2004	Launch of Facebook at Harvard (originally called "thefacebook")

Bibliography

Ambrose, Stephen E. *Nothing Like It in the World: The Men Who Built the Transcontinental Railroad*. New York: Simon and Schuster, 2000. An epic narrative of the epic engineering project.

Baldwin, Neil. *Edison: Inventing the Century*. Chicago: University of Chicago Press, 2001. A biography of the genius inventor with an emphasis on his personal life and family relationships.

Bayly, C. A. *The Birth of the Modern World, 1780–1914: Global Connections and Comparisons*. Malden, MA: Blackwell Publishers, 2004. A fascinating history that shows the world globalized earlier than assumed and reflects on modernity.

Bernstein, William J. *A Splendid Exchange: How Trade Shaped the World*. New York: Atlantic Monthly Press, 2008. A marvelous and rich account of economics on a global scale; highly recommended.

Blom, Philipp. *Enlightening the World: Encyclopédie, the Book That Changed the Course of History*. New York: Palgrave Macmillan, 2004. A clear exposition of the revolutionary impact of Diderot's project.

Boorstin, Daniel J. *The Discoverers*. New York: Random House, 1983. A gripping overview of the human urge to explore the world.

Bowler, Peter J. *Charles Darwin: The Man and His Influence*. Cambridge: Cambridge University Press, 1996. A clear and engaging explanation of Darwin and his ideas set against the context of his age.

Bown, Stephen. *Merchant Kings: When Companies Ruled the World, 1600–1900*. New York: Thomas Dunne, 2009. An accessible account of swashbuckling companies.

Brook, Timothy. *Vermeer's Hat: The Seventeenth Century and the Dawn of the Global World*. New York: Bloomsbury Press, 2009. Innovative history at its best, showing the global ties emerging after 1600.

Brown, Kevin. *Penicillin Man: Alexander Fleming and the Antibiotic Revolution*. Phoenix Mill, UK: Sutton, 2004. A biographic approach to a scientific revolution.

Brownworth, Lars. *Lost to the West: The Forgotten Byzantine Empire That Rescued Western Civilization*. New York: Crown, 2009. A vigorous argument for the importance of Constantinople as a neglected factor in Western history.

Cadbury, Deborah. *Dreams of Iron and Steel: Seven Wonders of the Nineteenth Century, from the Building of the London Sewers to the Panama Canal*. New York: Fourth Estate, 2004. A dynamic overview of the engineering urge of the Victorian age.

————. *Space Race: The Epic Battle between America and the Soviet Union for Dominion of Space*. New York: HarperCollins, 2006. An excellent and suspenseful narrative of U.S.-Soviet competition in space.

Crosby, Alfred W., Jr. *The Columbian Exchange: Biological and Cultural Consequences of 1492*. 2nd ed. Westport, CT: Praeger, 2003. The classic text that launched the concept of the crucial "Columbian exchange."

Crowley, Roger. *1453: The Holy War for Constantinople and the Clash of Islam and the West*. New York: Hyperion, 2005. A gripping account of the fall of Constantinople.

DeGroot, Gerard. *The Bomb: A Life*. Cambridge, MA: Harvard University Press, 2005. A clear and gripping narrative of the rise of nuclear weapons.

Dixon, Wheeler, and Gwendolyn Audrey Foster. *A Short History of Film*. New Brunswick, NJ: Rutgers University Press, 2008. A concise and accessible overview of major developments in film, with a global view.

Dryer, Edward L. *Zheng He: China and the Oceans in the Early Ming Dynasty, 1405–1433.* New York: Longman, 2007. Scholarly account of the larger context of the voyages of Zheng He.

Eisenstein, Elizabeth L. *The Printing Revolution in Early Modern Europe.* 2nd ed. Cambridge: Cambridge University Press, 2005. A historical classic that introduced the concept of the "print revolution."

Ellis, Jack C., and Virginia Wright Wexman. *A History of Film.* 3rd ed. Englewood Cliffs, NJ: Prentice Hall, 1990. A fascinating and readable history of film worldwide.

Findlay, Ronald, and Kevin H. O'Rourke. *Power and Plenty: Trade, War, and the World Economy in the Second Millennium.* Princeton: Princeton University Press, 2007. A stimulating and sweeping history of world economics and their effect on politics.

Fischer, David Hackett. *Fairness and Freedom: A History of Two Open Societies, New Zealand and the United States.* New York: Oxford University Press, 2012. A fascinating adventure in comparative history, including consideration of women's suffrage and settler societies.

Ford, Brian J. *Single Lens: The Story of the Simple Microscope.* New York: Harper and Row, 1985. A useful survey of Leeuwenhoek, his fellow scientists, and their technology.

Fowler, James, ed. *New Essays on Diderot.* New York: Cambridge University Press, 2011. These essays offer the latest research on Diderot and the ideas behind the *Encyclopédie.*

Goto-Jones, Christopher. *Modern Japan: A Very Short Introduction.* Oxford: Oxford University Press, 2009. In astonishingly concise form, an exploration of Japan's version of modernity.

Grimshaw, Patricia. *Women's Suffrage in New Zealand.* 2nd ed. Auckland: Auckland University Press, 1987. A lively and now classic account of how women won the vote in New Zealand.

Headrick, Daniel R. *Tools of Empire: Technology and European Imperialism in the Nineteenth Century*. New York: Oxford University Press, 1981. A now classic examination of how imperialism was engineered, on a world scale.

Himmelfarb, Gertrude. *The Roads to Modernity: The British, French, and American Enlightenments*. New York: Knopf, 2004. Fascinating insights into the contrasts between different national contexts for Enlightenment ideas.

Hitchcock, William I. *The Struggle for Europe: The Turbulent History of a Divided Continent, 1945 to the Present*. New York: Doubleday, 2003. A wonderful achievement: a comprehensive account of a half century of European upheaval and reconstruction.

Hobby, Gladys L. *Penicillin: Meeting the Challenge*. New Haven, CT: Yale University Press, 1985. Comprehensive and far-ranging history of how penicillin was deployed.

Hochschild, Adam. *Bury the Chains: Prophets and Rebels in the Fight to Free an Empire's Slaves*. Boston: Houghton Mifflin, 2005. An accessible and dramatic account of what the author considers the mother of all human rights movements.

Horvitz, Leslie. *Eureka! Scientific Breakthroughs That Changed the World*. New York: J. Wiley, 2002. Lively accounts of scientific discoveries.

Jensen, Oliver. *The American Heritage History of Railroads in America*. New York: American Heritage Publishing Co., 1975. Profusely illustrated with maps and key historical information.

Jukes, Geoffrey. *The Russo-Japanese War, 1904–1905*. Oxford: Osprey, 2002. The best brief account of this important but neglected conflict.

Karabell, Zachary. *Parting the Desert: The Creation of the Suez Canal*. New York: Vintage Books, 2004. A lively account of the personalities, intrigue, and engineering behind the 1869 Suez Canal project.

Kennett, Lee. *A History of Strategic Bombing: From the First Hot-Air Balloons to Hiroshima and Nagasaki.* New York: Scribner's, 1982. A gripping account of a terrifying phenomenon.

Kenney, Padraic. *1989: Democratic Revolutions at the Cold War's End: A Brief History with Documents.* New York: Bedford/St. Martin's, 2010. A thoughtful evaluation of global reform and revolutionary movements culminating in 1989, paired with original documents for the reader.

Kirkpatrick, David. *The Facebook Effect: The Inside Story of the Company That Is Connecting the World.* New York: Simon and Schuster, 2011. A detailed and fun narrative of a stunning technical and business phenomenon of our times.

Kowner, Rotem, ed. *The Impact of the Russo-Japanese War.* New York: Routledge, 2007. A long overdue evaluation of the worldwide impact of the 1904–1905 war.

Lawson, Philip. *The East India Company: A History.* New York: Longman, 1993. An elegant and concise overview of the history of "the Honorable Company."

Lester, Toby. *The Fourth Part of the World: An Astonishing Epic of Global Discovery, Imperial Ambition, and the Birth of America.* New York: Free Press, 2009. This study reads like a cartographic mystery; highly recommended.

Levathes, Louise. *When China Ruled the Seas: The Treasure Fleet of the Dragon Throne, 1405–1433.* New York: Simon and Schuster, 1994. A dramatic reconstruction of these epochal early voyages.

Lovell, Julia. *The Opium War: Drugs, Dreams, and the Making of China.* New York: Picador, 2011. A skillful, subtle, and learned discussion of the impact of the Opium Wars on China, ranging to the present day to illuminate how historical memory is deployed.

MacKenzie, Norman, and Jeanne MacKenzie. *H. G. Wells: A Biography.* New York: Simon and Schuster, 1973. A useful and insightful biography of a fascinating prophet of the future.

MacMillan, Margaret. *Nixon and Mao: The Week That Changed the World.* New York: Random House, 2007. A detailed and delightful reconstruction of a political trip and the world changes it unleashed.

Man, John. *Gutenberg: How One Man Remade the World with Words.* New York: John Wiley and Sons, 2002. Helpful illumination of the shadowy figure who has been called the most important man of the second millennium.

Mandiberg, Michael. *The Social Media Reader.* New York: New York University Press, 2012. A diversity of texts converging on the world of social media.

McDougall, Walter. *The Heavens and the Earth: A Political History of the Space Age.* New York: Basic Books, 1985. This fascinating space history won the Pulitzer Prize.

Mitter, Rana. *Modern China: A Very Short Introduction.* Oxford: Oxford University Press, 2008. In amazingly concise form, this book weighs whether and how China is modern, in its own terms.

Pomeranz, Kenneth, and Steven Topik. *The World That Trade Created: Society, Culture, and the World Economy, 1400 to the Present.* Armonk, NY: M. E. Sharpe, 1999. Links fascinating moments in economic history with vast consequences.

Reynolds, Glenn. *An Army of Davids: How Markets and Technology Empower Ordinary People to Beat Big Media, Big Government, and Other Goliaths.* Nashville, TN: Nelson Current, 2006. Provocative and bold speculation on where our technological society is headed next.

Rhodes, Richard. *The Making of the Atomic Bomb.* New York: Simon and Schuster, 1986. This Pulitzer Prize–winning book balances human detail with technology.

Robins, Nick. *The Corporation That Changed the World: How the East India Company Shaped the Modern Multinational.* London: Pluto Press, 2006. An impassioned account of a pioneering economic institution.

Ropp, Paul S. *China in World History*. New York: Oxford University Press, 2010. An admirably concise overview of a vital and big topic.

Schama, Simon. *The Embarrassment of Riches: An Interpretation of Dutch Culture in the Golden Age*. New York: Alfred A. Knopf, 1987. Already a historical classic; a brilliant cultural history.

Shirky, Clay. *Here Comes Everybody: The Power of Organizing Without Organizations*. New York: Penguin, 2008. A stimulating investigation of the new dynamics of organizing and viral spread of connectedness.

Spence, Jonathan. *Mao Zedong*. New York: Viking, 1999. A brief but substantial biography of a man who determined the fate of millions.

Stott, Rebecca. *Darwin's Ghosts: The Secret History of Evolution*. New York: Spiegel and Grau, 2012. Fascinating detective work to uncover the precursors to Darwin's insights into evolution.

Taylor, Frederick. *The Berlin Wall: A World Divided, 1961–1989*. New York: Harper, 2008. A vivid history of one of the most infamous human constructions of all time.

Waller, John. *The Discovery of the Germ: Twenty Years That Transformed the Way We Think about Disease*. New York: Columbia University Press, 2003. A model of clear science writing, this book illuminates giants of medicine.

Wedgwood, C. V. *The Thirty Years War*. New York: New York Review of Books Classics, 2005. The classic account of an increasingly meaningless conflict.

Wells, David, and Sandra Wilson, eds. *The Russo-Japanese War in Cultural Perspective, 1904–05*. Houndmills, Basingstoke: Palgrave Macmillan, 1999. Fascinating articles on the latest research on the literary, intellectual, and cultural impact of the war.

Wilson, Peter. *The Thirty Years War: Europe's Tragedy*. Cambridge, MA: Belknap, 2009. A sweeping and massive history of the factors at play in a war that lasted a generation.

Winik, Jay. *The Great Upheaval: America and the Birth of the Modern World, 1788–1800*. New York: Harper, 2007. With a flair for storytelling, Winik shows the interwoven destinies of American, French, and Russian societies in crisis.

Wohl, Robert. *A Passion for Wings: Aviation and the Western Imagination, 1908–1918*. New Haven: Yale University Press, 1994. A richly detailed account of how flying interacted with modern culture.

Notes

Notes